THE CHILD AND SOCIETY

DATE

The Child and Society

The Process of Socialization

FIFTH EDITION

Frederick Elkin
YORK UNIVERSITY, TORONTO

Gerald Handel
THE CITY COLLEGE AND GRADUATE SCHOOL
OF THE CITY UNIVERSITY OF NEW YORK

RANDOM HOUSE New York

Fifth Edition
98765432
Copyright © 1960, 1972, 1978, 1984, 1989 by Random House, Inc.

Cover Design by Sandra Josephson

Library of Congress Cataloging-in-Publication Data

Elkin, Frederick.
  The child and society
  Bibliography: p.
  Includes index.
    1. Socialization. I. Handel, Gerald. II. Title.
HQ783.E43 1988   303.3′2   88-18209
ISBN 0-394-38321-4

Manufactured in the United States of America

PERMISSIONS ACKNOWLEDGMENTS

Grateful acknowledgment is made to the following authors and publishers for permission to reprint selections from copyright material:

From William A. Caudill, "Tiny Dramas: Vocal Communication between Mother and Infant in Japanese and American Families," Chapter 3 in William P. Lebra (ed.), *Transcultural Research in Mental Health*. Copyright © 1972 by The University Press of Hawaii. Reprinted by permission of the publisher.

From Ernest G. Schachtel, *Metamorphosis: On the Development of Affect, Perception, Attention, and Memory*. Copyright © 1959 by Basic Books, Inc. and Routledge & Kegan Paul Ltd.

From Philippe Aries, *Centuries of Childhood*, translated by Robert Baldick. Copyright © 1965 by Alfred A. Knopf, Inc. Reprinted by permission of Alfred A. Knopf, Inc. and Jonathan Cape Ltd.

From *Night Comes to the Cumberlands: A Biography of a Depressed Area* by Harry M. Caudill. Copyright © 1962 by Harry M. Caudill. By permission of Little, Brown and Company.

From John U. Ogbu, *The Next Generation: An Ethnography of Education in an Urban Neighborhood*. Copyright © 1974 by Academic Press. Reprinted by permission of the author and the publisher.

From M. Kay Martin and Barbara Voorhies, *Female of the Species*. Copyright © 1975 by Columbia University Press. Reprinted by permission of the publisher.

Dedicated to Sylvia *F. E.*
and to
Ruth, Jonathan, and Michael *G. H.*

PREFACE TO THE FIFTH EDITION

Since the first edition of this book, the study of the socialization of the child has undergone an extensive development. In the successive editions we have sought, while maintaining our basic perspective, to integrate new ideas and new research into the enduring theories and concepts of the classical writers. This edition then has the same goal as that of the earlier editions: to provide a coherent account, from a sociological standpoint, of how children are socialized into modern society. We are interested in how the child as an active person incorporates a constantly changing society into his or her very being.

Extensive changes have been made in this edition. In discussing the processes of socialization, we have elaborated our analysis of the concepts of self, identity, and self-esteem and have given more consideration to the place of sentiments in development. We have introduced more material on the biological foundations and historical context of socialization. Throughout the volume, data have been updated. In discussing agencies of socialization, we have included new materials on day care, schooling for minority children, and peer influences. The section on the role of television in socialization has been completely rewritten. Our discussion of subcultural patterns has been elaborated with newer materials on social class, ethnic groups, black consciousness, and recent research on socialization among Old Order Mennonites. We have included new material on sex and gender. While we have sought throughout to be conscious of recent trends, we have not hesitated to retain discussions of less recent research and concepts where we believe they have merit.

Some topics in the study of socialization continue to be controversial. We have attempted, citing the evidence, to present the issues clearly and fairly. In some instances we indicate our evaluation of the evidence and view of the controversy; in others, we leave the matter open because we do not believe the evidence is sufficiently definitive to justify a conclusion. We are more interested in identifying major issues and stimulating thought in the student than in promulgating particular points of view or reinforcing the "correctness" of certain views.

We have been helped greatly in preparing this revision by the thoughtful comments from several anonymous reviews from Random House. We have adopted many of their suggestions and acknowledge our appreciation. Our thanks also to Sylvia Elkin for helping with the index.

F.E.
G.H.

CONTENTS

THE CHILD AND SOCIETY

CHAPTER 1

Socialization Defined

As children grow they develop in many ways. Physically, they become taller, heavier, stronger, and capable of such activities as walking, talking, writing, riding a bicycle, and, later, having sexual relations. Mentally, they become capable of such activities as memorizing poems, working out problems in algebra, imagining love scenes, and acquiring the knowledge necessary to carry through a job. Each child also acquires a more or less consistent personality structure, so that he or she can be characterized as ambitious, shy, sociable, cautious, and so on. However, these descriptions, useful as they may be, are of limited value in explaining how someone functions in society, because they do not reveal the interactions and relationships that a child has with others in the society. They do not tell us, for example, how a child learns what to expect from a doctor or a store clerk or learns the difference between behavior that is acceptable at a hockey game and behavior acceptable in church. In the course of growing up, a child must acquire varied knowledge and skills, such as what utensils to use when eating specific foods; how to greet strangers; how to show or conceal emotion in different settings; when to speak and when to be silent. As children grow they move into a widening world of persons, activities, and feelings—all shaped by encounters with others who help define a socially organized world. These others will establish standards of right and wrong, and as a result children will come to have certain feelings if they are inadvertently rude, fail an examination, upset a friend, or in some other way do not measure up to their own expectations or the expectations of others.

Babies, of course, know nothing of these ways of the society; but they have the potentialities to learn them. The potentialities are in fact wide and varied. In one setting children will speak English, in another, Russian; in one they will eat rice with chopsticks; in another, with a fork; in one they will be taught to empha-

1

size self-interest; in another, to focus on the interests of the group. In one setting a boy will be deeply respectful of his father; in another he will speak to him as a "pal." In one setting a girl will be taught that her future inevitably will involve being a wife and mother; in another, that she will have the freedom to choose her life style and commitments.

It is with such matters that the socialization of the child is concerned. Socialization may be defined as *the process by which we learn the ways of a given society or social group so that we can function within it.* As the examples above illustrate, many kinds of learning are encompassed within this general process. Some of what is learned is overt and visible, such as wearing appropriate clothes for different kinds of occasions. But even these overt behaviors can be understood only if we recognize that they come to be guided by more generalized learning, the effects of which are not directly visible but must be inferred. Put otherwise, children learn to be concerned with appropriateness as a general guide to their conduct. They develop a "sense of propriety," which not only governs their behavior in situations comparable to those they have already experienced but which also guides them in dealing with new situations that they encounter for the first time. Thus, when they enter a new group they do so with some sense of how to act, because they have learned to be concerned with acting appropriately in a group. When they take their first job, they are not at a total loss, because they have had experience in other situations that have the quality of "being supervised by someone with authority to supervise." Of course, people then go on to learn the specific requirements for membership in a new group or the requirements for being supervised as employees, which are different from the kind of supervision they received as children from their parents or as pupils from their teachers.

In addition to learning specific overt behaviors and a general sense of appropriateness, children also learn to experience certain specific emotions in specific kinds of situations. They may learn to feel possessive with property or feel indifferent to it. They may learn to feel proud at winning a fist fight or ashamed for having gotten into one, or a mixture of the two.

Some of what children learn in the course of being socialized is explicitly taught by people who have the obligation to teach them, as when they learn to use eating utensils or to feel patriotic.

Parents and teachers are specifically entrusted with the task of preparing the young to become qualified participants in society. But some of the learning that is included in socialization is self-motivated, and children develop and build on a constantly changing base. Having first become responsive to their parents, they have been prepared to be responsive to others. Early on, children begin to see in other people models for what they might like to become, and at home they are apt to take their parents as models for behavior in which they have not been instructed. If father brings home a briefcase, his five-year-old son may pick it up and carry it around "like daddy." Police officers and fire fighters are early heroes of many young children, and children see them, at least for a time, as models for their own later behavior.

Socialization takes place in many settings—at home and in schools, churches, and playgrounds. For the person interested in studying and understanding socialization, some of these settings are accessible only under special conditions; one cannot walk freely into someone else's home. But socialization can be observed fairly readily in public places. Some aspects of the process are well illustrated in the following episode observed in a neighborhood bank:

> While a young woman is engaged in her transaction at the teller's window, her little boy, approximately two years old, amuses himself with the velvet rope, supported by two posts, that the bank uses to regulate the waiting line. The boy straddles and rides the rope; one post is thus pulled down, startling the boy but not hitting him. Mother turns around, puts the post upright. The boy starts to straddle again, and she says, "Do you want to fall again and get hurt? You'll get hit on the head." He gets off.
>
> When the mother finishes her transaction, she and the boy head toward the door. He runs ahead and sits on an upholstered swivel chair near the door, turning from side to side. When his mother urges him to come, he says, "No, I like it." She says, "Good-bye, I'm leaving," and goes out the door. He follows quickly.

This little episode reveals some aspects of the socialization process. First, the mother seeks to influence her son's behavior by the use of threats. To control his behavior, she seeks to get him to believe that he will be badly hurt if he continues what he is doing. The teaching of such ideas is part of the socialization process—they may be ideas about physical objects, the supernatural, the political system, or anything else in society. Threat—an example of a negative sanction—is one procedure often used to attempt to attain a socialization goal.

The second part of the episode illustrates another aspect of the socialization process. The mother does not give the boy time to swivel on the chair. By proceeding to leave right away, she indicates to the boy something about adult goals and time spans. He is obliged to leave what interests him and fall in step with her or be abandoned. He must sacrifice his immediate pleasure and accept a definition of reality from the adult. By her actions, the mother defines the situation in these terms: it is now time to leave, not time to play. She uses the threat of abandonment to enforce her *definition of the situation*. Adults constantly define situations for children, and by so doing they create the social reality to which children respond. This episode illustrates that even a child of two can define a situation, but this definition may conflict with that of the adult, in which case the adults are likely to act to have their definitions prevail. They will not always succeed, but over the course of the many situations in which adult definitions of social reality are presented, they will usually succeed well enough that the new generation's social world will come to resemble significantly, though not duplicate exactly, that of the parents.

Socialization is, then, a process that helps explain two different kinds of phenomena. On the one hand, it helps to explain how a person becomes capable of participating in society. For it is clear that the newborn infant is not a social being. Most of the qualities we regard as human are present in the child only as potentialities. In the early days of life, the infant experiences hunger pangs, cries, gains satisfaction by sucking on a source of nourishment, experiences visceral tension, and gains relaxation by excretion. In short, the newborn's capacities for functioning with other human beings are exceedingly minimal. They are developed through socialization.

On the other hand, socialization helps to explain how society is possible at all. While certain species of animals lower in the evolutionary scale function in rudimentary societies, none of these approaches the complexity of human society, which takes so many different forms and is elaborated with infinite subtleties. Consequently, it is necessary to explain how vast numbers of organisms called human are able to attune their actions to one another in such a way as to make possible an ongoing social order. While a full explanation, insofar as one is possible, would take us far beyond the subject matter of this book, the socialization process is one key element of such an explanation. Social order is possible because human infants encounter adults who teach them and from whom they can learn to regulate their actions in accordance with various standards of appropriateness.

As implied in some of our earlier examples, the process of socialization is not confined to infancy and childhood. It continues throughout the life of the individual. The term "socialization" refers to learning the ways of any established and continuing group; a newly hired employee becomes socialized into the operations of the plant or office; the upwardly mobile person is socialized into a new social class; an immigrant becomes socialized into the life of his or her new country. The recognition of the continuing nature of socialization has led to the concept of *adult socialization.* The term recognizes the fact that adults are obliged to go through certain experiences and developments somewhat similar to those undergone by infants and children, although there is a basic difference in that later socialization is built upon an already acquired capacity to evaluate one's own behavior and function as a social being.

Having thus delineated the basic nature of socialization, it will be useful to indicate some problems that are not encompassed by this concept. First, it is not a problem of socialization to explain or speculate upon how a society or social group began. The society into which the child is born, with its common expectations, ways of doing things, standards of right and wrong, and current trends and issues, is the result of a unique historical evolution and exists before the child enters it. Socialization begins with the assumption of this ongoing preexisting society.

Second, socialization does not try to explain the uniqueness of individuals. Although it is true that no two individuals are alike and that each person has a singular heredity, distinctive experiences, and a unique personality development, socialization focuses not on such individualizing patterns and processes but on similarities, on aspects of development that concern the learning of and adaptation to the culture and society. In the course of development children go through two major processes simultaneously: individuation and socialization. In their earliest years children do not experience this distinction, but as they get older they inevitably develop individualities of their own and recognize their own uniqueness. But which aspects of this uniqueness become known and acknowledged—be they distinctive physical or personality characteristics or tastes or ways of doing things—and how these aspects are judged, are themselves results of societal definitions and the socialization process.

Third, socialization is not a one-way process, acting only on a child or a new member of a group. Socialization is always interactive. The entrance of a new member into a family, or any unit, changes the group. It is not just the old group with one added person, it is a *new* group with new relationships and a new organization. In a family, parents socialize their children and children socialize their parents. Parents, like their children, learn new roles, new knowledge, new skills, and new ideas. So, too, in a school do teachers and pupils socialize one another. In this book, however, our focus will be on the child as socializee, as the one who is socialized by parents, teachers, and others.

Finally, it is not a problem for socialization to prescribe what a society should become or the particular type of child rearing to achieve it. Socialization as such does not set a direction to be followed; it is a process in all societies whatever model is used for analysis. Whether society is seen as a system in which an established elite seeks to maintain the status quo or a struggle between groups seeking power or a system of adapting institutions and structures or some other arrangement, socialization remains a universal and necessary process for incorporating new members into ongoing social organizations. What they struggle for once they are part of the social organization becomes another question.

In recent years socialization has often come to be viewed from the perspective of the life span or life course.[1] This perspective emphasizes that human development continues throughout a lifetime and that there are always questions of what is constant and what changes; what aspects of development are continuous and what discontinuous; what aspects are timeless and what characteristics are peculiar to those brought up in a particular historical era; what links exist between the genetic, maturational, psychological, cultural, and social aspects of human development. This all-encompassing perspective is valid and necessary to understand human behavior and socialization in its entirety; such a perspective is also almost unlimited. In this volume we have chosen to focus specifically on socialization and specifically on childhood, although in the final chapter, as well as at various points throughout the work, we deal with the question of childhood's relationship to later life. Childhood socialization is *primary socialization*—first, and most important. The direction the person's development takes in later years cannot help but be influenced by the foundations established in childhood. This is not to say that the impacts of primary socialization always persist unchanged. They do not, but they do affect what happens later.

This study deals with the process of socialization, with the problem of how the child becomes a functioning member of the society. We shall use a wide range of illustrations, but generally they will come from North American society, with which we are most familiar. However, we shall also give some attention to socialization patterns that differ from the most familiar. Chapter 2 discusses the basic preconditions for socialization and is followed by a consideration in Chapter 3 of the processes, mechanisms, and techniques by which it occurs, as well as some of its outcomes. Chapter 4 considers socialization patterns of certain basic subdivisions in our society: social class, community, and ethnic group. Chapter 5 is concerned with the primary socializing agencies in our society: family, school, peer group, and media of mass communication. Socialization is intimately related to family life, and although the family is treated as such only in Chapter 5, ramifications of this relationship are discussed at various points throughout the book. Chapter 6 examines the many issues related to sex and socialization. The final chapter discusses later socialization and its relation to childhood.

CHAPTER 2

Preconditions for Socialization

For children to become socialized, two preconditions are necessary. First, they must have the *requisite biological inheritance*. If a child is feebleminded or suffers from a serious organic mental disorder, adequate socialization will be impossible. Certain other biological deficits do not make socialization impossible but cause it to be beset by serious difficulties. Children born blind, deaf, or mute encounter special obstacles and are necessarily excluded from certain kinds of opportunities available to others. Nevertheless, such children—and those with such other disabilities as the malformed arms and legs suffered some years ago by children of mothers who took the drug thalidomide during pregnancy—can, with special training, achieve levels of socialization that permit them to function more or less satisfactorily in the society.

This requisite biological inheritance includes the possibility, under the right social relationships, of developing a "human nature." Human nature is not readily given a compact definition, but some of its fundamental components can be specified. Of particular significance is the ability to establish emotional relationships with others and to experience such sentiments as love, sympathy, shame, envy, pity, and pride. Scarcely less important is the ability to transform experience into symbols, which makes possible speech, writing, and thought. Although writing is not, of course, necessary for adequate socialization—some societies have no writing at all, and in earlier periods of our own history a person could be adequately socialized without being able to read, let alone write—human socialization is not possible without speech; and speech depends upon the capacity to symbolize. How this human nature comes about will be considered in our discussion of the processes of socialization; without it, no child can really be considered socialized.

The second precondition is an *ongoing society*. Children are born into a world that already exists. They are "raw recruits" into the world, involuntary recruits, with no wish to be there and no knowledge of how to get along in it. From the point of view of society, the function of socialization is to transmit to new members the culture and motivation to participate in established social relationships. The society has a patterned consistency, so that one can predict, *within limits,* how people will behave, think, and feel. Both of these preconditions point up basic background material for an understanding of socialization.

BIOLOGICAL INHERITANCE

The first precondition for socialization is an adequate biological inheritance, or original nature. It is apparent that those who have certain serious hereditary deficiencies either cannot be socialized or will have distinctive problems in the process. Socialization depends, for example, upon memory. An adequate memory can develop only if the parts of the brain governing memory are sufficiently intact. A child born with serious injury to that area of the brain may be unable to develop the necessary level of memory. Thus, certain serious deficits in the biological organism preclude adequate socialization. Other organic deficiencies create problems but may be somewhat less fateful. Children born deaf will not learn to speak in the same way other children learn, since they cannot hear their own voices; but with special intensive training they can learn to speak. Children who are blind do not respond to colors or moving objects, but their parents and teachers can make greater use of touch and sound. It is worth noting at this point that the extent to which biological deficit precludes adequate socialization does not depend entirely upon the defect itself but upon society's response to it as well.[1] The deaf can be more adequately socialized today than formerly because our institutions chose to discover (with some success) ways of modifying deafness and its consequences. Intensified efforts have also been initiated in recent years to find ways to modify the deficit imposed by biologically induced mental retardation, so that this condition, too, may yield to the power of social organization. New norms and new institutions for coping with biological deficit yield new outcomes in socialization.

Although abnormal biological conditions present special

problems in socialization, problems that may be recast by social advances, socialization is also intimately involved with biology for the organically normal individual. Certain biological characteristics set the context for socialization. First, human organisms, although active, are completely dependent at birth. They cannot survive without the intervention of persons who give them care. It is evident that physical survival depends upon the provision of nourishment and protection against temperature extremes. However, there is also evidence, to be cited shortly, that these necessary rudiments of care may not be sufficient for the infant's survival, let alone for his or her adequate socialization. External stimulation and responsiveness from other people appear to be necessary for survival itself.

The newborn of many species is dependent at birth, but the human offspring has the *most prolonged dependency* of any. Lower forms of life—animals, birds, and insects—can often function well merely by following inborn patterns of goal-directed activity that have persisted relatively unchanged for thousands of years. No comparable built-in mechanisms exist in human beings, and in order to function within society, we must learn from others how to build homes, earn a living, and take care of our children.

Increasingly, however, modern research is demonstrating that the newborn infant is not an entirely passive creature, simply waiting to receive and absorb experiences. While the newborn is not equipped to do very much of what is expected of a socialized person, the indications are that it *participates actively* in the processes of becoming a person. The activities of which it is capable are preliminary to developing an empathy and the ability to know symbols. Infants bring considerable equipment that lends itself to socialization, the first perhaps being the rhythm of sucking and arousal which allows adults to anticipate their behavior. Very early, as well, the infant responds to and is selective of visual stimuli. In one study eighteen infants under five days of age were shown in several brief sessions six different visual stimuli; the length of time they looked at each was recorded by photographing eye movements. Eleven of the eighteen looked longest at a schematic drawing of a face; none looked longest at a white, a yellow, or a red stimulus that contained no pattern.[2]

Other research supports the notion that infants selectively fixate their eyes on some stimuli—faces, for example—in preference to others. Indeed, not only do newborns show preferences for different kinds of stimulation, they also show evidence of several capacities that underlie or are related to this selectivity, including alertness, visual discrimination and acuity, visual scanning in which they selectively respond to different aspects of the stimuli, and visual pursuit or following of a moving stimulus in order to keep it in view.[3] Thus, one investigator concludes that the studies of newborns' visual preferences show that "infants from birth have the capacity to receive and discriminate patterned stimulation, that they do attend selectively to parts of the environment, and that, therefore, *the acquisition of knowledge about the environment begins at the first look.*"[4]

The visual is but one domain of responsiveness. Infants are also sensitive to the distinctive features of human speech, and, like others, a baby born blind will smile in response to a human voice.[5] Likewise, the sound of another infant may promote crying in a newborn.[6] Infants, too, have the mechanism that enables them to imitate certain facial and perhaps hand movements, and they can make and break eye contact.[7]

In brief, the infant is ready to receive and respond to sights and sounds from the outer world and shows preferences from birth for some of these over others.

Another basic biological fact is *maturation.* The human organism develops according to a fairly set timetable, which varies within rather narrow limits. This timetable helps to shape the course of socialization. The newborn infant cannot immediately be trained to use eating utensils, whether these be chopsticks or knife and fork; a minimum level of eye-hand coordination must be achieved first. And, although a six-month-old infant may be "possessive" of a rattle, the social importance of "respect for property" can be communicated only when neuromuscular development allows walking and permits the toddler to reach for fragile lamps and other breakables.

The evolutionary development of certain specific organs is particularly important as a foundation for socialization. The development of the outermost layer of the human brain—the cortex—is a prerequisite to socialization. Vocal organs capable of highly varied speech (rather than merely a few grunts or tweets); the fact of being two-footed rather than four-footed; the fact that sexual drives are not restricted, as in many other animals, to a

periodic mating season—these are some of the organismic characteristics of the human that serve as determinants of or (looked
at in another way) resources for socialization.

Although the biological character of the organism and the
timetable of maturation set certain outer limits to human variation, a no less significant factor is the psychobiological *plasticity*
of the human body. Thus, children inherit certain "mass movements," impulses that are expressed in random undefined directions. For example, they make numerous different sounds and
move their fingers in a variety of ways. Whether these sounds are
eventually organized into the English, Spanish, or Chinese language, or whether the finger movements come to include the
ability to write, manipulate Ping-Pong paddles, or play musical
instruments, are functions of the specific definitions and guidance given by people in the surrounding world. Drives such as
hunger, thirst, sleep, and sex can be satisfied in many ways. The
need for food may be satisfied by eating meat, vegetables, insects,
or even people. Sex needs may be expressed directly or sub-
limated in dancing, art, or religious ceremonies; they may be
directed toward people within or outside certain groups; they
may be suppressed before marriage or encouraged and directed
to certain specific outlets. Which foods or which forms of sex
expression are preferred will reflect social and psychological influences. Such influences can be meaningful only because the
body allows variation.

Similarly, the development of intelligence and particular talents cannot be separated from the surrounding world. Indeed, in
no aspect of human development is it more futile to ask what
proportion derives from original nature and what proportion
from experience. Since *all* intelligence is "experienced" intelligence—that is, an indeterminate blend of native potentiality and
experience—there is no known way to measure "native intelligence." Whether a particular potentiality is actually developed
and what direction development takes depend upon the possibilities that are available, the encouragement that comes from others, and the growth of the personality structure. A society without
paints would not know Picasso, and neither Mozart nor Marx
would have become what they did in Mozambique. Nor would
they have succeeded if their personalities were so disturbed that

they could not focus their attention long enough to develop their talents and abilities.

Not to be overlooked are individual differences among infants. Children are born with certain temperamental tendencies toward passivity or activity, perhaps toward impulsivity or restlessness. They differ in irritability, how readily they are soothed and comforted, and how capable they are of self-comforting behavior. Such tendencies are evidenced from birth in a baby's movements, responses to touch, sleeping and crying habits, frustration tolerance, and responses to food. These temperamental tendencies gain further significance from the interpretation of their caretakers. An infant who is alert is more likely to evoke interactions than one who is not, an infant whose cues are easily "read" and whose behavior is highly predictable is likely to evoke more appropriate and effective reactions from caretakers than the infant whose signals are indistinct and not so predictable. Further, parents differ. An "active" baby will receive one kind of response if his or her parents enjoy an active baby and quite another response if they would be more comfortable with a placid and docile child.[8]

Even in a fairly homogeneous group of families there is considerable variation. "Thus one baby's first home might be quiet, with a low level of stimulation, while another baby might enter a complex, noisy, even hilarious and overstimulating household . . ."[9] Furthermore, it is necessary to distinguish between one household and another not only in terms of level of stimulation but also in terms of particular kinds of stimulation. "If one watches mothers with their babies and measures the sort of obvious things which people seem to regard as stimulation, like talking, smiling, touching, and so on, one is lumping things together under one global heading that do not necessarily belong together. A mother may show a lot of talking but little touching, and vice versa."[10]

Clearly, then, human biological nature—the form and transformation of the body through time—both allows and requires socialization; and certain biological requisites are necessary for adequate socialization. For purposes of analysis it is necessary to identify the biological substratum underlying socialization, but in actual situations biological factors become so closely linked with elements of the social world that it is often impossible to isolate empirically the hereditary from the environmental and to weight the importance of each.[11]

AN ONGOING SOCIETY

Many models have been proposed for analyzing ongoing societies. Some stress the continuity and adaptability of established institutions, others focus on fundamental conflict between groups; some stress evolutionary change, others the necessity of stages and revolutions; some stress political and economic spheres, others the social, cultural, and religious. Rather than considering particular models to understand our society, each with its unique set of concepts, it seems more useful to cite certain general social concepts, each of which points up distinctive features of our way of life.

First, there is the perspective of *norms* and *values*. A norm is an implicit rule defining the appropriate pattern of behavior in a recurring situation. "Being clothed" is the norm when presenting oneself in a public place. This example indicates that a norm is both a standard by which behavior is judged and also a prediction as to what behavior is likely to occur. People are supposed to be clothed in public, and one may predict that in any public place the people one encounters will probably be clothed. Such convergence of the two meanings of "expected" (what should happen and what is predicted to happen) is never fully realized. Students are expected to study throughout the term—that is, they should do so. But it is also expected that some will not; they will do no more than cram before an examination—that is, one may predict that this is how they will study. The two meanings of expectation are not always carefully distinguished, and for many purposes it is sufficient to make the rough assumption that what should be done is what generally is done. Many social problems, however, arise from divergence of what happens from what is supposed to happen, and it is then necessary to distinguish ideal norms from behavioral norms.

Values are more general than norms. They are best thought of as conceptions of the desirable or undesirable that serve as criteria for norms. A society in which freedom, for example, is a salient value will *tend* to develop norms consistent with that value in its economic practices, its educational methods, the relations between the sexes, the way it rears its children, and in other areas of life. This is not to say that all the norms in these situations are entirely consistent with freedom, for they are not. Other values tend to generate norms inconsistent with those of freedom, so that the norms governing any situation are not simple derivatives from a single value.

A second perspective is that of *status* and *role*. A status is a position in the social structure, and a role is the expected behavior of someone who holds a given status. We can cooperate with others because we know the rights and obligations associated with each status. The taxi driver has the right to ask you for your fare and the obligation to drive you to your destination; the physician has the right to ask about your symptoms and, in some instances, to ask you to remove your clothes; and the physician has the obligation to try to cure you. Similarly, role behavior is expected of the teacher, student, mother, father, daughter, grocery clerk, Roman Catholic, taxicab passenger, and doctor's patient. Each person has many statuses that define his or her expected behavior in given situations.

A third perspective is that of *institutions,* each of which focuses on a segment of life and consists of values, norms, and statuses. One such institution is the school, whose primary function is to transmit, in a more or less formal way, a large share of the intellectual heritage of a society. Within the school there is the value of learning and norms relating to attendance, sports events, courses, and holiday celebrations; and there are patterned status relationships among the teachers, students, principal, and cleaning staff. The church, hospital, stock market, and judicial system are other institutions that are the foci for the organization of many activities. Despite a regular turnover of personnel these institutions continue to operate over a period of many years, in great part because each new generation is socialized into the appropriate patterns.

A fourth perspective focuses on cultural and group subdivisions within the larger society. One major subdivision is *social class.* Individuals in our society vary in the amounts of wealth, prestige, and power they possess; and associated with these variations are differences in values and ways of life. Social-class rankings may partake of all of these elements. At one extreme may be the upper-class individual who is wealthy, has an important business position, lives in a luxurious home, sends his or her children to private schools, and vacations in Europe. At the other extreme may be the lower-class individual who works at an unskilled job, left school at the age of fourteen, lives in a slum area, and has "crude" table manners. Between these extremes there are other rough rankings, from the professional to the lesser business executive to the white-collar worker to the skilled laborer. It is evident that no single characteristic clearly differentiates class groups, that the lines between them are blurred, and that there is interclass movement. But a stratification system of a kind does exist.

Another major subdivision in our society, one that overlaps considerably with social class, is the *ethnic group.* The population of North America has been built up of immigrants from many countries. In coming here they have kept some of their old-country characteristics or responded distinctively in the new setting and thus may be thought of as "different" both by others and by themselves. Thus, we find Cubans, Italians, Greeks, Filipinos, Jews, Mexicans, Puerto Ricans, Chinese, and French Canadians, who are distinguished from others by their names, language, traditional foods, holiday rituals, occupations, folklore, patterns of child rearing, and loyalties. A related division is the *racial minority,* which is also likely to be thought of as "different" both by others and by themselves. The most prominent racial minority in our society are the blacks.

Still another perspective is that of *social change,* especially important today because of the rapidity with which it occurs. The society into which a child is born is not static; there are conflicting pressures, a diffusion of materials and ideas, and general trends that shift direction. New technology, new experiences, and new decisions reverberate in many directions, generating changes in values, norms, institutions, statuses, roles, and intergroup relationships. The reader will readily identify some of the familiar changes that have been under way for some time: the increasing number of young mothers taking jobs; the development of new careers in new industries, especially those of high technology; the increasing number of divorced men and women and of one-parent families; greater freedom in sex relations; a concern with sexually transmitted diseases; and the movement to provide better services for the handicapped. Among the most dramatic have been the upsurges of social action and citizen participation groups, especially the growth of the women's movement. In these, as in the other changes, socialization, inasmuch as it involves a receptivity to modification as well as given patterns of thought, feeling, and behavior, has a part to play.

There is, then, a complex and variable world, which may be approached from many perspectives, into which the children are to be socialized. In order to function within it, whether it be primarily as conformist, rebel, or compromiser, they must have at least a minimum of knowledge about this world and a minimum of what the culture defines as appropriate behavior and feelings. They must know what to expect from people of given statuses, how they themselves fit in with the various groupings, what is considered proper and improper in given situations, and the range of alternative behaviors possible in those segments of social life that are rapidly changing. This is the world that the socializers, knowingly or unknowingly, pass on to the newcomer.

The Case of Isolated Children

We take it for granted that a child is born into a family and an ongoing society which give it care. Without continuing care, we assume an infant cannot survive. As far back as the late Middle Ages, however, reports appeared from time to time of young children who had been isolated from society and who, in one fashion or another, had lived in a wild state. In some cases, supposedly, they had been reared by or at least lived in the company of wild animals.[12] It is instructive to review some of these cases to show both the limitations of development when a child grows up apart from an ongoing society and the degree to which deficiencies caused by early isolation from human contact can be overcome once social relationships are reestablished.

One of the few authenticated and the most celebrated of these cases is that of "the wild boy of Aveyron," discovered in south-central France in 1797. Recently psychologist Harlan Lane has come across some long-lost documents about the case and has written a review and analysis.[13]

The boy was first sighted running naked through the woods. Then, from time to time over a period of more than a year, he was seen digging up potatoes and turnips in fields and searching for acorns and roots. After being captured in a tree by some hunters, he was passed through the hands of several local governmental authorities and finally sent to Paris at the order of Lucien Bonaparte, Minister of the Interior and brother of Napoleon, to be placed in a school for deaf-mutes. In those years just before and after the French Revolution, issues concerning the relationship of individuals to society were at a new peak of interest, and the study of "savages" was believed to offer important clues to understanding human nature. The *sauvage de l'Aveyron* was closely studied as a case in point.

He was judged to be about eleven or twelve years old when found. His body showed various scars, but he was apparently free of any serious physical deformity. Of particular significance was the fact that he was "entirely without the gift of speech and makes himself heard only by cries and inarticulate sounds,"[14] although later evidence showed he was not hard of hearing. A committee of leading experts, including Philippe Pinel, who is sometimes spoken of as the first psychiatrist and is famous for removing the chains from inmates of insane asylums, delivered an extensive report to the Society of Observers of Man, a leading scholarly association of the time, in which they concluded that the boy was mentally retarded and ineducable. Pinel thought that the boy "was not an idiot because he was abandoned in the woods; he was abandoned in the woods because he was an idiot . . . recognized by heartless parents for what he was."[15]

However, Jean-Marc-Gaspard Itard, a former student of Pinel's who had been appointed resident physician at the school for deaf-mutes, disagreed, and set out to train the boy, to whom he later gave the name Victor. He hoped to achieve five objectives: (1) to interest the boy in social life; (2) "to awaken his nervous sensibility by the most energetic stimulation, and occasionally by intense emotion"; (3) to give him new, more social needs and thus extend the range of his ideas; (4) to teach him to speak; (5) to develop his ability to reason, at least in a rudimentary way.[16] Itard reported some progress. At the outset,

the boy was indifferent to temperature and rejected clothing even in the coldest weather; he would put his hand in a fire; his eyes did not fixate; he reached alike for painted objects, objects in relief, and the image of objects reflected in a mirror; he did not sneeze, even with snuff, nor did he weep; he did not respond to loud voices; he did not recognize edible food by sight but by smell; he preferred uncooked foods and had no taste for sweets or hard drink; he had no emotional ties, no sexual expression, no speech; he had a peculiar gait and would occasionally run on all fours.[17]

After three months of Itard's regimen, Victor removed his potatoes from the fire with a spoon instead of by hand; he liked to stroke velvet; he began to wear clothes; he would get up at night to urinate instead of sleeping in a cold, wet bed. He also evidently learned to sneeze; Itard says that "I judged by the fright that seized him the first time this happened that this was a new experience for him. He immediately ran away and threw himself on his bed."[18] Victor later learned to sit at a table, wait for food to be served, and eat with utensils. He developed emotional expression, at times embracing Itard and the woman house-keeper who took him for walks and cared for him in many other ways. He gave evidence of having developed sentiments such as gratitude, remorse, pleasure in pleasing others, but he failed to show any evidence of pity.[19]

Itard worked with Victor over a period of six years. His great-est disappointment was that Victor never learned to speak de-spite Itard's strenuous efforts and specialized training program. (Itard is considered the founder of what is known today as Special Education.) Various explanations for the failure have been pro-posed by diverse experts from Itard's time to our own. Following an evaluation of these explanations and a review of the evidence, Lane himself concludes that Victor was probably neither men-tally retarded nor autistic. "Victor's symptoms, then, including his mutism, may overlap with those of congenital retardation or autism, but are explained by neither; instead they are the result of his isolation in the wild, as Itard maintained all along. This is the view that prevails among diverse environmentalists."

Lane then goes on to ask why Victor didn't "readapt to society once he returned and, indeed, received intensive rehabilitation. . . . Why didn't Victor recover language and progress much further in his intellectual development and socialization?"[20]

While some elements of a human nature proved recoverable with the establishment of a primary-group relationship in Itard's household and with Itard's training program, vocal speech, beyond a few sounds, was not. Thus, Lane suggests a second explanatory factor in addition to isolation: "The prolonged isolation deprived him of the crucial skill by which children and adults profit from social experiences that are not explicitly designed for their instruction, namely, the skill of imitation."[21] Whatever the reason, although Victor learned to imitate other actions sufficiently to communicate in nonspoken ways, and even learned to read and write simple sentences, he never did learn to speak, although he lived to an age of more than forty years.[22] Perhaps, as some modern students of language are suggesting, there is a "critical period" for learning spoken language, and a child who is deprived, by isolation, of the opportunity to learn and use spoken language during this phase of maturation is unable to learn it thereafter.[23] Such may have been Victor's fate, although we cannot be certain of it.

In addition to the explanations for Victor's muteness discussed by Lane, at least four others have been proposed as possibilities. One, originally mentioned by Pinel, was that Victor was an idiot, but the boy's very development belies this theory. Second, as the boy had a large scar on his neck, perhaps his vocal organs were injured—but Itard concluded that the deeper injury was unlikely. Third, possibly the boy developed a serious psychological disturbance before his abandonment, but we lack further evidence to support this. Finally, it has been suggested that Itard's methods of training were too rigid and traumatic—he allowed Victor little opportunity to learn for himself through free activity and sometimes he used scare tactics; thus, he added to Victor's difficulties in overcoming the initial absence of speech due to early isolation.[24]

In more recent times the best-authenticated cases of isolated children are those of Anna, Isabelle,[25] and Genie. Anna was an illegitimate child, confined to one room from infancy. She had very little contact with other human beings. The mother brought her milk but otherwise paid little attention to her, not ordinarily taking the trouble to bathe, train, supervise, or cuddle her. When Anna was found, at the age of six, she showed few, if any, signs of human nature. She was described as completely apathetic; she lay on her back, immobile, expressionless, and indifferent. She was believed to be deaf and possibly blind. She lived for another five years, first in a country home and later in a foster home and school for retarded children, and in this period developed only to the level of the normal two-year-old. Whether the lack of development was due primarily to mental deficiency, to the deprivations of early life, or a combination of the two is not clear. Isabelle's circumstances were relatively more fortunate. She, too, was an illegitimate child kept in seclusion. However, her deaf-mute mother was shut off with her, and the two were able to communicate by gestures. When Isabelle was found, also at the age of six, she, too, lacked a manifest human nature. She seemed utterly unaware of ordinary social relationships and reacted to strangers almost as an animal would, with fear and hostility. She made only a strange croaking sound, and in many respects her actions resembled those of deaf children. In contrast to Anna, Isabelle was given a systematic and skillful program of training and, after a very slow beginning, began to develop quite rapidly. By the time she was eight and a half years old, she had reached a normal educational level and was described as bright, cheerful, and energetic. Thus, with an appropriate environment she was able to develop into a girl with normal habits and feelings. That Isabelle attained this level of socialization indicates that she had an adequate intelligence potential, but only intensive and focused social interaction brought it to actuality. It is significant that Isabelle, in contrast to Anna, did have close, although limited, human contact when she was a baby.

The most recently reported case of a "wild child" is that of Genie, a thirteen-year-old girl discovered in 1970 in California.[26] From the age of twenty months, when her family moved into her grandmother's house, Genie lived in nearly total isolation. She was kept in a small room, sitting on a potty seat, naked and restrained by a harness that her father had made. She could move only her hands and feet. At night she was put into a sort of straitjacket in a covered crib with wire-mesh sides. Her father made only barking sounds and growled at her. If Genie made any noise, her father beat her.

When found, Genie was taken to Children's Hospital in Los Angeles where she was treated and studied by a variety of physicians and psychologists. Her improvement was not spectacular. During her first seven months at the hospital she did learn to walk with a jerky motion and became more or less toilet trained. But she still had many disconcerting habits, especially salivating and spitting.

A major research emphasis has focused on her language development. In spite of special attention by therapists, her speech development was abnormally slow. After some months, she began to string two words together but, unlike the language development of normal children, this was not followed by a rapid and explosive development in speech. Four years later, Genie understood little grammar and her speech was like a somewhat garbled telegram. The fact that Genie learned so little language after puberty argues in favor of the theory of the "critical period." With a limited understanding of grammatical principles— for example, not distinguishing among pronouns or between active and passive verbs—it seems that Genie will remain limited in her social and intellectual development. Whether we will ever gain more information is uncertain since, in 1978, Genie's mother became her legal guardian and withdrew her from professional assistance and research.

Childhood as a Product of Social Change

Socialization always takes place in a specific historical time period. This is obvious. What is less obvious is that the very concept of childhood itself changes from one historical period to another. As we shall discuss more fully in Chapter 3, there is evidence to suggest that the notion of childhood as a distinct period of life emerged as recently as 400 or 500 years ago. Prior to that time, infancy was thought of as a stage that lasted from birth to about seven years of age, after which the child was admitted to, and freely mingled with, adult society. Schools existed only for a privileged few. Girls worked at home. Boys either labored in fields or began an apprenticeship at age seven or eight with a master craftsman with whom they lived and boarded while learning a trade. Although the term "child" (or equivalent) was used, it signified a family tie or kinship, not age. The notion of childhood as a time for keeping children segregated from adult activity and expecting them to spend much of their time with age-mates did not exist.

Once the concept of childhood began to emerge in the late Renaissance, there were debates and disagreements among leading thinkers of the time and later concerning the nature of children. Historian J. H. Plumb states that about the year 1600, there was a new attitude that considered children as innocent, requiring special protection from the adult world. The child became an object of respect.[27] Sociologist Anthony Synnott, in a more comprehensive review, sees this as only one of the attitudes that was emerging. As the title of his study, "Little Angels, Little Devils," indicates, another attitude, deriving largely from John Calvin, one of the originators of Protestantism, was that children were inherently evil and had to be severely disciplined and harshly punished to make them conform to God's will. A third view, derived from John Locke, a late seventeenth-century British philosopher, was that the child is a blank slate, neither good nor evil; the child is largely molded by the kind of education it is given, although biologically given talents also were believed to have some effect.[28]

Ideas about children—what they are like, what they are capable of, what they require—affect their place in society. After the onset of industrialization in the middle of the eighteenth century, children, like adults, were pulled out of the home and into factories. The first Factory Act limiting child labor was passed in England in 1833. For the first time children under the age of nine were prohibited from working in factories, and children between nine and thirteen were limited to eight hours of work a day.[29] In the United States, a national law limiting child labor was not adopted until 1938, although some of the individual states had taken such steps earlier. Children who worked in factories—and also those who worked on farms—were valued especially for the economic contribution they made to the family unit. But over a period of time another view emerged; instead of being appreciated because they were useful, children were to be loved for their own sake. Sociologist Viviana Zelizer, who studied cultural factors that led to this redefinition, describes the basic change in these terms:

> While in the nineteenth century, the market value of children was culturally acceptable, later the new normative ideal of the child as an exclusively emotional and affective asset precluded instrumental or fiscal considerations. In an increasingly commercialized world, children were reserved a separate non-commercial place. . . . The economic and sentimental value of children were thereby declared to be radically incompatible. Only mercenary or insensitive parents violated the boundary by accepting the wages or labor contributions of a useful child. Properly loved children, regardless of social class,

belonged in a domesticated, nonproductive world of lessons, games, and token money. It was not a simple process. At every step, working-class and middle-class advocates of a useful childhood battled the social construction of the economically useless child.[30]

At the conclusion of her study, Zelizer raises the possibility that we may be at the very beginning of another historical change. The great increase in working women has led to a decline of the full-time housewife. Although men resist becoming part-time househusbands, there is some slow movement in that direction, and there may be some movement toward children becoming part-time "housechildren."

> The world of children is changing and their household responsibilities may be redefined by changing family structures and new egalitarian ideologies. The notion, inherited from the early part of this century, that there is a necessarily negative correlation between the emotional and utilitarian value of children is being revised. The sentimental value of children may now include a new appreciation of their instrumental worth.[31]

Some support for her view comes from Robert S. Weiss's study of single mothers. He reports that children in these families grow up a little faster than those in two-parent families, particularly if the mothers work full time. Four- and five-year-olds are sometimes expected to make their own beds, eight-year-olds may vacuum floors and clean up the kitchen. Other changes are more subtle.[32]

While changing ideas and practices affect children's status in society and therefore influence the socialization experiences they are likely to have, changing technology (which also, of course, is the product of ideas) likewise can have a direct impact. Although social scientists do not yet have a very detailed knowledge or profound understanding of how such products as computers or video-cassette recorders are affecting socialization, some incidental consequences of new technology have been pointed out by communications theorist Joshua Meyrowitz. For example, he cites the influence of television on the position and authority of the teacher. At one time teachers could assume that young children had been shielded from topics appropriate only for adults and knew little about problems of the larger world. But now the child who has watched thousands of hours of television may have witnessed innumerable examples of adult struggles, misbehavior, and anxieties and may also know about many things the teachers have never heard of. Teachers, as a result, can no longer expect children to view them as all-knowing authorities.[33]

Another example concerns parental discipline. Meyrowitz writes:

> At one time, parents had the ability to discipline a child by sending the child to his or her room—a form of "excommunication" from social interaction. Such an action, however, takes on a whole new meaning today if the child's room is linked to the outside world through television, radio, telephone, and computer.[34]

Consumer electronic technology thus seems to have modified parental discipline by giving children resources that enable them to maintain more control over their social situation than was previously possible.

The study of socialization derives in part from the emergence of the concept of childhood and the ideas about the nature of children that began to receive active consideration about 500 years ago and have continued ever since. It also derives in part from early twentieth-century ideas about the nature of society. Emile Durkheim, one of the founders of sociology, was particularly concerned with explaining the nature of social order—how it is that social life takes on a certain degree of predictability. He recognized that socialization is an essential process for maintaining an ongoing society. Thus, questions about the nature of children and the nature of society must both receive part of their answer in the study of socialization.

CHAPTER 3

The Processes and Outcomes of Socialization

Although it is sometimes useful to speak of *the* process of socialization, just as we speak of the process of urbanization or industrialization or bureaucratization or modernization, the fact is that each of these terms is no more than a convenience for certain purposes. Each points in a general direction and identifies certain large-scale effects. When we study these phenomena, we quickly become aware that each of these terms encompasses diverse events. Socialization is not a unitary phenomenon, but rather a term for a variety of processes. The relationships among these specific processes are by no means fully worked out and understood; a unified and comprehensive theory of socialization has yet to be achieved. Nevertheless, we shall try, in this chapter, to identify and discuss the major processes. In so doing, we must approach our topic from several angles of vision, each of which illuminates the subject in a somewhat different way. Our goal here will be to present a general "model" of socialization that is broadly applicable and independent of specific cultures.

To begin, recall our definition of socialization: the process by which we learn the ways of a given society or social group so that we can function within it. By unraveling this definition, we can fashion a framework that helps us locate component processes of socialization. Learning involves developmental change in the organism; it occurs primarily in interaction with others who play important roles in that person's life. Such interaction necessarily entails communication of one kind or another, which is most meaningful in the context of emotionally significant relationships; and such relationships are always shaped by the social groups of which the person is a member. Succinctly, then, we may say that socialization

1. occurs over time,
2. through interaction with "significant others,"
3. by means of communication,
4. in emotionally significant contexts,
5. which are shaped by social groupings of varying scope.

It will be convenient to begin with the last point and move through the framework in reverse order.

SOCIETY AND SOCIALIZATION

Most commonly, socialization processes have been considered in face-to-face contexts such as the family, school, or peer group. Indeed, we shall focus on these contexts in Chapter 5. Yet it is clear that such groupings are agencies of the larger society. Parents not only raise their children to function in the family but also prepare them to leave the family and function in other settings. The school does the same. The values and techniques of peer-group relationships and the mass media, although less obvious, likewise have their long-term applications. Furthermore, although families, schools, and other social groupings often express divergent expectations toward those being socialized, they also often have convergent expectations. From this perspective, then, it is reasonable to say that *society specifies certain outcomes or ranges of outcomes of socialization.* For example, every society, just to maintain itself, expends some of its resources to produce children who will become law-abiding adults. Children who do not become law-abiding are likely to be judged socialization failures. Another socialization outcome specified by the society is loyalty. The society seeks to engender loyalty to itself, and its institutions and groups contribute to this outcome in various ways.

Families, schools, peer groups, and other agencies of socialization may vary in how attentive they are to socially desired outcomes, how they go about trying to bring about these outcomes, and how effective their chosen procedures are. Despite these variations, we can say that society—any society—endeavors to bring about certain desired and recognizable results in the socialization of its young. (Indeed, at various times society "gives recognition" when the desired results have been achieved—in the form of titles, prizes, badges, diplomas, promotions, and so forth.)

The most basic result sought is a *motivated commitment to sustain responsive participation in society.* Another way to put this is to say that children should become people who recognize and accept legitimate claims made upon them by others. These claims are multiple and diverse, and they differ according to a person's location in the social structure. Some, however, are general. For example, people should accept and function within the limits of communication and emotional expression that are defined as appropriate in different situations. Thus, they may scream at a football game, but not in a supermarket. They may laugh at home, at a movie, at a party, but not at a funeral. Another general type of claim may be expressed in this way: people should accept the obligations of their roles. If they take a job, they should do the work and meet its other legitimate requirements. If they enter into a friendship, they should be friendly according to the norms of that particular friendship, whatever they may be.

Even in those special cases where people are later trained for patterned withdrawal from general society—for example, nuns or monks who take vows of silence—the pattern of behavior is responsive to certain norms. It is not idiosyncratic withdrawal. Such an outcome falls within the range of socially acceptable results of socialization; although it represents a deviant role, it is not defined as a lack of motivated commitment to sustain responsive participation in society. In contrast, the role of "junkie"—a drug addict, especially one addicted to heroin—is one type of "dropping out" of society. By definition, this behavior represents a failure from the perspective in which we are now viewing socialization.

The difference between the role of the monk who takes vows of silence and that of the junkie can be understood more fully by stating another socially specified outcome. As has been pointed out by sociologist Alex Inkeles[1] and social psychologist M. Brewster Smith,[2] society expects the development of some kind of *competence.* Different societies require different kinds of competence, and any one society requires different kinds of competence for its diverse social roles. Nevertheless, it seems possible to formulate certain general requirements that transcend this diversity. Inkeles does so in the following way:

> Every individual must learn to be reasonably responsive to the pattern of social order and to the personal needs and requirements of the other individuals with whom he is in immediate contact. In other words, he must be basically socially conforming. He must have the ability to orient himself in space and time and have sufficient command of the rudimentary physical requirements of his setting so as not to destroy himself or be an undue burden on others. The requirements of society and of its specific statuses seem usually to involve certain motor and mental skills and techniques, and some kind of specialized knowledge and information; certain ways of thinking about the world, organized in a set of opinions and attitudes and constituting a distinctive idea system; a set of goals or values to guide action, and beliefs about the appropriate and acceptable paths to the goals; a conception of oneself which gives an identity and forms the basis for a system of social relations which include distinctive ways of relating to immediate authority, to intimates and peers, and to the larger community; some pattern for the organization of psychic functioning which favors and facilitates certain distinctive modes of defense or moral functioning; and a particular cognitive, conative, and affective style.[3]

Applying this conception to our example, we may say that our society recognizes certain kinds of "religious competence" and allows the development of institutions in which that competence may be practiced, even when that practice takes the form of withdrawal from verbal communication in order to engage in meditation. In contrast, drug addiction is defined by our society as willful destruction of a person's social competence and is therefore not generally accepted as a legitimate outcome of socialization in this society.

Now it is necessary here to introduce certain modifications of what has just been said. We have argued that many groups in a society have convergent expectations; that is, in any given society, family, school, church, and youth group, for example, press toward the same general outcomes. Because there is such convergence, we are justified in saying that society specifies certain outcomes. But two important modifications need to be stated: First, the fact that various institutions in a society tend to be mutually supportive in what they expect does not mean that they are entirely so. There is conflict as well as support among institutions. Parents often do not approve of what the school does, and vice versa. The youth group may encourage activities on which the authorities frown. Accordingly, socialization is not a smooth process. The child is subjected to conflicting as well as mutually supportive expectations.

Second, in arguing that society seeks to generate a motivated commitment to sustain participation and certain general forms of competence, we ignored certain phenomena that also are among the processes of socialization. Earlier we spoke of "dropping out" as a failure of socialization. What needs to be added here is that whereas some socialization failures may be attributable to particular socializing agents, other failures may be due to society's own contradictory organization. Thus, society may expect all children to learn certain things but may order its institutions in such a way that some are prevented from learning what they are expected to learn. In the United States, for example, one of the goals of the elementary school is to teach children of diverse backgrounds how to get along with others. But many institutional arrangements have resulted in segregating whites from blacks in their schooling, so that there is a systematically fostered limiting of competence. To take another example: There has been a "rediscovery" of hunger and malnutrition in various sections of the United States. Political and economic institutions do not deliver food to all who need it, and many suffer from malnutrition. These nutritional deficiencies very likely impair mental ability and thus prevent children from learning things they are expected to learn.[4] This again is an example of how the pattern of institutions can generate failures in socialization. More generally, although every society expects various types of minimal competence and seeks to foster more than minimal competence in those activities it most values, no society succeeds in eliciting even minimal levels among all its children, in part because the institutional pattern interferes.

These, then, are the two general goals of socialization: a motivated *commitment* to sustain responsive participation in society and forms of *competence* that the society accepts as appropriate. These goals are generic; they are universally applicable. Of course, when we become more specific, we find that the same kinds of commitment and competence are not expected of all members of society. The artist and the career soldier differ not only in their kinds of competence but also in the kinds of commitment to social participation expected of them. The soldier will participate in a set of relationships governed by rigid rules of obedience to command. The artist will participate in a set of relationships governed by efforts to attract an audience that will appreciate the uniqueness of his or her vision and skill. Society expects the socialization process to enable every new member eventually to find *some* appropriate adult status(es) within some legitimate set(s) of relationships. As we noted in Chapter 2, each status entails a role. We can add that a role (such as the occupational role of soldier or artist) involves a particular type of commitment to social participation and a particular type of competence.

While socialization is expected to result in the fulfilling of various specialized roles, it must also, as Inkeles points out, make it possible for persons to participate in a variety of ways with others whose statuses and roles are quite different from their own. The late Robert Hutchins, an educator and social reformer, used to deride a certain engineering school that maintained a Department of Engineering English because, as he put it, "nobody else talks engineering English." Whatever the merit of his derisiveness, the point he was making was that socialization can sometimes result in such an intense commitment to a particular form of social participation as to hamper social participation across role boundaries. A similar point had been made earlier by social critic and economist Thorstein Veblen, who spoke of a "trained incapacity."

Any society provides a variety of statuses and roles. Usually it also has more or less explicit rules governing access to at least certain statuses and roles. The social class into which a child is born, for example, may decisively determine the statuses and roles open to that child in later life. As early as 1944, W. Lloyd Warner and his colleagues showed that the type of education young American children receive is determined to a large extent by their social class.[5] Their conclusions have been borne out by much subsequent investigation. Ethnic group membership and religion are often decisive determinants of the kinds of social participation that will be allowed and the kinds of competence that children will be able to acquire. Thus, for example, blacks in the United States, untouchables in India, blacks and other nonwhites in South Africa, native Indians in North America, and political refugees and illegal immigrants from many countries have been restricted in certain kinds of social participation and often prevented from gaining the kinds of competence the societies value most highly. These groups have, in their respective societies, been depreciated by more dominant groups who have effective control of many institutions including, importantly, the schools, which affect socialization outcomes. With more or less stringency, the children of these depreciated groups have been socialized toward the less valued statuses and roles, often toward those that sociologist Everett Hughes has characterized as the "dirty work" of the society. Conversely, children born into more favored segments of society are socialized toward more favored statuses and roles. Generally, then, we may say that society has criteria for distinguishing among children, often based upon the status attributes of the families into which they are born, and procedures for directing different groups of children into different sequences of experiences that eventuate in different socialization outcomes.

Thus, we see that society organizes itself in such a way as to develop in its children both a general commitment to participate in society and a general competence for doing so, and also a variety of commitments and competences that are considered relevant to particular statuses and roles. And, to the degree that different groups in society have different opportunities, positions, and values, they may also have different measures of competence and different methods of child rearing for developing this competence.

EMOTIONALLY SIGNIFICANT RELATIONSHIPS

Where does socialization begin? We have given one answer to this question by saying that society specifies desired outcomes that are to be brought about by its agencies—its families, schools, churches, youth groups, mass media, and other institutions. From this perspective, socialization begins with the specification of the range of outcomes toward which all newborns will be directed.

But the newborn, of course, knows nothing of this. If we look at the question from this perspective, it receives a different answer: Socialization begins with *personal attachment.* Born active but helpless, vocal but without speech, with only the potentiality to become human, needing care, infants begin to be socialized by being cared for by one or more persons who are committed to caring for them. At birth, children evoke sentiments of pride, love, apprehension, tenderness, responsibility, hope, and so forth, in those who receive them as new members of the group. Most important among them usually is the mother. She responds on the basis of the sentiments her child evokes in her.[6] Her response has many aspects. She touches and holds the child in a certain way, perhaps self-confidently, perhaps nervously, perhaps with a certain annoyance. She may be diligent or dilatory in responding to its cries. She may breast-feed and sing to her child, or she may routinely give it a bottle and let it feed in solitude.

From the perspective of the individual child starting out in life, the mother-child relationship is where socialization begins. What happens in this relationship that initiates socialization? Many different things.

This is the infant's first relationship with another person. It is therefore the first significant encounter with what it means to be human. Being cared for is one's first experience of social life. As such, and coming before a child can evaluate it, the relationship with the mother is virtually all the social life an infant has and therefore presents his or her first expectation of the social world. The infant whose mother spends much time with it, singing, playing, feeding, will have a different expectation of social life than the infant whose mother gives only minimal and cursory care.

Not less important, in this first attachment the child has the beginnings of a sense of self. One fundamental fact of the mother-child relationship is that the adult has far more power than the infant. But this is not to say that the infant is necessarily powerless. If its cries of discomfort succeed with some consistency in evoking parental response that allays the discomfort, then, we have reason to believe, the infant is launched on a path of experiencing itself as effective. On the other hand, when the infant's cries do not bring a satisfying response, or do so only inconsistently, its sense of powerlessness is intensified.

That the mother-child relationship is important for socialization has long been believed, but efforts to identify the crucial aspects of this relationship have met with uneven success. Psychoanalysis, a theory formulated on the basis of closely attentive observation of adults being treated for emotional disturbances, argued that the child's earliest feelings about feeding and excreting were influential—often decisive—in shaping the child's later development. Academic research workers were challenged by this theory presented by nonacademic clinicians and sought to test these ideas in a way that would justify accepting or rejecting them. What was important about feeding? Was it the difference between breast-feeding and bottle-feeding? Was it the suddenness or gradualness of weaning? Since toilet training seemed to be the first clear imposition of society's demands upon the unsocialized infant, did the age at which such training was begun make a difference? And was it better to start early or late? Should the mother be gentle or stern in the way she went about it?

These and numerous related questions prompted a voluminous quantity of research. In a meticulous review of this research—a review which itself fills nearly eighty pages—Bettye M. Caldwell concludes that the results remain inconclusive.[7] The research does not justify the conclusion that feeding and toilet-training practices have no effect, but neither is it clear that the practices as such have definite effects.

Of greater interest in recent years has been the question of the attachment of the child to the mother. That children form attachments as early as three or four months is indicated in an early study by Leon J. Yarrow. Infants of this age who were moved from foster homes to adoptive homes showed disturbances such as withdrawn behavior, increased apathy, and disturbances of sleep and feeling. "More overt social disturbances—excessive clinging or definite rejection of the new mother—occurred with increasing frequency after six months."[8]

Jerome Kagan refers to two other studies that also show the strength of mother attachment, even for young children who spend considerable time with substitute caretakers. In one, a group of children, from the age of three and one-half months, attended a day-care center in Boston five days a week. When the children were twenty months old, each was placed in an unfamiliar setting with the mother, the primary day-care teacher, and an unfamiliar woman. On two occasions, the child was deliberately made uncertain by having the three adults suddenly exchange seats. When the children were apprehensive because of this provocation or when they were tired or bored, they all went to their mother for comfort.

In another comparative study, researchers report on children, age nine to thirty-one months, who had been in day care since infancy and who spent at least half of their waking time each day with caretakers in a pleasant, stimulating, and reinforcing environment. Still, when they had a choice in a play situation of interacting with their mothers or their caretakers, or when faced with a mildly difficult problem, they were significantly more likely to go to their mothers.[9] Kagan concludes: ". . . that the number of hours a child is cared for by an adult is not the critical dimension that produces a strong attachment. There is something special about the mother-infant relationship."[10] We shall refer to this point again when we discuss the family as an agent of socialization.

We have been assuming that the primary infant-care functions are largely carried out by one person, the mother. This has been the usual situation. Some cultures, however, and increasingly our own, apportion such care among several people, including the father, grandparents, and caretakers at day-care centers. One study of father-infant interaction showed that children between the ages of one and two, depending upon the degree to which fathers have cared for them, may be equally attached to mothers and fathers.[11] There is some evidence, however, that the infant is likely to form a closer attachment to one among the multiple caretaking figures,[12] and, as we have noted, attendance at day-care centers does not seem to weaken attachment to the mother.

In sum, by being cared for, by evoking response and being responded to, the infant obtains its first sense of self, first sense of another person, first experience of a social relationship. In this relationship the infant develops its first expectations and thus its first sense of social order. A rudimentary temporal order emerges from such experiences as the interval between crying and being responded to; the interval between feedings; the alternation of sleeping and wakefulness. In being cared for, the infant has its first experiences of those sentiments that Cooley identified decades ago as the hallmark of human nature.

The child's attachment to the earliest caretaking figure is the first of many emotionally significant relationships that the child will form in the course of his or her life with *significant others*. This will be followed by various attachments to a diversity of significant others, who may include other adult figures, siblings, age-mates and older children in neighborhood and school, relatives, teachers, friends, and "enemies." A child will form a somewhat different kind of relationship with each of these people; because of this, and because each has a different status in society and a different role in relation to the child, each will make a different kind of contribution to the child's socialization. These differences will give rise to problems for the child from an early age, with the conflict between parents and age-mates typically being one focus of stress. Four-year-olds encouraged by playmates to cross the street in pursuit of adventure may experience distress before they follow the suggestion or only after their parents have discovered that they have done so. In either case, they are experiencing an early form of the conflict of norms and expectations that impinge on them from socializing agents who occupy different statuses.

COMMUNICATION

Now we face a paradox. Society presses toward certain outcomes, yet socialization begins in a two-person relationship of mother giving care to an infant who cannot speak or think or even understand instruction. How can an infant traverse the path from this beginning to that of a participating member of society? How can he or she be set upon this path?

The relevant facts here are that speechless newborns can see, hear, feel, and communicate, and these resources can get them started. At the outset infants can feel discomfort and comfort. When they feel discomfort, they cry. A mother or mother substitute hears the cry, *interprets* it as a sign of discomfort, and *responds* with activities that she hopes will restore the infant to comfort or at least keep it quiet. She will evaluate, or interpret, her own effort as successful when the child ceases to cry. Her initial efforts may not be "on target" because she may incorrectly interpret the source of the discomfort and the actions that will be effective in assuaging it. She may assume the child is hungry, only to find that it does not nurse. Further trial and error will lead to a "correct interpretation"—that is, one that leads the child to stop crying and leads the mother to judge that she has responded appropriately.[13]

Symbols, Language, and Interaction

The situation we have just described is the prototype of social interaction from which more complex forms evolve and through which the infant will develop into a person who can function in society. In this rudimentary interaction, the child makes a sound that is not simply a noise to his or her mother. The noise is significant to her—on two bases. First, she accepts the noise as having a legitimate claim upon her attention, because of her relationship to the child. The cry will not go unnoticed as might the noise of an airplane passing overhead, because *for her* it signifies or *symbolizes her* attachment and responsibility to the child. It does so independently of how she chooses to respond to the cry. But the second meaning of the cry is a responsive or *interactive* meaning. She may decide that the cry should be interpreted as meaning she should attend to the infant right away. Alternatively, she may decide to interpret it as one that allows her to wait until a more convenient moment to respond. Or she may decide not to respond immediately, with the express goal of teaching the child to tolerate more discomfort. Whatever her particular response, she engages in an imaginative process—which may take no more than an instant—in which she represents to herself what the child is probably feeling and what should be done about it. Her overt response to the child's cry occurs only after the process of inner representation.

The capacity to interpret communications from others and to represent to oneself what others may think, feel, and do is fundamental to all of social life. Newborns do not have this capacity, and this is what they must develop. At the outset they experience discomfort but do not know how it can be assuaged. Crying is involuntary; it is not a communication to *the infant.* But in time, as cries succeed in bringing mother and comfort, they begin to be more under the infant's voluntary control. Whether the infant develops, in this preverbal period, the capacity to form mental representations of her is a moot question. Some psychoanalytic writers postulate that preverbal infants do have the capacity to imagine their mothers coming to them. Most scholars, including most psychoanalytic writers, remain skeptical because there is no reasonable way at this time to ascertain whether a preverbal infant does or does not imagine anything. Nevertheless, the child becomes increasingly able to anticipate the mother's appearance. By the time the child becomes able to stand in a crib, he or she is also able to look toward the door through which mother will enter and to greet her entry by rocking on his or her feet, reaching out, and changing vocalization—before the mother ministers to the child. The child has developed some expectations that are responsive to the mother's expectations as she comes to tend to him or her. The child is on the way to becoming socialized. The child begins to learn how to function in society by learning how to function in the relationship with his or her mother (or mother substitute).

There is some evidence that even during this preverbal period of the newborn's life mother-infant interaction varies from one society to another in ways that are already preparing the infant for membership in the particular society. William Caudill, a long-time student of Japan, observed mothers and infants in thirty Japanese middle-class homes and in thirty American middle-class homes. He found in these samples differences between the two societies in mothers' caretaking style and in the infants' behavior, differences that were related to the general organization of the two societies. The American mothers were lively in their caretaking, more often in and out of the baby's room than were the Japanese, and engaged in active vocal interaction with their infants. The Japanese mothers sought to soothe and quiet their babies while lulling and rocking them. Physical contact was more prominent than vocal interaction. Caudill writes:

> In America the mother views her baby as a potentially separate and autonomous being who should learn to do and think for himself. For her, the baby is from birth a distinct personality with his own needs and desires which she must learn to recognize and care for. She helps him to learn to express these needs and desires through her emphasis on vocal communication so that he can "tell" her what he wants and she can respond appropriately. She de-emphasizes the importance of physical contact such as carrying and rocking and encourages her infant through the use of her voice to explore and to learn to deal with his environment by himself. In the same way that she thinks of her infant as a separate individual, she thinks of herself as a separate person with needs and desires which include time apart

from her baby so that she may pursue her own interests. . . . For this reason the pace of her caretaking is quicker than the Japanese mother's, and when she is caretaking, her involvement with the baby is livelier and more intense. This is true partly because she wishes to stimulate the baby to activity and response so that when it is time for him to sleep, he will remain asleep and allow her time to do other things. . . .

In Japan, the mother views her baby much more as an extension of herself. . . . The mother feels that she knows what is best for the baby, and there is no particular need for him to tell her what he wants because, after all, they are virtually one. Thus, in Japan, there is greater emphasis on interdependence, rather than independence, of mother and child, and this emphasis extends into adulthood. Given this orientation, the Japanese mother places less importance on vocal communication and more on physical contact; also, for her, there is no need for hurry as the expectation is that she will devote herself to her child without any great concern for time away from him. . . . As we know from other research . . . the Japanese child will ordinarily sleep with his parents until he is approximately ten years of age.

Given the differences in these two styles of care, we believe that the infants have learned to respond to each respective style in culturally appropriate ways by three to four months of age. . . . This learning process takes place well before development of the ability to use language in the ordinary sense; hence, these infants have acquired before then some aspects of the "implicit culture" . . . of their group—that is, those ways of feeling, thinking, and behaving that go on largely out of awareness and that, in general, characterize the actions of people in a given culture.[14]

Joy Hendry, a social anthropologist whose children spent their preschool years in Japan, confirms this picture of much bodily contact and the importance of nonverbal communication. She writes:

Traditionally, mothers took babies into their own bedding or provided a small mattress beside their own for a young child . . . if they use a cot, they keep it next to their own bed and rarely put the baby into it until they have lulled it carefully off to sleep first. . . . the Western practice of putting a baby into a cot in another room and leaving it to cry itself to sleep [is] shocking to most Japanese mothers. . . . a good mother is supposed to be able to anticipate her baby's requirements, the beginning of the art of non-verbal communication which she should later pass on to her children for dealings with other people.[15]

With the gradual acquisition of language, socialization accelerates and becomes qualitatively transformed from its preverbal beginnings. Language is, of course, part of the heritage of a society, and facility in the use of its language is one of the kinds of competence toward which society directs its newborns. But while *language facility* is one of the expected outcomes of socialization, *language acquisition* is of enormous importance as one of the component processes of socialization long before full facility is achieved.

Recall our account of mother-infant interaction. When the infant cries, the mother interprets this as a sign of need. But she must discover for herself whether the infant is hungry, wet, cold, has caught its foot in the slats of the crib or is in some other state of discomfort. The infant's cry is an interpretable symbol to its mother but only imperfectly so; and it is not at all a symbol to the infant.[16] As infants acquire the ability to use common gestures and language, they are acquiring the ability to symbolize—the ability to identify and name things, people, and feelings. In place of nonspecific cries, they are able to point or tug or name their wishes to another. But in order to be able to do this, they have to be able to identify wishes to themselves. When children are able to present to themselves the same symbol for an object that they present to others, they have taken a large step toward regulating their own behavior and simultaneously a large step toward participating responsively with others. A qualitative change of great importance has thus taken place when, instead of nonspecific cries, children can designate their wishes with words that communicate specifically: "bottle," "wet," "pick me up," and so on. They now have at their disposal specific symbols whose meaning *they know* and that they know their mothers know. They are entering into a social world of shared symbols. Their capacity for social interaction is thus expanding enormously as they master an expanding array of shared symbols. In this process they are gaining the capacity to move beyond the circumscribed world of the mother-child relationship into a larger social world of widely shared symbols.

Recent research on the acquisition of language indicates that it is a far more complicated process than had previously been supposed. Indeed, like socialization generally, it involves many component processes. Two deserve brief mention here. From one point of view, language consists of words, and learning language involves learning words. Infants begin to speak by making random sounds and their repertoire in the first six months, it is claimed, contains all sounds present in human language.[17] When they make a sound that approximates a word in their "native language," their parents and others encourage them by repeating the sound as the "correct word" that they almost hear. By responding in an interested and pleasurable way and by providing the child with "correct pronunciations" of words they imagine the child is struggling to say, the significant others reward and encourage the child's further efforts. Since much of this activity goes on in relation to specific objects and experiences in the child's world, the random sounds develop both into "real words" and into symbols for objects and experiences. Sound and meaning come to be associated.

This view of language learning has been held for some time. It seems satisfactory as far as it goes, but it does not go far enough. A number of linguistic scholars, most prominently Noam Chomsky, have pointed out that language consists not simply of words but of sentences.[18] Further, there is no limit to the number of sentences that can be formed. Even children will, at some point, begin to speak sentences they have never heard before and that therefore cannot be explained simply as the result of their being directly taught in the fashion described in the preceding paragraph. Accordingly, these scholars argue, in some fashion children learn *"productive rules* that enable the speaker to produce the infinite variety of sentences that he produces and to understand the infinite variety of sentences that he hears."[19] How the child learns these rules is not yet understood, but more is involved than learning textbook grammar. The available evidence does indicate, according to James J. Jenkins, that

> the child is very systematic in his approach to language. It may be that he moves from one system to another, testing, changing, testing, trying again, or it may be that he chooses one system and progressively differentiates it into finer and finer portions; but the evidence that he is doing *something* systematic is overwhelming. . . . there is evidence that the child is struggling with a system for generating language at every stage and in very complex ways.[20]

These insights into the child's learning of language emphasize that in the course of socialization he or she is engaged in an effort to develop an inner regulation of behavior, an internal order that in some adequate way corresponds to an external social order.

Language is, then, an example of social order, just as the arrangement of houses on streets or the exchange of money for goods and services are examples of social order. All of these regulate the relationships among people in accordance with rules, and the child will have to learn the relevant rules for these and many other aspects of social order.

But language plays a particularly significant part in organizing a social order and in the child's socialization into that order. Language is, among its other functions, a system for classifying objects and events in ways that are socially significant. Thus, if a child sits on a table, he or she may be told "that's not a chair." The table surface lends itself to sitting just as does the seat of a chair; but despite their physical similarity in this respect they are socially defined as completely different objects, and this difference is embodied in a verbal classification that organizes behavior in relation to the objects. The way in which things and events are verbally classified defines their social nature, and these classifications become a fundamental part of our way of thinking and acting. Our very perception is shaped by our language categories. In time the child will not even see the table as offering the possibility for sitting, because his or her knowledge of it as being within the category "table" will preclude the possibility.

Categorization of social reality takes more complex forms. A common example in our society is the disposition to see many situations in "either-or" terms. The child may encounter this at the dinner table in the form of "Either eat your vegetables or go without dessert." Another situation of similar form is "Practice the piano (do your homework, clean up your room) or you can't go out to play." Desired activities are thus incorporated in an "either-or" way of thinking that makes them contingent on the performance of some undesired activity—"or else."

Finally, one further indication of the way in which language shapes experience is of particular interest. Freud called attention to "the peculiar amnesia which veils from most people (not from all) the first years of their childhood, usually the first six or eight years."[21] He was impressed with the fact that childhood experiences are often vivid and that they include love, jealousy, and other passions. Yet despite the intensity, memories of these experiences in later years are fragmentary at best. Following up

Freud's observations, but dissatisfied with his explanation of this massive failure of memory, Ernest G. Schachtel proposed the following explanation: Memory organizes past experiences in the service of present needs, fears, and interests. Adult memory is organized into categories that are shaped by society. These categories "are not suitable vehicles to receive and reproduce experiences of the quality and intensity typical of early childhood," because they are shaped by the biases, emphases, and taboos of adult culture. Adult memory is essentially conventionalized, and therefore early childhood experience—in which everything seems new, fresh, and exciting—is incompatible, hence forgotten. The conventionalization of memory proceeds so far that, as Schachtel puts it:

> the memories of the majority of people come to resemble increasingly the stereotyped answers to a questionnaire, in which life consists of time and place of birth, religious denomination, residence, educational degrees, job, marriage, number and birth-dates of children, income, sickness and death. . . . the average traveler through life remembers chiefly . . . what he is supposed to remember because it is exactly what everybody else remembers too. . . . Experience increasingly assumes the form of the cliché under which it will be recalled. . . . This is not the remembered situation itself but the words which are customarily used to indicate this situation and the reactions which it is supposed to evoke. . . . There are people who experience a party, a visit to the movies, a play, a concert, a trip in the very words in which they are going to tell their friends about it; in fact, quite often they anticipate such experience in these words. The experience is predigested, as it were, even before they have tasted of it. Like the unfortunate Midas, whose touch turned everything into gold so that he could not eat or drink, these people turn the potential nourishment of the anticipated experience into the sterile currency of the conventional phrase which exhausts their experience because they have seen, heard, felt nothing but this phrase with which later they will report to their friends the "exciting time" they have had.[22]

Thus, Schachtel maintains, language not only shapes memory into conventionalized categories; in extreme cases it even conventionalizes the experience before it passes into memory. But even in ordinary cases, conventionalization is so powerful that most early childhood experience is not accessible to memory.

Although society provides linguistic categories for organizing our thoughts and ideas, conversations themselves may have a problematic aspect for the participants because much of what is said assumes many things left unsaid. Social interaction depends upon interpretive procedures that help the person "make sense of" or "understand" what is going on. To illustrate the constantly ongoing interpretation in social interaction, Harold Garfinkel reproduced a conversation between a student and his wife (left-hand column) together with the meaning that was understood in each statement (right-hand column). We quote it in the same format that Garfinkel used:

HUSBAND: *Dana succeeded in putting a penny in a parking meter today without being picked up.*

This afternoon as I was bringing Dana, our four-year-old son, home from the nursery school, he succeeded in reaching high enough to put a penny in a parking meter when we parked in a meter parking zone, whereas before he has always had to be picked up to reach that high.

WIFE: *Did you take him to the record store?*

Since he put a penny in a meter, that means that you stopped while he was with you. I know that you stopped at the record store either on the way to get him or on the way back. Was it on the way back, so that he was with you, or did you stop there on the way to get him and somewhere else on the way back?

HUSBAND: *No, to the shoe repair shop.*

No, I stopped at the record store on the way to get him and stopped at the shoe repair shop on the way home when he was with me.

WIFE: *What for?*

I know of one reason why you might have stopped at the shoe repair shop. Why did you in fact?

HUSBAND: *I got some new shoelaces for my shoes.*

As you will remember, I broke a shoelace on one of my brown oxfords the other day, so I stopped to get some new laces.

WIFE: *Your loafers need new heels badly.*

Something else you could have gotten that I was thinking of. You could have taken in your black loafers which need heels badly. You'd better get them taken care of pretty soon.[23]

Such interpretive procedures must be, and evidently are, learned fairly early in the course of socialization, although just when and how are not yet understood. A child learns quite early in life that when a telephone caller asks, "Is your daddy there?" the child is not only being asked a question but is also expected to call daddy to the phone. Nor is it a question when the mother says, "How many times have I told you to close that door!" Nor is the nursery-school teacher just making announcements when she says, "It's nap time" or "It's clean-up time now."[24] In all these instances, the child is expected to interpret and to then act appropriately. Each sentence spoken carries a wider range of meaning than is actually stated, and conversational language must be continually interpreted by the participants.

Gregory Bateson and his co-workers have pointed out that all communication involves something said and a modality in which it is said—words are said seriously, jokingly, commandingly, questioningly, and so on. The participant in a conversation must interpret the modality being used as well as what is said. Very young children are sometimes unable to do this. For example, they may not understand that parents are commanding, not asking. Certain kinds of playful comments made by older children or adults may not be understood as playful by the very young child, who may burst into tears. When this happens, the older children or adults may engage in a detailed explanation of what was intended. In the course of socialization, most children develop the ability to interpret (and later to use) modality appropriately most of the time. Still, there are times when anyone may be uncertain and may ask: "Are you serious?" or "Are you kidding?" Adequate socialization makes such occasions infrequent. We are able to recognize the modality by the combination of words spoken, tone of voice, and the social context in which the words are spoken. But even when we understand the modality, we still must continually interpret the words, as our examples demonstrate.[25]

THE SIGNIFICANCE OF SIGNIFICANT OTHERS

With our discussion of emotional attachments and of communication as background, we are now in a position to identify some additional processes that make significant others significant to the child and that help the child develop from the primarily biological organism he or she is at birth into a person as well.

When we say that the task of socialization is to enable the child to learn to function in society, we refer to a complex type of adaptation that cannot be understood as a kind of mechanical conformity. As our brief sketch of human biological nature in Chapter 2 makes clear, human socialized behavior is not analogous to the behavior of the trained rat running a maze and receiving rewards for making correct turns in correct sequence. Socialization is not simply a process of making correct motions prescribed by trainers. Running in a rat race or jumping through a hoop are, when applied to humans, terms for caricaturing certain distortions of socialization.

As suggested by our discussion of learning language rules, the essence of socialization is the person's *internal regulation* of his or her own behavior in ways that are adequate to the interpersonal situations and to the larger social order in which he or she participates. The capability for internal regulation develops as a result of interaction with significant others.

Significant others present themselves to the child in two essential ways:

1. By what they do
2. By what they say (and how they say it)

Doing and saying are, of course, organized in terms of roles. Thus, a mother at home presents herself to her child by feeding, changing diapers, offering toys, addressing the child with words of endearment, and perhaps also these days, if she is working, by carrying a briefcase and driving the child to a day-care center. The father may do many of the same activities as the mother, but likely will also be taller, have a deeper voice, talk with different inflections and a different vocabulary, more often watch football, and be brusquer in his handling. An older brother may run and shout, throw a ball, have his own toys, use a still different vocabulary, and be subject to the authority of the parents.

As infants become aware of the activities going on around them, they become interested in these activities; and because these are the activities of people to whom infants are emotionally attached, infants want to do what those around them do and, indeed, to be as they are. For example, not long after a mother begins giving her child nonliquid food, the child wishes to feed her as he or she is being fed. The child tries to take the spoon from her and feed her. As the range of observation expands, the child tries other activities that seem interesting: turning light switches on and off, opening the refrigerator, and the like. And while the child's significant others are engaged in such activities, they are also engaged in saying things—naming the objects they handle ("Drink your milk."), describing what they are doing ("Here's your doll."), playing word games ("Where's your nose? Show me your nose."). Children begin to repeat the words they hear and to carry out the actions they see others carry out. In short, they perceive their significant others as *role models,* sources of the patterns of behavior and conduct on which children pattern themselves. It is through interaction with these role models that children develop the ability to regulate their own behavior.

The basic fact that the child's regulation of his or her own behavior develops from interaction with role models has been noted by numerous interpreters but explained variously by them. No single account of this process and its consequences is fully satisfactory, nor has anyone yet developed a satisfactory composite interpretation. We shall therefore draw upon several sources that seem necessary for an adequate understanding of this process but which do not yet fit well together.

For George Herbert Mead, an influential figure in American sociology, the principal outcome of socialization that makes self-regulation possible is the development of the *self.* The self, in his view, is the capacity to represent to oneself what one wishes to communicate to others. Language plays a crucial part in development of the self. This is why, from Mead's point of view, the child's change from simply crying to being able to use socially shared symbols such as "I want bottle," "Go outside" (for "I want to go outside") is such a significant transformation.[26] Only humans can self-consciously and purposively represent to themselves that which they wish to represent to others; this, for Mead, is what it means to have a self and what it means to be human. The child who can do this is on his or her way to becoming human, that is, to being simultaneously self-regulating and socially responsive.

According to Mead's analysis, the self is both a structure and a process. It consists of two parts or phases, which Mead called the "I" and the "me." The "I," which is a feature of the human being as a biological organism, is the self as an acting subject; it is also that part of the self that enables us to be aware of who we are. The "me" is the self as the object of one's own actions; it is the accumulation of attitudes toward the person expressed by diverse others that are taken over by the person. To help clarify this distinction, consider the following example.

A mother tells her little daughter, Susie, "You have brown hair." Having brown hair is part of the mother's attitude toward her daughter; that is, it is part of the mother's ideas about her and something she believes Susie should know. When Susie hears it, it becomes part of her "me." It may take awhile before Susie can make this information part of her usable knowledge about herself, but before long she will be able to say to someone else, "*I* have brown hair." When she can do this, Susie has become an acting subject toward herself (as well as toward the person she addresses). Her "I" recognizes something about herself, something originally put into words by her mother. This capacity to be aware of oneself, to act toward oneself, is called *reflexivity*. It is essential for self-regulation. During Susie's early childhood, her mother will comb her hair. At a later period, Susie will look in the mirror and decide, "I've got to comb my hair before going out." That is a reflexive action (she acts toward herself), and it is also part of an interaction because the hair combing is done in anticipation of being with other people who will see her. In Mead's terms (which sociologists still use today), Susie has "taken the role of the others" whom she anticipates seeing, and their attitudes became part of her "me." As an "I," she regulated her own action by combing her hair. How did Susie become able to take the role of the others? Mead had an explanation. Language, which he considers paramount, is part of the explanation: "Combed hair" and "uncombed hair" are symbols Susie shares with others. But there is more to role-taking than language.

In addition to language, Mead also recognizes the importance of the child's observations of others' activities. He postulated that children, following a stage in which they mimic without comprehending, go through two stages of observation toward the development of self. In the first, or *play stage*, children take the roles of others: They play at being the others who are significant to them. They want to push the broom, carry the umbrella, put on the hat, and do all the other things they see their parents do, including saying what parents say. The story is told of the four-year-old playing "daddy" who put on his hat and coat, said "good-bye," and walked out the front door, only to return a few minutes later because he didn't know what to do next. He had taken as much of his father's work role as he could see and hear—the ritualized morning departure. What is noteworthy in the illustration (as in all play) is that the child is now able to govern his own behavior to a certain extent. When he first heard adults say "bye-bye" to him, he did nothing because the sound had no meaning to him. Nor did it mean anything when he first learned to repeat the sound. Now when he says "good-bye," he directs himself to walk out the door.

In the play stage children play at many roles that offer interesting models to them, not only imitating their parents and other children but also playing "cops and robbers," letter carrier, space pilot, and so on. During this stage they progress to taking two complementary roles at a time. Thus, they may say things to themselves that their mothers have said to them, then reply in their own roles of children. If no playmates are around, they may enact the roles of both cop and robber in alternation.

With further development the child enters the *game stage*. The importance of this lies in the fact that games involve an organization of roles, and the child participating has to take the role of everyone else. In Mead's famous example of the baseball game, the child

> must have the responses of each position involved in his own position. He must know what everyone else is going to do in order to carry out his own play. He has to take all of these roles. They do not all have to be present in consciousness at the same time, but at some moments he has to have three or four individuals present in his own attitude, such as the one who is going to throw the ball, the one who is going to catch it, and so on. These responses must be, in some degree, present in his own makeup. In the game, then, there is a set of responses of such others so organized that the attitude of one calls out the appropriate attitudes of the other.[27]

Then, as Mead puts it:

> This getting of the broad activities of any given social whole or organized society as such within the experiential field of any one of the individuals involved . . . is . . . the essential basis and prerequisite

of the fullest development of that individual's self: only in so far as he takes the attitudes of the organized social group to which he belongs toward the organized, cooperative social activity or set of such activities in which that group . . . is engaged, does he develop a complete self. . . . And on the other hand, the complex cooperative processes and activities and institutional functionings of organized human society are also possible only in so far as every individual involved in them . . . can take the general attitudes of all other such individuals with reference to these processes and activities and institutional functionings, . . . and can direct his own behavior accordingly.[28]

Thus, once children have developed selves, they can act cooperatively with others. They may imaginatively take the position of others and know what is expected of them in their various roles— as pitcher on a baseball team, as passenger on a bus, as clown in a school play, as "good and polite" child visiting grandmother, as best friend, as caretaker of younger sister, as newspaper delivery boy or girl. The explanation of such role-taking is a subject of some disagreement among contemporary sociologists. Some would emphasize that performing a role is explainable as learned conformity. The baseball pitcher, in this explanation, learns the rules of baseball and what the pitcher is supposed to do in relation to the batter, the catcher, and the other players. The pitcher does his or her part according to the rules. Other sociologists emphasize that carrying out a role is a creative and interpretive activity. As Ralph Turner, one of the leading writers of this view, puts it, much role-taking should be regarded as role-*making* because it involves "devising a performance on the basis of an imputed other-role."[29] The pitcher is not merely pitching according to a set of rules. In addition, he or she imputes a role to each batter—this one swings at every pitched ball, that one waits for a pitch to his liking, and so on—and decides how to try to pitch to each one. If the bases are loaded and there are two outs, the pitcher will devise one kind of role performance if the next batter is a good hitter and another type of role performance if the next batter is not a good hitter. This view of role performance as role-making, as continually developing as the situation changes, is based on Mead's notion of the "I" as active rather than simply as conforming. In Mead's words,

The "I" is the response of the organism to the attitudes of the others . . . this response of the "I" is something that is more or less uncertain. . . . The "I" gives the sense of freedom, of initiative.

The situation is there for us to act in a self-conscious fashion. We are aware of ourselves, and of what the situation is, but exactly how we will act never gets into experience until after the action takes place.[30]

For young children, the opportunity to experience and develop role-taking occurs especially in family relationships, but is also evident in their relationships with toys.[31] Children commonly impute identities to their stuffed dolls and toys. They give them parts to play, converse with them, and act toward them. These toys may be given roles of surrogate companions, they may be sources of comfort and security or targets of love, hostility, sympathy, and other sentiments. The children, in their relationship with their toys, explore their own feelings and play with self-images of power, age status, and sex roles. Even computers—as Sherry Turkle demonstrates—are given "life," considered to have minds of their own, and become objects of interaction.[32] The children are thus acting and devising performances on the basis of the roles they impute to others. They are "role-making." Toys and games in this sense facilitate the process by which children engage in imaginative behavior and prepare for subsequent roles and relationships.

In taking the roles of others, children come to learn that sometimes they can "manage the impression" that they are making. Thus, they may prepare a performance, practice what they will say, put on the right clothes, and act with the right demeanor. Sometimes they may know what others expect but, for whatever reason, choose to act otherwise. Sometimes, because of a miscalculation or slip-up, they are embarrassed or ashamed and seek to cover up or "save face." Such miscalculations reflect inaccurate role-taking. As Sheldon Stryker explains,

> One takes the role of others by using symbols to put oneself in another's place and to view the world as others do. Role-taking is the process of anticipating the responses of others with whom one is involved in social interaction. Making use of symbolic cues present in the situation of interaction, prior experience, and familiarity with the particular other or with comparable others, one organizes a definition of others' attitudes, orientations, and future responses which is then validated, invalidated, or reshaped in ongoing interaction. . . . Accuracy in role-taking is based at least in part on common experience which creates a fund of common symbols; but accuracy in role-taking is variable.[33]

Mead's explanation of the development of the self, shaped by language and role-taking, remains one of the basic building blocks in our understanding of how man functions in society. In certain respects it is unexcelled to this day, more than fifty years after his death. But it contains some important omissions. For example, Mead does not distinguish among different kinds of utterance. His approach finds no significance in the difference between a parent's saying "Here's your ball" and "Don't do that!" The latter expression is important in ways that the former is not, even though both are statements made by the same role model and both help the child to categorize the world in linguistic terms. But the latter statement is made *authoritatively.* It is more than a simple categorization. It is a statement of a *rule,* and it carries with it the suggestion of a *sanction.*

Role models who can present themselves to the child with authority to state rules and to enforce them with positive and negative sanctions play a particularly decisive part in the development of the child's self. An admired uncle who pilots a plane may catch the child's imagination more than his or her own father who works at a nine-to-five desk job. But the father, as the model who wields the more effective authority over the child's life, is likely to have greater influence in shaping the child's social participation. He, along with the mother, makes the child aware of limits to acceptable behavior. In short, the child has impulses and attempts actions that are unacceptable to those who have effective authority to interpret his or her behavior in the light of norms and values and to offer rewards and impose penalties to encourage appropriate conduct. (Effective authority does not rest only with adults. When children play with their peers, they come under a system of norms and sanctions that define "playing fair" and "cheating.") The self is established, then, not only on the basis of taking the role of the other but also through the process of *internalizing the values and norms* that are effectively presented by authoritative role models. In one sense socialization can be summed up by saying that what was once outside the individual comes to be inside the individual. Society comes to exist within the individual as well as outside of him or her. This is the developmental change that makes all the difference.

But we must consider developmental change from another angle of vision as well.

SOCIALIZATION AND TIME

Socialization is an extended process. It takes time, obviously. Less obviously, it takes different kinds of time. To begin, let us make a basic distinction between *life-cycle time* and *social time,* after which we shall note some of their complexities.

By life-cycle time we mean a sequence of biological stages based on maturation. Everywhere humans are born small and helpless. They then pass through a decade and a half or so of increasing size and strength. Sometime during the second decade puberty is reached and sexual maturity attained. For several decades thereafter, adult levels of energy are sustained, followed by a period of more or less precipitous decline. This sequence of stages is universal. The age at which changes occur varies according to many influences, but the sequence itself is not alterable.

Adequate socialization requires the development of cognitive capabilities (capacities to learn, understand, and think) and these, too, require time. The late Swiss psychologist Jean Piaget, who conducted many studies of how the minds of children work, concluded that they develop in four main stages.[34] At first, as infants, children deal with the world simply through sensations and movements—seeing, tasting, and touching or moving toward and handling things. They learn that objects have permanence; a toy out of sight is not necessarily a toy out of mind. Piaget called this the *sensorimotor stage.*

Then, at about eighteen to twenty-four months, children begin to develop simple concepts that refer to tangible objects. A two-year-old child, for example, may learn the concept "dog" and then apply it to any animal it sees; the child does not yet have the concept "animal" which is abstract and does not refer to any particular creature, yet includes dogs, cats, and squirrels. Children at this stage are also egocentric, unable to view themselves from the position of others. They may not understand, for example, that, to their siblings, they are brothers or sisters. This second phase Piaget calls the *preoperational stage.*

From about the age of six or seven, the child moves on to the third *stage of concrete operations,* so called because the child thinks in terms of concrete specific examples. Children at this stage can think logically and classify things, but have difficulty with more than one classification at a time. To recognize that at the same time one can be American, Mexican, Californian, Catholic, and a Democrat is hard to grasp.

From the age of twelve or so, children enter into the fourth *stage of formal operations*. Now they can think in abstract concepts, using not only such simple ones as "animal," but also more difficult ones such as "nature," "space," "our country," and "love." The child can think logically about all kinds of problems, build ideals, and imagine things contrary to fact. The changes from one stage to another do not occur at precise ages but, according to Piaget, must follow his four-stage sequence. This entire process of cognitive development is linked, in a general way, to life-cycle time because it depends partly upon biological maturation. However, it is also linked to social time, because it depends partly upon experience.

Social time may be generally defined as the organization of events into socially meaningful units. As society changes, the organization of time is likely to change. For example, when people worked a six-day week, they had one day of rest called the Sabbath. With a five-day work week now standard, the nonwork unit is of two days' duration and is called the weekend, although it could conceivably have been called "double Sabbath." The weekend is not simply twice as long as the Sabbath but is very different in social meaning as well.

Every society, in organizing its social life, takes note of the biological states, a phenomenon known as *age grading*. In our society we set certain age-level guides for going to school, learning to drive a car, taking a full-time job, marrying, and retiring. Age grading is thus one type of social time. But every society does not make the same age distinctions, nor does every society consider them of equal importance. Furthermore, as a society changes, its age grading is also likely to change. Thus, it may be said that the biological life cycle constitutes a substratum upon which society imposes its own distinctions as an overlay.

Social change is relevant to socialization. We discover from the work of Philippe Ariès, a sociologically minded historian, that the very notion of a distinctive period of life conceived of as childhood is of fairly recent origin. The many facts of childhood that seem so compellingly distinctive to us and lead us to differentiate the early years from those that follow did not have this impact in Western countries before about the sixteenth century.

This was shown in many ways in earlier times. For example, once infants were out of swaddling clothes, they were dressed just like "the other men and women" of their social class; there was no distinctive dress for children in medieval society. After the age of three or four, children played the same games as adults, including card games and games of chance for money. Documents from the early seventeenth century reveal that adults did not refrain from gestures and jokes with children that would today be regarded as immoral or perverted. Ariès notes:

> In medieval society, the idea of childhood did not exist; this is not to suggest that children were neglected, forsaken or despised. The idea of childhood is not to be confused with affection for children; it corresponds to an awareness of the particular nature of childhood . . . which distinguishes the child from the adult, even the young adult. In medieval society, this awareness was lacking. . . .
>
> In the Middle Ages, at the beginning of modern times, and for a long time after that in the lower classes, children were mixed with adults as soon as they were considered capable of doing without their mothers or nannies, not long after a tardy weaning (in other words about the age of seven). They immediately went straight into the great community of men, sharing in the work and play of their companions, old and young alike. The movement of collective life carried in a single torrent all ages and classes.[35]

The awareness of childhood as a distinct period of life is, then, a historical creation. Once this awareness developed, the nature of childhood and what should be done about it became a matter of ideological controversy, and it has remained so down to our time. At some periods and among some groups, the child has been regarded as basically tender and innocent. In opposition to this has been the notion that the child is wild and needs to be tamed. These two images continue to have their respective adherents.

Within any given society in a given historical period, the child passes through various kinds of sequences. Ariès describes how the school year has become a time unit for socialization:

> Today the class, the constituent cell of the school structure, presents certain precise characteristics which are entirely familiar: it corresponds to a stage in the progressive acquisition of knowledge (to a curriculum), to an average age from which every attempt is made not

to depart, to a physical spatial unit, for each age group and subject has its special premises . . . and to a period of time, an annual period at the end of which the class's complement changes.

The extremely close connection between the age of the pupils and the organic structure which gathers them together gives each year a personality of its own: the child has the same age as his class, and each class acquires from its curriculum, its classroom and its master a distinctive complexion. The result is a striking differentiation between age groups which are really quite close together. The child changes his age every year at the same time as he changes his class. In the past, the span of life and childhood was not cut up into such thin slices. The school class has thus become a determining factor in the process of differentiating the ages of childhood and early adolescence.[36]

Of course, while the child is passing through these school-determined age statuses, each with its own contribution to socialization, he or she is also passing through other gradations that are not institutionally determined or precisely delineated but which nevertheless mark significant steps. Such distinctions are numerous: for example, the progression from the play to the game stage in Mead's analysis. Or consider the progression from being a child who must come in when it gets dark to one who is allowed to stay out after dark with peers; or the farm child old enough to own a pony, the city child old enough for his or her first two-wheel bicycle. Language plays its part in these gradations, as well; children are told they are too old to cry or too young to have some object they want. *In some situations their age status is negotiable:* They may persuade their parents that they are old enough to go to the movies alone or to have a shotgun. The negotiation of age status as an interactive process between parents and children has not received much study.

In a process of *anticipatory socialization,* children prepare themselves for roles they might play in the future. They rehearse actions, values, and feelings before they actually enter into a particular status or adopt a new role. The child of four, in play and imagination, practices at being a child in school; a girl of ten, dreaming of being a teenager, tries on the clothes of her older sister; a boy of eleven, imagining himself in the school marching band, begins trumpet lessons. As viewed by parents and other adults, anticipatory socialization is often more long run. Thinking of future occupations, for example, they may encourage their children to play with computers or chemistry sets. If the role is truly on the horizon and the rehearsal appropriate, the processes of anticipatory socialization may well ease the adjustment into future roles.[37]

All these progressions lead the child toward maturity, a concept that has relevance both biologically and sociologically. Indeed, one of the important considerations for an understanding of socialization is that biological maturation usually presents a challenge to society or its agents. The child who becomes able to walk wants to walk in places that are "off limits" (for example, on sofas or in mud puddles) and therefore evokes negative sanctions. In similar fashion, other aspects of biological maturation, from eating to sexuality, present a challenge to society and its agencies and a challenge also to the growing child's own self. With each new step in biological maturation, the child feels ready to do things that once were done for him or her or wants to do things that his or her role models do, whether or not they feel the child is ready. The child says "let me do it" when the adult would rather do it more quickly or judges that the action is one the child should not yet do at all, even slowly—as when a three-year-old wants to use a sharp knife or carry something too heavy. Thus, from one perspective, socialization can be regarded as the process through which an individual's biological potentialities are brought into relationship with society: They are developed and transformed through time and made social.

No writer has achieved a more comprehensive view of this process than Erik Erikson.[38] In a sweeping look at the whole life cycle, he has proposed that it can be divided into eight stages, each of which presents the person with a basic socialization issue or dilemma. The manner in which each issue is resolved will shape the child's social participation as well as his or her happiness.

1. The first issue facing the helpless newborn is that of *trust versus distrust.* The emotional attachment to the mother is crucial in determining how this issue is resolved. From this standpoint, the first social achievement of the infant is its ability to let the mother out of sight without becoming anxious or enraged. This is possible when the mother has become "an inner certainty as well as an outer predictability."

2. The second year of life is marked by rapid gains in muscular maturation, visual and auditory discrimination, and verbalization. All of these give children the possibility of greater control over their own actions, and they begin to experience a sense of autonomous will. At this time, during which children are often also expected to gain bowel control, they are subjected to closer scrutiny. The issue posed by this level of development, according to Erikson, is that of *autonomy versus shame and doubt.* If children are subjected to too much parental control, their sense of their smallness becomes overwhelming and they become vulnerable to shame or doubt about their ability to be self-directing.

3. In the next stage, about the third year of life, the child has mastered walking and is able to move about freely. His or her language capacity "becomes perfected to the point where he understands and can ask incessantly about innumerable things, often hearing just enough to misunderstand them thoroughly." Children's capacities for both language and locomotion enable them to imagine actions and roles that may frighten them. Thus is posed an issue of a *sense of initiative versus guilt.* Children explore and get into things, both verbally and in action. Their sense of rivalry with others is heightened. They also become aware of sex differences. Successful passage through this stage enables children to feel that their own purposes have validity, that it is all right for them to move on their own toward things that seem interesting. If they are made to feel too frightened by their initiatives, they develop too stringent a conscience, dominated by a sense of guilt.

4. The next stage, extending over a period of several years, which Erikson calls the school age, is marked not so much by distinctive biological changes as by a more firmly modulated emotionality. Children are ready to learn; they form attachments to teachers and parents of other children; they are interested in people practicing occupations that they can grasp—police officers, plumbers, garbage collectors, and pilots, for example. They are also capable of fuller cooperation with others (Mead's game stage). There is growing acquaintance with the objects and practices of the society's technology. The issue presented by this developmental stage is called by Erikson *industry versus inferiority.* Successful development through this stage gives children a sense of their ability to work at tasks, both individually and in coopera-

tion with others. If things do not go well, children develop a sense of inferiority. This can come about in various ways:

the child may still want his mommy more than knowledge; he may still prefer to be the baby at home rather than the big child in school; he still compares himself with his father, and the comparison arouses a sense of guilt as well as a sense of inferiority. Family life may not have prepared him for school life, or school life may fail to sustain the promises of earlier stages in that nothing that he has learned to do well so far seems to count with his fellows or his teacher. . . . It is at this point that wider society becomes significant to the child by admitting him to roles preparatory to the actuality of technology and economy. Where he finds out immediately, however, that the color of his skin or the background of his parents rather than his wish and will to learn are the factors that decide his worth as a pupil or apprentice, the human propensity for feeling unworthy may be fatefully aggravated . . .[39]

5. The next period, adolescence, is the crucial period in Erikson's analysis of socialization. The period is initiated by puberty and is marked both by sexual maturation and by rapid growth in height and weight leading to the attainment of adult size. These changes set the basic task for developing adults: They must begin to find their own specific place in society. This is a period in which people must work out for themselves some integration of role models, values, norms, beliefs, emotional feelings. The issue of this period is that of *identity versus role diffusion.* Successful resolution of this issue produces individuals with a coherent sense of themselves and their relationship to society. Those who are not able to utilize this period to find and establish a coherent sense of identity may be unable to find adult statuses and roles that are both personally satisfying and socially acceptable. They may be unable to settle upon an occupation and generally unable to find a worthwhile way of life. Such socialization failures may be induced by socialization agencies that do not give adequate scope to diversity: "Youth after youth, bewildered by the incapacity to assume a role forced on him by the inexorable standardization of American adolescence, runs away in one form or another, dropping out of school, leaving jobs, staying out all night, or withdrawing into bizarre and inaccessible moods."[40]

The remaining three stages of the life cycle in Erikson's

scheme go beyond the major concerns of this book. For the sake of completeness, we mention them briefly.

6. As people emerge from their identity struggles, they face the issue of *intimacy versus isolation.* This involves the ability to enter into relationships that in some sense involve self-abandon within a framework of trust: love, friendship, erotic encounters, experiences of joint inspiration.

7. The biological capability for parenthood does not necessarily lead to parenthood as a satisfying social role. The issue of this mature adult stage is *generativity versus stagnation,* generativity being "primarily the interest in establishing and guiding the next generation or whatever in a given case may become the absorbing object of a parental kind of responsibility."[41] Thus, Erikson does not mean that stagnation results from not being a parent in the literal sense. Rather, he means that the adult stagnates if he or she is not in *some* kind of role that involves fostering development, whether of a business or scientific research or a garden. (Indeed, sociologist Alice Rossi argues that parenthood in the literal sense—or at least motherhood—is an inappropriate role for many women and that American culture presses many women into maternity who are not very maternal and perhaps should not become mothers. Her view is gaining support.[42])

8. The process of aging confronts the person with the issue of what kind of life he or she has lived, the issue of *integrity versus despair.* Integrity in this sense means a sense of wholeness:

> an emotional integration faithful to the image-bearers of the past. . . . the acceptance of one's one and only life cycle and of the people who have become significant to it as something that had to be and that, by necessity, permitted of no substitutions. It thus means a new and different love of one's parents, free of the wish that they should have been different, and an acceptance of the fact that one's life is one's own responsibility. It is a sense of comradeship with men and women of distant times and of different pursuits who have created orders and objects and sayings conveying human dignity and love.[43]

Erikson is the only modern social science theorist who has attempted a unified analysis of socialization through the entire life cycle from birth to death. For this reason his analysis is helpful in thinking about some of the complexities of this topic. Two issues concerning time have come to be recognized as troublesome: First, to what extent, if at all, does early socialization affect adult social behavior? Erikson views socialization as a cumulative process in which the resolution of the central issue at one stage affects the resolution of the issues presented by succeeding stages. He does not make any simple claim that the mother's treatment of her infant in the first year of life determines what kind of social being her child will be when adult. Rather, he is saying that the child's socialization in any one stage generates certain expectations, which the child brings with him or her into new socialization settings. The socializing agents in the new settings have their own expectations, which they direct toward the child. These agents become new role models that the child adds to those he or she already has. The child, then, has the task of creating some internal order out of the expectations of the various socializing agents. The task is made easier, of course, when the expectations are similar, but as we pointed out early in this chapter, every child encounters some divergence of expectations.

The second question involves the relation of life-cycle time to historical time: How can parents (and other socializing agents) prepare their children to be adults in a society that will be very different when the children reach adulthood? The answer to this question is not simple—and is far from completely available. But certain things can be said. One is that social change is sometimes so great that socialization has in fact not fit children for the changed conditions. Erikson, for example, describes the identity problems and social disorganization of Sioux Indians in North Dakota, who were still being socialized to the values, skills, and way of life relevant to hunting buffalo although all the buffalo had been wiped out decades earlier.[44]

Yet, clearly, in many situations adults do function in a society that makes available statuses and roles that did not exist when those adults were children. One explanation, offered by Albert J. Reiss, is that early values learned in the family setting are not internalized; the individual's behavior changes as he or she moves from setting to setting and encounters different values. To illustrate this, Reiss points out that the same individual was able to function successfully in Germany under the post–World War I Weimar Republic, the dictatorial Nazi regime, and the post–World War II democratic political system.[45] But although it is true that the same individual might have, under successive regimes, filled different roles for which there had been no specific preparation, the argument given by Reiss does not deal with the possibility that certain kinds of early socialization may prepare a child to function adequately under successive drastic changes. For example, if the prime value inculcated in the German child had been obedience to whatever authority held effective sway, he or she might in this way have been socialized to change roles in later life as the political institutions changed.

Recently the question of the relationship between socialization and social change has also been interpreted in terms of a *cohort* perspective. A cohort is a set of people who have a common social characteristic—for example, all those born in a given year or all those who experience a particular historical event. Thus, one cohort of children experienced the Great Depression of 1929 to 1939. For another, World War II was a major event of early experience. The postwar baby boom and resultant overcrowding of school classrooms in the 1950s and 1960s affected a later cohort. Recent cohorts experience the widespread diffusion of computers into their education and their recreation. These historical changes in the society are the sources of changes in people's lives.[46] One reason that children do not become carbon copies of their parents is that each cohort is affected differently by the events of its time. The parents' efforts to socialize their children are necessarily modified by the historical events to which they and their children are responding.

Lillian Troll and Vern Bengtson, in reviewing a number of studies, have applied a variation of this cohort perspective and found that parent-child similarity in values, attitudes, and action varies by life sphere. For example, children of high school and college age tend to have the same religious affiliation and orientation as their parents, but more liberal attitudes about sexuality. The liberalization of sexual attitudes in the larger society thus was somewhat more influential than parental attitudes. But the authors qualify this conclusion in two ways: (1) Effects of parental socialization are still evident, for the most liberal children tend to come from the most liberal parents; (2) this is one area of activity in which the young had a socializing impact on their elders; some parents became more accepting of nonmarital sexual cohabitation, influenced by their children's attitudes and behavior.[47]

On the other hand, we have research from a longitudinal study in Berkeley that pays less attention to historical events and changing social ideas and suggests that problem behavior and unstable family relationships pass down from one generation to another. Writing of a study of four generations (G1 to G4), Glen Elder, Jr., Avshalom Caspi, and Geraldine Downey propose:

> From the G1 to G2 generation, unstable personalities are reproduced in part through marital tension and parent hostility. This socialization environment linked unstable parents to a similar style of behavior in their middle-aged sons and daughters. Likewise, unstable parents in the G2 generation markedly increased the likelihood of ill-tempered, difficult children by increasing marital tensions and the arbitrariness of parents. The pattern repeats itself in the G3 generation during the active years of parenting. Weak family ties were characteristic of the adolescents (G4) who ranked highest on a lack of self-control.[48]

This research, which is based primarily on correlations in test and questionnaire scores rather than intensive family analyses, points to the importance of personality factors in socialization.

The relationship between socialization and social change is obviously enormously complex. Perhaps Erikson again, here speaking of the identity problems of youth, best captures the intricacy of the problem:

> each generation of youth must find an identity consonant with ideological promise in the perceptible historical process. But in youth the tables of childhood dependence begin slowly to turn: no longer is it merely for the old to teach the young the meaning of life. It is the young who, by their responses and actions, tell the old whether life as represented to them has some vital promise, and it is the young who carry in them the power to confirm those who confirm them, to renew and regenerate, to disavow what is rotten, to reform and rebel.[49]

Some of the various ways in which time and conceptions of time affect socialization are illustrated in the following chapter.

OUTCOMES OF SOCIALIZATION

The most general outcome of socialization is a person capable of functioning in society. It is important to emphasize that "functioning" does not necessarily mean "conforming" or "fitting in." To function in society means to be able to take action that has social relevance. Thus, a bank robber can be described as socialized because he or she knows that money is valued, knows what social establishment keeps a supply in a fairly accessible place, probably has acquired some skill in using a product of society's technology, a gun—and can put all this together in a socially relevant act, a bank robbery. His or her socialization is, however, deviant from the majority's in ways that lead the robber to take actions that threaten the social order. He or she disregards the socially important distinction between legitimate and illegitimate procedures for obtaining money. This disregard represents something missing in his or her socialization, which may thus be considered incomplete.

We run into problems, however, if we try to specify what "complete" socialization would be. We can't say that it involves conformity with all major values and norms because most people deviate sometimes in their adherence to one or another major value or norm. Further, certain kinds of nonadherence to usual patterns are purposive and creative. They may be effective in bringing about changes, so that an act that was deviant or illegitimate at one time is not at another.

While we cannot give a definition of "complete" socialization (even though we sometimes recognize cases of seriously incomplete socialization), we can say more about the outcomes of socialization. The functioning person—whether bank robber, workaholic, revolutionary, or loyalist—has an inner organization that has been produced, in part, by a socialization which makes it possible to take the particular kinds of actions that link him or her to the society. No single concept encompasses all of a socialized person's inner organization, and the several concepts that are relevant overlap. We shall, however, attempt to distinguish them as sharply as we can within the limits of contemporary usage.

The Self

Of the several types of inner organization that result from socialization, the self is the most general. The self makes us human but it does not make us into a specific kind of person. By enabling us to take the role of the other, the self makes it possible for us to interact with people unlike ourselves—those of the opposite sex, of different ages, of different social stations, of different societies, or even, in our imagination, with people of earlier times. The self enables us to experience shared humanity even when the other person is socially very different.

The self is, then, a structure that gives the person the capacity to function in society. For example, within the space of an hour, a six-year-old child completes a school day, plays with other children on the way home, then enters his or her home. In that brief time, the child has switched from the role of pupil to the role of playmate to the role of son or daughter. In enacting its own role, the child takes the role of a series of others in succession— teacher, playmates, mother. These social accomplishments are possible because the child already has a self, which gives it the capacity to take the roles of others in context, grasping the social situation and expressing role-appropriate behavior and senti- ments—deference to the teacher, friendliness to playmates, af- fection to mother. The development of a self enables the child to become self-regulating and thereby capable of coordinating his or her activities with others.

The activities of the self, many of which have been studied by Erving Goffman, are complex and numerous. For example, in any adult interaction, a person seeks to control the impression that he or she makes on others. The person endeavors to act in ways that are appropriate to the situation and that convey a particular impression.[50] This kind of self-management in social interaction develops slowly among children in the course of socialization, and we allow them much more leeway in expressing feelings of fear, pain, delight, self-congratulations, and other emotions. Norman Denzin points out that "The young child violates nearly all rules of deference and demeanor. They make claims for self- respect in statements like 'Mommy, look at me, aren't I pretty?' Proper interactants, Goffman claims, must not make claims for self-respect. They must wait for others to confer (voluntarily) such judgments on them."[51] As Gary Alan Fine notes, "Central to the process of growing up is learning ways of displaying one's social self in public. Adults fear that children will say the wrong thing in public."[52] The ability to manage the impressions one wishes to make is one of the capacities of the self.

Another activity of the self that Goffman studied is the self's use of rules in social interaction. Goffman noted that "the person in our urban secular world is allotted a kind of sacredness that is displayed and confirmed by symbolic acts."[53] By this Goffman means that persons are entitled to a certain amount of respect, which is shown by approaching them according to rules. One keeps a certain physical distance from others, for example. One also observes rules in the use of names: First names are used for family and friends; persons who are not close are addressed by a conventional title of respect—Mr., Ms., Mrs., or Miss. Interactions are begun with a ritual greeting—"Hi" or "Hello" or some such—and terminated with a ritual of departure—"So long" or "Good-bye," or "Have a good day." A child of eighteen months or two years who wants the attention of someone may tug on the clothing or body of the person; the child does not yet know the proper access rituals. William Corsaro, building on Goffman's work, undertook to study when and how children develop the ability to use access rituals in approaching others. Over a period of several months, he studied two groups of nursery school children, one two to three years of age, the other three to four, with about twenty-five children in each group. His observations focused on how children join other children in activity, their "access strategies." He noted that three of the strategies were verbal and adultlike; these were: request for access ("Can I play?"); questioning participants ("What ya doing?"); and greeting ("Hi"). But these were not the most frequently used. Most common were nonverbal strategies, such as silently coming alongside children playing and starting to do what they are doing. Thus, nursery school–age children are beginning to develop the social and communicative skills that characterize adult self- and social regulation, but the skills are not yet very widespread.[54]

Self-Concept, Identity, Self-Esteem

We have noted that the self is both a structure and a process and has two parts or phases, the "I" and the "me." As a process, the phases interact with each other whenever a person acts in any situation. Consider as an example the situation of a pupil in class who does not understand something the teacher has just said. If, say, that pupil's parents (who are "significant others" for the child) have always told her that she asks too many questions, that judgment is part of her "me"; she was that kind of an object to her significant others and is also now that kind of an object to herself. In the classroom situation, she has a quick inner dialogue in which the "I" is aware of the "me" as a too-frequent questioner. The pupil's silent action in the situation may therefore take the form "I don't understand what the teacher is saying, but let it pass. I'm not going to ask for an explanation." This is, of course, only one possibility. Another pupil may have as part of the "me" the attitude that asking questions is an appropriate part of the pupil role, plus the additional attitude, based on previous experience in this class, that this teacher criticizes pupils who interrupt with questions before the presentation is completed. Taking the role of the teacher, the pupil anticipates that the teacher will criticize him for interrupting. The teacher's attitude is already incorporated in the pupil's "me." The pupil's "I" is aware of it and decides to wait until after class to ask the question. The "me" says: "Don't interrupt; you'll be criticized." The "I" is aware of this constraining attitude incorporated from a significant other (the teacher) and decides to wait until after class to ask the question.

The "I" and the "me" are not separate little things inside a person's head; they are two phases of the process of self-awareness. We have simply tried, in the above examples, to present in slow motion what is in fact usually a very rapid reflexive activity in which an initiating phase and a constraining phase of an imminent act combine to shape the action that is actually taken. Once the child's self has started to develop, the reflexive activity goes on frequently, though we cannot say whether it goes on every minute of the day. But a changing stream of interactions leads to a stream of evaluations that become part of the "me." A child's mother sends him off to school with a hug, a nonverbal symbol that he understands means she loves him, and he feels good about himself. On the way to school he encounters a child who doesn't like him and calls him a name—"nerd" or some other derogatory term—and he feels bad about himself. At school the teacher tells him he made too many mistakes on his arithmetic test, but she is glad to see that his handwriting is improving— mixed information and a mixed evaluation. At recess he joins his friends in a race to see who can run around the schoolyard the fastest and he wins. Again, he feels good about himself, but on a different basis from his mother's morning hug; his view of himself now includes "fast runner." The child's daily activities involve many interactions that result in a more or less mixed bag of evaluations, which the child is aware of *and which the child himself or herself evaluates.* If the child who called the boy the bad name is one he cares about, he may feel bad about himself for some time; if he is indifferent, the name-caller is not a significant other for him and the remark is quickly forgotten with no enduring effect.

The reflexive activity of the self is ongoing and transient; every moment of it passes. But out of this activity arises a structure that is more stable and enduring.[55] This product is the *self-concept* or *identity.* These two terms, unfortunately, are not fully standardized, so that they may be taken as synonyms or as having meanings that are related but not synonymous. Morris Rosenberg defines self-concept as "the totality of the individual's thoughts and feelings having reference to himself as an object."[56] Betty Yorburg defines identity as

> the total conception that people have of who they are. It includes all the beliefs that make up the individual's conception of self. It also includes the beliefs that people have about their worth as human beings—beliefs that determine self-confidence and self-esteem. . . . Identity is the product of the roles individuals have played and the definitions of self contained in these roles.[57]

Yorburg's definition includes "conception of self" plus "self-confidence and self-esteem," and her usage is similar to Erikson's as the most inclusive statement about what a person is. Sociological usage, however, seems to be coming around to regarding identity not as an inclusive term but as part of the self-concept, with the notion that a person's self-concept includes several identities. We shall adopt this latter usage, as we try to sort out these various terms that conceptualize the results of socialization interactions.

According to Morris Rosenberg, the content of the self-concept includes (1) a person's beliefs about his or her physical characteristics, (2) dispositions, and (3) identities. Physical characteristics of the self-concept include beliefs about how one looks, whether one feels one is too tall or too short or the right height, and any other such beliefs about one's appearance. Dispositions in the self-concept include beliefs about one's personality, abilities, and, generally, one's "tendencies"—sports-loving, chocolate-loving, ambitious, religious, or whatever. Identities are the groups, statuses, and categories to which a child is socially recognized as belonging. The newborn baby belongs to a family, a sex, an age category, a race, a religion, thus starting out with a set of ascribed identities.[58] In time, the child learns that these identities have been assigned to him or her, and they become gradually built into the self. As social experience continues, children develop additional identities, such as best reader in the first grade; tough kid on the playground; beginner at piano lessons; Tommy's best friend; fan of Bruce Springsteen, of the Toronto Maple Leafs, or of the New York Yankees; and so on.

Some identities are specific to childhood and must be abandoned. This is particularly true of identity based on age grade. As Erikson notes:

> All through childhood tentative crystallizations take place which make the individual feel and believe . . . as if he approximately knew who he was—only to find that such self-certainty ever again falls prey to the discontinuities of psychosocial development. . . . An example would be the discontinuity between the demands made in a given milieu on a little boy and those made on a "big boy" who, in turn may well wonder why he was first made to believe that to be little is admirable, only to be forced to exchange this effortless status for the special obligations of one who is "big now."[59]

Of course, the reverse may happen: A child may announce that he is a big boy now, while his parents still consider him a little boy. Thus, establishment of an identity involves two processes: (1) being assigned an identity by others, and (2) claiming an identity for oneself. Gregory Stone proposed that "One's identity is established when others *place* him as a social object by assigning him the same words of identity that he appropriates for himself or *announces.* It is in the coincidence of placements and announcements that identity becomes a meaning of the self."[60]

Lee Rainwater has further refined this analysis. Noting that a person may sometimes announce an identity that he does not really believe is his, Rainwater proposes the concept of *valid identity*:

A valid identity is one in which the individual finds congruence between who he feels he is, who he announces himself to be, and where he feels his society places him. Individuals are led to announce a particular identity when they feel it is congruent with their needs, and the society influences these needs by its willingness to validate such announcements by a congruent placement. As individuals seek to build identities valid in terms of their own needs, they use the resources—the values, norms, and social techniques—which their culture makes available to them. Each individual tries on identities that emerge from the cultural material available to him and tests them by making appropriate announcements. If these announcements meet with success, he will maintain his identity until it is no longer validated by others or no longer congruent with his inner promptings.[61]

Identity formation goes on throughout life, but typically the person has some sense of himself or herself as maintaining continuity. People go through school, marry, change jobs, convert from one religion to another, migrate from one country to another. These changes in social condition all involve changes in identity, but ordinarily they are not total.

The self-concept consists not only in one's knowledge and beliefs about who one is but also in one's evaluation of oneself. The basic evaluative judgment that a person makes about himself or herself establishes the level of self-esteem. Self-esteem is the product of social interaction. The child who goes to school more poorly dressed than any other is likely to experience a lowering of self-esteem as a result of comparing self to others. The child who shows a talent that is valued by others is likely to experience increased self-esteem. As these examples suggest, a person's level of self-esteem can change as a result of changes in social participation and social interaction. If, say, the poorly dressed child discovers and is recognized as having an ability that the other children value, its manifestation may well result in their favorable evaluation, which may then result in increased self-esteem, perhaps sufficient to overcome entirely the poor self-esteem experienced because of inferior dress.

One reason a change in self-concept is almost never total is because, as already noted, a person has many identities at once, reflecting his or her various social memberships and roles. Sheldon Stryker, following up Mead's idea that the complete self is made up of multiple identities ("elementary selves" was Mead's term), has suggested that these identities necessarily are organized in a *salience hierarchy*. Salience refers to how prominent an identity is, how likely it is to be the governing identity in a situation, and in how many situations it is considered important.[62] We can illustrate this conception in the following way: Consider three families with children in school. All three belong to a church. The children in all three engage in some athletic activity. In one family, being a good Christian is the most important goal, and the children are socialized to that identity in many ways. The family says grace before meals, the children attend a Bible class two or three times a week. Although expected to do reasonably well in school, the children's role as students is not emphasized, and being academically superior is not as important as being a good Christian. The children participate in recreational sports, but sports identity is not stressed. In another family, sports participation is central; the children compete in athletic contests. Their religious and academic identities are less salient than their identities as athletes. And in the third, commitment to the student role is more important than to religious or athletic roles, and the children's identities as good students in science or languages or social studies are more salient than the religious or athletic. The salient identity is the one that the person feels is more important than others, and it is operative for more times and over a wider range of situations than less salient ones.

Sentiments and Emotions

The concept of self, as we have presented it, derives largely from the work of George Herbert Mead, who emphasized that the self is cognitive in nature. In Mead's view, the self is what makes us distinctively human, and the key aspect of that is the ability to know ourselves and act toward ourselves as objects. Although Mead did say a little about emotions, knowing—not feeling—was his central focus.

Mead's perspective has to be supplemented with that of Charles Horton Cooley, his contemporary in the early part of the twentieth century. Where Mead insisted on the importance of our ability to *symbolize* as the human capacity that makes possible reflexivity and taking the role of the other, Cooley stressed the importance of our ability to *sympathize,* by which he meant to understand what another person is feeling. (Since "sympathy" in recent times often has come to mean feeling compassion for someone who is troubled or suffering, the term "empathy" is usually used today in the broader sense that Cooley intended. We will use empathy.) Cooley believed that human nature consists of sentiments and that empathy is the most basic, because it enters into all others. Sentiments such as love, ambition, resentment, envy, patriotism, hero worship, "school spirit," and what Cooley called the "feeling of social right and wrong" all include empathy, understanding what others are feeling. Cooley wrote: "Human nature in this sense is justly regarded as a comparatively permanent element in society. Always and everywhere men seek honor and dread ridicule, defer to public opinion, cherish their goods and their children, and admire courage, generosity, and success. It is always safe to assume that people are and have been human."[63]

From our present perspective, more than seventy years after Cooley, and with much intervening experience and research, we know that the situation is more complex than he described it. Some people will brave ridicule rather than dread it; not all defer to public opinion, nor do all cherish their children. But certain of his fundamental observations are durable: Such sentiments as honor and ridicule, courage and generosity are distinctively human and possible in all human societies and thus are not limited to certain cultures, although they receive varying emphasis and are expressed differently in different cultures.

The capacity to create and communicate complex meanings, cognitive and emotional, which we find among human beings everywhere, is without equal elsewhere in the animal kingdom. Similarly, the wide range of human sentiment is without equal in other species.

It was Cooley's significant insight that the sentiments that he saw as the core of human nature were not inherited. Rather, human nature develops in primary groups,

> those simple face-to-face groups that are somewhat alike in all societies; groups of the family, the playground, and the neighborhood. In the essential similarity of these is to be found the basis, in experience, for similar ideas and sentiments in the human mind. In these,

everywhere, human nature comes into existence. Man does not have it at birth; he cannot acquire it except through fellowship, and it decays in isolation.[64]

Although Cooley's insight (based in part on observation of his own children) perhaps outran the evidence then available to support it, several lines of more recent evidence tend to support and amplify his view. In various ways, they indicate that human nature is a product of involvement with other human beings.

There has been considerable debate about whether emotions are part of human biology or whether they are formed and shaped in social relationships.[65] At one time psychologists would have argued for the biological origin and sociologists for the social, but the two fields no longer divide in this way. Sociologists such as Thomas J. Scheff and Steven L. Gordon, citing data on the newborn and very young, recognize a biological source of emotional expression,[66] and psychologists such as Carol Zander Malatesta and Jeanette N. Haviland stress that early emotions are transformed by socialization.[67] The arguments on emotion and sentiments are complex, and various formulations have been offered. Drawing on various analyses, we present what seems to us a reasonable view.

The evidence seems to indicate that humans are born with a few basic emotions—anger, fear, sadness, happiness. These not only become socialized but become differentiated into a wide variety of sentiments. Discussing the transformation of emotion, Malatesta and Haviland write:

> Emotion finds expression in physiology, feeling states, and motor behavior. In the course of development, any or all of these aspects may undergo transformation to varying degrees. In unsocialized human beings, such as infants, affect expression is a whole body experience, presumably involving all aspects. Later, under the impact of environmental contingencies, as well as of self-directed modulation and the development of symbolic function, favored modes of expression develop. Socialization may be directed at training in one or all of these channels.[68]

In infancy, the key socializing factor is mother-infant interaction, particularly the mother's face-to-face play with the infant.[69] At later ages the tone and content of utterances become more important. Preschoolers, having gained some mastery of the symbols of language, have learned a vocabulary for emotional states and emotional expressions. In the course of childhood, children also learn *feeling rules,* that is, what emotions are expected or acceptable in what situations and how to display or refrain from displaying emotions.[70] One of the important outcomes of socialization is that people have to learn to manage their feelings.

The term "feelings" or "affective state" includes both emotions and sentiments, but sentiments are more numerous and specifically social than are emotions. Steven Gordon defines a sentiment as "a socially constructed pattern of sensations, expressive gestures, and cultural meanings organized around a relationship to a social object." He goes on to point out that:

> Most of a culture's vocabulary of named affective states are sentiments rather than emotions. Sentiments develop around social attachments, such as parental love, romantic love, friendship, and loyalty. Grief, sorrow, and nostalgia reflect social losses. Compassion and pity are sentiments based on empathy, whereas jealousy and envy reflect notions of possession. Moral sentiments that we feel when judging others include indignation, resentment, and contempt, but also gratitude and pride. Our reactions to how others judge us include shame, guilt, and embarrassment. Patriotism and religious reverence are sentiments for social institutions. Humor, impatience, and enthusiasm are relatively transient sentiments, but are learned socially and are expressed within more enduring relationships to which they contribute meaning.[71]

The work of both sociologists and psychologists is thus further developing Cooley's important insights into the socialization of sentiments.

Incipient Adult Roles

In childhood, children are assigned children's roles, but at the same time they are being prepared for adult roles. By the time a child passes from the age grade of child to that of adolescent, a considerable amount of such preparation has already taken place. In Chapter 6 we shall examine preparation for adult sex roles. Here, we shall briefly look at preparation for three other adult roles: citizen, worker, and consumer.

The role of *citizen* connects the person with the political system and government of the society. As noted earlier in this chapter, every society seeks to engender loyalty, including loyalty to the prevailing system of government. The study of this aspect of socialization has come to be known as political socialization. In one study, Sandra K. Schwartz found that some political socialization has taken place by the time a child is five years old. In her sample of seventy-nine nursery school children, most not yet five, she found the beginnings of awareness of political symbols and governmental authority. The children were shown a picture containing nine flags, including the American and the Liberian, which resembles it. Asked which flag they liked best, 60 percent chose the American, 19 percent the Liberian, and 20 percent a different flag. Eighty-three percent knew which was the American flag. With regard to agents of governmental authority, some of the children have heard of the president, but they are more familiar with the policeman. About half of them mentioned that he directs traffic, about a third identified him as enforcing laws, and about a third mentioned his role in helping lost children.[72] In kindergarten and elementary-school years, children, according to several studies, have a very positive image of the president. In a California study, Moore, Lare, and Wagner suggest that this image has its origin in religious sensitivities. The most common reply of kindergarten children to the question "Who does the most to run the country?" was God or Jesus. The authors go on to say that "an early religious orientation predisposes children to have more positive feelings toward the President and other civil authorities."[73]

A number of studies have found that, during the elementary-school years, children have a very idealized view of political authority. Fred Greenstein suggests an explanation for this outcome (which, however, changes during adolescence):

> While there is no explicit norm in the United States that children should be "protected" from politics, it is likely that adults—even politically cynical adults—more or less unconsciously sugarcoat the political explanations they pass on to children. As Easton and Hess have suggested, politics may be in the same class as sex—one of those sordid aspects of adult existence from which it is thought that young children are best shielded.[74]

However, children from segments of society that suffer from discrimination or economic deprivation are less likely to believe that political leaders are so benevolent. In the above-cited California study, kindergarten children were asked, "If you were playing in front of your house, and a policeman stopped to talk to you, what do you think he would say?" Almost one-quarter of the non-Anglo children, mostly Mexican, gave a remark that was threatening, compared to only 7 percent of the Anglos.[75] Another study of black inner-city children showed that by the fourth grade they have developed "a marked degree of malevolence and distrust toward political leaders."[76] A study of children in the Appalachian region of eastern Kentucky, a poor rural area (discussed more fully in Chapter 4), found that children "are dramatically less favorably inclined toward political objects than are their counterparts in other portions of the nation."[77]

As we noted earlier in this chapter, socialization is intended to lead to various kinds of competence. Most children are expected to become capable of doing some kind of economically useful work in their society. Goldstein and Oldham have studied socialization of children for the adult *worker* role. Their study covered 900 children in the first, third, fifth, and seventh grades in five New Jersey communities with different social characteristics—from working class to upper-middle class. Their study examined (1) beliefs and perceptions, (2) values, (3) attitudes and feelings, and (4) work experiences.

About 80 percent of first graders and 89 percent of fifth graders have some understanding of the concept of work and its relation to money. Occupational stereotyping is also fairly definite even in the first grade. Asked their reactions to "typically male" and "typically female" occupations, 74 percent of the boys and 29 percent of the girls said they would feel positively about being a construction worker; 79 percent of the girls and 24 percent of the boys said they would feel positively about being a nurse. Children have fairly realistic ideas about occupational income differentials, though not about income levels. Thus, even first graders know that bankers and doctors earn more than teachers and secretaries. Awareness of income differentials increases during the elementary years until it becomes quite accurate.

Interestingly, many children ascribe negative feelings about work to the general population, although they tend to be quite positive about their own chores. The researchers believe that this contrast may reflect the fact that children perceive negative adult attitudes and that in time they, too, will come to like work less.

Children are also aware of social class differences. Even first graders are aware of prestige differences among people—usually explaining such differences on the basis of the importance of the role to the community or on the fact that some people work harder. As children get older, wealth, fame, and power are recognized as the bases for prestige differences.

Children's own work experiences increase with age. "Childwork" (paid work done by children outside the household or for their own family) was done by 13 percent of first graders, 39 percent of third graders, and 75 percent of seventh graders. Neighbors are usually the first employers; yardwork, baby-sitting, newspaper delivery are the most common types of work. In addition, children do chores at home, which are usually sex-typed: Three times as many girls as boys report doing dishes; four times as many boys as girls report taking out the trash.

The authors summarize their study with these generalizations:

> The process of occupational socialization during childhood has been shown to be developmental in nature, and to follow an age-related pattern largely in accord with that which has been shown or presumed to govern children's growth in general. In other words, while work itself in the formal sense may be largely a phenomenon of late adolescence and adulthood, preparation to assume one's place in the world of work and growth into an occupational self-identity begin far earlier than that.[78]

Socialization to work has gone on for centuries in all societies; survival requires that the young be prepared to work. Probably only in fairly recent times, however, with the rise of a broadly based market economy offering a wide array of goods for sale, do we find socialization for an adult *consumer* role. And not until very recently has anyone begun to study the process. One research team that has begun to do so defines consumer socialization as "the gradual development of a broad range of attitudes, knowledge, and skills which are related to consumption, e.g., attitudes toward television commercials, knowledge of the purpose of commercials, knowledge of brands and products, and skills, such as how to most effectively allocate discretionary monies."[79] Children develop information-processing skills, skills in selecting, evaluating, and using information relevant to purchasing.

Children are introduced to the consumer role within their families, both through watching television and through family communications. They receive a great deal of information about products and brands of merchandise available in their society through TV commercials. By kindergarten age, 60 percent of children (in samples studied in Boston and Minneapolis/St. Paul) ask their parents for soft drinks by brand name; this reaches 84 percent by sixth grade. As many as 93 percent of kindergartners ask for cereal by brand name. Understanding of the selling purpose of commercials increases with age, as does the judgment that advertising is not always truthful. Although few mothers engage in purposive consumer training, children's requests for products often initiate interactions with a parent, and in this way families may mediate the impact of television advertising on the children. About half the 615 mother-child pairs studied were found to engage in such discussions.

A Store of Social Knowledge

In summarizing the principal outcomes of socialization, we have thus far focused on the inner structures that are created through socialization—a self, an identity, and incipient roles. In discussing these structures we have alluded to such aspects of social life as rules, symbols, attitudes, feelings, communication, and information. These are, so to speak, the materials or resources that the socialized person must make use of in functioning, no matter what particular pattern he or she develops. In concluding the chapter, it is useful here to make explicit the fact that these materials or resources are part of a large store of social knowledge that the socialized person begins to acquire soon after birth and continues to acquire throughout the life course. The social world is made up of an immense number of social objects—work, money, politics, God, family, material goods, knowledge, pleasures, discipline, crime—the list could be extended. Each of these social objects can be further divided and specified in different ways. The socialized person inevitably acquires some kind of knowledge about some of these objects, more about some than about others, including how to think and feel about the object, what to do about it, if anything, what are preferred or approved actions with regard to each, and what are disapproved. Such a store of knowledge is an outcome of socialization required by every socialized person who functions in the society. In the next chapter we shall examine how a child's location in society influences the kind of social knowledge he or she is likely to acquire.

CHAPTER 4

Socialization and Subcultural Patterns

Any society that is large includes within it many different ways of life. To be sure, there are also important elements shared in common. Thus, in North America, for example, clothes, foods, tools, advertisements, kitchen appliances, drugstore displays, automobiles, popular sports, and many other elements are widely shared. Indeed, these elements are shared not only across two North American societies—Canadian and American—but in varying degrees across many others, as well. But there are differences in the emphasis that societies give even to these common elements. For example, the United States accepted—or embraced—commercial advertising and gave it far greater value than did other industrial societies. This showed up in several ways. Our newspapers are much thicker than newspapers elsewhere, especially with department store and supermarket advertising; our highways are dotted with billboards; our radio and television stations devote more time to commercials. Nor elsewhere have so many special programs and advertising campaigns been directed by advertisers to children. Advertising agencies and marketing research groups, as well, have become major business enterprises. In short, although commercial advertising is common and valued in many societies, it has received greater attention in the United States than elsewhere and has been more influential in affecting various kinds of social and economic decisions.

This example illustrates a concept of great importance for socialization, the concept of *culture*. This concept originates in anthropology but has proved extremely useful in all the social sciences. Like all such concepts that try to capture a complex reality, it has been variously defined and interpreted. But the following definition would receive wide acceptance among an-

thropologists and sociologists and is suitable for our purposes:
*A culture is a way of life developed by a people in adaptation to the physical
and social circumstances in which they find themselves. It tends to be passed
on from generation to generation, but it changes as circumstances change.
It includes some elements that are highly valued by the people themselves and
other elements that are accepted as necessary or "realistic" adaptations but
are not especially valued.*

One problem always presented by the term "culture" is that
of the unit it represents. We may speak of cultures of nations,
regions, social classes, ethnic groups, generations, or religious
and occupational groups, in each case focusing on the com-
monalities of thought, attitudes, behavior, and objects. This
question of what a culture refers to is of considerable importance
for understanding differences in socialization. Does the child
growing up in an isolated and poor rural hamlet in Kentucky have
the same culture as a child growing up in the middle of New York,
Chicago, or Houston? Does the child growing up in the slum
have the same culture as the child growing up in the affluent
suburb? Does the child of Italian immigrants in an Italian section
of Boston or Toronto have the same culture as the child of
long-established families of English descent? The easiest answer
to these questions is "No." The visible differences are so great
that it has become common to insist that the children in these
different settings are in fact being socialized into different cultures. Closer examination suggests, however, that some cultural
similarities are simply less visible than the differences and that
the differences are more likely to be necessary adaptations to
circumstances than differences in values.[1] As an example, let us
take the value of career success. There is no question that career
success is a more dominant concern in some segments of society
than in others. There are segments of American society, which we
shall discuss shortly, in which men and women have no evident
interest in career success, contrasted with others in which careers
seem all important. It was fashionable at one time to regard their
lack of interest in a career as evidence of a value difference.
Closer examination has shown, however, that these people are
not unmindful of the value society places on one's occupation.
They have, however, for reasons that lie largely beyond their
control, lost all possibility for success or even a steady job. They
share in the value that others hold, but the value has lost meaning

for their own day-to-day lives because there seems to be no way in which they can implement it.

This complex relationship of being both a part of a large society yet in some ways marked off from it, participating in a larger culture yet having a distinctive version of it, is expressed in the terms *subsociety* and *subculture*. Charles Valentine emphasizes both the distinctiveness of subcultures and their interplay with the larger culture:

> It is perhaps reasonable to assume that any subsociety may have a configuration of more or less distinguishable lifeways of its own. This configuration constitutes a subculture that is distinct from the total culture of the whole society in a . . . special and limited sense. The wider sociocultural system has its own coherence to which subsocieties and subcultures contribute even with their distinctiveness.[2]

What is the importance of subcultures for socialization? First, children are socialized into a particular subculture, not into a culture as a whole. This means that initially children learn not the ways of their society but the ways of a particular segment of it. They develop outlooks and assumptions that are not necessarily shared by those outside that segment. If they spend their entire lifetimes associating only with those who share the same subculture, they may have difficulty understanding the thoughts, actions, and situations of those from other subcultures. The point may be illustrated with a hypothetical example. We might imagine a child in comfortable circumstances meeting a very poor child and asking "How much allowance do you get?"—not realizing that in some parts of society children do not receive a weekly allowance. This is an example of a situation that affects all children in their early socialization but which most eventually leave behind as their experience widens: The things that are believed, valued, and done in one's own way of life lead to the implicit question "Doesn't everyone?"

A child's encounter with a different subculture can also take the reverse form. Instead of the revelation "I didn't know that everyone doesn't do what I do," the child may have an experience that takes the form "I didn't know other people do that." Thus, a young black woman whose mother cooked for a white family reports a childhood discovery: "Sometimes Mama would bring us the white family's leftovers. It was the best food I had ever eaten.

That was when I discovered white folks ate different from us. They had all kinds of different food with meat and all. We always had just beans and bread."[3] A child's "emergence" from his or her own subculture into an awareness of diversity may come early or late in life, and for some living in isolated and homogeneous communities it may never come at all.

Of course, with increasing urbanization, mobility, education, and the widespread influence of television, a smaller and smaller proportion of children grows up so completely insulated within a subculture as to be unacquainted with other ways of living in the same society. Even the very small towns come under the influence of urbanization and its divergent ways.[4] These changes mean that more and more children are learning at some point in the course of their socialization that the answer to the question "Doesn't everyone?" is "No, everyone doesn't." Everyone does not belong to a country club; everyone does not go to church Sunday morning; everyone does not live in a neighborhood of crowded apartments; everyone does not believe that the most important thing is to get a good job that leads to advancement and a house in a nice suburb; everyone does not live in decaying wooden houses in muddy hollows.

The general implication of the fact that socialization starts within a particular subculture is that *every* child's socialization in some measure *limits his or her ability to function in the larger society.* The values, beliefs, assumptions, and ways of life that come to be "second nature" to children make it difficult for them to function effectively in some kinds of social situations involving persons who have been socialized in other subcultures. The limiting effects of socialization are currently receiving considerable attention in the Western world and indeed have become a matter of political conflict. On the one hand it is stated that lower-class children are socialized in such a way that they do not know how to function in a middle-class society. More recently, on the other hand, the contrary is also asserted: Middle-class people are so "locked in" by their values and norms that they do not understand the different subculture of lower-class people. This issue finds its most intense expression between black people and white people; the long-held belief on the part of many whites that blacks cannot acquire many necessary kinds of competence because of their inferior way of life finds its answer today in a growing insistence by blacks that the socialization of whites renders them incompetent to meet the needs of blacks and to serve as socializing agents for black children. The same arguments are made by native Indians in Canada and the United States. These bitter problems are but the latest form of what early sociologist William Graham Sumner saw many years ago as a universal social characteristic, which he named *ethnocentrism*: "Each group thinks its own folkways the only right ones. . . . Ethnocentrism leads a people to exaggerate and intensify everything in their own folkways which is peculiar and which differentiates them from others."[5] As two more recent sociologists, Tamotsu Shibutani and Kian M. Kwan, have noted, ethnocentrism is one version of "trained incapacity"; it limits social competence.[6]

Although all cultures and subcultures necessarily generate some measure of ethnocentrism, some do so more than others. Isolation from other subcultures intensifies ethnocentrism, but so also do conflict and discrimination. Ethnocentrism is, in principle, modifiable, and many programs designed for its reduction are carried out by agencies concerned with human relations. Many social scientists go so far as to affirm that all socialization outcomes that limit social competence are modifiable by appropriate action programs.[7]

The importance of subcultures for socialization can be further appreciated by reference to concepts introduced earlier:

1. A person's *status* in society is partly determined by the subculture in which he or she participates.
2. A child's earliest *role models* are drawn from his or her own subculture, although by school age the child may have encountered some role models from outside it.
3. Since a child's *self* is formed in large part by taking the role of others, and since the child's earliest significant others tend to be from his or her own subculture, the child's self has an anchor in a particular subculture.

Subcultures are based on different types of social differentiation. In the remainder of this chapter, we shall consider three of particular importance—social class, community of residence, and ethnic group—and ask how each of these affects socialization. In Chapter 5 we shall consider the relationship between subcultures and the major agencies of socialization.

SOCIAL CLASS

Although social class is variously defined in social science literature, virtually all social scientists recognize the existence of socioeconomic strata in our society and acknowledge that different groups possess unequal amounts of wealth, influence, prestige, and "life chances." Such inequalities have consequences and ramifications that sociologists feel justified in interpreting as aspects of social class. The general public, too, recognizes that people in our society have different social standings based primarily on income, occupation, and education, and less obviously on moral standards, family background, community participation, social skills, and physical appearance.[8] Our use of such terms as "rednecks," "jet set," "yuppies," "hard-hats," "nouveau riche," and "moral majority," as well as "middle class" and "lower class," shows that we evaluate differently all these categories of people.

Children become aware of social class differences even at elementary-school age. In a photograph-matching and interview study of children in grades one, three, and six in Toronto, Bernd Baldus and Verna Tribe found that children in the first grade could match cheap and expensive cars with the appearance of the people likely to drive them. The older children could also match the houses they lived in, the furniture they used, and the appropriate party guests; by sixth grade, few of the children of both middle and working class made any mismatches.

Baldus and Tribe go even further to suggest that children, by the ages of eight and nine, have the rudiments of an ideology that legitimates inequality and makes it seem natural. The older the children, the more certain they were in their choices and the more evaluative was the language used. In response to stories about the children of well-to-do and working-class fathers, the subjects judged the children of the former to be more popular and successful while those of the latter were more likely to have reading problems, lie to their mothers, and start unprovoked fights. These judgments were made by all the grades and surprisingly by all the children, no matter what the social position of their parents. Thus, the children seem to be internalizing a set of standards for judging social respectability and social accomplishments—the high-status position is desirable and rewarding; the lower-status position is unpleasant and disreputable.[9]

Social Class as a Way of Life

From the point of view of socialization, perhaps the most important aspect of social stratification is a group's "way of life" or subculture. There are many ways of life associated with social class, ranging from a very small "upper-upper" class with its genealogy, mansions, servants, yachts, debutantes, and private school education down to tramps and outcasts who live off the handouts and discards of others. For purposes of illustration and contrast, in this section we shall focus on socialization in three social class groupings—the upper-middle class and the blue-collar working class, which we shall discuss together in the next section, and the destitute lower class. We shall touch only briefly on the upper class, which, by almost any criterion, makes up a very small proportion of the population. We shall also not give major attention to the lower-middle class as such, which, by most definitions, is made up of a varied group of white-collar workers, including salespersons, clerks, small shopkeepers, lower management supervisors, and perhaps grade-school teachers. In the research literature on socialization, the lower-middle class is not clearly distinguished from the upper-middle class. It seems, in fact, as we shall see, that although the lower-middle-class people have fewer years of schooling and do not live as well as the upper-middle class, they tend to hold similar values and aspirations for their children.

Perhaps the readiest means of identifying a person's social class membership is by occupation. The upper-middle class consists primarily of families whose breadwinners are relatively affluent professional and business people, almost all with a college education. The working class includes workers in manufacturing, trades, and service occupations (such as hairdressers), usually with a high school education, who are generally employed steadily and whose way of life is seen as stable by both themselves and others. Often they belong to labor unions and, except perhaps in periods of economic depression, have some sense of being able to influence decisions that affect their own lives. In the lower class, the breadwinners are generally unskilled laborers who work irregularly. In these days, when unskilled labor is increasingly replaced by machines, it includes men and women (and their families) who, having no skill, may be chronically unemployed. The lower class also includes families, often led by single mothers, whose income derives largely from public assistance. Thus, not the least important fact about the lower class is that it is poor, but the differences between it and the classes above are not simply income and what it buys. Social classes are ways of life and therefore socialization environments for the children born into them.

At the same time, as we have observed, the lines between particular subcultures are not always clearly drawn. This is particularly true with regard to values. There has been some controversy in recent years as to whether all social classes in a society are oriented to the same or different values. Considerable light on this controversy has been cast by Hyman Rodman, whose analysis of several research studies leads him to conclude that the lower class develops a "value stretch." As he puts it, "The lower class value stretch refers to the wider range of values and the lower degree of commitment to these values to be found within the lower class."[10] The implications of this will be discussed in this and the following chapters.

Upper-Middle and Working-Class Subcultures

The distinctive characteristics of these two subcultures are best seen as contrasts. First, the income of the upper-middle-class family, although increasingly dependent upon two incomes, is likely to be considerably higher, and the family lives at a superior level of material comfort. The family residence is likely to be substantial, though not palatial, and it is well stocked with a wide range of consumer goods, some of which are likely to be rather costly. The dwelling usually is large enough for each child to have a separate room; when this is not the case, the family is likely to look forward to the time when its income will increase sufficiently for this standard to be attained. Privacy is a value, and it is felt that even children require privacy. Privacy in this form costs money, and the upper-middle family generally has enough money, sooner or later, to buy it.

In working-class families, the standard of living also increasingly depends upon two incomes, but neither matches those of their upper-middle-class counterparts, and, in unstable economic conditions, these incomes may be uncertain. The working-class family does not live as well. The neighborhood, though perhaps clean and respectable, is less spacious and attractive, and the houses are smaller and more cheaply furnished. With a somewhat higher average birth rate in working-class families as well, the children will more often share rooms, and privacy as such is not considered so important.

The upper-middle-class way of life usually involves its members in a variety of institutions outside the family. The father's or mother's occupations, for example, may require them to be in contact with many organizations in addition to the ones that employ them. If they are in business, they are involved in buying-and-selling relationships with people in other firms. If they are professionals, they are associated with hospitals or courts or universities or government agencies, where they meet others with whom they collaborate or whom they help, persuade, teach, or supervise, as the case may be.

In addition to occupational contacts with many organizations, the husband and wife are likely to have roles in numerous other formal organizations—associations of business or professional people (medical societies, law groups, chambers of commerce, and so on), church groups, country clubs or swimming clubs, and perhaps some civic betterment association. In addition to activities in these formal organizations, there is likely to be considerable entertaining at home, largely arranged by the wife, as well as such out-of-home entertainment as dining in good restaurants and attending the theater, concerts, and the like.

The upper-middle-class child picks up information, knowledge, vocabulary, and attitudes concerning all this activity. At dinner and at other times, he or she is introduced to the world of business deals or court cases or giving lectures, as such matters are discussed or alluded to. The concerns, activities, and meetings of this or that association may also come up. Thus, in the upper-middle-class home the child is likely to learn that life involves some kind of responsibility not only in an organization but *for* the organization.

Children growing up in this class undergo a *sponsored independence,* to use Bernard Farber's term.[11] They begin early to have a diversified social participation, much of it directed by adults. They are likely to belong to one or more organizations such as the Boy Scouts, the Girl Scouts, athletic teams, church and synagogue groups, hobby clubs, and community-center groups. Their schools sponsor many extracurricular activities; in a study of an upper-middle-class suburb, one school principal reported that there were forty-two extracurricular organizations in his school.[12] In addition, children go away to summer camp and, during the school year, may take lessons in music, dancing, swimming, skiing, or tennis. It is part of the value system of this class, to quote one research report, that:

> Parents and adult leaders of children's associations expect the cooperation and gratitude of the child "for all that is being done for him." Such associations should, in adult eyes, satisfy all the child's recreational needs. Adult reaction to the child-centered, child-controlled associations which do develop outside the orbit of adult control is one of marked suspicion and some anger, the elders' direct response to a rejection of their well-meant efforts.[13]

In contrast to the wide participation of upper-middle-class men and women in organizations and institutions, the working class plays a much less active role in the larger society. Except for labor unions, church groups, and some fraternal organizations, working-class people are much less likely to be involved in organizations concerned with politics, fund raising, health, welfare, youth activities, women's rights, or other "causes." If they do become involved, they are less likely to take on positions of leadership, a not surprising result in view of their lesser confidence in such areas and their lesser verbal and interpersonal skills.[14]

Working-class children, too, are likely to follow different organizational patterns. They may well be members of sponsored scout or neighborhood teams and active in such school sports as football, basketball, baseball, and track, but in general, when they are not attending class or carrying out family responsibilities, they are on their own, independent of the watchful and guiding eyes of their parents and other adults. They are less likely to participate in individualized sports or to take private music or other fee-charging lessons.[15] Farber's term is *unsponsored independence.* Nor, in contrast to the upper-middle class, do they have role models of their parents to set an example of organizational leadership.

Researchers Lydia O'Donnell and Ann Stueve have investigated the ways in which mothers participate in their school-aged children's after-school activities, and report important differences between middle-class and working-class mothers as social agents linking their children to the community. In a Boston-area suburban town of 50,000 people, they found eight major sources of formal children's activities: (1) public school–sponsored programs, (2) scouting, (3) boys' clubs, (4) church-related activities, (5) private lessons, (6) recreation departments, (7) sports teams and sports clubs, and (8) low-income programs sponsored by the town housing project. Although children from working-class families participated in activities specifically geared to residents with limited incomes, they were much less likely than those from middle-class families to participate in activities open to all. Children from the two social classes also tended to use public services differently. A group of working-class boys, for example, would stop by the gym at the boys' club when they felt like it; middle-class boys were likely to participate on a more scheduled basis, for example, taking a carpentry class regularly twice a week.[16]

The more scheduled commitments and more regular participation of the middle-class children reflected the more active involvement of their parents as social agents helping their children to establish these community connections. The work that parents, usually mothers, perform in integrating their children into community life includes a variety of commonplace, seldom-noted activities, including

> Trying to line up parent volunteers for a school fund raiser; attending the early morning practice of the hockey team; calling half a dozen day camps to locate one that is affordable, appropriate, and not already booked; scheduling an appointment for a teacher conference to discuss a child's progress; being a room mother, Brownie leader, Sunday school teacher . . . taking responsibility for choosing, coordinating, and chauffering children to their daily round of activities.[17]

Working-class mothers were less active than middle-class in interacting with the organizations and groups that sponsored children's activities. The middle-class mothers valued having their children participate in regularly scheduled structured activities more than did the working-class mothers, who believed it was more important that their children spend free time with friends.

The researchers found that the maternal activity as social agents for their children was not related to whether or not the mothers worked outside the home. Instead, they found that employed mothers often managed to arrange their working hours so as to be able to monitor their children's activities and connect to the organizations they were involved in.

Of special importance in understanding socialization in upper-middle and working classes are the values and aspirations that the two groups uphold and seek to pass on to their children. Upper-middle-class men and, increasingly, upper-middle-class women are greatly concerned with developing successful careers, whether as independent professionals or as salaried executives working in large organizations. This means that they are oriented to the future and look to expanding responsibilities, prestige, and income—at least until that time in life when they recognize that they have achieved their maximum.

One of the important distinguishing characteristics of middle-class as compared with working-class occupations, according to an analysis by Melvin Kohn,[18] is that they require greater initiative, independence, and self-direction. To carry on such occupations with even a moderate amount of success requires a certain kind of self: a belief in one's ability to face and solve problems and to make judgments and decisions. Confidence that one's own actions make a difference in how things turn out is also required. Although there are uncertainties, anxieties, and disappointments in pursuing a career, and many people fall short of "making it" as they had hoped, numerous upper-middle-class lives are dominated by a concern with career and future. As they pursue these goals, upper-middle-class people are exerting a considerable degree of control over themselves and their situations.

The upper-middle-class woman is as likely as the man to think of herself as an effective "doing" sort of person. In earlier days, she was often involved in some kind of volunteer activity. More likely today she is employed instead, or possibly doing both. She works because she chooses to. Quoting one woman corporate executive: "I made a choice to work and I like it. . . . [Most men] never really had that choice. They've always known they were going to work. They were going to support a family, and they never were able to make a choice. But I did. It's very important to me, or I wouldn't have made the choice."[19]

Another woman with her own career told her husband, before they married: "I made the point—which he completely agreed with and obviously completely understood—that career was my way of life. And, that although I wanted a family also, I in no way considered this a matter of alternatives or substitutes, but a matter of both. And he completely agreed."[20]

Working-class people, often employed in manual labor and factory jobs, live under different conditions of life and experience the world differently. Rather than manipulating ideas and symbols and dealing with interpersonal relationships, they are concerned more with the manipulation of physical objects, and they require less in the way of interpersonal skills. Their work, be it working in a factory, repairing cars, driving trucks, or cutting hair, is also likely to be more standardized compared to that of the professional or business executive, and requires less thought, judgment, and flexibility.

Working-class men and women are also likely to be more closely supervised by foremen or managers watching over their performance. Thus there is relatively less emphasis on self-direction and internalized standards of behavior and relatively more on orderliness, conformity, and externally imposed rules.

These values, derived from the occupational experiences of the parents, are carried directly over to the treatment of the child. The upper-middle-class parent is intensely focused on the child's future and directs a great deal of effort to attempting to prepare children for the tasks to come. At the same time, upper-middle-class people generally expect that their children's future will be quite different from their own current adulthood, although they do not know in what ways it will differ. Partly for this reason, they place a great emphasis on independence and self-direction.

For the working class, these particular values are less important. For one thing, the parents have fewer resources to set aside to guarantee a future for their children; they are more immediately concerned with maintaining a stable, respectable, and adequately comfortable life. Lillian Rubin, who carried out an intensive study of working-class families, writes:

> Parents in professional middle class families have a sense of their own success, of their ability to control their world, to provide for their children's future, whatever that might be. For them the prob-

lem is not . . . *whether* they can go to college or professional school, but *which* of the prestigious alternatives available to them ought to be encouraged. For working class parents, however, the future is seen as uncertain, problematic. For them, the question is most often *whether,* not *which*—and that "whether" more often asks *if* the children will finish high school; *if* they will grow up without getting "into trouble"; *if,* even with maximum vigilance, they—the parents—can retain some control over their children's future.[21]

In summary, Kohn's analysis goes as follows: Values are products of life conditions. While many such conditions affect values, one that is particularly salient is the general structure of the parents' work. Upper-middle-class occupations are distinguished from working-class occupations in that the former involve more self-direction and self-reliance, less close supervision, and—with certain exceptions—greater involvement with ideas than with things.

At first glance there appears to be a contradiction between the Kohn analysis and the previously noted O'Donnell and Stueve report that found that middle-class mothers encourage and arrange structured after-school activities for their children while working-class mothers leave their children free to do as they wish. But the findings are not necessarily contradictory. The middle-class mothers are following the principle of *sponsored independence*—they believe they are helping their children to develop knowledge, skills, and resources of personality that will enable them to take broader responsibility and to make decisions of wider scope as adults. The working-class mothers on the contrary are following the principle of *unsponsored independence.* They are less conscious of any connection between after-school activities and adult careers and may merely be viewing the activities of the children as a welcome respite from the constraint and supervision of school.

Supporting Kohn's interpretation with its emphasis on occupations and values is the type and style of discipline of upper-middle-class and working-class families. Kohn argues that, in applying discipline, middle-class parents are more concerned with the motives and intentions of their children's acts, whereas working-class parents are more concerned with the overt consequences. To illustrate, a five-year-old girl trips her younger sister, who falls and bursts out crying. The upper-middle-class parent is likely to ask him- or herself whether the tripping was accidental or whether the older girl was angry at her younger sister and, in her anger, deliberately tripped her. Only in the latter case would the child be punished, for the child must learn to internalize appropriate standards and not lose self-control. The working-class parent, on the contrary, is more likely to react to the outcome; the tripping is hurtful to the younger sister and disrupts the peace of the household, so the older girl should be punished. The working-class parent wants the child to conform to rules and behave properly. Lillian Rubin explains this for the working class as follows:

> Those who must work at such [standardized] jobs may need nothing so much as a kind of iron-willed discipline to get them to work every day and to keep them going back year after year. No surprise, then, that such parents look suspiciously at spontaneity whether at home or at school. No surprise, either, that early childhood training tends to focus on respect, orderliness, cleanliness—in a word, discipline.[22]

According to Wallace Lambert and his colleagues, who studied parental values in ten national groups, a harsher discipline by working-class than middle-class parents is a worldwide characteristic, but the difference is especially notable in North America, among English and French Canadians and Americans: ". . . middle-class North American parents are much more permissive and lenient than working-class parents when the child's behavior calls for discipline. In fact, North American middle-class parents prefer to divert, distract, or at the most scold rather than threaten or actually punish a child who misbehaves."[23]

Further supporting this general picture of different emphases in socialization between the upper-middle and working class is their use of language. As we pointed out in Chapter 3, language is one of the important ways—some sociologists believe the most important—in which social reality is organized. Insofar as social classes use language differently, they are organizing their worlds differently. Befitting the fact that upper-middle-class parents live more in the world of ideas and abstractions and give greater emphasis to verbal skills, they are more likely to explain and give reasons to the children for their actions; the working-class parents are more likely to express directly what they have in mind without explanation. Thus, whereas the working-class parent may simply say "No, you can't" to a child who wants to stay up late to watch a television show, the middle-class parent may say "It's probably not a good idea because if you stay up you won't get enough sleep and then you won't be alert for your test tomorrow."[24]

With the upper-middle class, too, according to Basil Bernstein, language becomes the object of special attention and elaboration. The structure and syntax of middle-class speech are particularly complex and make possible a more subtle and complex grasp of reality than is the case in the working class. Bernstein illustrates with a homely example, an English middle-class mother saying to her child, "I'd rather you made less noise, dear." Middle-class children have learned to interpret "rather" and "less" as requiring a particular response. Bernstein believes that working-class children do not have available this kind of sentence structure and would have to translate the foregoing sentence into a form that they know from their own experience— "Shut up!"[25] Another study reports that middle-class mothers use many more words than do working-class mothers in talking to their children, that more of the words are abstract, and that the sentences are longer and more complex.[26] This general difference in language, we shall see later, also serves upper-middle-class children well in school.

Socialization in the upper-middle class to emphasize self-direction and a future orientation was once characterized as deferring basic gratifications in order to attain future goals. This *deferred gratification pattern,* as it was called, included such diverse aspects as the postponement of paid employment in order to attain more education, saving money rather than spending it freely as the spirit moves, controlling aggressive impulses, and avoiding sexual intercourse until one is married and settled.[27]

This picture of austerity, ascetism, and self-restraint in the upper-middle-class child is certainly no longer valid; in its socialization, the middle class allows its children considerable pleasure. However, it is doubtful that the earlier picture is completely outdated. It seems likely that despite the greater indulgence of upper-middle-class children today, they nevertheless remain more closely supervised and more intensively guided toward adult roles than the children of the lower or working class. Also, preparation for an upper-middle-class occupation still requires sustained application and more or less rigorous self-discipline. And the child—in the terms Allison Davis used almost five decades ago—has "learned" to experience an *"adaptive"* or *"socialized anxiety"*—the child feels anxious lest he or she not succeed.[28]

In this section we have focused on differences in child-rearing values and techniques between the working and the middle class. There appear to be trends in values, however, especially among the working class, which bring the two social class groups closer together. Less value is being placed on conformity and more on independence. Duane F. Alwin, reviewing a trend survey in Detroit of the average ranking of five valued "child qualities" from 1958 to 1983, finds that, in the working class, "to obey" decreased from 3.43 to 2.97; in the business class, it decreased from 2.81 to 2.62. Meanwhile "to think for oneself" increased in the working class from 3.89 to 4.26, which is not far from the 1983 score of 4.55 of the business class.[29]

In a replication study of "Middletown," the Indiana city first studied in the 1920s, Alwin found the same general trend. Among the working class, the selection of "strict obedience" as one of the three most important emphases in child rearing decreased from 46.2 percent in 1924 to 20.7 in 1978, not far from the 13.6 percent of the middle class. "Autonomy" meanwhile as one of the three most important emphases increased in the working class from 17.3 to 67 percent, much closer to the 1978 figure in the business class of 83.7 percent.[30] Alwin finds the same general trend in a recent review of national U.S. historical survey materials.[31] Thus, he speaks of a general trend away from the child-rearing values of conformity and obedience and an increase in and convergence toward the formerly middle-class values of autonomy and independence. Unfortunately, however, we lack the studies that might tell us whether and, if so, how, these values are being put into practice.

Lower-Class Subculture

The term "lower class" has two principal meanings. Its more neutral meaning denotes those in a society—the unskilled and often erratically employed, the badly underpaid, the elderly with little money, and many single mothers—who have the least benefits the society distributes, including income, education, housing, prestige, and influence. The term has additional connotations, particularly to many middle-class people: It is used to refer unfavorably to the way of life followed by people so situated. Thus, *lower class* implies ignorance; instability of employment and family life; "premature" initiation of heterosexual activity and subsequent promiscuity; "low standards" of personal grooming, housekeeping, and language usage—in short, a wide array of behavior that is unacceptable to middle-class people. These judgmental connotations make it difficult for middle-class people to consider lower-class life with detachment and therefore raise some questions about continued use of the label. We use the term of course in its first meaning.

Because lower-class people are intensively preoccupied with problems of survival in the present, the child is brought up in a subculture that is not strongly oriented toward the future. Albert K. Cohen and Harold M. Hodges, in their study of lower-class life on the San Francisco Peninsula, identify four main aspects of the lower-class person's life situation.[32]

1. *Deprivation.* Lower-class people feel deprived. They have inadequate resources compared with their felt needs and levels of aspiration. Although it is possible to feel deprived at any level of life, lower-class people feel more chronically deprived of more things than do people at other class levels. These include not only income and what it can buy but also such valued goals as education, satisfying work, happy marriage, and enjoyment of life. They have few resources, material and otherwise, to pass on to their children.

2. *Insecurity.* Lower-class life is especially unpredictable, entailing high vulnerability to sickness, injury, disability, death, and entanglements with the law. And when these misfortunes occur, there are fewer resources to deal with them. People have neither the funds nor the necessary skills, knowledge, and access to institutions that can help.

3. *Simplification of the experience world.* Lower-class people move in a more narrowly defined world, both geographically and socially, than do people of other classes. They have experienced a relatively limited range of objects and situations and have limited perspectives from which to define, classify, and evaluate their experiences.

4. *Powerlessness.* Lower-class adults have little "leverage" in

society. Their relatively low level of skill makes them easily re-
placeable in employment; they have "the least access to and
control over strategically important information." Representatives of established society such as the police, welfare workers,
and school officials often intervene in their lives, and they feel
little ability to influence the course of their own lives. Not only
have lower-class people experienced little previous success in
shaping their own lives, they expect little in the future. Their
pessimism is summarized by Cohen and Hodges:

> "A body just can't take nothing for granted; you just have to live
> from day to day and hope the sun will shine tomorrow." No theme
> more consistently runs through the pattern of the LL's [lower-class
> person's] responses and distinguishes him from the others. In his
> view, nothing is certain; in all probability, however, things will turn
> out badly as they generally have in the past.[33]

Furthermore, lower-class people know that they are "at the
bottom of the heap" and looked down upon by people more
favorably situated in society. Thus, they face the problem of
evolving a way of life that will, insofar as possible, reduce insecurity and serve as a defense against moral criticism. One way
in which this is done is to maintain a network of relationships with
people situated as they are, primarily neighbors and kin. In this
way they are able to call upon others in time of need. Another
aspect of this way of life is to place heavy reliance on fate, chance,
or luck; belief in such factors as causes of their destiny helps to
relieve the sense of failure. Yet these and other adaptations to a
harsh reality do not always eliminate despair and a sense of
ineffectiveness. Eleanor Pavenstedt describes what she saw in
lower-class homes that she studied:

> The outstanding characteristic . . . was that activities were impulse-
> determined; consistency was totally absent. The mother might stay
> in bed until noon while the children were kept in bed as well or ran
> around unsupervised. Another time she might decide to get them up
> and give them breakfast at 6, have them washed and dressed and the
> apartment picked up by 8:30. Or the children might get their break-
> fast from the neighbors . . . None of the children owned anything;
> a recent gift might be taken away by another sibling without anyone's
> intervening. The parents often failed to discriminate between the
> children: a parent, incensed by the behavior of one child, was seen

dealing a blow to another child who was close by. Communications by words hardly existed. . . .[34]

This quotation emphasizes the disorganization of lower-class home life. Yet closer reading indicates some effort, even if only episodic, to live up to norms that are shared by the wider society—for example, washing and dressing the children, picking up the apartment. Inconsistency of behavior in the lower class, including inconsistency in socialization of its children, has been one of its readily recognizable aspects since sociologists began studying differences in the ways of life of the different social classes. More recent observations and analyses have directed our attention to the fact that the lower-class subculture includes values and norms that are central to middle-class culture but which often cannot be sustained under the conditions of lower-class life. The lower-class person's actions oscillate between conformity to values and to countervailing circumstances. In speaking of this "lower-class value stretch," Rodman writes:

> Without abandoning the values placed upon success, such as high income and high educational and occupational attainment, [the lower-class person] stretches the values so that lesser degrees of success also become desirable. Without abandoning the values of marriage and legitimate childbirth he stretches these values so that a non-legal union and legally illegitimate children are also desirable. . . . They share the general values of the society with members of other classes, but in addition they have stretched these values, or developed alternative values, which help them to adjust to their deprived circumstances.[35]

Moreover, some of the characteristics that were often thought to be distinctive of lower-class culture are now more fully understood not simply as "their way" but as adaptations to deprivation. Thus, Cohen and Hodges, as have others, note that "toughness" is an important quality in lower-class life. This includes a "dog-eat-dog" ideology; pride in the ability to "take it"; and a general posture of assertiveness, a "don't-push-me-around" touchiness. But while toughness sometimes manifests itself as belligerence, other observers have emphasized another aspect, the capacity to endure hardship. One mother explains why she kept her children home from school: "There was no food in the house and I didn't want them to have to go to school hungry and then come home hungry too. I felt that if I kept them home with me, at least when they cried and asked for a piece of bread, I would be with them to put my arms around them."[36]

We have little systematic research on the socialization of the children of the lower class but find some suggestive ideas of how teachers reinforce class characteristics in a report by Valerie Suransky on a predominantly black federally funded, low-income urban day-care center. Most striking, she says, in contrast to middle-class day-care centers, is the merging of spatial and temporal structures. Areas are not demarcated for free play or motor and cognitive areas, and various activities take place simultaneously.

> Not only were spatial boundaries low—as evinced by the *integrated,* rather than *separated,* use of space—but many activities coexisted in time: a late breakfast, snowflake making, "play" fighting were all events in time which were unbounded by the rigors of a schedule. A spontaneous decision to go on an outing changed the noisy atmosphere within seconds, and a further time transformation took place. The "present" rather than "future" time orientation of the staff was conducive to that spontaneity. Events "happened" as opposed to "being planned" in advance.[37]

The spontaneity in this school was in marked contrast to the very orderly and structured programs Suransky found in two day-care centers with a middle- and upper-middle-class pupil population. In both of these centers, the children's activities were firmly scheduled by the staff. Routinization of activity was stressed in one of them; in the other, based on educator Maria Montessori's idea that absorption in work leads to self-discipline, Suransky observed preschoolers being socialized to work alone and to be possessive about their own work.[38]

Conflict was also handled differently in the middle-class and lower-class centers. In the two middle-class centers, teachers suppressed children's physical aggression.[39] In the center with lower-class children, conflict—pushing, punching, hairpulling, biting, hitting—was easily tolerated by the staff as "natural for kids at that age." Conflict here was viewed as a norm, a part of life, and the staff intervened only when an escalation of the conflict presented a physical danger to the child.

Suransky also notes the "socialization of a collective ethos" in the low-income center. To be possessive or fiercely individualistic was not considered desirable or legitimate, and children were strongly encouraged to share and play together. If children squabbled over possession of a toy, the teacher might well take the toy away. Even the language of the staff reinforced a collective orientation. Whereas in a middle-class school, the teacher might compliment a child on her new shoes, at this school a teacher might more likely say "I have shoes like yours" or "What do we have the same today?"[40]

COMMUNITY OF RESIDENCE

Our discussion of social class subcultures has been based on work carried out primarily in metropolitan areas and in small towns. We were not concerned with community of residence as a basis for differentiating subcultures, although the residential community is increasingly linked to social class. Thus, many upper-middle-class people live in suburbs (although, to repeat, not all suburbs are upper-middle class). Lower-class people live in slums in the "inner city" areas of large cities and in run-down areas in small towns. To an important extent, then, analyzing a subculture from the standpoint of social class and from the standpoint of community of residence are simply two different approaches to the same task. We believe that the social class approach contributes fuller understanding (although not all sociologists would agree). Nevertheless, a community's history, geography, and economy do contribute to subcultural variation and, therefore, to socialization, particularly if the community is relatively isolated. Let us present a brief sketch of one subculture in a relatively isolated area.

The Subculture of a Depressed Area

We shall describe some aspects of the subculture of the Cumberland Plateau, a mountainous area consisting of nineteen counties in eastern Kentucky, as it was portrayed by Harry M. Caudill in the early 1960s.[41]

The Cumberland Plateau is an area of steep ridges and narrow, winding valleys, part of the Appalachian Mountains. It is inhabited by about half a million people, most of whom are descendants of English, Welsh, Irish, and Scottish pioneers who first settled the area long before the Declaration of Independence. The people who live in the area are part of that backwoods group derogatorily referred to in other parts of the country as "hillbillies."

Families and neighbors were divided by the Civil War. Cousins, brothers, and even fathers and sons often took opposing sides. When the occupants of a mountain cabin learned that a relative had died in the war, they took revenge against the nearest available family whose members were sympathetic to the opposite side. A tradition of hatred and violence was established, and it developed into the ferocious Kentucky mountain feuds that lasted unchecked until 1915. "Thus the mountaineer came to inherit the hatreds of his father along with his name. . . . The mountaineers' hatreds became so many-layered, so deeply ingrained and so tenaciously remembered that they were subconscious, and as such they have, to a remarkable degree, been transmitted to his present-day descendants."[42] The transmission of hatreds of ancient origin is one illustration of the way in which historic events can shape the socialization process.

Between 1875 and 1910 the mountaineers lost most of their land to big-city entrepreneurs from the North and East. Being isolated from the rest of the country, they were unaware of the growing industrialization and consequently of the value of the timber and coal on their lands. Also, being illiterate and unsophisticated, many had not adequately registered and secured title to the land, some of which had been given as a veterans' benefit at the close of the Revolutionary War. Much of the land slipped from their hands either through acceptance of nominal payment or through court action.

Absentee-owned coal companies came to dominate the economy; the mountaineers were recruited to work in the newly developing mines. Since there were no towns in the region—the largest town was often the county seat with no more than 150 people—the companies built camps to house the miners. In many of them the housing was ramshackle, built of unseasoned lumber, so that in a few years the houses began to sag and sway. Miners were required to live in these company-owned houses as a condition of employment and to pay rent to their employer. Although the coal companies also built school buildings, the schools were inadequately financed because the companies were powerful enough to keep their taxes low. Since there was not enough money to pay qualified teachers, most left the area and were replaced by children of mountaineers whose training went no further than a semester or two at a state teacher's college.

During the early years of the coal towns, some efforts were made by both companies and residents to keep them clean. This proved to be a losing battle as coal dust seeped into everything. The polluted atmosphere peeled paint from the walls and turned clothing yellowish gray. Despite best efforts, the communities turned "coal-camp gray." Caudill describes the effects on the women:

> Many women fought the dirt-and-grime battle through the best years of their lives and surrendered to it only in old age, long after the Big Boom and the Great Depression were history. . . . Realizing that the contest could not be won, they slowly capitulated to the unremitting clouds and allowed their homes to lose the sparkle and shine which had characterized the new towns. The spick-and-span gave way to the dull and disordered, and the women sat down on the front-porch swings and in chairs before the fireplaces and allowed the victorious enemy to run riot through the towns. There appeared the first symptoms of the vacuity, resignation and passivity which so marks the camp dwellers today, traits which could only deepen as the years brought new defeats and new tragedies.[43]

The boom period in coal mining ended in the late 1920s, and the economy of the area never really recovered, although there was a brief upsurge after World War II. One important factor was that coal mining became mechanized, so there were few jobs for men who knew no other skill but mining. By the end of 1957 more than half the people in some counties were regularly existing upon food supplied by government relief. Efforts of many men to find jobs in cities such as Cincinnati, Detroit, or Chicago were fruitless. Many younger people did succeed in leaving the area for jobs elsewhere, thus leaving the area depleted of energy and ability. The great unemployment and "the flight from the plateau of its hardier people" resulted, Caudill states, in "the growth of 'welfarism' on a scale unequaled elsewhere in North America and scarcely surpassed anywhere in the world."

One of the central features, if not indeed the dominant one, of this subculture was a sense of demoralization. Men over forty could find employment neither in the area nor elsewhere. Many of the homes were rotting and almost beyond repair. The area had one of the highest birth rates in the United States, and this, together with the extensive unemployment, led to widespread and often devious efforts to become eligible for one or another program of public assistance. Children who managed to graduate from high school usually left the area; by a year after graduation, no more than 4 or 5 percent of the graduates remained in their home counties. Some of the important consequences of this subculture for socialization were revealed in an interview with a fifty-six-year-old jobless miner:

I hain't got no education much and jist barely can write my name. After I lost my job in 1950 I went all over the country a-lookin' fer work. I finally found a job in a factory in Ohio a-puttin' televisions inside wooden crates. Well I worked for three years and managed to make enough money to keep my young'uns in school. Then they put in a machine that could crate them televisions a whole lot better than us men could and in a lot less time. Hit jist stapled them up in big cardboard-boxes. I got laid off again and I just ain't never been able to find nothing else to do.

But I kept my young'uns in school anyway. I come back home here to the mountains and raised me a big garden ever' year and worked at anything I could find to do. I sold my old car fer seventy-five dollars and I sold all the land my daddy left me and spent the money on my children. They didn't have much to eat or wear, but they at least didn't miss no school. Well, finally last spring my oldest boy finished up high school and got his diploma. I managed to get twenty-five dollars together and give it to him and he went off to git him a job. He had good grades in school and I figured he'd get him a job easy. He went out to California where he's got some kinfolks and went to a factory where they was hirin' men. The sign said all the work hands had to be under thirty-five years of age and be high-school graduates. Well, this company wouldn't recognize his diploma because it was from a Kentucky school. They said a high-school diploma from Kentucky, Arkansas, and Mississippi just showed a man had done about the same as ten years in school in any other state. But they agreed to give the boy a test to see how much he knowed and he failed it flatter than a flitter. They turned him down and he got a job workin' in a laundry. He jist barely makes enough money to pay his way but hit's better than settin' around back here.

I reckon they jist ain't no future fer people like us. Me and my wife ain't got nothin' and don't know nothin' hardly. We've spent everything we've got to try to learn our young'uns something so they would have a better chance in the world, and now they don't know nothin' either![44]

This man's case is not atypical in the area. The interview suggests that the values in this subculture—at least with respect to preparing children for adult roles—are not very different from those of middle-class subculture, although there are differences in many norms. The interview also indicates some of the ways in which even a relatively isolated subsociety is part of the larger society. And it brings out significant effects of economic conditions on a subculture and socialization into it. Stories of the relative success of some who have moved away and the view of the world offered by television provide some role models that are more diverse than those present locally and thus stimulate aspirations; but the resources actually operative in the subculture are insufficient to develop in the young more than a minimal competence to occupy adult roles in an industrial society. As Richard A. Ball points out in his analysis of Appalachian subculture, the young learn to expect defeat, and much of the culture can be understood as consisting of efforts to seek relief from insoluble problems.[45]

The effects of isolation on the socialization process are vividly brought out in a report from another part of Appalachia:

Mountain people are indeed reared in a society of the "known," a rural environment providing little stimulation or opportunity, and thus acquire neither the attitude of mind nor the few skills needed for meeting new and different situations. There are few broadening experiences available to them—few simple experiences like sitting with people you don't know on a bus, asking for change from a busdriver, doing business with strangers in stores or supermarkets, meeting and playing with strange children in the park. . . . Because mountain children are surrounded by a culture that contains only what is known, they are often extremely reluctant and afraid to attempt any unfamiliar experience.

For example, a group of men from our area were being housed in a YMCA in a city where the church was seeking to relocate them.

One night a member of the group stopped in the lobby for a candy bar while the others went on up to their rooms. Following along afterwards, he entered the automatic elevator, which had always been operated by someone else in the group. Finding himself alone with the doors closed, he panicked. He yelled and screamed and beat on the sides of the elevator until someone on the outside punched the button, opening the doors for him. He was so shaken by this experience that the next day he boarded a bus for home. . . . Here was a young man in his early thirties who was so overwhelmed in this new situation that he could not handle his fear.[46]

Following widespread publicity about the Appalachian way of life in 1963 and 1964, many efforts were initiated to rehabilitate the region but, according to a later work by Caudill published in 1976, these were of little avail. The more able young people continued to migrate out, the industrial and political powers-that-be continued to resist any significant changes that threatened their positions, and those who remained received welfare. The atmosphere for the children growing up in the region, suggests Caudill, remained one of degradation and degeneration.[47]

Specialized Communities

Other communities also have distinctive characteristics that may cut through class, ethnic, and other subcultural divisions. Summer resorts in which the local residents distinguish between themselves and tourists (who may be viewed as "fair game") represent one example; Indian reservations in which the distinction between the resident Indian and the outside white underlies all interaction are another; relatively isolated one-industry or mining towns in Canada in which residents look to the company or the government to serve their needs are still another.[48] The child in such communities grows up in a world of distinctions and social definitions that differ from those in other types of communities.

Specialized communities can maintain themselves over a period of time only through maintaining boundaries between themselves and outside influences and effectively socializing the generations to come. One good example of such a specialized community is found among the Old Order Mennonites, centered in Waterloo County, Ontario, Canada, many of whom trace their origins to migrations from Pennsylvania following the American Revolution and again from 1825 to about 1875.[49]

Mennonites have a long and complicated history. Originally formed during the Protestant Reformation, the Mennonite groups moved to avoid persecution, from Holland and Switzerland to Germany and Russia and later to the United States and Canada. Since then there have been continued migrations and splitting into factions, with many Mennonite groups becoming relatively modernized and secularized. The Old Order Mennonites of Southern Ontario, as described by John F. Peters,[50] remain one of the most conservative and traditional of the groups. The great majority are farmers, with some 7 percent of the men working in shops making or repairing shoes, harnesses, furniture, buggies, or stoves. The group has lived in this region for many generations, semiautonomous, and always maintaining an economically viable existence.

The Old Order Mennonites have kept their traditional ways and their distinctiveness, refusing in many respects to adapt to the modernized world around them. They do use small tractors in the fields, but only horses and buggies for transportation, no automobiles. They speak a German-Swiss dialect and have no central heating, telephones, radio, or television in their homes. Women wear long dark dresses, black shawls, black shoes, stockings, and a white "prayer bonnet" to "show their obedience to God and submission to their husbands." Men wear dark trousers with suspenders, long-sleeved shirts, and hats.

Sex roles remain rigid, with the men carrying on the farming and the women helping on the farm and maintaining responsibility for the household, baking, food preservation, and child care. The father is the dominant figure.

Through mutual aid in case of illness or hardship, the group can maintain its independence from the larger society. Peters writes:

> In the event of fire, the community assists by reconstructing the building, assuming 75% of the material costs and all labour. Medical expenditures are similarly carried by the community. Should a farmer be temporarily physically handicapped, neighbours will assist by planting or harvesting. The poor are also assisted. Most of the elderly live adjacent to a son or daughter. When continuous bed care is necessary, neighbour folk watch in 12 hour cycles.[51]

The entire way of life is strongly supported by a stern religious practice and ideology based on the Bible. There is little time for leisure except for attending church and social visiting, which is a weekly Sunday afternoon routine.

The traditional patterns are passed on to the children through consistent socialization processes supported by all the authorities and institutions of the society. The family is the basic and primary socializing agency. The parents introduce the children into their ideology and way of life in the normal course of their day-to-day lives. No one ever disputes the authority of the father, and discipline is rigid. Boys tend to identify with the father and males of the household and are brought into their activities. Girls identify with the mothers and other females and participate with them.

The families are strongly moralistic. Religion permeates their everyday activities and serves as the ideological authority for all behavior. The children are so identified with their families that they are known as "Josiah's son or daughter, not as the person Susan Martin." The children accompany their parents on family visits, and there is no free time for them to spend with peers.

Other institutions all support the family. The school is not an independent institution in which peers ever spend time with one another free of supervision. The teachers live in the community and reinforce the teachings of the family. In school the children do learn English, but the German dialect remains the language of the home, the church, and the community. The church likewise serves to support the values of the family. Children attend church with their parents rather than a separate Sunday school. The minister, along with parents, teachers, and the elderly, serves as an authority figure who represents traditional morality and values. For the young children there is in effect no leisure time and no separate or independent peer-group existence. Not until the children are age fourteen or fifteen do they participate in activities independent of adults, and this begins with a Sunday evening singing and game-playing session at someone's house.

The Old Order Mennonites have followed this way of life with relatively little change or influence from the outside world. The children grow up in this community experiencing no other way of life and having little experience with or pressure from the outside community to change their ways. And they in turn "are socialized to recognize that outsiders change their ways frequently, and that this change brings group instability, personal dissatisfaction, insecurity and religious disintegration."[52] Theirs is a specialized community that so far—to a great degree because it has been economically viable and has been accepted as another multicultural group by the surrounding society—has managed to shelter its children and maintain its ways.

A few years ago another type of community setting—the *commune*—received considerable attention. The term is used broadly to refer to a group of adults, not related by kinship, who have made a primary commitment to their group and who organize themselves into a "total institution," separate from conventional society. The members generally share their resources, their household, and their work. Communes vary considerably in several respects. For example, they may be rural or urban; economically, they may seek to be self-sufficient, specialize in one type of product, or live off the largesse of others; they may withdraw from the surrounding society or they may affirm a "mission" that requires interaction with others; they may be religious or secular, politically conservative or radical, authoritarian or anarchic. The variations are many.

The vast majority of communes have been short-lived. For one reason or another, or more likely a combination, they have often collapsed within a few months of their establishment. Disruptive personality clashes, the lack of capital or skills to carry out their proposed projects, the complexity of the organizational problems all play a part. Perhaps, above all, the commitment to the group or its ideology just wears thin.[53]

Communes have not ordinarily been established with the considerations of children in mind. Broad ideologies and utopias loomed large in earlier days. In more recent years communes have represented an alternate life style in which the participants seek to "realize" themselves and obtain a more satisfying life. They are oriented more toward the structuring of alternative families rather than alternative societies.[54] In those communes in which there are children, socialization is necessarily very different from that in conventional society. In the Israeli kibbutz—which besides being long-lasting is also distinctive in that it is part of a larger political system to which it makes a significant contribution—the kibbutz itself assumes responsibility for the physical and economic well-being and training of the child. Although kibbutzim vary considerably, the usual pattern is that, from birth, children sleep, eat, and later study in "children's houses," overseen by nurses, teachers, and other caretakers. But mothers and fathers still play an important role; they are recognized as parents and give their children nurture and affection, and the emotional bonds that develop are often quite strong. Psychoanalyst Bruno Bettelheim questions the depth of the personal relationships that can develop among children brought up in this type of arrangement, but others point to the good adjustment, independence, and productive overall functioning of the kibbutz-born young adults, and to the stability of the communities that have persisted through several generations. In recent years the kibbutzim have been moving toward a more traditional and individualistic parent-child pattern with infants and children sleeping in the parental residence and spending much more time with their parents. Thus, there is less "collective mothering," and parents have relatively more influence and peers relatively less.[55]

North America's more informal rural "hippie" communes, which grew up in the 1960s and 1970s, present a very different picture. In theory, the child belongs to the commune rather than to the mother or the mother and father. The child has a variety of relationships with adults, and all the older members of the commune may serve as role models. Sex roles are different from those in traditional families, since the mother and father roles are redefined with an emphasis on the sharing of child-care tasks. Perhaps the most intensively studied of such communities with children is "The Ranch" in California—so called by researchers Bennett Berger and his colleagues—which endured at least twelve years and with a membership at times as high as two dozen adults.[56] What most impressed Berger about the child-rearing practices of The Ranch was the "decline of age grading," which is somewhat akin to the medieval conception that we quoted from Ariès (see Chapter 3). In ideology, the children were "small persons," equal in status to adults and with the rights of other members of the commune to drugs, sex, and resolving disputes among themselves. Children should be allowed to develop in tune with nature, unspoiled by the repressive institutions of the middle-class world.

In practice, of course, there are limitations, for at least with young children, age and status cannot help but make a difference.

One problem derives from the disparity between the ideology and the obligations of parenthood. Berger quotes one mother, exasperated with the toilet training of her two-year-old child: "What I wanted was a baby, but a *kid,* that's something else!"[57] Having babies was viewed as good, it was organic, natural, and beautiful, besides representing the potential of the human being free from all the corrupting influences of the repressive institutions in the larger society. The ideology provided few supports for the arduous tasks of child rearing, particularly in those situations in which interaction with the child was not immediately gratifying to the adults.[58]

In these communes, as children get older they become less the responsibility of the mother and more the responsibility of the commune as a whole. Berger writes:

> Infants and "knee babies" are almost always in the charge of their mothers, particularly if they are nursing. . . .
>
> Children aged two to four frequently "belong to the commune" in a stronger sense than infants and knee babies because they are less dependent upon continuous monitoring. Nevertheless, even with children of this age the conventional pattern of sharing their care was primarily in the hands of the group of mothers-with-children, any one (or more) of whom would do collective baby-sitting to give the other mothers a break from child care. . . .
>
> I do not mean to imply that small children did not get a lot of fathering. They always did at The Ranch, although it was not necessarily by their biological fathers or their mothers' current lover. Over the years the men have increasingly shared child care as they became adapted to and accepting of the increasingly strong currents of feminism among the women at The Ranch. . . .
>
> But such fathering behavior also depends to some extent on the personal predispositions of the men. In the first few years of my association with The Ranch, there did not seem to be strong norms *requiring* the attentiveness of men to the young children. Some of the men are fond of children, are good with them, and gravitate naturally toward nurturing functions; some are not and do not. . . .
>
> For children older than four or five, the supervisory responsibilities of either parents or other adult communards are much attenuated. Children are regarded as intrinsically worthy of love and respect, but not necessarily of special restrictions or privileges or attentiveness or close monitoring. As they grow out of primitive physical dependence upon the care and supervision of adults, they

are treated (and tend to behave) like other members of the communal family.[59]

In an earlier report, Berger and his colleagues also noted that at this age, the children would be offered (and would take) an occasional joint of marijuana as it passed around the family circle.[60]

Once the children were five or six years old, they had considerable autonomy and came and went largely as they pleased. They were encouraged to participate in useful work and to express their views on commune affairs at family meetings. They attended school, at first in a nearby village, and later on The Ranch grounds where they were joined by other children from the vicinity. The school was relatively egalitarian, with the curriculum determined in part by "bargaining and discussion in which the subjects that available adults are competent to teach are balanced against what students ask to learn."[61] In 1979, at the time of writing, Berger notes that the community had moderated its originally strong "counterculture" quality and now looked unfavorably on dope smoking among children and childhood sexual activity. Apparently the growth of the children and the establishment of the school had had its effect.

We cannot generalize about child rearing in communes. In one Christian community children were regularly disciplined by spanking,[62] and in others adults seemed quite indifferent to children's needs.[63] But in all instances in which we have adequate data, from the point of view of theory and research, communes serve as valuable experiments that help to focus questions about the complex processes of child rearing and socialization. We may wonder, for example, how commune-reared children will fare when they become adults in a society that is likely to remain highly individualistic and competitive. Will these children, when adult, continue a communal way of life? To take another point, adults in the communes Berger and his colleagues studied appear to use a different notion of age grading than does modern conventional society—children are not a special object of adult concern, and they mingle more freely with adults. Will this result in an easier, less conflicted socialization? It is too early to know, but the later outcomes of communal socialization will be awaited with great interest.[64]

ETHNIC GROUPS

An ethnic group, in contemporary usage, is a distinctive minority segment of society. The members of such a group have *a shared identity* based on (1) *a common ancestry* and (2) *a common culture.* Each of these terms condenses several elements, which should be identified.

A *shared identity* can be based on the members' own beliefs and feelings, or on the beliefs and feelings of nonmembers who attribute such an identity to others, or on the beliefs and feelings of both members and nonmembers. Most ethnic groups include some people who have minimized or are in the process of minimizing their identity with the group. Nevertheless, nonmembers as well as members may still consider them part of the group, and this attributed identity may continue to have some impact on the socialization of the children. But the core of an ethnic group is usually made up of members who choose to identify themselves as members.

The concept of a *common ancestry,* although widespread in popular usage, is more complex than it seems. It seems to imply a common biological background, and there is partial truth to this. But few people, if any, can trace their biological ancestry more than seven or eight generations at most, at which point we lose track of who contributed to our genetic inheritance. People may say "I'm mostly Irish, with a little English and German mixed in," by which they mean that they know of some specific English and German contributors to their biological inheritance, know of many more Irish contributors, and assume that the ancestors far back beyond their knowledge were mostly Irish, in conformity with the recent majority they know of. The point here is that the notion of a common ancestry shared by members of an ethnic group rests on (a) their shared belief concerning their biological inheritance combined with (b) a sense of the group's having inhabited a given geographical area and, therefore, (c) their sharing in a distinctive group history.

A *common culture* here means a culture that is distinctive to the minority group in the midst of a dominant culture. Ethnic-group cultures usually involve one or more of the following cultural elements: (a) a language that is different from the dominant language in the society; (b) a religion; (c) a shared awareness of a historical background that is preserved in stories, legends, ceremonies, songs, costumes, holidays; and (d) some values and norms that are distinguishable from those of the dominant majority.

These diverse components of what has come to be called *ethnicity* combine in different ways to result in different kinds of ethnic groups. Nationality groups, such as Italian, Polish, and Lithuanian, are distinguished by their origin in and ties to a particular political unit, a country of origin. There is in such nationality groups a sense of common biological inheritance, but this is usually less prominent than the sense of coming from a politically designated geographic place where people spoke their own language and participated in a culture identified with that place. In contrast, a sense of biological distinctiveness is more prominent in what are thought of as racial minorities, such as blacks, Indians, and Inuit (Eskimo).[65] Other groups, such as Hutterites, Quakers, and Mennonites, have a shared identity based predominately on their distinctive religions, which serve them as bases for distinctive ways of life. Jews have had a shared identity based on a distinctive religion—in this respect they are like the religious minorities—but also based on a shared awareness of a distinctive historical background and language—in this respect they are like the nationality groups.

Except for the Indians and Inuit, who were already here, and the blacks, who first came as slaves, the population of North America derives from immigrants of many countries. First came the original colonizers, primarily from England, France, Spain, and Holland; then immigrants from northern and western Europe and from China; then immigrants from southern and eastern Europe. In the United States, free and open immigration was halted by legislation in the early 1920s, when it was replaced by a restrictive quota system based on national origins; some nationalities were preferred over others. In 1968 the national quota system was replaced by one giving priority to preferred occupational skills and to kinship ties. Also, from time to time, special acts of Congress have permitted refugees to come from countries in political turmoil. In recent years relatively more immigrants have come from Latin America (especially Mexico), the Philippines, Asia, and the Caribbean. In Canada in recent years, immigrants have also come primarily from non-European countries—from Hong Kong, Jamaica, the Philippines, Latin America, the Near East, and other countries in Asia. Refugees have also been admitted in large numbers.

Of course, the largest ethnic group in the United States is not an immigrant group at all; blacks, who number over 28.5 million and make up almost 12 percent of the population, have been in the country almost as long as whites. (In 1790, when the first census was taken, blacks made up 19.3 percent of the population.) For generations, whites regarded blacks as a distinctive minority group by virtue of their common African ancestry; increasingly, in recent years blacks have also come to so regard themselves, accepting the definition the larger society has thrust upon them. Accompanying the new self-definition has come a change in feeling from one of derogation to one of racial consciousness and pride: "Black is beautiful." The very same redefinition that focuses on an assumed common ancestry and on similarities rather than differences among individuals and subgroups has also been occurring among North American Indians who, generations past, saw themselves only as Iroquois, Creek, Dakota, Cree, Hopi, Crow, Ojibway, Arapaho, or whatever other particular tribal group they stemmed from. To indicate that they were the original inhabitants of the land, Indians have also come to adopt the term "Native Americans" or in Canada, "Native Peoples."

From the perspective of socialization, the wide variation among ethnic groups and the rapidly changing social context make for a complex, confusing, and uncertain picture. The fourth- and fifth-generation children of Scandinavian and German immigrants may now see themselves only as American, hardly, if at all, aware of their ethnic origins. The third- and fourth-generation children of immigrants from southern and eastern Europe are more likely to be aware of their ethnic origins and, as we shall see, may or may not identify strongly with their ethnic groups. The children of more recent migrants from Mexico, Puerto Rico, Cuba, Vietnam, Hong Kong, and elsewhere cannot help but experience some dual-culture problems, akin in many respects to those experienced by earlier immigrant children.[66] Still another dimension is introduced for such groups in the United States as blacks, native Americans, and some Hispanics, who are part of active ethnic social and political movements fighting for increased recognition of their rights. It would be far too complex to discuss each generation or each type of ethnic group separately. Rather, through the analysis of the two key concepts of *identity* and *culture,* with an emphasis on the role of the family, we shall seek to clarify some of the basic problems of ethnic socialization for the members of any ethnic group.

Identity

The ethnic identity of children, we have noted, derives from the "racial," religious, or national collectivity of which their parents are members. Children come to identify themselves as Hungarian, Jewish, Irish, Puerto Rican, Italian, or whatever. From the perspective of the social structure, these are positions or statuses; from the point of view of the individual, they are identities. They are self-designations that define an individual's position linking one to and setting one apart from others. Children learn their ethnic statuses before school age when they are still very much a part of the family. One researcher suggests that children can be aware of their ethnicity by age three, following awareness of their sex;[67] another says that the "spontaneous use of an ethnic attribute when describing oneself may occur as early as five years of age."[68]

Studies among black and white children show that by the age of five, racial attitudes may already be quite complex. Using a doll-choice game technique, Judith Porter carried out an intensive study of 359 black and white children, ages three to five, attending nursery schools and kindergartens in the greater Boston area. She concludes:

> By five years of age, children of both races have clear knowledge of racial differences and their racial attitudes are already rather sophisticated; white children may realize that blatant and overt expressions of prejudice are somehow unacceptable, and the black child may be developing complex feelings toward both his own and the opposite race. But even at age four, children have internalized the affective connotations of color and begin to generalize these meanings to people. Although the three-year-old white child does not, on the whole, invest color with social meaning, the black child of this age does perceive vaguely that color differences are important and may be personally relevant.[69]

When young children think of ethnicity, they think first of such external attributes as festival celebrations, language, or a particular school; as they get older, belief systems, values, and feelings of pride and attachment become more important.

The ethnic self-definition may, depending on the particular context, encompass a broad or narrow range and may or may not correspond with the definitions of others. When do Chicanos in San Antonio consider themselves Mexican, Texan, or Mexican-American? Under what circumstances do Jews define themselves by the subidentity Orthodox, Conservative, or Reform; and when as American Jews, or just Jews, without national identification? When are Iroquois in upper New York State Indians, when American Indians, and when Iroquois of the same tribe as the Iroquois of Canada? When are Serbs, "Czechs," and Bulgarians "Slavs"; when are they not? Identity is a concept that allows considerable flexibility; it varies among members of an ethnic group, it expands and contracts, it changes over time, it looms large or small depending upon the particular context and possibly on the advantage to be gained from manipulating the ethnic label.[70] Children, in the course of growing up, learn their ethnic identities and subidentities and the uses of each.

A second major dimension of identity is affective. To know and recognize one's ethnicity is cognitive; to feel its sentiments and emotions is affective. The two, of course, are closely linked; yet the distinction between them is useful. Some ethnic-group activities are clearly cognitive. Children may be taught the language, history, and culture of their group and develop an information base that enables them to delineate those who do and do not share their common ancestry. Other activities are clearly affective, focusing on rituals, group singing or dancing, ceremonies, and other types of group participation that serve to develop a feeling of belonging and an emotional attachment to those one recognizes as sharing a common ancestry.

Closely associated with the affective identification with one's group is what Gordon Allport has called *ego-extension,* that identification with any object, persons, causes, and collectivities that are thought of as "mine."[71] Psychologically, the group and its symbols become part of one's self. In the same way that one's school, local football team, new bicycle, or hometown may be an extension of one's self and arouse feelings of pride, exhilaration, shame, or anxiety, so, too, may one's ethnic group. The process is well known. We need only note the intense interest of North American Jews in the fortunes of Israel, or Poles in the activities of a Polish pope, or the enthusiastic demonstrations in 1982 of Italians to the success of Italy in World Cup soccer play. Attacks on ethnic-group members may be considered personal insults. For example, the smearing of "Jew" on the poster of a Jewish candidate for political office may anger other Jews. Negative stereotypes, too, such as the identification of the Italian with the Mafia or the Irish with excessive drink may rouse a sense of outrage.

Ego-extension, in the process of socialization, can become even more than an emotional projection of one's self onto an ethnically associated symbol. It can lead to a particular way of viewing the world, suggesting what is important and how particular phenomena should be viewed. Blacks, for example, have long been aware of their difficulties in getting good jobs, education, and housing, and when they consider lines of action, the leaders in the black community often stress human rights and the need to ban discrimination. A quite different kind of extension is found among Jews, whose concern for ethnic survival leads them to give importance to the position of Israel in the Middle East. Thus the relevance and significance of issues depend on the orientation and concerns of the particular ethnic group. Children of different ethnic groups in this sense live in different worlds.

How does ethnic identity take root? The foremost agency of ethnic socialization is certainly the family, in which the child first experiences close and intense emotional relationships.[72] Unless children learn and experience their basic ethnic identity within the family or other early primary groups, it is unlikely that they will ever strongly feel it thereafter. Ethnic parents may or may not deliberately set out to teach their children an ethnic identity. Perhaps the most effective device is the ethnically defined activity of everyday life. Following a study of Italian, German, Ukrainian, and Polish Canadians, Jeffrey Reitz writes: "Whatever the intentions of parents, children raised in an environment conducive to language retention are far more likely to remain within the ethnic fold than those who are not."[73]

Immigrant families, in the course of their everyday activities, express their distinctive speech, religious practices, holiday celebrations, food customs, characteristic gestures, and ordinary topics of conversation. Writing of the Greek family, Antoniou says:

> Work and play, eating, conversation, celebration are in terms of the family and the way through which belongingness is taken on. Contacts with the outside world are made through the family and its extensions. A child's friends are the family friends and their children. He goes visiting and to social gatherings with the family, by day or by night, no matter how late. He goes to church with his parents, to social gatherings or wherever his parents are invited . . . The expectation is that the child will adjust the rhythms and pace of its life to that of the family's.[74]

Young children in such circumstances—in which they are taken-for-granted members of a practicing ethnic unit—learn their ethnic identity along with their cultural heritage. At first, they know no other culture or ethnic identity, and it would not ordinarily occur to them that life could be otherwise. In daily situations the parents, knowingly or unknowingly, often reward their children for behavior associated with their ethnicity. They may, for example, compliment them, smile, or pay more attention to the children when they recognize the ethnic symbols, understand or speak the ethnic language, join in ethnic ceremonies, or in other ways express an ethnic identification. Parents in such instances may also encourage an ethnic identity through serving as positive models of identification themselves.

A related way in which parents "teach" ethnicity is to distinguish between those who are and those who are not members of the ethnic group. The way of life of participating ethnic group members then tends to set apart those who belong from those who do not. The boundaries and the differences in interaction patterns may or may not be explicit; they may be evidenced in the topics of conversation, use of the ethnic language or ethnic phrases, different degrees of self-awareness, facility of expression, and general feeling of ease and rapport. Speaking of Orthodox Jewish socialization in Toronto, Kallen writes:

> Traditional Judaic prescriptions and proscriptions provided strong boundary maintaining mechanisms ensuring that social relationships with outsiders were confined to the public sphere of business, school, and market-place. On the other hand, continuing and comprehensive interaction with ethnic insiders was encouraged. Primary

relationships were confined to fellow Jews, and private Jewish institutions remained largely insulated from the cultural influences of Anglo-Canadian society.[75]

In learning boundaries and in experiencing different interaction patterns between their own group and others, children cannot help but become aware of their ethnic identity. Cognitively, whether they view themselves from the position of their own group or from the position of others, they are designating their ethnicity; and emotionally, in experiencing different self feelings with their own group and others, they reinforce a sense of difference.

Parents also indirectly help "teach" children their ethnic identity by controlling their external environment. They may, for example, choose to live in a neighborhood in which ethnic culture and contacts will be reinforced. They may sponsor and send their children to such activities as language classes, church programs, or youth clubs in which they learn ethnic culture and associate with others of the same heritage.

Such efforts to control and guide the environment, to the degree that they are successful, undoubtedly help reinforce an ethnic awareness and identity, although it may be a different version of identity from that of the parents. Children participating in such programs view themselves as ethnic-group members. Insofar as others in the group, teachers, for example, become "ethnic reference points," people whose roles the children take and from which they view their own behavior, that ethnic identity is further reinforced.

Children learn the symbols that tend to set their ethnic groups apart and that permit a differentiation between the outsider and the insider. One prominent symbol for many ethnic groups in the United States and Canada is language. It is also a relatively easily identifiable ethnic indicator. Names, pronunciations, accents, distinct vocabularies, and twists of the language may all at times, for example, serve to identify and set the Spanish-speaking apart from the English-speaking. A Mexican-born social scientist, in an autobiographical account, has described the sociolinguistic problems he had when his family migrated to Sacramento, California:

> The Americanization of Mexican me was no smooth matter. I had to fight one lout who made fun of my travels on the *diligencia,* and my

barbaric translation of the word into "diligence." He doubled up
with laughter over the word until I straightened him out with a kick.
In class, I made points explaining that in Mexico roosters said "qui-
qui-ri-qui" and not "cock-a-doodle-doo," but after school I had to
put up with the taunts of a big Yugoslav who said Mexican roosters
were crazy.[76]

On a broader sociopolitical level, language in Canada has
become a symbol of the struggle of French Canadians to survive
as an independent ethnic group. To the child who lives amid the
struggle, the issue is more than simply the wider use of French;
the French language becomes a symbol of a movement of increasing ethnic identity and solidarity.

Numerous other aspects of life may also become symbols of
ethnic-group identification. Religion may loom important, for
example, for the Greek Orthodox, Mennonites, or Ukrainian
Catholics; so, too, may dietary practices, special clothing, national folk traditions and ceremonies, or voluntary associations
such as the Polish Boy Scouts.

For children, ethnic identity, with the group boundaries that
are implied, has both functional and dysfunctional aspects. Perhaps the most obvious function of ethnic-group identification for
children is that it may offer comfort and security in a mass society
characterized by impersonality and thus counteract influences
toward a feeling of anomie. Ordinarily, within their own group,
children will experience less social distance and will feel at
greater ease. They may communicate more easily with insiders
and enjoy participation in their activities and their causes.

Such group identification and the accompanying participation
may also be a protection against the dangers of what has been
termed "self-hatred."[77] In a heterogeneous society in which ethnic groups are ranked on a scale of power, privilege, and prestige,
members of the lower-ranked ethnic groups often come to adopt
the perspective of the higher-level groups. That is, the higher-
level group is used by the members of the lower-ranked group as a
reference group. A reference group is one whose standards one uses
to judge one's own group and behavior.[78] Viewing themselves
from the higher position, they rank their own ethnic group low
and look down upon and perhaps even despise that which they
themselves represent or are assumed to represent. Solidarity with
an ethnic group can reinforce one's positive feeling of self-worth
and reduce the impact of the outsiders' negative definition.

This analysis was applied originally to Jews facing intense hatred during the 1930s and 1940s when Nazism stirred and amplified anti-Semitism in Germany. More recently, however, we recognize that the relationship between a reference group orientation—which underlies the idea of self-hatred—and self-esteem is much more complex and varies by ethnic group and social class. The question of self-esteem has been especially prominent in writings about black children, with writers often in sharp disagreement.

On the one hand we have surveys that consistently show that black children, although they may recognize that many Americans rank blacks low, rank themselves high in measures of personal identity and self-esteem. Morris Rosenberg explains this by noting that a child's self-concept derives less from the reflection of the broader society than from the child's significant others, and the appraisals of these significant others are favorable. He writes:

> . . . it is imperative that we see the world . . . from the viewpoint of the child. . . . The reflected appraisals that shape the black child's self-concept are not the reflections of the broader society but the child's significant others—mother, father, siblings, friends, etc.; these reflected appraisals are every bit as favorable as those received by white children. Similarly, the comparisons that children make are not comparisons with distant and unknown others but with those who enter their immediate experience; like white children, black children's socioeconomic and academic comparisons tend to be with their peers. Finally, the self-attribution principle is supported by the fact that blacks are aware that many of the observed socioeconomic outcomes are attributable to external causes—racism in its diverse expressions—rather than to personal deficiencies.[79]

On the other hand, we have ethnographic studies of the black slum child that, while also recognizing the strong influence of the family, stress the deprivations and sense of frustration in a chaotic, hostile, and destructive world with a resulting negative self-concept. Lee Rainwater reports on a three-year study of about 10,000 lower-class blacks in a slum housing project in St. Louis:

> It is in the family that the child learns the most primitive categories of existence and experience, that he develops his most deeply held beliefs about the world and about himself. From the child's point of view, the household is the world; everything he meets as he moves

out of it and into the larger world is interpreted in terms of his particular experience within the home. The painful experience of a child in the Negro slum culture is therefore interpreted as in some sense a reflection on this family world. The impact of victimization is transmitted through the family, and the child cannot be expected to have enough sophistication to see exactly where the villains are. . . .

In Negro slum culture, growing up involves an ever-increasing appreciation of one's shortcomings, of the impossibility of finding a self-sufficient and gratifying way of living. . . . As the child's sense of frustration builds, he too can strike out and unmask the pretensions of others. The result is a peculiar strength and a pervasive weakness. The strength involves an ability to tolerate and defend one's self against degrading aggressions from others and not to give up completely. The weakness involves a reluctance to embark hopefully on any course of action that might make things better, and particularly any action that involves cooperation with and trusting attitudes toward others. . . .

Parents' conceptions of children make them constantly alert to evidence that their child is as bad as everyone else. This reflects basic views in lower-class culture that human nature is essentially bad, destructive, immoral. . . . In the child's identity development he is constantly exposed to labeling by his parents as a bad or potentially bad person. Because he does not experience his world as gratifying, it is easy for him to conclude that this lack of gratification is due to the fact that something is wrong in him, and this can readily be assimilated to the definitions of himself as a bad person that are offered by those with whom he lives. In this way the Negro slum child learns his culture's conception of being in the world, a conception that emphasizes inherent evil in a chaotic, hostile, destructive world.[80]

Thus, in some circumstances—especially it would seem in lower-class settings—the child in a depreciated ethnic group may feel trapped.

On a less destructive level, ethnic identity may lead to a turning inward within the group. The child may live in an ethnically homogeneous neighborhood, attend a private ethnic or religious school, join ethnically exclusive clubs, and consume ethnic mass media, thus restricting his or her range of knowledge, contacts, and experience. The result may be a relatively comfortable and secure existence, but lead to a rejection of certain other opportunities and a limited development of latent potentialities. It may, for example, impede children from taking the psychological risk of venturing into new occupational spheres where they might develop untapped possibilities and conceivably achieve great personal success. This assumes, of course, that the ethnic child has a choice. It may well be, segregation and ethnic solidarity being what they are, that the child will have little choice. His or her very locale may place limitations that the child cannot possibly transcend.

Marginality refers to a situation in which a person has strong links to two or more divergent socio-cultural groups, but does not identify fully with either; he or she remains on the margins of both. In the context of majority-minority relationships, the child of the ethnic minority group has two statuses, an ethnic one and a status as a citizen or prospective citizen in the larger society (United States or Canada), which identifies the child as a prospective American or Canadian. As a person of Greek, Japanese, or any other background, the child may be proud of his or her national heritage and religion; as an American or Canadian, the child may be aware of the family's foreign-sounding name and his or her parents' strong accent. The child lives on the margins of two cultures, has loyalties to both, but does not fully and exclusively identify with either. As Shibutani and Kwan observe:

> Many of the problems confronting such individuals arise from their having to perform for two different and incongruous reference groups. Since contradictory demands are made upon them by the two audiences, they experience inner conflicts. When a man lives in two social worlds, each of which is a moral order, he cannot live up to all of his obligations. Where standards are inconsistent, he will be wrong in the eyes of one of the groups no matter what he does. He may be plagued by a sense of guilt even when he has done his very best. Some persons sometimes have difficulty developing a consistent self-conception. As Cooley pointed out, a man comes to conceive of himself as a particular kind of human being in response to the manner in which others treat him. But what happens to a man who looks simultaneously into two mirrors and sees sharply different images of himself?[81]

Developing a consistent self-conception or identity is, as we noted earlier, a task for every child, but it is accentuated for the child who is marginal to two cultures. The comment of a Mexican-American girl, made more than a generation ago, is as applicable for some immigrant families today as it was then:

My mother and dad got too many old-fashioned ideas. She's from another country. I'm from America, and I'm not like her. With Mexican girls they want you to sit like *moscas muertas,* dead flies, like that. If you tell them what the teachers say, they say the teachers don't know. . . . I remember when me and my sister told my mother we wanted to dress neat and American they beat us and said no.[82]

In varying degrees, marginality was a problem for all immigrant ethnic groups, especially when the ideology of the "melting pot" was prevalent. It is tempered today by the greater acceptance of ethnic diversity and multicultural values, but it is far from eliminated. Following a reference to recent Chinese immigrants, historian Selma Berrol writes: ". . . the schools today no longer try to deracinate the immigrant child. Dick and Jane are long since gone, ethnic pride and bilingualism are 'in'. Nevertheless, older attitudes reappear, and marginality remains a problem. Human nature, it seems, is stronger than educational trends."[83]

In cases of dispute between children and immigrant parents, it is generally the parents, unable to draw on the broader culture and social system to support their position, who make the major adaptation. In the terms of Erikson (in the quotation on p. 63 in Chapter 3), the children are not "confirming" their parents; the life that the parents hold out as correct does not represent a "vital promise" in the new environment, as the children see it. What is happening is that the children are changing their reference groups. The parents and their ethnic group are no longer regarded as suitable reference points. The children increasingly judge themselves by the standards of their American or Canadian age-mates or peers, because, of course, they are being judged by them on the street and in school.

Such ethnic marginality may be so easily handled by some individuals that it is hardly noticeable; on the other hand, it may involve a complex set of thoughts and feelings in which almost every ethnically associated situation becomes a dilemma of uncertainty and anxiety. On the positive side, marginal children have access to alternate ways of life and the opportunity thereby to enlarge their range of experience. Marginality may thus bring special insights into the problems of several groups, including those who are deeply committed to the preservation of their distinctive ethnic culture and those who feel caught in ethnic pressures and counterpressures.

Socialization of course, as we have observed, is not a simple

one-way process. Immigrant parents also—influenced by neighbors, workmates, previously arrived relatives, community leaders, and especially their own children—become socialized into
the ways of the new social worlds they enter. Over the years even
their patterns of child rearing may change. Researchers have
noted, for example, that immigrant parents may be considerably
stricter and more demanding of their older children than of their
younger ones.[84]

Culture

For any ethnic group the distinctive culture that makes up the
content of socialization is not easily defined. For one thing, the
culture varies among members within an ethnic group according
to such factors as socioeconomic status, age, occupation, and
region of origin. Not all Poles or Mexicans, for example, uphold
the same values or adopt the same life styles. Nor is any culture
ever static; there are always drifts, trends, and counterbalancing
forces, with inevitable differences between those in the vanguard
and those in the rear guard of particular changes.

An ethnic culture, too, is likely to take on the features of its
immediate geographic setting. Hylan Lewis describes the array of
specialized institutions that make up the urban black ghetto to
which many thousands of rural blacks migrated:

> Carry-out shops, laundromats, and record shops have recently come
> to the ghetto in numbers. They join taverns, pool halls, liquor stores,
> corner groceries, rooming houses, second hand stores, credit
> houses, pawn shops, industrial insurance companies, and store front
> churches as part of a distinctive complex of urban institutions that
> have undergone changes in adapting to the effective wants, limited
> choices, and mixed tastes of inner-city residents.[85]

And linguist Walt Wolfram writes of the Puerto Ricans:

> it seems safe to generalize that Puerto Ricans in Harlem and other
> centers of concentration in the city use both English and Spanish:
> . . . A Spanish domain is most completely approximated in the home,
> particularly (1) if the parents speak little English or are fairly new
> arrivals in the city, or (2) if there is frequent contact with new arrivals
> from the island. Children of preschool age apparently learn English
> from their siblings and companions on the street rather than from

their parents, and many youngsters who are fluent in English speak Spanish to their parents and other relatives. In the neighborhood both English and Spanish are used, depending on the age and the Puerto Rican orientation of the speaker.[86]

Wolfram then goes on to discuss the English of Puerto Rican children, which varies depending upon whether they have extensive or restricted contact with blacks.

Further, as we have observed, children do not passively accept all aspects of an ethnic culture. To a great degree they build their own reality, and the ambivalence and conflict that are part of the process of socialization may well include ethnic dimensions. As one aspect of a more general resistance to authority, children, perhaps with the support of peers and mass-media models, may reinterpret or reject the ways and expectations of their ethnic socializers, possibly perceiving them as cowardly, parochial, docile, or just old fashioned. Sometimes a child stumbles innocently into a conflict with authority, as happened to this Italian-American:

> Immigrants used "American" as a word of reproach to their children. For example, take another incident from my childhood: Every Wednesday afternoon, I left P.S. [Public School] 142 early and went to the local parish church for religious instruction under New York State's Released Time Program. Once I asked one of my religious teachers, an Italian-born nun, a politely phrased but skeptical question about the existence of hell. She flew into a rage, slapped my face and called me a *piccolo Americano,* a "little American." Thus, the process of acculturation for second-generation children was an agonizing affair in which they not only had to "adjust" to two worlds, but to compromise between their irreconcilable demands. This was achieved by a sane path of least resistance.[87]

Recognizing such complexities in particular cases, what are the general features likely to be transmitted in ethnic socialization practices? Perhaps most obvious are the more visible aspects of a distinctive cultural heritage, such as traditional recipes, language, ceremonial and religious practices, certain gestures, particular interests and skills such as lace making or soccer, and a knowledge of the group's legends, myths, and heroes.

` Less manifest, but equally recognizable, might be certain more subtle aspects of personal relationships, the distinctive conceptions of male (the *machismo* of Latin America) and female, the protective role of the older brother, the obligations of the god-parents, the father's right to swear, the respect paid to the priest, the domesticity of the mother and perhaps her care in preparing a traditional holiday dish, and expected kinship patterns of hospitality and loyalty.

Also included may be a distinctive world view and codes of behavior that provide the raison d'être for the behavior of the group. French-Canadian children in Quebec, for example, had long been taught that it was their sacred mission in the New World to maintain their distinctive language, religion, and traditional rural way of life. Currently, children of Estonians, Latvians, Lithuanians, and North American Indians are likely to be taught that they have been deprived of lands that are rightfully theirs.

Feelings and sentiments enter into all aspects of such transmission of cultural practices, ideas, and beliefs, including those that form part of daily routine and those that are part of heightened ceremonial occasions. Some groups have stringent rules governing diet, and their members feel revulsion in situations in which they might have to violate the rules: Hindus served beef or Moslems served pork, for example. Some solemn ceremonies call forth deep emotion, as when Ukrainian groups gather to honor the heroes and martyrs of the Ukrainian struggle for independence or when Jewish groups gather to commemorate the six million Jews annihilated in death camps by the Nazis in the early 1940s. Traditional deep-seated antipathies toward other ethnic groups may also be part of the heritage; for example, the antipathy of Irish Catholics to the English in Northern Ireland, and Greeks and Turks to each other. The origins of such feelings, passed on culturally from one generation to another, may lie in the remote past.

Other studies show that ethnic groups have varied considerably in their attitudes toward education and orientation toward achievement. In the early decades of the twentieth century, no ethnic group placed more emphasis on education and achievement than the East European Jews. For the immigrant generation Jewish mobility rested on entrepreneurial success; in later generations it rested more on extended education. The wish to succeed, the value of learning, and the ability to adapt to the educational methods of the schools were all relevant factors.

The Slav and Italian immigrants did not fare as well, partly for economic reasons, partly because they valued education less. Schooling was not generally considered essential to their needs and boys were encouraged to acquire job skills. Also, the families emphasized sharing and the common good, and the children, as a matter of course, would give their earnings to the family.

Recent reports of immigrant Chinese children present another picture. Education and scholastic achievement are highly valued, and the children are described by their teachers as earnest, well disciplined, and hard-working. They earn good grades despite language problems and the need to work part time.[88] The success of Chinese and Chinese-American children has been attributed to their socialization in the family. Chinese-American women believe that taking care of a home and educating their children are more important than having a job, and they supervise their children more closely than do white parents. The children are integrated into family activities and tend to develop a mutual dependence upon the family rather than focusing on themselves. This results in their tendency toward a greater compliance with adult demands than is found in Western cultures. The parents press the children to achieve, and they, in turn, having been taught to give up pleasure or comfort in order to meet family expectations, become motivated to do well. When a Chinese student does not do well in school, the parents are likely to believe that the child is not trying hard enough, whereas white or black parents in a similar situation often believe that the teacher or school is not doing its job. Until high school age, Chinese children tend to remain isolated from the dominant, wider culture. This pattern of socialization, with its strict home environment, produces stress and anxiety in the children, as well as achievement and upward mobility. One scholar predicts that as a result of the wider participation in American culture that occurs at the high school and college levels, this Chinese cultural pattern will become less influential, and, in time, the family patterns that have set the Chinese apart will become undermined.[89]

Sometimes an ethnic minority culture can include practices and beliefs that unintentionally create difficulties for children at school and actually hamper their achievement. Stephen T. Boggs illustrates such an occurrence in his discussion of the "speaking routines" among "part-Hawaiian" children from low-income families.[90] "Part-Hawaiians" are those residents of Hawaii who have some Polynesian ancestry and retain some traditional sub-cultural patterns that differentiate them from other cultural groups in the state.

Boggs cites the example of the "direct question" in the handling of discipline. The part-Hawaiian parents use direct questions when they are about to punish, "in order to accuse a child of wrong-doing, and to extract from the child's own lips the incriminating evidence."[91] The resulting wariness of the children to direct questioning carries over to the school situation, and when teachers ask direct questions—as they often do—the child answers minimally and warily. Boggs concludes that

> Routines that resemble those used by adults at home often do not call for the same kind of response in school and teachers often do not respond as parents would when children act as they do at home. . . . the lack of fit between routines and the participation structures learned at home and those encountered in school is the principal cause for the poor performance of part-Hawaiian children from low income families in school.[92]

Running through all these elements that enter into an ethnic culture is the previously discussed concept, identity. In learning a language, participating in ceremonies, following family patterns, and the like, a child's identity with his or her ethnic group can be reinforced. Children are aware of and feel they belong to a collectivity that links them to some and sets them apart from others.

The studies we have noted indicate that ethnic groups in the United States and Canada can vary considerably in the patterns they follow and the values they emphasize. They do not, of course, inasmuch as they deal with particular groups at particular times, necessarily serve as good predictors for subsequent generations. Some years ago, for example, studies on the values Italian parents upheld for their children pointed to their low expectations for self-reliant behavior and low occupational aspirations as compared with, among others, white Protestants.[93] This is now an outdated picture. Richard Alba, citing responses to a General Social Survey carried out by the National Opinion Research Center between 1975 and 1980, writes: "There is no meaningful difference between Italians and WASPS [Protestants of British ancestry] on this scale [which measures the desirability of traits associated with conformity and self-direction]. Both averaged a bit more than $+1$ [a score that indicated a slight leaning toward self-direction]."[94]

Except for the racially defined ethnic groups, the traditional image of immigrant adaptation in the United States was the melting pot—over a period of time, the various ethnic groups would lose their distinctiveness and become part of a common blend. Even as late as 1953, W. Lloyd Warner, one of America's most prominent sociologists of the time, wrote:

> The number, size, and importance of ethnic groups and sects in American life increased almost yearly. Many of them are disappearing, and others yield much of their cultural substance to the influences of the other American world. All increasingly adjust to the later outlines of American society. . . . it seems likely that most, if not all of them, will ultimately disappear from American life.[95]

The situation, as it has developed, is more complex than that. Certainly to a great degree, from a cultural point of view, Warner's prediction is correct. Relatively few of the third- and fourth-generation descendants of immigrants to the United States and Canada speak the language of their forebears or follow the traditional customs and patterns of their family groups. They have attended standardized schools, mixed with children of all groups, and participated in the same popular culture of television shows, advertising, sports, movies, supermarkets, drugstores, popular music, and motor travel. Their professed core values, too, are the standard North American ones of individualism, materialism, egalitarianism, the work ethic, and political freedom.

In the late 1960s and 1970s many researchers began raising questions about this traditional image of the melting pot and the nature of ethnicity. For example, in the first edition of their book, *Beyond the Melting Pot,* published in 1963, Nathan Glazer and Daniel P. Moynihan argued that the national aspect of most ethnic groups rarely survives a third generation, although the religious aspect could still serve as a basis of subcommunity and subculture.[96] But the second edition, published seven years later, reported a renewed importance in ethnic identification, particularly as a basis for pursuing political goals. A later book edited by the same authors published in the mid-1970s continues this line of analysis.[97] A comparable analysis by a sociologist in Canada also noted the continued importance of ethnic identity, albeit with variations, viewing ethnic groups as "forms of social life, rather than survivals from the past, as mobilizers of interests rather than bearers of cultures or traditions, and collectivities with which people choose to identify rather than as groups into which they are born and from which they struggle to escape."[98]

In line with such emphases, commentators pointed to relatively circumscribed areas of some ethnic communities—ethnic clubs and organizations, specialized food centers, and special classes to teach ethnic children their native languages and ceremonies. Certainly many of the third and fourth generation—especially in Canada where multiculturalism is official government policy—feel a strong sense of identity with fellow members of their ethnic groups.

Some more recent analyses, however, have focused more on structural forces that point to a movement toward assimilation and "the twilight of ethnicity." Richard D. Alba, for example, writing of Italians in the United States born after World War II, cites their high rates of occupational mobility, entrance into higher education, and movement into the suburbs, all of which—especially for Italian men—are little different from national and even "WASP" averages. Perhaps above all, rates of intermarriage have been increasing. Alba writes: "depending on how one defines an intermarriage, somewhere from two-thirds to four-fifths of young Italian Americans intermarry."[99] Similar trends apply to other ethnic groups. Intermarriage rates are up among Jews, and even among the Japanese Americans, over a third of the third-generation are marrying non-Japanese, usually whites.[100]

Ethnic groups may not deny their ethnic origins—as the old melting-pot theory might have suggested—but, following an analysis of Herbert Gans, this identification with the ethnic group, especially for the upwardly mobile, is not really very deep. Gans speaks of *symbolic ethnicity,* that is, the ethnic members select a few symbolic elements from their ethnic heritage that do not seriously interfere with their everyday behavior. They construct personal identities that contain some ethnic "spice," but they do not seriously experience their ethnic heritage or an ethnic-group cohesion.[101] Alba cites examples:

It can take the form of curiosity about the immigrant experience, often viewed nostalgically as a bittersweet authenticity in which the too assimilated third- or fourth-generation ethnic American cannot share, or it can be expressed by participation in a political movement with ethnic themes, perhaps concerned with the homeland or the group's standing in American society. Or it can be cast in the form of small details: objects in the home that have an ethnic meaning; occasional participation in ritual; or fondness for an ethnic cuisine.[102]

For the European immigrant groups, we may sum up the historical trend in these terms. A situation that began with the introduction of quite different ethnic cultures has evolved into a mosaic of loose ethnic groupings each representing somewhat different versions of a larger North American culture. Currently these groupings do not seek to gain security by following traditional ways; rather they are forms of life in which members choose to participate. Some members may become active participants in maintaining ethnic ties and symbols, others may construct ethnic variations of their own, and still others may have nothing to do with their ethnic heritages.

The implications for the socialization of children are important. Children in an ethnic grouping may well come to learn and experience their ethnicity, but they are not bound by it in their future behavior. They may choose, in all or part of their lives, to participate with members of their own or closely related ethnic groups; or they may live a life in which ethnicity plays little part.

For the children of non-European immigrants and for blacks and native peoples, the picture is even more complex. For the relatively recent immigrants from Hong Kong, India, Pakistan, Korea, Mexico, the Philippines, the Caribbean and Latin America, the patterns of adjustment are somewhat akin to those of the European immigrants of three and four generations ago. They must learn a new culture. Added to which are the complications for most of them, as for the blacks and native peoples, of being a visible minority. The blacks and native peoples in North America have the additional problem of a unique history of deprivation and subordination that has affected their way of life and their life chances.

The subcultures that provide the content of the child's socialization are brought to him or her by particular groups and institutions—agents of socialization, the topic to which we now turn.

CHAPTER 5

Agencies of Socialization

Socialization occurs in many settings and in interaction with many people, organized into groupings of various kinds. Each grouping exerts particular kinds of effects on children, and each has more or less distinctive functions in preparing children for social life. Each may therefore be called an agency of socialization.

While each agency has its own functions in socialization, functions that in certain respects may be contradictory, various agencies also reinforce each other's efforts. Common cultural images of the child affect many agencies. Thus, when "getting along with others" was a dominant goal in socialization, as was true in the forties and fifties in the United States, family, school, church, voluntary associations, and even informal peer groups worked toward this end.[1] During the 1960s socialization concerns changed in some degree; academic competence became a more important goal for many sections of both the middle and working classes, particularly those parts of the latter made up of urban ethnic minorities. The middle class placed a somewhat greater emphasis on individuality and creativity as goals. These emphases were widely diffused, so that many socialization agencies reflected the changed values and goals. Thus, family and school tended to share the increased emphasis on academic achievement although they may often have differed on implementation. Convergence and divergence of expectations coexisted side by side.

During the 1970s there was again something of a shift in socialization emphasis. Although academic competence remained important in families, in schools, and elsewhere—and still is important—it was not the focus of intense concentration that it had been earlier. No other single concern quite replaced it, yet the changes in society have yielded new emphases. One significant contender for the new dominant concern in socialization is that of revising or repealing old stereotypes, particularly sex-role stereo-types. Until recent years socialization took place within a frame-work that led fairly clearly to different socialization paths for boys and for girls. Increasingly in North America, more slowly in some other countries, these stereotypes are being revised. The tele-phone company publishes photographs of women climbing tele-phone poles to make repairs and of men working as telephone operators. Whereas each of these occupations was formerly re-stricted to the other sex, now both are open to both sexes.

This is but one illustration of a wide movement to change traditional expectations and therefore socialization experiences that had been sex-specific. This is not to say that everybody concerned with socialization is in agreement on the changes; the point is, rather, that the question of whether boys and girls should be confined to traditional sex-specific experiences is a question that is emerging near the center of attention for all persons who are in any way concerned with socialization. This question follows upon, and to some extent competes with, an earlier concern with revising minority-group stereotypes.

Also contending for increased attention in the late 1970s and early 1980s were the disabled, including the children who were hard of hearing, crippled, mentally retarded, or handicapped in some other way. In part this was a result of an increased interest in the handicapped—1981 was the United Nations–designated International Year of the Disabled—and in part a result of a general movement for the rights of children. Handicapped chil-dren, it is affirmed, should by right, insofar as possible, have the same opportunities as other children—to a good early education, to any public facilities, to entertainment and sporting activities, and later, without discrimination, to higher education and jobs. It is also affirmed that normal children without disabilities should recognize the human dignity and rights of those who are handi-capped and not stigmatize or discriminate unfairly against them.

Also receiving considerably more attention in the 1980s are those children whose parents have veered from traditional pat-terns. These above all are the children of single parents—divorced, separated, or never married. Another nontraditional category that is beginning to receive some attention consists of the children of stable marriages in which both parents work out-side the home and the children attend day-care centers and nursery schools. As we shall see, the number of such children of nontraditional families has increased enormously in the 1980s, to the point that in some sectors of society, they are the normal— that is, typical—children.

In sum, if we look back over the last forty or fifty years, we can recognize several shifts of attention and concern in socialization beliefs and practices, from getting along with others to an emphasis on academic competence to a still newer emphasis on revising certain minority and sex stereotypes and adapting to new family types. The earlier concerns are not discarded; they are edged away from the center of attention and worked into newer patterns.

Before proceeding to our discussion of particular agencies, it is important to make clear that some socialization outcomes are consciously sought by the agency of socialization, whereas others are unintended. Socialization always takes place in overlapping time frames. For example, when a parent tells a child to take his or her feet off the furniture, the parent is most likely concentrating on keeping the furniture clean and unscratched. The parent may or may not also be thinking at that moment about developing in the child "respect for property," "respect for authority," "self-restraint in disposing one's body," "neatness," and any number of other long-term objectives that might be considered socially desirable. But even though the parent may not have these latter objectives in mind, they may nonetheless be among the consequences of the interactions whose goal is simply to save the furniture. We are, then, alluding to an important distinction between *purpose* and *function*. [2] A purpose is a goal that a person or group wants to accomplish; it is an "end-in-view." A function is a consequence, or effect, of action and interaction. Purposes and functions may sometimes coincide; thus, knowledge of arithmetic is one of the goals, or purposes, that the elementary school endeavors to attain. It is also a function, that is, a consequence of teaching. If purposes and functions never coincided, socialization would probably be impossible. Nevertheless, it is important to bear in mind that socialization agencies have functions that are not necessarily among their purposes.

One reason functions and purposes do not entirely coincide is that although the family, school, and others are agencies of the society, they also "have a life of their own." When we say that society—through law, custom, and public opinion—delegates certain socialization functions to specific agencies such as the family or the school, we are not describing a process that is the same as an army captain directing a subordinate to carry out an assigned task. Agencies of socialization necessarily have more leeway in how they achieve the goals assigned to them than does the captain's aide. Agencies of socialization are accountable to the society only within rather broad limits. A school that does not include arithmetic in its curriculum will be examined by a state agency or criticized by parents, and it will be required to meet at least a minimum standard. But a great deal of what goes on in schools, in families, or in other agencies of socialization is not scrutinized, not subject to sanction by society.

It is therefore not entirely useful—but useful up to a point— to think of agencies of socialization as carrying out society's mandates. Such agencies are not like machines processing a raw material into a predetermined product. Even in a society that attempts to predetermine with great exactness the outcomes of socialization, many things go awry. As sociologist Allen Kassof observes, the efforts of the Soviet Union to mold the attitudes of its young people through closely regulated youth programs do not, for various reasons, result in uniformly starry-eyed enthusiasts.

> In spite of all the resources at its command, in spite of its monopolistic advantage, in spite of its unprecedentedly vigorous efforts to indoctrinate entire generations, the youth program does not work well when it is undermined by the actual conditions of the larger society. . . . It is too much to expect that more than a small minority should emerge from the youth program with such unblemished views of a society where the noise of busy construction is interrupted only by the rhythm of happy dancing and skating.[3]

The fact that socialization agencies develop purposes of their own and that persons being socialized also develop individualities of their own should keep us from thinking too literally of society as some kind of tightly integrated "system" and from developing what sociologist Dennis Wrong has called *"the oversocialized conception of man* in modern sociology."[4] Although all socialization occurs through some form of interaction, and although all interaction is patterned by values and norms of some kind, interaction also evolves in directions that are not necessarily specified in advance.

The concept of "agency of socialization" needs, then, to be understood in this somewhat complex way. Any such agency generates processes, purposes, and functions of varying import. Some are most relevant to society as a whole, some to a particular subculture, some only to the agency itself. In some respects, society's mandates are quite specific and agencies are expected to be diligent in carrying them out. For example, all families are expected to carry out society's prohibitions of incest. All elementary schools are expected to teach children to read and write. All peer groups are expected to refrain from undue violence against authority.

In other respects, society's mandates are general and even vague, leaving socialization agencies a great deal of leeway. For example, the family and the school are jointly expected to prepare children for gainful employment on reaching maturity. The school probably has more directly assigned responsibility for achieving this outcome, but the family is expected to cooperate with or at least not hamper the school in carrying out this mandate. But the mandate to the school is vague enough to be influenced by particular subcultures and by the educators in particular schools and school systems. Thus, the school may have the general obligation to help children develop their talents to the fullest extent possible so that, among other outcomes, they may qualify for "the best jobs" of which they are capable. But in one subculture this may mean that the school should encourage and reward capacities for independent thought, whereas in another subculture the expression of such capacities might be regarded as evidence that the school is failing in its obligation to foster respect for authority, thereby disqualifying the children for jobs as well-appreciated participants in bureaucratic organizations.

With this understanding of the complex relationship between agencies of socialization and society, let us turn to an examination of some of the most important agencies in our society.

THE FAMILY

The family is the first unit with which children have continuous contact and the first context in which socialization patterns develop. It is a world with which they have nothing to compare and, as such, it is the most important socializing agency. True, the family is not as all-encompassing in our society as it once was, and its effects may be modified (some easily, some not so easily) by other agencies. Children may now be placed in day-care centers in infancy, attend nursery school or summer camp at the age of three, and watch television from the time they can focus on a moving picture. Schools, hospitals, government agencies, and service industries have taken over many activities that were once conducted by parents or relatives such as grandparents, uncles, and aunts. Nevertheless, despite the greater exposure of the contemporary child to outside influences, the family remains crucially important for his or her socialization. This may be seen from several vantage points.

The Family in the Community

The family into which a child is born *places* the child in a community and in society. This means that newborns begin their social life by acquiring the status their families have, and they will retain this status certainly throughout the first few years of their lives, very probably until they reach adulthood, and only somewhat less probably as they move through adulthood.

To be born into a particular family, then, is to acquire a status (or set of statuses) in the community and in the society. The child's family-given status is an important determinant of the way others respond to him or her. One obvious example is the child of royalty, such as Prince William, son of England's Prince and Princess of Wales. At the other extreme, the case of a boy named Johnny Rocco provides a pointed illustration:

> Johnny hadn't been running the streets long when the knowledge was borne in on him that being a Rocco made him "something special"; the reputation of the notorious Roccos, known to neighbors, schools, police, and welfare agencies as "chiselers, thieves, and trouble-makers" preceded him. The cop on the beat, Johnny says, always had some cynical smart crack to make. . . . Certain children were not permitted to play with him. Wherever he went—on the streets, in the neighborhood, settlement house, at the welfare agency's penny milk station, at school, where other Roccos had been before him—he recognized himself by a gesture, an oblique remark, a wrong laugh.[5]

Although these examples reveal how family fame or notoriety may be conferred on children who have not brought such fame or notoriety on themselves, the basic principle of status-conferral holds for other kinds of statuses as well. Children of unmarried mothers or dual-career parents, daughters of clergy, sons of police officers or garbage collectors—all have particular images to contend with in the social worlds in which they live.

The family's status in the community affects not only the way others respond to the child and the kind of formal education he or she is likely to receive; it also mediates for the child the culture available in the larger society. Any family participates directly in a limited number of subcultures and networks (one based on social-class position, one based on ethnic-group membership, possibly others based on kinship, occupations, or interests). These are the versions of the larger society that are made most directly available to the child through example, teaching, and taken-for-granted daily activity. At the same time, any family is likely to be aware of at least portions of other subcultures that may serve as subjects of emulation or derogatory comment. In these ways the families into which children are born present them with selective versions of the larger society, with the result that children may become impressed early with the importance of religious devotion, or baseball, or school achievement, or making money, or sexual intercourse as a primary focus of attention, depending upon the emphasis of the subculture(s) in which their families participate.

In sum, the family is not simply a passive transmitter of a subculture to its children but plays an active part in screening in and screening out elements of available subcultures. This is accomplished (1) by means of activities—for example, going to church, inviting guests, visiting friends, going to football games—and (2) through comment and comparison—evaluating such activities and the people who do or do not participate in them and evaluating the groups and subcultures of which these activities are a part.[6]

The family's position in the community also affects the age-grading of children. This is to say that what is expected of a child at given ages depends to some extent upon the family's social position. Families thus differ in the rate at which they *pace* their children toward maturity. Generally, childhood is of longer duration in middle-class than in lower-class families. In the latter, children take on serious responsibilities at an earlier age. For example, in a study of very poor black families living in a public housing project, David Schulz found that firstborn daughters are given responsibility for caring for their younger siblings when they themselves are very young and, by the age of nine, may even be doing much of the grocery shopping and cooking in their households.[7] Although later-born girls are less likely to have such heavy responsibilities of caring for younger siblings, they are likely, as is their eldest sister, to begin having children of their own when in their teens. Child-care responsibilities thus begin at a much earlier age than is the case in the middle class, whether black or white. In a sociological sense, it can be said that childhood ends at an earlier age.

In Schulz's findings we see an illustration of the distinction between intended and unintended outcomes of socialization. The mothers intend that their firstborn girls take care of younger siblings and also become competent in shopping and cooking. The mothers do not, however, wish to see their daughters begin giving birth to children of their own in their teens and, indeed, endeavor, however ineffectively, to prevent this from occurring. But since the mothers themselves began having children when they were adolescent, they provide models with which their daughters identify and which, therefore, weaken the impact of their strictures. Further, the subculture does not apply strong negative sanctions against early motherhood, in or out of wedlock. Most importantly, the discrimination practiced by whites against blacks, and especially against those who are poor, functions in various ways to prevent many young and poor black girls from developing effective goals for adulthood that would enable them to delay motherhood. Becoming a mother provides some feeling of self-esteem in a subculture with many deprivations and many norms shaped by discrimination.[8]

In sum, then, a child is born into a family, and the family locates the child in society. From the moment of birth, before there is any opportunity to take independent actions, the child is located in society—as middle class or working class, child of teacher or truck driver, Christian or Jew, member of a dominant or subordinate ethnic group, member of a family respected or scorned by neighbors. The family's—and therefore the child's—

location in these social groupings affects the experiences the child will have as he or she matures. It will determine, to a significant degree, not only what form socialization opportunities will take but also at what ages, in what order, and with whom. It will also play an important part in determining the child's later location in society when he or she has become an adult.

The Family as an Interaction Structure

Although one of the family's functions is to place children in the society and thereby directly or indirectly affect their experiences outside the home, this is not its only importance in socialization. The family has an organization of its own that has its own direct effects on children.[9]

From this perspective, perhaps the most important function of the family in socialization is that it introduces children to intimate and personal relationships. Since children's first social relationships are family relationships, it is in this group that they acquire their first experiences of being treated as persons in their own right. They receive care for their dependency and attention for their sociability. Because newborn children are both without experience and very needing of care and attention, their initial outlook is assumed to be egocentric. The kind of care and attention they receive during their first and second years of life affects their resolution of the issues of trust versus distrust and autonomy versus shame and doubt—and therefore their capacity for establishing later ties with people outside the family.

At the outset newborns are unaware that they are separate and distinct persons. As time goes on, they become aware, first, that they and their mothers (or other caretaking persons) are separate and, then, that there are other members of the household—father and, possibly, siblings. Children learn that others have wishes, interests, and ways of their own and that it is advantageous to adapt to them. Others do not invariably appreciate children and their needs and wishes—indeed, the appreciation varies according to how responsive a child is. Living in a household shared with others, children learn that they must share the resources of the household—the space, the furnishings and other objects, the time and attention of parents and siblings. They learn the ways in which their cooperation is sought and welcomed and the ways in which they may compete for what they want when it conflicts with what other family members want. In interacting with children, parents may be more or less expressive of their feelings, more or less authoritative, more or less protective. The mother, in dressing a young child, may demand or plead for cooperation; the father, in disciplining the child, may be angry or businesslike. Siblings may be more or less jealous, more or less interested in accepting a brother or sister as playmate and companion.

Through these various kinds of interaction with family members—such as showing affection, being cared for, resisting, being disciplined, being accepted as a companion and playmate—the child develops initial capacities for establishing relationships with others. These capacities will find both later expression and further development in relationships with non-family playmates, co-workers, authority figures, friends, and, ultimately, a spouse and children.

The family into which the son or daughter is born is the child's first *reference group,* the first group whose values, norms, and practices the child adopts and refers to in evaluating his or her own behavior. What this implies, as Talcott Parsons and Robert F. Bales have argued, is that the child identifies with the family as a group, so that its ways become part of his or her own self. These authors have thus amplified the concept of identification beyond the original meaning Freud gave it when he spoke of the child as identifying with the parent of the same sex.[10] This means, for example, that not only do the particular members of the family constitute models for the child's own behavior but *the pattern of interaction among the members* itself becomes a model. The child's socialization is affected not merely by having a hard-working or an alcoholic father, a loving or indifferent mother, a domineering or distant older sibling. It is affected also by whether the interaction in the family is characteristically relaxed and good-natured or tense and guarded, whether it emphasizes or minimizes the distance between parents and children or between males and females, whether it is typically cooperative or competitive.

The impact of family interaction pattern, even during a period of dramatic social change, can be seen in a study by Troll and Bengtson of student activists in the late 1960s. This study showed that the student activists were often perpetuating a family theme—that of manifesting a dedication to causes—even though the students' actions were, in a literal sense, different from their parents:

> the parents may have been dedicated to "modernizing" the practices of the Catholic Church or eliminating reading problems by adapting a phonetic method of teaching, and their children to promoting interracial housing or opposing the war in Vietnam. The *modus vivendi* of the parents may have been committee meetings and public speaking, and of their children marches and "sit-ins," but for both generations the core value of dedicating one's life to righting wrongs and improving the world seemed to be the same. Dedication to causes persisted as a "family theme" . . . though the particular wrongs to be righted and the particular means of trying to do so were different with each new lineage generation.[11]

This example illustrates how values can be inculcated during the family socialization and yet be expressed in innovative fashion by children who must interpret the existing situation in their own time; they may feel their time calls for different actions than were required or appropriate in their parents' time.

One way to see differences in family interaction patterns is to select relatively consistent and clear types. For purposes of analysis, Herbert Gans describes three such types of families in North America.[12] One is the *adult-centered,* in which the family is run by adults for adults, a pattern not uncommon in the working class and which Gans found among certain Italian groups in Boston and Jack Weller found among the Anglo-Saxon mountain people in Appalachia.[13] In this type of family, the wishes of the children are clearly subordinate to the wishes of the parents. When the children are with adults they must act as adults want them to act: to play quietly in a corner or to show themselves off to other adults in ways that reflect well on the parents. But once the children are with their peers, they have considerable freedom to act as they wish as long as they do not get into trouble. Parents in these families are not very self-conscious or purposive in their child rearing. They

> are not concerned with *developing* their children, that is, with raising them in accordance with a predetermined goal or target which they are expected to achieve. [They] have no clear image of the future social status, occupational level, or life-style that they want their

children to reach. And even when they do, they do not know how to build it into the child-rearing process.[14]

Gans's second type is the *child-centered family,* in which parents subordinate their own pleasures to the demands and the happiness of their children. Some high-school-educated lower-middle-class and immigrant families would come close to this type. In this family, unlike the adult-centered, children are planned and serve as the parents' most easily shared interest. Family companionship is important, parents spend time playing with their children and give up some adult pleasures for them. They want their children to have a happier childhood than they had. Each child adds to the shared enjoyment and family unity, at least while the children are young. Sometimes, although the parents are not necessarily permissive, Gans writes, the children dominate their parents unmercifully.

A third type, which Gans says is an upper-middle-class pattern, is the *adult-directed.* The child's wants are less important. Parents are generally college-educated and know what they want for their children much more clearly than do parents in the child-centered type. Emphasis is placed on individual growth. Children are taught to strive for self-development in accordance with their own individuality, and parents exert considerable pressure on their children to do well in school. A recent variation of this pattern, we shall note, is the dual-career family, in which both the father and mother have high-status professional or business positions and in which the parents, while directing the child, also assert their own rights and require the child to adapt to their career interests.[15]

Although family interaction styles unquestionably tend to vary with social class, it also needs to be said that insufficient attention has been paid to variations *within* a social class or other social category. When such variation is the focus of research attention, the results suggest how family interaction patterns have effects on socialization that do not derive from social class. Ezra Vogel and Norman Bell, for example, in an almost classic exploratory study, have analyzed how families who are rather precariously balanced psychologically might make a scapegoat of one child in their interactions with one another. One child is picked out and blamed for almost everything that goes wrong in the family, and this child becomes the target for the aggression of parents and siblings. This type of interaction can be independent of social class.[16]

One other aspect of family structure needs to be considered: the significance of persons in specific family statuses. The importance of the mother has been discussed in an earlier chapter. At this point we need only reiterate that the mother is ordinarily the first socializing agent. As such, she is the first representative of society to the child and, through the care she provides, initiates the development of the sentiments and symbols that give the child a human nature and enable the child to become a responsive participant in society.

Primarily because the man's paramount role in our society has been his occupation, the father's contribution to the child's socialization for a long time was relegated to the background. Recently, however, partly as a reaction to this relative neglect, the father has received much more systematic attention. In explaining the increasing interest in the role of the father, Michael Lamb writes that "the focus on mother-infant and mother-child relationships became so extreme and imbalanced that researchers were forced to ask whether fathers could legitimately be deemed irrelevant entities in socialization."[17] The father's influence is not only direct, it is also indirectly mediated through the husband-wife relationship. Studies suggest, for example, that emotional support from the husband and a satisfying marital relationship enhance the mother's competence and sense of well-being, which in turn influence the mother's behavior with the child.[18]

The role of the father in our society is undergoing some change. Perhaps the major change is that the father's role is less stereotyped than it once was. Fathers were once thought to be— and often were—uninterested in babies, and therefore they did not interact much with their children until they could talk, play games, and benefit from fatherly instruction. The traditional father was one whose major role was to provide economic support and to assist sons to acquire appropriate sex-typed behavior to enable them to become breadwinners and authority figures.[19] There is growing recognition that fathers can and often want to be warmly interactive with their children as soon as they are born.[20] Also, divorced fathers are sometimes gaining custody of their school-age children; it is estimated that about 10 percent of children of divorced parents were living with their fathers.[21] Another indication of increased father involvement in parenting of very young children is the publication of a national guide to programs, services, and resources for fathers. According to this guide, a limited number of child care classes for school-aged boys are available, but more numerous are support and discussion groups for fathers.[22] The available evidence suggests that expectations for the father's role are currently undergoing change, but the consequences for socialization are not yet very clear.

Although change is under way, one continuing fundamental contribution of the father is that he provides a basic model of masculinity. For his sons, this model becomes a basis for developing their own male identity. For his daughters, the model provides a basis for developing images of male companions and perhaps a desirable husband. For children of both sexes, these images are influenced not only by the father's actual conduct but by the mother's evaluations of him, as well. In recent years the meaning of masculinity, however—outside of meaning to be sexually a male—has become much more uncertain than it was in the past. "Masculinity" used to imply a syndrome including such personality traits as courage, decisiveness, venturesomeness, and grit in the face of adversity. The boy who sought to be masculine would hold back his tears, play roughly in team sports, and suppress any feelings of fear. Now, however, the image has become tempered, and men, in films, newspaper photos, and other areas of popular culture, are more often portrayed as expressive of warmth, dependent upon others, hesitant, and sensitive to the needs of others. This change is in part undoubtedly a reaction to the women's movement, and it puts into question the psychological tests that define masculinity by its traditional characteristics.

However masculine and feminine may be defined, the mother and father, according to some recent studies, act toward the child with different styles. Both are responsive, but whereas the mothers are primarily responsible for emotional support and caretaking, the fathers more actively engage in physical stimulation and playful interactions.[23]

Finally, entering into any patterns of influence are the siblings, who may add considerable complexity to family relationships. In a review of sibling relationships in the family,

Schvaneveldt and Ihinger[24] observe that siblings form various coalitions that, depending upon the particular groupings and their perspectives, may have both integrating and disruptive effects. Children, for example, may conspire against their parents, older siblings may gang up on younger ones, or family lines may be drawn on the basis of gender. Norms grow up in the *sib subsystem*: Siblings negotiate, bargain, and learn how far they can go and in what direction. For each sibling the family climate is different, with the older siblings often serving a pioneering function for the younger. The older siblings, be it in asserting independence from the parents or joining in certain peer-group activities, blaze the trail for the younger siblings.

Especially important in affecting the interaction are the size and composition of the sibling group. James Bossard and Eleanor Boll compared one hundred families each with two children with one hundred families each of which had six or more children. They found that there tended to be more "regimentation" and assigning of jobs in the large families than in the small and that in the small families "the children were often spared from all household chores in the interests of concentrating on their education, outside activities, and social life."[25] They also reported that siblings in the small families were more dependent upon their parents for security, whereas the children in the large families were more likely to find security "in the numbers of siblings who formed a cohesive group for defense, playing, confiding, teaching, even plotting against parents."

The sex composition of the sibling group is also important, since the small family is much more likely to have children all of one sex, and growing up in a house with siblings of one sex is a different experience from growing up in a house with siblings of the opposite sex. Sociologist Orville Brim, analyzing data collected by psychologist Helen Koch, sought to confirm this in a large study of personality traits of children in two-child families. Making use of George Herbert Mead's theory of social interaction, Brim reasoned that "taking the role of the other" should result in a greater frequency of typical cross-sex personality traits in children who have a sibling of the opposite sex than in children whose only sibling is of the same sex. When he examined Koch's data from this perspective, he found that his prediction was substantially correct. Thus, a girl with a brother was more likely to have "high masculinity traits" (such as ambition or competitiveness) than a girl whose sibling is another girl. Similarly, the boy whose sibling is a sister is somewhat more likely to show "high femininity traits" (such as affectionateness or obedience) than the boy whose sibling is a brother. What is significant here are not the particular traits, which today may seem arbitrary, but the finding that there is a greater overlap of traits in cross-sex-sibling families than in families without opposite-sex siblings.[26]

Variations in Interaction Patterns

The discussion of the family as an interaction structure has taken the two-parent nuclear family as the case type. The nuclear family, usually consisting of parents and their biological children, had for a long time been considered the "normal" (that is, preferred) and the typical (that is, most prevalent) unit for the primary socialization of children. It is still the most frequently found family form (63 percent in 1982)[27] and is still probably most widely preferred, but, in a trend that began during the 1960s, children increasingly are being socialized in other types of units as alternative forms come into being alongside the traditional nuclear family. In 1984 as many as 23 percent of children under eighteen years of age were living with only one parent, the vast majority in mother-child units.[28] Approximately 10 percent were with fathers. Others live in foster homes and still another large group—13 percent in 1977 and considerably more today—live in remarried or "reconstituted" or "blended" families in which at least one of the two adults is not the biological parent.[29] By the age of eighteen, according to one estimate, 60 percent of all children born in 1984 will have lived for a period of time with just one parent.[30] In Canada, with its lower divorce and unmarried-mother birth rates, in 1981, the percent of single-parent families was less than 12 percent. The general trends, however, are in the same direction as in the United States.

A child may live in several types of families before reaching adulthood. The child might be born into a three-generation household, then live in a nuclear family when his or her parents set up their own household, then in a single-parent family after the parents divorce, and finally in a reconstituted family when the parent he or she lives with remarries.

Thus, although the nuclear family remains the most common family unit in North America, and the majority of children continue to grow up in households consisting of two parents, an increasingly large minority receive at least part of their socialization in other kinds of family or household units. The child in these other kinds of families or household units is likely to undergo distinctive socialization experiences.

The most common of these families, we have noted, is the single-parent, the great majority of which are created by separation or divorce. The child of divorce in the new single-parent family must make many adjustments. In the intact nuclear family in which all goes well, the family observes many routines, some everyday and some on special occasions during the year; both parents share household tasks and have a hand in disciplining the child; both give attention and affection to the child; and each parent gets some psychological support from the other. In a family broken by separation or divorce, the routines are upset, the uncomprehending children are uncertain about both day-to-day events and the future, and they may even be called on to take sides. The single parent with custody—especially if it is the mother—is likely to feel overburdened, alone, and harassed, and especially concerned about giving direction and discipline to the child. Wallerstein and Kelly, who studied 60 divorced families over a five-year period, write:

> for children, the transition from a married family to a post-divorce family is complicated because they have little control over the changes in their lives. Not only did many youngsters have to adjust to new locations, new and more stringent economic situations, and the changed availability of the mother, but there were the more difficult adjustments that they had to make to the changed attitudes and behavior of their parents. . . .
>
> One half of the mothers found the role of disciplinarian extremely difficult to assume. . . . A high number were unable to say no to demanding children or enforce rules for fear the children would reject them in favor of the other parent, or the other parent's lover, or the new stepparent. . . . Many women felt severely threatened by their children's rebelliousness and were reduced to tears, nagging, or screeching. Only gradually, as their fear of rejection by their children lessened, did they learn to stand firm and to assume the parental role and its prerogatives along with its responsibilities.[31]

Not having immediate father and mother role models at hand also complicates the child's problem of self-identity. Children, we have observed, adopt models from the environment in which they live and they share in the characteristics of those with whom they feel strong emotional ties. Their values and self-images derive in part from these identifications. In the shift to the one-parent family, problems in self-identity may well arise. Speaking of the thirty-one children in their sample who were first seen during the preadolescent ages of nine and ten and again one year after the separation, Wallerstein and Kelly write:

> during latency years the child's normal conception of his own identity is closely tied to the external family structure and developmentally dependent on the physical presence of parental figures—not only for nurture, protection, and control, but also for the consolidation of age-appropriate identifications. Specifically, the self image and identity which in latency is still organized around "I am the son of John and Mary Smith" is profoundly shaken by the severance of the parental relationship. Some children expressed this confusion and sense of ruptured identity with anxious questions, comparing physical characteristics of their parents and themselves, as if trying in this manner to reassemble the broken pieces into a whole.[32]

Serving to ease the situation for the child of divorce in recent years is the large increase in the size of the divorced population in the society at large. When divorces were less common, the child of divorce often felt ashamed and stigmatized before his friends. Currently the divorced child is one of many and, if he or she does require help and support, it may often be obtained in the schools or through self-help groups with other children in the same situation.

In divorced families, patterns of some kind are likely to become established over time, but not without stress and difficulty and sometimes failures. Wallerstein and Kelly speak of one-third of the children in their sample managing very well after five years; another third were "unhappy, still angry at one or both parents, still yearning for the presence in the family of the departed parent, still lonely, needy, and feeling deprived and rejected";[33] and another third were in the middle range. The variations among the families were too great to allow of easy generalizations, but one factor that seemed to be of special importance after the divorce in contributing to the child's growth and stability was the continued and regular contact with both parents. Also having important long-run implications is the age of the child. The preschool child has a very limited repertoire of coping mechanisms "with fantasy, denial, self-blame, displacement and somatic symptom development being the primary ways in which they respond to stress in their lives."[34] Children in the school years can better identify the complexities of interpersonal relationships and have additional resources outside of the home to help buffer the stress.[35]

Accompanying the increase in the number of one-parent families is the increase in number of reconstituted families. For the child, relationships in these families can become exceedingly complex. A son may have a new stepfather married to his mother. Living with him may be natural brothers and sisters, stepbrothers and sisters, and later half brothers and sisters. His father may also remarry, which gives him other stepbrothers and sisters and perhaps later half brothers and sisters. He may also now be in touch with four sets of grandparents. The number of pair relationships in such families runs into dozens, and the possible combinations involving two or more persons into tens of thousands.

For the child in the reconstituted family, the changes are far-reaching. One problem that may well arise is that of discipline. The natural father who no longer lives with the child is in no position to impose discipline, and the stepfather may be reluctant to fully assume the role of parent and the authority that goes with it lest he weaken the possibility of forming close bonds with his new family unit. Also, if he has children of his own, he may be wary lest he discipline his wife's children more than his own. The natural father, too, may resent the stepfather's attempts at or methods of discipline.[36] Thus, compared to the role expectations for a parent in an unbroken nuclear family, the situation is fraught with dilemmas. But, as one of the present authors has argued, it is a mistake to attempt to infer the quality of interaction in families by looking only at the formal membership composition. Every family, regardless of its membership composition, must construct its own patterns of interaction, which in turn influence socialization.[37]

The child in the reconstituted family has to solve complex problems posed by having several different parental figures in his or her life. Wallerstein and Kelly in their study found that most of the children in the remarried families made every effort to conceptualize the father, stepfather, and mother together and that the stepfather did not replace the departed father. Only when the child, through his or her own active choice, *voluntarily* rejected the father and disidentified with him did the child place the stepfather in the father's role. In those cases where the father and stepfather were bitter rivals, the role-model and identity problems for the child were immeasurably more difficult.[38]

The increase in variant family forms serves to call attention to one major issue concerning socialization in families. Many students of society have pointed out that in the nuclear family, in contrast to the extended family, the burden of socialization falls on a very small group. Generally, two parents bear the responsibility of child care and provide the child with a restricted range of immediate role models. An increasing interest in communes arose partly from efforts to counteract these alleged disadvantages. On the other hand, the single-parent family concentrates the responsibility and restricts the range of parental models even more than does the two-parent nuclear family. The reconstituted family increases the range of models, since a stepparent is added to the displaced natural parent, but may add to the parental burden as new relationships between the child and stepparent are being constructed.

While alternative family forms have become increasingly prevalent, the nuclear family has also been changing in significant ways. Most notable has been the increasing number of working mothers. A couple of generations ago almost all women left the labor force when they gave birth to a child. In 1940 only 8.6 percent of married women in the United States with children under the age of eighteen were in the labor force. By 1983 the figure was almost 60 percent. Especially dramatic in recent years has been the increase of working mothers with children below age six. In 1950 the figure was 12 percent; in 1983 it was over 50 percent.[39] It was even over 50 percent in 1983 for those with children under two.[40] The figures for Canada are comparable. In 1985 almost 55 percent of married women were working for pay, including 56 percent of those with preschool children and almost 66 percent of those with children age six to fifteen.[41] Thus, the socialization experiences for a high proportion of young children are considerably different today from those of a generation ago.

What is the effect of the mother's employment on the child? Unfortunately the question does not allow of a definite answer because maternal employment is too broad a variable—it includes women of the middle and working class, women with children of various ages, women (including single mothers) who work of necessity and women who work primarily out of choice, women who enjoy their jobs and women who don't, women who feel comfortable leaving their children in the hands of others and women who feel guilty doing so. Still other relevant considerations are the wide variation in child-care arrangements while the mothers are working and the changing attitudes toward the employment of wives that, for many, make it a stigma to be "just a housewife."

Yet many of the studies, according to Lois W. Hoffman, who has critically reviewed the research on working mothers, point in the same direction and allow some limited conclusions. One is that the employment of mothers has no known negative effects on preadolescent children. Research does not show, for example, any significant differences in personality adjustment or educational achievement between children of working mothers and children of full-time housewives.

One finding for which there is considerable support is that the daughters of working mothers tend to have less traditional views of marriage and sex roles and are more independent, with higher achievement aspirations, than daughters of mothers who do not work. This is especially true for daughters of high-achieving mothers. But again, with all the variables that might be relevant, the explanation of why this is so is not clear:

> If the daughters of working mothers are found to be more independent or higher achievers than daughters of nonworking mothers, one cannot tell whether these attributes are products of the working mother as model, the fact that the father is more likely to have had an active part in the girl's upbringing, the fact that the father in working-mother families is more likely to approve of and encourage competence in females, or because the girls were more likely to have been encouraged by their mothers to achieve independence and assume responsibilities. All these intervening variables [possible links between mother's employment and daughter's characteristics] have been linked to female independence and achievement.[42]

Another review of the research on working mothers by Rallings and Nye concluded that the mother's employment has these socializing impacts on sex roles: (1) The child of a working mother is more likely to favor equality for women; (2) a working mother has a positive effect on the child's evaluation of female competence; (3) lower-class boys whose mothers work have less esteem for their fathers than lower-class boys whose mothers don't work; (4) among middle-class boys, those whose mothers work tend to see their fathers as warmer, more expressive, more nurturant.[43]

In the 1960s most researches reported that, when wives worked, husbands did not increase the time they devoted to household tasks and child care. More recent data, however, suggest otherwise. One 1977 report on fathers in Syracuse, New York, says they spent 25 percent more time on housework and child care than they did ten years earlier.[44] Another survey, based on national time diaries, concludes that between 1965 and 1980 the average proportion of the total family work done by men increased from 20 percent to 30 percent.[45] Included in this increased participation is an increase in time spent with children. A long-term replication study in "Middletown," Indiana, reports that in 1924 about 10 percent of fathers did not spend any time at all with their children while two-thirds spent over one hour a week; in 1978 the "no-time-at-all" percentage was below 2 percent while the over-one-hour-a-week was over 75 percent.[46]

When fathers do participate more in housework and child care, according to one study, it does have an effect on socialization. Bonnie Carlson, using two indices—one she called PICCI, Parental Involvement in Child Care Index, and one PRPT, Parental Role Perception Test—compared families with children ages three to six in which fathers did and did not share household and child-care duties with their wives. The fathers who shared also scored higher in nurturance, displaying more love to the children both physically and verbally.[47] One major conclusion of the study was that "children whose fathers assume greater responsibility for child care and housework are significantly less likely to see their fathers in sex-stereotypical terms."[48] A father's participation does affect his children's perception of his role.

Currently, in popular writings, fathers are encouraged to participate more in child care. We can only speculate on how far this will go, although it may well be helped by the growth of "flextime"—in which employees, within limits set by their employer, plan their own work schedules—which in 1980 covered about 12 percent of American nonfarm workers and, it is estimated, will cover 30 percent by 1990. One study of federal employees who chose flextime found that they were able to spend more "P.M. time" with their families and had less difficulty in engaging in family recreational, social, and chore-related activities.[49]

Day Care

In evaluating the significance of maternal employment for socialization, we have noted that one important variable is the arrangement made for the care of the child. Day care was originally designed as a privilege for the poor, but it has now become a necessary service for both women who have to work and women who choose to work. The greatest proportion of preschool children of working mothers—some 77 percent—are in "family" or "home-based" care, that is, minded in the homes of other mothers. But 23 percent are in organized day care or preschools (about 15 percent in Canada). Among children under three years of age (as of June 1985), 45 percent were cared for by a relative and 24 percent were in family day care.[50] These figures represent a considerable increase in the last decade, and, with the continuing rise in the number of working and single mothers, the number is expected to increase much further still.

Day care raises many important questions for socialization. First we note that the increase in the use of day-care centers contributes to the trend of introducing the child to other-than-family influences at a younger and younger age. A few generations ago a child stayed at home with the parents until he or she attended school at the age of six. Kindergarten and nursery schools brought this down to ages five, four, and three, and day-care centers now increasingly take toddlers and infants.

One question relevant for socialization concerns relationships with the mother. If, as a full-time employee, a mother spends less time with the child, does this affect the child's attraction to her and the development of a sense of security and trust? Might this affect the child's feelings about self and capacity to form relationships with others? Is it to the child's advantage or disadvantage to spend most of his or her time in day care? The answer is far from clear. Most researchers agree that during the first months of life, babies do best when tended by a mother or some other one person. But beyond that, the experts vary sharply in opinion. In one major study reported in 1978 by Jerome Kagan and his colleagues in Boston, comparing three- and four-year-old children in a well-staffed day-care center with children at home, no differences were found in the attachment of the children to their mothers. The authors speculate that the impact of the mothers is greater than that of the day-care center personnel because the experiences at home are more salient and more affectively charged. The mother is more emotionally involved with the young child than the caretakers and is likely to intrude more with punishment, praise, affection, and commands. She is also more likely to be around when the children are experiencing great joy or when they are ill and experiencing great distress.[51] With the infant, too, the mother at home is likely to be more responsive—perhaps, for example, reacting to meaningless sounds that a caretaker might ignore. Thus, although the working mother may spend less time with her child, her influence need not be any less.

But this report is based on a high-quality day care. What of centers with a poorly trained staff, constant turnover of personnel, crowding, and poor facilities? Psychologist Jay Belsky, who with Lawrence D. Steinberg in a 1978 review of research concluded that good day care had no adverse effects on a child and, in fact, might even be beneficial,[52] completely reversed his position in 1986. Following new research and a reanalysis of earlier studies, Belsky now argues that babies who spend their first year in nonmaternal day care, even in high-quality centers, may well have a less secure attachment to their mothers. He also cites evidence that these children in their early school years may be less cooperative and more aggressive than children who stayed home with their mothers. But other experts disagree. They question some of Belsky's interpretations of research studies and cite the relevance of such other factors as the family situation and the stability and quality of the day-care arrangements. The questions, it is evident, are many, emotion-laden, and controversial.[53] We hope for more definitive answers when we can do research in years to come on those who, as infants and toddlers, experienced different types of child-care arrangements.

Peer-group experiences in day-care centers also raise important questions for socialization since, in a center, a child has earlier and more prolonged contact with other children. According to some studies, children in a day-care center become more peer-oriented and are more physically active and aggressive (as well as getting more colds and flu) than other children; however, other extraneous factors such as the size of the day-care center, the ratio of adults to children, the turnover of personnel, and the knowledge and skills of the caretakers enter into any analysis.[54]

Nor can relationships with peers be considered apart from relationships in the family. Through alleviating the hassle and anxiety of constant child care, day-care centers can certainly reduce tension for the parents. Also, through introducing new routines, new possibilities for exploration, new relationships, and new female models, day-care centers, early in life, extend the range of a child's experience. On the other hand, difficulties may also arise—relatively shy children, for example, might find themselves isolated and their shyness reinforced, or the patterns and authority styles of the day-care center might run counter to the patterns and authority style of the home, with resulting conflicts. In one day-care center, for example, in which caretakers treated boys and girls alike, some parents were horrified to hear that their sons played "dress-up" and doll games.

Day care may also be the child's first experience with non-family rules and rituals. We observed in Chapter 3 that learning rules and rituals in social interaction has a strong emotional as well as cognitive component; the child experiences feelings of some kind toward others and toward himself or herself. Martha Power, citing an "apology ritual" in a day-care center, points to one example of how we "socialize our children to control, to hide, to reinterpret, redirect and reconstruct their emotions so that interactions can progress smoothly and with a minimum of emotional disruption."[55]

> Dwain, for no readily apparent reason, hits Gwen. Gwen starts to cry and a teacher, Val, goes over to the two of them:
> Val–Dwain: "Dwain, that's not nice. You shouldn't hit your friends. Now give Gwen a hug and tell her you're sorry."
> Dwain (as he gives her a hug)–Gwen: "I'm sorry."
> Gwen immediately stops crying and they go off their separate ways to play.[56]

Thus, children are taught to say "please" and "thank you" to adults, to refrain from running around during story time, and, on a larger scale, to act and feel excited at Christmas, Easter, Halloween, and their birthdays.

Specific incidents and issues at day-care centers in themselves are not likely to be major or determining influences in the socialization of children; as patterns, however, that may be repeated in various ways in neighborhoods, schools, and other settings, they can play a significant part in the development of attitudes, interpersonal relationships, sex roles, and identification models.

Another variant family type that is rapidly increasing in numbers is the dual-career family. Traditionally it was only the father who followed a professional or business career, but now the mother, too, may be equally committed to her job as doctor, lawyer, artist, architect, engineer, or business executive. Reporting on one pattern of dual-career couples in the corporate world, Rosanna Hertz writes:

> In their efforts to cope with career, family, and household, they look to themselves, to the marketplace, and ultimately to their checkbooks for solutions.
> To compensate for two equal sets of demands on their time and physical energy, they hire somebody else to clean the house. Because they cannot be home to supervise their children, they hire someone else to do so.[57]

In such dual-career families, we ask, Is there anything unique about socialization? At this point, we can only speculate. We have considerable information on the relationships between husbands and wives in dual-career families,[58] but practically nothing on their children. In many respects—for example, in their concern for their children's independence and self-reliance—we would expect these families to be very much like other upper-middle-class families. In other respects, however, we might expect some differences. For one thing, with the model of a professionally committed mother, we might expect a greater emphasis on occupational aspirations and achievement, especially for daughters in the family. Also, with the children called upon to adapt to the demands of the mother's as well as the father's career interests, we might expect a great deal of emphasis on mutual adaptation.

For any definitive answers, however, we must await the results of relevant research.

In sum, then, although an increasing number of children are growing up in families that differ from the traditional nuclear family that has been the prevalent type of family in North America, little is yet known with any assurance of the consequences of these changes for socialization. There are many questions, but only the beginnings of some answers.

THE SCHOOL

The importance of the school as an agency of socialization has already been suggested in several illustrations. Now we wish to treat this agency more systematically. For the sake of convenience, we shall divide our discussion into four subtopics: the school and society, the classroom, the teacher, and the school and neighborhood. Although this division is somewhat artificial because each of these subtopics is fully understandable only in relation to the others, the distinctions will nevertheless be helpful in organizing our discussion.

School and Society

When children begin to go to school, they ordinarily come, for the first time, under the supervision of people who are not their kin. They thus move from a milieu dominated by personal ties to one that is more impersonal (although the degree of impersonality is theoretically less at the nursery-school and kindergarten level than it becomes later). By involving children with teachers and classmates, the school plays an important part in lessening the emotional dependence upon the family. Furthermore, the school is likely to be the first agency (in a literate society)—except perhaps for the church—that stimulates children to develop loyalties and sentiments that go beyond the family, that link children to a wider social order. The school is society's principal agency—at least its principal formally designated agency—for loosening children's ties to their parents and initiating children into social institutions that cut across kin and neighborhood groupings.

The school as an agency of socialization needs to be recognized, then, first as an organizer of social relationships and stimulator of sentiments. Some of the social relationships will be discussed in the following section on the classroom. As an example of its role in organizing sentiments, we may observe how the school stimulates loyalty to the existing political and social order. In a review of numerous studies of how the American school functions as an agent of political socialization, Philo C. Wasburn found that the school communicates messages about five main concepts: nationality, authority, citizenship, information worth knowing, and democracy. The main messages communicated to schoolchildren can be summarized as follows:

> Nationality: "Being an American is better than belonging to any other nationality."[59]
> Political authority: "Established authority deserves respect."[60]
> Citizenship: "Good citizens are those who obey the law, vote, and pay their taxes."[61]
> Information worth knowing: "Knowledge of some historical facts and the formal structure of government is important."[62]
> Democracy: "As an abstract principle, democracy should be supported."[63]

Wasburn's review of the literature leads him to conclude that

> The political messages about nationality, authority, citizenship, information worth knowing, and democracy encourage the development of future citizens who tend to be loyal and at least somewhat nationalistic. They have little understanding of political controversy and define citizenship in passive terms. They have only a vague understanding of, and little personal commitment to, political democracy. . . . During the present period of rapid social and economic change, the call for "better" schools which will provide students more effectively with marketable skills undoubtedly has broad popular support. . . . A call for providing "better" political education in the schools which would provide students with a realistic political perspective and practical political skills for keeping government reasonably responsive to their expressed needs in the future is likely to find some popular support as well.[64]

Orienting children to and fostering their respect for the established social and political order is one of the ways in which the school functions as a conservative socializing agency. It seeks to pass on to children the knowledge, sentiments, skills, and values that have been built up over time and presumably thereby provide children with the resources they will need in their adult roles.

At the same time, there is growing recognition that the pace of social change in contemporary industrialized societies is so rapid that transmitting a particular heritage of the past is not sufficient for socialization. A professor in Britain once said that "in most countries of the world nearly all the education consciously given is already out of date. It is sometimes out of date at the time when education is taking place. It is more usually out of date in terms of the children's prospects."[65] A more complex picture is provided by an American sociologist who argues with reference to the United States that

> as a society we have decreed that the responsibility of our schools shall not end with the maintenance of the status quo nor even with the socialization of individuals who are able to adapt easily to a changing social and physical environment, but instead shall extend to the maximum encouragement of the creative abilities of new members of the society. Thus, paradoxically, educational institutions have assumed a major role as agents of innovation and change along with their conservative role in assuring the cultural continuity of the society.[66]

He further argues that many of the issues in American education can be understood as debates over the relative weight that should be given to the school's conservative as opposed to its innovative function. Many observers have pointed out that socializing children for a society in such rapid change is a new task, one not encountered by any society before, and it is not surprising that no one is entirely sure how to do it. The problem is exacerbated by the fact that the school seems to change more slowly than other aspects of the society.[67] There are undoubtedly many reasons for this, among them being school responsiveness to conservative community pressure. Such pressure can in part be understood in terms of socialization, for socialization has the general effect of giving people a more definite picture of society as they *have* experienced it than as they *will* experience it in the future. Community pressures on the school system to socialize children for society as it has been known are therefore likely to be generally stronger than pressures to socialize for a society whose form is as yet unknown.

Although the British professor quoted above may be correct that almost all education is out of date by the time it is to be used, many observers note that the schools nevertheless seem to prepare some children better than others, whether preparation be defined in minimal terms as learning to "read, write, and reckon" or in more sophisticated terms such as learning how to cope with unforeseen problems. The reasons for this are multiple and complex, and a full exploration would take us far beyond the scope of this book. But the basic situation can be summed up as follows: *The effectiveness of the school as a socializing agency depends to a major degree upon the kinds of families its children come from.* Generally, the school tends to be less effective in educating children from families that are poor and of low status. Such children are often, though by no means invariably, from minority groups. Although there is wide agreement that schools are not as successful in socializing children from poor and low-status families as they are with those of higher income and status, there is wide disagreement concerning the causes of the discrepancy. Some observers attribute it to differences in what the schools give the children, whereas others attribute it to what the children bring to the school in the way of home-based socialization. There is evidence to support both viewpoints.

Considerable evidence has accumulated by now to indicate that in the elementary grades the school tends to reinforce the child's family-given status. This is brought about in a number of direct and indirect ways. Schools in neighborhoods where poor families predominate have often received smaller allocations of educational resources than those in higher income and status neighborhoods.[68] Further, schools that serve children of various status levels and that also have more than one classroom or section for each grade level often group the children in sections according to the status of their families, even though ability or achievement is ostensibly the sole basis for grouping. The practice of grouping students by supposed ability, for teaching purposes, is known as "tracking" or "streaming." In Britain, one study reports that

> although teachers genuinely intended to stream children according to their measured ability, they nonetheless allowed these judgments to be influenced by the type of home the children came from. . . .

> Even where children *of the same level of ability* are considered, those from middle-class homes tended to be allocated to the upper streams and those from the manual working-class to the lower streams. Furthermore, children who were dirty or badly clothed or who came from large families also tended to be placed in lower streams, regardless of ability.[69]

Some American studies report comparable practices in which factors associated with social position influence treatment of students. In a study in the early 1970s, sociologist Ray C. Rist reports:

> Throughout the various levels of the St. Louis educational system we found commonly shared assumptions about "how things really are." The basic tenets may be summarized as follows: Middle-class students can learn, lower-class students cannot; white schools are "good," black schools are "bad"; control is necessary, freedom is anarchy; violence works, persuasion does not; teachers can save a few, but will lose many; the school tries, the home will not; and finally, only the naive would dispute these beliefs, as the wise know. *The outcome of this set of attitudes, assumptions, and values is that the school as an institution sustains, in a myriad of ways, the inequalities with which children first come to school.* The school's response to issues of color, class, and control all mesh together to make two nets—one to catch winners and one to catch losers.[70]

Not surprisingly, there is also some evidence that children placed in lower ability groups perform at lower levels and experience a stigma that adversely affects their self-esteem. They are labeled "slow learners" by teachers and classmates alike.[71]

Speaking specifically of teachers, Christopher Hurn completes a review with: "There is mounting evidence that, at least as far as elementary school is concerned, teacher judgments of students' behavior and deportment, in addition to sheer intellectual competence, are of great importance in their evaluations and their future treatment of students."[72]

Thus, it seems that school personnel often perceive children of poor and low status as having less ability to benefit from education than children of higher status and do not put forward their best efforts in educating them.

Other studies, not necessarily inconsistent with the above, suggest that such pupils tend to fare poorly in school partly because they begin school poorly prepared by their early socialization in the family. The children do not have the experience and training that enable them to be successful in their schoolwork and to take advantage of what the school has to offer. In our earlier discussion of language, we referred to Basil Bernstein's analysis of linguistic codes. Working-class children, he says, tend to learn a "restricted code," a way of speaking in which contexts are assumed to be understood by the listener and meanings are implicit. In telling a story, for example, the child might say "he" without explaining who "he" represents. In contrast, the middle-class child learns, in speaking with adults—although not necessarily with peers—to use an "elaborated code," with a higher level of conceptualization. Middle-class children are more explicit in their speech if the listener would not otherwise understand and also can express more subtle shades of meaning.[73] It is the "elaborated code" that teachers appreciate more.

The problem of communication styles that work against the lower-class child at school has been identified in several studies. For example, in a study of black lower-class families, Robert D. Hess and Virginia Shipman speak of mothers who control the behavior of their children by commands rather than by considering particular situations. The behavior is "neither mediated by verbal cues which offer opportunities for using language as a tool for labeling, ordering, and manipulating stimuli in the environment, nor mediated by teaching that relates events to one another and the present to the future."[74] The previously cited work of Melvin Kohn on child-rearing practices points in the same direction. Working-class children are taught to conform to external rules; middle-class children are encouraged to shape the environment through their own efforts.

The relevance of such arguments here is not that the middle-class experience and training are "better" than the working- or lower-class pattern, but that the latter are not as helpful for the attitudes and abilities that are called for in the school situation and on which children are evaluated.

Many researchers, with data gathered on a large scale and using quantitative indices, point in the same direction, to the limitations in early background and family experiences that set up barriers to school achievement. James Coleman in a 1966 publication and Christopher Jencks in the early 1970s found that the quality of schools was not significant in determining student performance. The ability to do well in school, they concluded, was essentially dependent upon the home and the socioeconomic background.[75]

Some subsequent researchers, however, generally using case materials and more qualitative and longitudinal data, have disputed these conclusions and point to programs that have been successful in improving the performance of disadvantaged students. Schools can be effective, they say, if principals set good standards; if school personnel have significant personal involvement with the students; if teachers provide models, set high expectations, and conduct their lessons well; and if schools work with parental organizations.[76] (In a 1982 report on high schools, Coleman came to a conclusion opposite to that of his 1966 study; the later study concludes that the quality of the school as a learning environment does significantly influence student performance.)[77]

While the school generally functions to sustain children in the statuses to which they are born, it also functions to encourage upward mobility. Most Head Start programs of the 1960s, which sought with government funds to help young children of disadvantaged groups, were not long-run successes, but some were.[78] Certainly, too, many immigrant groups—Jews, Chinese, Japanese, and others—have used their educational opportunities to great advantage. Children who do well in school, whatever their family backgrounds, are likely to win awards and be encouraged to go on to higher education and higher-status positions. A British study by birth cohorts over a forty-year period shows a constantly increasing proportion of children of working-class fathers attending university,[79] and a U.S. report with data into the 1970s by David Featherman and Robert Hauser estimates that 20 percent of the sons of manual workers attain management or professional positions.[80]

The Classroom and Socialization

For young children the school classroom constitutes a social situation without parallel. Ordinarily students spend about 1,000 hours per year in a classroom, and will spend approximately 7,000 hours in school between kindergarten and the end of sixth grade.[81]

The structure of the classroom has both short-run and long-run implications for children. Since most of what children do in a classroom is done in the presence of others, they have to learn to cope with a more or less formalized multiperson situation. They have to learn to wait their turn, and this means not only waiting to satisfy one's wishes to speak or perform but often abandoning those wishes if the activity moves on to something else. Also, children must learn to ignore and not be distracted by those around them. As one observer of classroom functioning notes:

> if students are to face the demands of classroom life with equanimity they must learn to be patient. This means that they must be able to disengage, at least temporarily, their feelings from their actions. It also means . . . that they must be able to re-engage feelings and actions when conditions are appropriate. In other words, students must wait patiently for their turn to come, but when it does they must still be capable of zestful participation. They must accept the fact of not being called on during a group discussion, but they must continue to volunteer. . . . In most classrooms, powerful social sanctions are in operation to force the student to maintain an attitude of patience. If he impulsively steps out of line, his classmates are likely to complain about his being selfish or "pushy." If he shifts over into a state of overt withdrawal, his teacher is apt to call him back to active participation.[82]

Anthropologist R. Timothy Sieber, in a study of first graders, gives a number of examples of teachers calling on children to be still and listen: "Bobby, we can do without smart alecks in this class! Now, sit up straight!"; "Let me see all your faces! I don't see Lois's face because she's not listening"; "Hey! You at the back table! I want you looking up here!"; "Jeremy, you should be watching, not talking with Hannah!"; "I'm waiting until everyone's quiet and ready . . . I'm waiting . . . I'm waiting."[83] These are good illustrations of how children are induced to sustain responsive participation in society, which we discussed briefly in Chapter 3.

The time schedule that governs classroom activities has another effect on children: The beginning and ending of activities does not necessarily correspond to children's interest in them. Activities may begin before children are interested and may end before they have lost interest—sometimes "when it's just getting interesting."

These various aspects of adapting to the crowded classroom —learning to delay or suppress desires, to tolerate interruptions, and to turn aside from distractions—are part of what is referred to as the classroom's "hidden curriculum." This term has gained favor as a way of calling attention to the informal and unofficial matters that are taught, matters generally unnoticed by those who have responsibility for teaching the official curriculum. While the pupils are learning skills (such as reading and hand-writing) and subjects (such as arithmetic and geography), they are also interacting with fellow pupils and the teacher in ways that reinforce their membership in society.

Since pupils differ in the rate and quality of their learning and in the various kinds of social facility that are encouraged in the classroom (for example, promptness, cooperativeness, and cheerfulness), their progress toward desired goals is evaluated. Although the teacher is the main source of evaluation, children also evaluate themselves—they know when they can't spell a word or solve a problem. Kindergarten children in one "low" evaluated group called each other "stupid," "dummy," and "dumb-dumb."[84] Also, the class as a whole may be asked to evaluate a student's work, "as when the teacher asks, 'Who can correct Billy?' or 'How many believe that Shirley read that poem with a lot of expression?' "[85] The classroom environment is one in which children are being evaluated in a variety of ways—by teacher comments, self-judgments, classmates' judgments, re-port cards, marks and comments (and perhaps gold stars, red stars, or blue stars) on exercises and papers, classroom displays of the "best" papers, requests that they stay after school or bring their parents in for a conference. Sometimes there is organized competition (as in spelling bees, which may pit boys against girls, thus emphasizing sex identity along with competitiveness and learning of the official curricular material), which adds to the evaluational process.

Evaluation begins in kindergarten. Rist followed a group of children, in a virtually all-black school with an all-black faculty and staff, from their registration for entry in kindergarten until about midway through the second grade. He found that the kin-dergarten teacher made permanent seating assignments on the eighth day of school. In seven days the teacher had sorted out the children.

> Within a few days, only a certain group of children were continually being called on to lead the class in the Pledge of Allegiance, read the weather calendar each day, come to the front for "show and tell" periods, take messages to the office, count the number of children present in the class, pass out materials for class projects, be in charge of equipment on the playground, and lead the class to the bathroom, library, or on a school tour. This one group of children, who were always physically close to the teacher and had a high degree of verbal interaction with her, she placed at Table 1.[86]

These children were all dressed in clean clothes that were relatively new and cared for. The children at Tables 2 and 3 were more poorly dressed, in some cases dirty. The children at Table 1 also displayed greater ease in interacting with the teacher, greater familiarity with standard American English, and also tended to come from families that were middle class. (The teacher had access to preregistration forms filled out by the parents and to a list of children from families receiving public welfare payments. Also, teachers exchange information about families, so that many children bring with them into kindergarten family reputations established by their older siblings. The case of Johnny Rocco [p. 139] is not unique.)

This ongoing and multifaceted process of evaluation contributes to socialization in three main ways. The first is that *the evaluations become processed into the child's developing self.* Children learn certain of society's values and norms, and in this way their selves are transformed: They learn to be neat, prompt, able to follow instructions, and so forth—or they learn that they are not very good at being neat or prompt or at following instructions. They learn to think of themselves as being good in math or not so good in math, good or not so good in reading, and so on. These evaluations of children's achievements in skills, subject matters, and social performances thus gradually accrue to their emerging selves. Children thus come to know themselves as particular kinds of social beings, ones who may aspire to certain kinds of future opportunities but not to others.

While their selves are thus evolving, *children are also acquiring an academic reputation that affects the way teachers treat them.* Numerous studies point to the advantages teachers offer those students whom they perceive, for whatever the reasons, to have greater ability. One study finds that good readers are allowed to make mistakes without being interrupted and corrected while poor readers are not; another finds that teachers wait longer for answers to questions from good than from poor students; and still another finds that teachers are more likely to praise a good performance from a high-expectation than from a low-expectation child.[87]

Still another way in which evaluation affects socialization is that children while acquiring a reputation among teachers are also *building up a semipublic "cumulative record."* The quality of this record (and reputation) serves as a ticket of admission (or refusal) for later opportunities. At any given point during the formation of this reputation and record, their quality at that point affects children's progression to the next step—for example, whether they will be put into a fast, slow, or average section, whether they are doing well enough in classwork to be allowed participation in school team sports, whether they have done well enough in lower grades to be admitted to college-preparatory curricula in high school, whether they have done well enough in high school to be admitted to a college (and, if so, to what kind of college, with how much encouragement in the way of scholarships, and the like). In short, the school classroom functions as a system of selection for sequences of interlocking opportunities leading to particular kinds of adult roles.[88]

The Teacher's Functions

Many readers of this book will perhaps recall a particular elementary school teacher as especially influential or helpful; other readers will have no such recollections, all their teachers being dimly fused in one anonymous blur. How influential are teachers? Is there any evidence—apart from subjective recall—that teachers can be significant in the socialization of children? Some recent research suggests that they can be.

One study of particular interest examines and tests a basic sociological axiom formulated by W. I. Thomas: "If men define situations as real, they are real in their consequences." In a somewhat elaborated formulation, the process has been called "the self-fulfilling prophecy."[89] This means that one's beliefs lead one to act in such a way that the beliefs cannot help but be reaffirmed. A study by Robert Rosenthal and Lenore Jacobson in the late 1960s explored "how one person's expectations for another person's behavior can quite unwittingly become a more accurate prediction simply for its having been made," and it asks specifically "whether a teacher's expectation for her pupils' intellectual competence can come to serve as an educational self-fulfilling prophecy."[90] To test the validity of this idea, the investigators conducted an experiment in a school whose pupils were mostly of lower-class background. First, they administered to all the pupils an intelligence test, which they disguised with the highfalutin name "Harvard Test of Inflected Acquisition." They told the teachers that this test could predict academic "blooming" or "spurting," and they asked the teachers not to discuss the test with pupils or parents. Then, in a completely random way entirely unconnected with the test results, the names of about 20 percent of the students were selected and, at the beginning of the following school year, given to their teachers with the explanation that they might like to know which of their pupils were "about to bloom." Since the names of these pupils were drawn from a hat, in effect, "the difference between the children earmarked for intellectual growth and the undesignated control children was in the mind of the teacher."[91] Retesting showed that at the end of the school year the children with the "special" designation gained an average of more than twelve IQ points, whereas the others averaged a gain of about eight points. The differences were much greater than this at the first- and second-grade levels than at higher grades. Further, later retesting when the children had moved on to new teachers indicated that there was some persistence in the differential gain. Significantly, then, children who were expected by their teachers to "bloom" did so, much more than those for whom teachers did not have this expectation.

This research has been criticized for its methods and has not been successfully replicated, in part perhaps because teachers are now suspicious of what researchers tell them about "blooming" students. But other studies confirm that teachers do develop different expectations of their students—naturally occurring expectations rather than experimentally induced—and behave toward them according to these different expectations.[92]

If teachers' expectations can be influential, and if the classroom is one of the important places in which children compete and are prepared for their adult statuses and roles, it is pertinent to ask whether children in one classroom have as good a chance as children in another to come under the influence of teachers who will have favorable expectations. Or, conversely, is there some social process at work that tends to make it more likely that certain kinds of children will come under the influence of teachers with less favorable expectations and that they will accordingly experience less "bloom-promoting" teacher-pupil interaction? We provided a partial answer to this question when we noted that teachers of lower-level students are likely to be less qualified than teachers of higher-level students. We might infer from this and other related studies that the children of these teachers tend to be evaluated more negatively than middle-class children. But can we go beyond inference and actually see teachers communicating different kinds of expectations to children, based on the children's status?

A study by anthropologist Eleanor Leacock examines this question.[93] She observed second- and fifth-grade classrooms and interviewed the teachers and pupils in four city schools, each located in a different kind of neighborhood. The predominant pupil background of the four schools was, respectively, lower-income black, lower-income white, middle-income black, middle-income white. Although she found certain similarities in the four schools—traceable to such factors as similar teacher training, similar educational philosophy, and the fact that the schools were all part of the same school system and therefore subject to similar administrative practices—certain differences were also significant.

The differences Leacock found among the teachers do *not* fall into any simple pattern; she did not find that all the "bad" aspects of teaching were in the lowest-status classrooms and the "good" aspects in the higher-status ones. For example, the second-grade teachers were somewhat more positive than fifth-grade teachers in evaluating pupil participation, and this was as true in the low-income black school as in any of the others. Teacher pleasantness or unpleasantness to pupils was unrelated to the status of the pupils in this study, as also was teacher competence. But one difference that did emerge was the teachers seemed to expect less of their pupils if they were from the low-income group. In the middle-income schools, the teachers were likely to work more actively with a child having difficulty with a problem, whereas those in the low-income schools would more quickly give up and turn to another child, making little effort to see that the first child understood. At the fifth-grade level the teacher in the low-income black school was observed to have difficulty explaining arithmetic, but made the pupils seem responsible for failure to understand. One general conclusion reached by the study goes counter to some currently fashionable interpretations of school life:

> What we observed in the [low-income black] classroom was not the attempt to "impose middle-class goals" on the children but rather a tacit assumption that these goals were not open to at least the vast majority of them. *The "middle-class values" being imposed on the low-income Negro children defined them as inadequate and their proper role as one of deference.* Despite the fact that some teachers in the low-income schools stated their felt responsibility to set "middle-class standards" for the children, their lowered expectations were expressed by a low emphasis on goal-setting statements altogether. In a three-hour period, clear-cut overt goal-setting statements numbered 12 and 13 for the low-income Negro school, 15 and 18 for the low-income white school, and 43 and 46 for the middle-income white school.[94]

Thus, the evidence of this and other studies converges to suggest that pupils from low-income and low-status families are more likely to be met by lower levels of expectation for accomplishment from their teachers. The likely result of these lower levels of expectation is a reduction in levels of aspiration, levels of accomplishment, and probably even levels of intelligence.

School and Neighborhood—A Case Illustration

A study by anthropologist John Ogbu adds some important new findings and ideas to the literature on the school as a socializing agent. In his investigation of "Burgherside," a low-income neighborhood of Stockton, California, in which 92 percent of the elementary-school population consists of blacks and Mexican-Americans, he sought to understand why so many children from that neighborhood failed in school. Like Leacock in New York, Rist in St. Louis, and other observers elsewhere, he found that teachers expect low-income children to fail. He found that Burgherside parents have high educational aspirations for their children and that the children also have these aspirations. But he found, in addition, something that had not often before been reported as a central finding by an observer sympathetic to low-income children: "Burgherside children lack a serious attitude toward their school work. . . . *Burghersiders do not fail in school because, although they try, they cannot do the work. . . . Rather, Burghersiders fail in school because they do not even try to do the work. They are not serious about their school work, and therefore make no serious effort to try to succeed in school."*[95]

In pursuing this, Ogbu found that the children were acquiring the belief that schooling was no use because it would not open up the opportunities that good school performance ought to.

> In general, Burgherside parents appear to be teaching their children two contradictory attitudes toward education. On the one hand, they emphasize the need for more education: *You are not going to grow up to be like me. Get your education.* On the other hand, they teach their children both verbally and through their own lives that it is not easy for Burghersiders who have "made it" in school to "make it" in society. They believe that for one of them to get a good job he must be "twice as qualified" as a Taxpayer competing for the same job. A Burghersider who merely has the same qualifications as a Taxpayer has no chance of success in a competition with a Taxpayer. That is why, Burghersiders say, they become discouraged and give up, saying *Oh, I know I will never make it.* [96]

(Taxpayers are whites living in another neighborhood who not only pay taxes but are publicly acknowledged as and consider themselves to be Taxpayers. They consider themselves the bearers of mainstream culture and also the bearers of the costs of running the city. Although Burghersiders pay taxes, they are often publicly described and treated as Nontaxpayers.)

An important element in Ogbu's analysis is his distinction between subordinate minorities and immigrant minorities. Subordinate minorities are those that were incorporated into the United States against their will—American Indians, blacks, Mexicans of the Southwest incorporated by conquest after the Mexican War. The immigrant minorities are those that came to the country looking for religious, political, or economic betterment.

He notes that "subordinate and immigrant minorities appear to differ in the way they perceive American society and in how they respond to the educational system."[97] He considers it essential to understand the historical relationship of the subordinate minority group to American society in order to understand their children's high rate of school failure. Reduced effort in school is a mode of adaptation to a longtime limited level of opportunity for social rewards.

> The educational dilemma of subordinate minorities is that their children are expected to work as hard as whites in school for fewer ultimate rewards from society. . . . Faced with this educational dilemma, subordinate minorities apparently chose to stop working hard in school since they could neither expect more for their hard work nor force society to change its discriminatory practice. They thus have reduced their anxiety about having to work hard for little by adjusting their efforts downward to a level commensurate with what they think they will actually get for their education.[98]

Over time, the blacks and Mexican-Americans developed the belief that they couldn't "make it" in society; the whites developed the belief that these minorities were "inferior." Both sets of beliefs become the basis for behavior in the school. The black and Mexican-American children in Stockton maintain this pattern of school-failure adaptation by such practices as frequent absence from school and not taking schoolwork seriously. Taxpayers, including teachers, do their part in maintaining the pattern by adopting a patron-client relationship with Burghersiders.

> Teachers, as representatives of Taxpayers and of the dominant ethnic group, represent the power structure. Teachers decide when, where, why, and how they will interact with parents. Many regard themselves as service-oriented patrons and expect Burghersiders to reciprocate with manifest interest and cooperation if their "problems" are to be solved. Burghersiders do not accept the situation as defined by teachers; but, since they need what teachers have to offer, and since they have relatively little power to insist otherwise, they comply with teachers' expectations.[99]

The teachers often regard the Burgherside children's problems as psychological, while the parents more often see the problems as matters of instruction and educational guidance.

Under these circumstances, according to Ogbu's analysis, remedial programs that are entirely focused on the children in their school setting cannot succeed. Compensatory education programs in Stockton in the 1960s, he believes, were naive in trying to change attitudes and behavior patterns in eight months that had been developed and transmitted over several generations. Burgherside parents and schoolchildren perceive schooling in terms of its "payoff" in later employment opportunities. From this viewpoint, improved school performance by children of subordinate minorities depends upon enlarging the definition of equal educational opportunity to include not merely equally favorable learning conditions for all children but also "the equal enjoyment of the benefits or rewards of education by individuals and segments of the society according to their educational achievement."[100]

Thus, the school, the subordinate minorities, and the political and economic authorities in the society become involved in a mutually reinforcing set of self-fulfilling prophecies: (1) White employers believe black and Mexican-American workers are inferior and, for this reason, discriminate against them in employment even when they have requisite educational qualifications (Ogbu documented cases of such discrimination); (2) parents, knowing of such discrimination directly or indirectly, discourage their children from expecting occupational success; (3) children learn from their parents and others not to expect much economic reward even for good educational qualifications and so do not try to do well in school; (4) teachers see the poor performance of subordinate minority children, and this confirms their already-existing belief in these children's inferiority, a belief they share with other "taxpayers," including prospective employers. Each category of person in this cycle has an expectation or "prophecy" about some other category of person and acts in such a way as to bring about the result that is anticipated.

In a subsequent analysis, Ogbu goes beyond his Burgherside analysis to argue for a "cultural-ecological" perspective which stresses that the black urban ghetto requires very different competencies from those of the white middle-class world, competencies identified by such categories as mutual exchange, the street man, entertainment (including athletes), pimping, hustling, clientship (Uncle Tomming), and collective struggle. He writes: "From a cultural-ecological perspective, black childrearing is organized to inculcate the instrumental competencies which have proven functional in the exploitation of conventional and street economy of the inner city and to ensure that black children grow up competent in these adult tasks."[101] This perspective may help explain some of the socialization outcomes in the black urban ghetto, outcomes that are very distant from those the school system tries to foster.

THE PEER GROUP

While the family and the school are socializing agencies organized primarily by adults, the child also comes to be socialized into a world in which adults are peripheral. This world is generally designated by the term *peer group*. The term is a bit misleading, since it does not designate a single group in which a child participates but rather all those groups made up of children in which any particular child participates. Any given child is likely to belong to more than one peer group, although there may be overlapping membership. Thus, a peer group may consist of the children on one's block or in one's apartment building. Another may include one's playmates at school. A third may be the children in the same Boy Scout troop or those who go to the same summer camp or music school. Yet another may be made up of the cousins whom one may see as a group at periodic intervals. It would therefore be more accurate to speak of one's "peer world," since the child's actual peer groups might differ in significant ways and the child might have different roles within them. For example, adult values might be more prominent in a Boy Scout or Girl Scout troop than in the neighborhood backyard or back alley peer group. We shall use the conventional term, however, and the reader will be able to judge from the context when we are referring to a particular type of peer group and when we are more generally discussing the peer world.

The peer group as a socializing agency has certain distinctive characteristics: (1) By definition, it is made up of members who have about the same age status and roughly the same position in relation to adult authority; (2) within the peer group the members have varying degrees of prestige and power; (3) the peer group is centered about its own concerns; whereas adult authority figures instruct the child in traditional norms and values with an awareness that the child must learn to function in adult society, the peer group has no such responsibility; (4) thus, any long-run socializing implications are largely unintentional. Children participating in peer groups do not do so with the aim of preparing themselves for adult society, though the peer group experiences do have such import.

The child's peer-group participation may be said to begin in a very rudimentary way in the day-care center or sandbox at about the age of two or so, although egocentricity, rather than any form of cooperation, is still the order of the day. This play may be followed by the formation of rudimentary pairs and later by a succession of peer groups. With increasing age, the peer groups gain in solidarity and complexity, and usually in size, while the activities and interests on which they focus change with the children's maturation and social development.

The Peer Culture

While children are absorbing the adult culture at home and in the school, they also—on the street and in the playground—sustain an age-limited subculture of their own. It consists of a range of interests and activities, rules, traditions, distinctive expressions and gestures, and ways of making and breaking peer relationships. The richness of this subculture is suggested by studies conducted in Britain by Iona and Peter Opie. One of these reports on some 2,500 games played by children ages six to twelve. While many of these are simply slight regional variants of basic games (none of which requires even such minimal equipment as a ball), children nonetheless sustain a great variety of games that can be roughly classified into eleven different types: chasing, catching, seeking, hunting, racing, dueling, exerting, daring, acting, guessing, and pretending. Excluded from the study were party games, scout games, team games, and any sport that required supervision.

This study, carried out over a ten-year period in many parts of Britain, discloses that certain kinds of rules appear repeatedly. There are, for example, rules for starting a game. Two or three children on a street or playground initiate the idea and then, to round up enough to play, they issue a traditional "summons" to others around. In one region, for example, children call out, "All in, all in, a bottle of gin; all out, all out, a bottle of stout."[102] While there is considerable local variation in the particular wording of the call, the practice of some such traditional way of starting a game is widespread.

Similarly, there are rules for avoidance of a disliked role. The investigators observed that

> the chief impediment to a swift start is the fact that in most games one player has to take a part that is different from the rest; and all children have, or affect to have, an insurmountable objection to being the first one to take this part. Tradition, if not inclination, demands that they do whatever they can to avoid being the chaser, or the seeker, or the one who . . . is "it."[103]

To avoid being first, children shout out some particular phrase or engage in some particular gesture. By general agreement, the last one to do so is first to be "it." And just as there are rules for choosing the first child who will be in a role that pits him or her against the others, so there are rules for changing roles. Thus, in chasing games, a touch results in a change of role. To temporarily remove themselves from the game—perhaps to tie a shoelace, go to the bathroom, or to catch one's breath—children in the United States may cross their fingers and call "Times!"[104]

It appears that games of this kind were once played by grownups and children together and that they did not become distinctively children's games until about the start of the eighteenth century.[105] Today they are virtually restricted to children and taught by children. The rules are sustained by children, as is the interest in them. The Opies note that games go through periods of rise and decline in popularity: "it is no coincidence that the games whose decline is most pronounced are those which are best known to adults, and therefore the most often promoted by them; while the games and amusements that flourish are those that adults find most difficulty in encouraging (e.g., knife-throwing games and chases in the dark)."[106]

Not all aspects of peer culture are as organized as games with their often elaborate sets of rules. In an earlier study the Opies documented a vast amount of "lore and language" known mostly to children, circulated largely by them, and passed down from one generation of children to another. This takes such various forms as nonsense rhymes, tongue twisters, riddles, recitations, jeers, trick bets, "codes of oral legislation" (such as "finders keepers, losers weepers"), and others.[107] The study turned up many parallels in the United States and some on the European continent, suggesting that at least certain aspects of the peer culture transcend ethnic and national boundaries. Parallels of the Ladybird (or Ladybug) rhyme—Ladybird, ladybird, fly away home / Your house is on fire / And your children alone—have been reported in France, Germany, Switzerland, Denmark, and Sweden.[108] Sue Parrott, in a study of the recess activities of second-grade boys, speaks of two other categories of activities. One she calls "tricks," such as splashing or tripping someone, tapping someone and hiding, or looking under a girl's skirt; the other she speaks of as "goofing around," including jumping into piles of snow, friendly fighting, or sucking icicles—all of which, in distinction from games, lack teams, rules, competition, or goals.[109]

Gary Fine, deriving his material from a study of baseball Little Leaguers, ages nine through twelve, in New England and Minnesota, speaks of a preadolescent subculture. Using language to illustrate the content, he cites expressions not part of adult or even older adolescent vocabularies that are widely known and used by these preadolescents. Some of the terms are local, but others are regional or even national. Examples are "doofy" meaning foolish or awkward, "mutt" referring to a disliked girl, or "ding dong ditch" referring to a prank of ringing a doorbell and running. Such terms, Fine suggests, are diffused primarily through interlocking social linkages, through individuals who share membership in several groups, and sometimes through the mass media of communication. Fine also notes that preadolescent subcultures are gendered, that is, boys and girls maintain distinctive subcultures to some extent.[110]

These peer-group subcultures remain largely apart from the world of adults although, as we shall note in the next section, some aspects clearly oppose the adult world. Adults couldn't care less about the proper way to avoid being "it" in a game, nor are they especially concerned about the language games of children, the tricks, or the "goofing around," if these are not seriously disruptive of ongoing relationships and do not unduly threaten the values and proprieties the adults are trying to teach. Socialization, however, is not all of one piece, and while many aspects of the peer-group subculture reflect this world apart and separate from adults, it must also be noted that some peer groups *are* organized around adult values and draw upon adult models. In our discussion of middle-class subculture we mentioned that children participate in many groups sponsored and controlled by adults. Working-class children also participate in such groups, often based in such institutions as churches, settlement houses, scout troops, and Little League baseball teams. Parental encouragement is often considerable. It should also be noted that parents sometimes intervene in child-organized peer groups, for example, by prohibiting their child to play with another child or to participate in a group that they consider undesirable, while encouraging the child to play with others they consider more suitable. Such parental intervention is often based upon social class and ethnic evaluations, with the result that the child is led unwittingly to take on parental sentiments and attitudes toward other social classes and ethnic groups.

The link between the games of children's peer groups and the world of adults is probably nowhere as evident as in sports. In our culture, sports are not only a major form of leisure activity, they are held up for children as a means of achieving physical health; as a way of learning leadership skills, loyalty, and other desirable traits; and as valuable training in competitiveness and give-and-take relationships. The value, however, that stands out the most both in sports and in the surrounding world is pride in achievement. As socializers of young children, adults are likely to stress the importance of self-development and fair play, but as children become older and more sophisticated, they tend to give more weight to success and achievement. Adult sport stars themselves serve as models. If these stars perform outstandingly—be it hitting a home run, scoring a touchdown, shooting the winning goal, or winning a tennis match—they dramatically express their delight by shouting, jumping and waving their arms. The values of suppressed emotional expression and modesty in achievement have been replaced by expressiveness and self-congratulations. Children thus have a license to follow this same pattern.

Parents also serve as models in valuing success and achievement. Especially in their behavior as spectators and supporters of the home teams—including the local teams in which their children participate—they readily overlook the questionable calls by the referees or the fouls the referees do not see, as long as they favor the home team. Harry Webb speaks of the professionalization of children's attitudes—"the substitution of 'skill' for 'fairness' as the paramount factor in play activity, and the increasing importance of victory."[111] Children are socialized to want to win at almost any cost and to feel badly if they lose.

In a study of children in the public and parochial schools of Battle Creek, Michigan, Webb found that the higher the grade, the greater the importance placed on "beating one's opponent" and the less the importance placed on "doing one's best" or "playing the game fairly." He concludes by drawing a parallel with the business world, saying that to insist

> on play's contribution to the development of such "sweetheart" characteristics as steadfastness, honor, generosity, courage, tolerance, and the rest of the Horatio Alger contingent, is to ignore its structural and value similarities to the economic structure dominating our institutional network, and the substantial contribution that participation in the arena thus makes to committed and effective participation in the wider system.[112]

In discussing the school, we noted that academic achievement may be an avenue of mobility, of achieving a higher socioeconomic status than one's parents. Ability in sports is undoubtedly another such avenue, of which children soon become aware. The heroes of the sports world—especially in such television-publicized sports as football, basketball, and baseball—are honored and acclaimed in the child's as well as the adult's world. The pattern is not only North American. Speaking of soccer in Brazil, which she describes as "an all-consuming commitment bordering on fanaticism," Janet Lever writes:

> Soccer-playing begins very young in Brazil; one often sees four- and five-year-olds using small rubber balls to mimic their older brothers. By the time a boy is in his early teens, he is conscious that soccer might be his road to success, and many play as though they felt the eyes of the scouts boring into their backs.
>
> There are also, in Brazil, the equivalent of little leagues, where many middle-class boys spend hours on the soccer field perfecting their skills. But it is the poor boys, perhaps, who in the tradition of rags-to-riches American sports story, most desperately want to make it to the "juvenile teams" and then on to pro status. Too poor to

afford soccer balls, these youths will practice the whole day through on beaches or empty lots with only tightly rolled stockings for a ball.[113]

In the United States, colleges and universities serve as training grounds and screening devices for professional sports, and outstanding athletes are given athletic scholarships. Thus, sports may become a means of obtaining a college education, which in turn may become a basis for possible success in the business or professional world. In Brazil, as in most countries of the world, universities place little emphasis on organized sports, but the professional soccer clubs in Brazil do sponsor their "little leagues" for children ages ten and up, and these children may be housed by the clubs and given a better education than they would otherwise receive.[114] So, for a limited number of children,— including those who do not become highly paid professional athletes—sports in Brazil can be a means of upward social mobility. The more basic point for the socialization of the child, however, is that in North America, Brazil, and elsewhere, outstanding athletic achievement is a significant ideal for lower-class boys (less so for girls) who aspire to rise in social status.

Functions of the Peer Group

Philippe Ariès has stated that "The development of mass education is undoubtedly the most important social change that has ever taken place."[115] The reason he gives such emphasis to this development is that it has had the effect of setting children apart from adults, of making them a special group in society. True as this is, and significant as it is, this judgment overlooks the fact that the school is organized by adults and is specifically governed by the purpose of preparing children for adult life. So while the children are defined as a group apart, the school does not really keep them apart from adults and the adult world. The only social setting in which children are in fact separated from adults in any meaningful sense is in the peer group, governed as it is by the rules, rituals, interests, and logics of children. From this point of view, then, it would seem that one of the functions of the peer group is to keep children from being completely immersed in the process of socialization. But this conclusion must be qualified.

Although it is probably true that the peer group retards socialization in the sense of keeping the child from being totally concerned by the rules, values, and norms of the adult world, there are other ways in which it contributes to socialization.

First, the peer group gives children experience in egalitarian types of relationships that are qualitatively different from relationships with authority figures. In peer groups children engage in a process of give-and-take not ordinarily possible in relationships with adults. In the family and in school, children necessarily are subordinate to parents and teachers, however benign this subordination may be. Any activities—physical or verbal—between adults and children are not the same as in relationships between equals, and, even if they approach such interactions, these are not likely to be sustained for long periods of time as is the case in peer groups.[116]

The peer group, we have observed, is likely to have its own subculture, with its norms and established patterns of behavior, and children entering the group are likely to be interested in the companionship, attention, and goodwill of its members. For behaving in the appropriate or valued manner, the group rewards its members by bestowing attention, approval, or leadership or by giving permission to participate or to employ certain symbols. For behaving otherwise, the peer group punishes by disdain, ostracism, or other expressions of disapproval. Responding the same way as they do toward other socializing agencies, children come to view themselves as objects from the point of view of the group and in some measure to internalize its standards. The standards of the group are reinforced by the feelings of solidarity and support that children obtain from one another. Yet, at the same time, the children are likely to feel that, as participating equals, they have a part in setting and establishing the norms.

The way in which games contribute to this process has been nicely described by Devereux in his essay on children's play and backyard baseball:

> because there was no official rule book and no adult or even other child designated as rule enforcer, we somehow had to improvise the whole thing; this entailed endless hassles about whether a ball was fair or foul, whether a runner was safe or out, or more generally,

simply about what was fair. We gradually learned to understand the invisible boundary conditions of our relationships to each other. Don't be a poor sport or the other kids won't want you to play with them. Don't push your point so hard that the kid with the only catcher's mitt will quit the game. Pitch a bit more gently to the littler kids so they can have some fun, too; besides, you realize that you must keep them in the game because numbers are important. Learn how to get a game started and somehow keep it going, as long as the fun lasts.[117]

The reciprocity inherent in such relationships among peers is very different from interactions with adults who "know" the norms and rules of the game and are in a position to define them.[118]

Although such interactions among peers are but part of the experience determining subsequent development, they may also, suggests William A. Corsaro, be viewed as direct roots of particular adult relationships. In nursery school "insult routines," for example, in such comments as "You got poo-poo on your head" or "I could poke your eyes out with my gun," three- and four-year-olds are learning about opposition status relationships and competitive interaction skills.[119]

A second function of the peer group stems from the fact that its characteristic equality actually holds only for some contexts but not for others. A game of tag or hide-and-go-seek may include children of both sexes and span an age range of about seven to twelve; all are equal, and they are likely to experience themselves as such. But when the group is practicing basketball or choosing sides for a baseball or hockey game, the differences in skill associated with age level are likely to become prominent. Age differences of a year or two become significant, and the older child who skates faster or catches a ball more reliably or takes the lead in organizing games can become a role model for the younger one. In the same way that children identify with reference groups and derive their standards of thought and judgment from these groups, so, too, might children identify with *reference individuals* and derive standards of behavior and values from them.[120] Thus, in some contexts, the age differences within the peer group (and associated skill differences) become more significant than the basic age similarity. The younger children see in the older ones a model of what they might become *soon* (while still children), while the older children become aware that they can be a model to younger ones.

A third function of the peer group is that it provides a setting within which children develop close relationships of their own choosing. Within the larger peer group of equals, children, perhaps at about the age of eight or nine, often establish special friendships with someone of the same sex, which Harry Stack Sullivan, in an almost classic analysis, called *chums*. [121] These chum relationships are the first experience of peer intimacy and validate the child's sense of acceptability and worthwhileness. Each child reinforces the other's self-esteem by accepting without question the other's role identity. They are also opportunities to value someone else as well as to be valued. Gary Fine adds that such preadolescent friendships also operate as staging areas for behavior; friends learn interactional skills and develop their self-image so they can better handle social situations. Chums will tend to have interests in common—the child interested primarily in athletic achievements is not likely to have as a chum the child who is a computer addict and disparages sports activities.

Various studies show that boys and girls tend to follow different patterns of friendship. Girls tend to pair off into dyads or, at the most, triads, and to experience close, exclusive, and intimate relationships. Boys are more likely to have several friends and to develop less intense and more extensive ties. This is a pattern that seems to continue on to adolescence and even into college years and later. One theory seeks to explain this through socialization processes. The daughter can maintain a primary identification with her mother and have a more continuous development while the son must be differentiated from his mother and must deny dependency needs and close intimate identification. [122]

Still another function of the peer group derives primarily from their subordinate position vis-à-vis adults. As representatives of the established order, adults are not in a good position to teach in those areas that are sensitive and taboo, and the task in great part falls to the peer group. This is most readily seen in the area of sex. Alfred Kinsey, in his 1948 report on male sexual behavior, reports that "Children are the most frequent agents for the transmission of the sexual mores." [123] Willard Hartup speaks of the inevitable limitations of adults as educators of sex:

Blinded by the belief that the peer culture is an unreliable context for socialization, many adults have felt that it would be better if more sexual information were given to the child by parents and/or teachers than by other children. In spite of their best efforts, though, sex educators cannot provide the child with the trial and error, the modeling, and the vast store of information needed for ultimate determination of the individual's sexual life style. Given the taboos that have evolved to prevent sexual activity between adults and children, it is only through interaction with agemates that these opportunities can be found.[124]

Finally, membership in the peer group serves as a step in the developing independence of the child. In peer groups children establish new emotional ties and identify with new models. In seeking acceptance and respect from others at their own level, they pull away from their parents and other adults and gain strength to resist parental wishes and demands. (In later years, ideally, they also gain sufficient strength to become independent of their peers.)

The peer-group subculture in which the children become involved, as we have observed, is a world largely apart from adults and at times in opposition to adults. It includes ways of talking that adults frown on and various acts that adults would disapprove of if they knew about them. It includes attacks on authority and sometimes ridicule of adults. Examples are common in the lore and games of children. For example, they recite: "Ladies and gentlemen, take my advice, pull down your pants and slide on the ice."[125] Or: "No more pencils, no more books, no more teachers with dirty looks." Mary Ellen Goodman cites the conversation of two four-year-old boys who, in a caricature of adult women, were "convulsed by their own wit":

JACK: It's *lovely* to see you!
DANNY: I'm so happy to see you.
JACK: How *are* you? How have you *been?*
DANNY: Sorry I have to go so quick.
JACK: I hope you have a good time falling down and bumping your head.[126]

Brian Sutton-Smith suggests that such play, in which conventional roles are mocked, may serve not only to encourage independence but also to develop potentialities of innovation and creativity.[127]

The patterns of behavior and values of the peer group that—depending upon the age level and the particular group—may include popularity, success in games, cleverness, audacity in provoking adults, dancing ability, sexual exploits, good grades in school, leadership in clubs, and drugs, become prime considerations in the child's idealized image of self. As the peer group defines the culture and the heroes of its time—the fashions in clothes, the computer games, the slang, the popular songs, the athletes, the musical groups, the movie stars, the TV performers, the pop singers—children establish a solidarity with their generation. When they reach adulthood and see their children and *their* peer culture, they become aware that their own childhoods were passed in a particular time and under historically limited circumstances that make them members of a particular generation.

THE MEDIA OF MASS COMMUNICATION

The media of mass communication comprise newspapers, magazines, comic books, radio, television, movies, and other means of communication that reach large heterogeneous audiences and in which there is an impersonal medium between the sender and receiver.[128] Unlike the other agencies, the mass media do not directly involve interpersonal interaction. Nevertheless, as Donald Horton and R. Richard Wohl point out:

> One of the striking characteristics of the new mass media—radio, television, and the movies—is that they give the illusion of face-to-face relationship with the performer. The conditions of response to the performer are analogous to those in a primary group. The most remote and illustrious men are met *as if* they were in the circle of one's peers; the same is true of a character in a story who comes to life in these media in an especially vivid and arresting way. . . .
>
> In television, especially, the image which is presented makes available nuances of appearance and gesture to which ordinary social perception is attentive and to which interaction is cued. . . . The audience . . . is . . . subtly insinuated into the program's action and internal social relationships.[129]

Since the media include a wide range of materials, they should not be viewed from a single perspective. In content, *The New York*

Times, a comedy television show, a soap opera, and a science fiction comic book do not have much in common. Nor can the mass media be considered in isolation. They are ordinarily seen or heard in group settings, and the family and peer group have a considerable influence in guiding exposure to, and generally defining, their content.

Themes and Implications of Mass Media Content

The mass media, by their content alone, teach many of the ways of the society. This is evident in the behavior we take for granted—the duties of the detective, waitress, or sheriff; the functions of the hospital, advertising agency, and police court; behavior in hotel, airplane, or cruise ship; the language of the prison, · army, or courtroom; the relationship between nurses and doctors or secretaries and their bosses. Such settings and relationships are portrayed time and again in films, television shows, and comic strips; and all "teach"—however misleadingly—norms, status positions, and institutional functions. They provide the child with images of what it might be like to be in such situations and relationships. Until he or she encounters these situations in actuality, and unless the images are counteracted by other images or by the child's significant others, the images serve as effective "knowledge" of them.

That children learn from mass media is nicely shown in a study of their knowledge of occupations by Melvin L. DeFleur and Lois B. DeFleur. Using cartoonlike representations of occupations classified according to whether children know them through personal contact (such as teacher, supermarket clerk), television (judge, butler) or general culture (accountant, skilled printer), 237 children, age six to thirteen, were tested on their knowledge of and their ability to rank sets of occupations. Personal contact, as expected, was found to be the most effective learning source, but children also obtained a considerable amount of information from television, especially about occupational status rankings. The authors in fact conclude that TV is the most potent of the three sources for learning about the social status of occupations. But the authors add, citing a related study by Melvin DeFleur, that TV portrayals do tend to stereotype— lawyers are very clever but usually unorthodox, truck drivers are burly and aggressive, artists are temperamental and eccentric—and they suggest that television "provides children with much superficial and misleading information about the labor force of their society."[130]

The mass media tend also to present recurrent themes and story types, each with their own sets of values and ideals. The Western story form, for example, generally assumes that a law enforcement officer fights for justice and that people who dishonestly seek great wealth are evil; the soap opera sees family and friendship relationships as replete with personal crises that good people with spiritual strength and support from others are able to surmount; the romantic musical implies that love, rather than wealth, makes one happy, and that the world of show business is exciting and glamorous.

The mass media also present models of behavior—of heroes, villains, and comics; of occupational, ethnic, and personality types. The models presented by the media wax and wane with the changing times, but certain of their qualities persist through their change of dress. Tarzan faded, but his agility and courage lived on in such successors as Batman, Spiderman, and Superman, whose mode of levitation was more appropriate to the start of the space age. Although the Western hero still survives as a model of good judgment and self-reliance, he gradually gives way to the detective, the woman police officer, the space astronaut, the emergency-room doctor, and other urban types who take up the twin causes of good character and social order.

As values and norms change, the media follow, usually cautiously, but nevertheless with an ongoing effort to keep current so that their communications will be perceived by the audience as relevant and up-to-date. Television programs still largely refrain from using "street language," even though profanities are used in conversation more casually than twenty years ago. But the content of programs has changed. Sexual topics such as menstruation, teenage pregnancy, cohabitation, rape, homosexuality, and sexually transmitted diseases that were once unmentionable are freely discussed on news and discussion programs and are often central themes in dramas. Interethnic relations, a taboo subject before the civil rights movement of the 1960s, are also portrayed: Majority and minority persons are sometimes seen as neighbors or co-workers, and occasionally a minority person may even be portrayed as a supervisor of majority persons. Such changes in media content, which reflect normative changes in the society, are more evident in programs aimed at adults than at children; but, as we shall see, many children watch adult programs. One specific change that has been noted in children's programs in the United States is that about 20 percent of the commercials now include both white and nonwhite characters. Before the late 1960s, the characters in children's commercials were almost exclusively white.[131] We will note other changes in TV content.

Socializing Influence of the Mass Media

The nineteenth-century crusader against vice, Anthony Comstock, began his comprehensive survey of Satan's schemes for victimizing children, *Traps for the Young*, with two chapters on "Household Traps." Among the most sinister of these, in his judgment, was the daily newspaper. An example of how the newspapers do their dirty work of corrupting the young is provided in this account:

> The daily papers are turned out by the hundreds of thousands each day, and while ink isn't yet dry the United States mails, the express and railroad companies catch them up, and with almost lightning rapidity scatter them from Maine to California. Into every city, and from every city, this daily stream of printed matter pours, reaching every village, town, hamlet, and almost every home in the land. These publications are mighty educators, either for good or evil. Sold at a cheap price, from one to five cents each, they are within the reach of all classes. More: they enter the homes—often files of them are preserved—and are especially within the reach of the children, to be read and reread by them. The father looks over his paper in the morning to ascertain the state of the market, to inform himself as to the news of the day. His attention is attracted by the heavy headlines designed to call especial attention to some disgusting detail of crime. A glance discloses its true character. He turns away in disgust, and thoughtlessly throws down in his library or parlor, within reach of his children, this hateful debauching article, and goes off to business little thinking that what he thus turns from, his child will read with avidity.[132]

Comstock does not tell us whether the home newspaper files were kept by the father in spite of his disgust or whether they were preserved by children who scavenged debauching articles in the parlor after they had been thrown down by the father.

No commentator today still considers the newspapers to be a debaucher of children, although some for a time did assign that role to comic books.[133] Many, however, still express concern about television. Children, it is said, as watchers of TV, may become hyperactive, have a reduced attention span, be weak in verbal ability, and perform poorly in reading. Their values, too, may become corrupted because they see so much violence and immorality.[134] More recently concern has been raised by explicitly sexual lyrics and increasingly dramatic violence communicated in rock-and-roll music via MTV—music television presented by cable—and in phonograph records and albums.[135]

While television may have replaced the newspaper in the minds of critics as a corrupter of the young, the newer and the older view both assume that these media of mass communication can affect children and in ways that are considered to impede their preparation for productive membership in adult society. If Comstock's view seems ridiculous today, are his modern-day successors more justified in their concern about the effects of television?

Before attempting to answer this question, it should be noted that children are exposed to a wide variety of media: TV, movies, radio, comic books, magazines, and newspapers. Since children begin watching television before they can read and before they go to school, and because children spend many hours watching, even after they have begun school, this medium has been felt to be far more significant in its impact than the other media. It has, accordingly, in recent years attracted the most attention from both critics and social scientists. We shall therefore focus our own attention primarily on television.

Content and Children's Use of Television

Children spend a good deal of time watching television. Almost all American and Canadian homes have television sets (and it won't be long before they all have VCRs, as well), and virtually all children in North America watch at some time or another.

Reports on the amount of television viewing have been fairly consistent over the years. The A. C. Nielsen Company, which does audience measurements that are turned into TV program ratings, reported for 1986–1987 that children in the age category two to five watched an average of just under three and one-half hours per day while those age six to eleven watched over three hours per day.[136]

Some studies report differences by ethnic and social class groups, with lower-income and minority ethnic-group children generally watching more. Jack Lyle and Heidi R. Hoffman, writing of particular grades in a predominantly working-class community near Los Angeles with a sizable Mexican-American minority, noted a tendency for sixth-grade Mexican-American girls to spend more hours per week viewing television than did "Anglo" girls and, in a direct comparison of social class levels, found that blue-collar children in the sixth and tenth grades tended to watch more television than white-collar children.[137] Bradley S. Greenberg and Brenda Dervin also concluded in their study of fourth and fifth graders in East Cleveland, Ohio, that black and low-income children watched longer than high-income children. The black children from low-income groups in their sample averaged almost seven hours of viewing on a given weekday in comparison to four hours for white youngsters from high-income families.[138]

The television programs children prefer, as might be expected, also vary by age. During preschool years, children's favorite programs tend to be those with animals, cartoon characters, or puppets. During the early school years, children's program interests broaden to include child-oriented adventures, family situation comedies, and what some researchers have called "hip adventure programs."[139] Some differences are also reported in program preferences between boys and girls as early as the first grade; boys show greater preference than do girls for action programs that feature a strong male character, while girls show greater preference for family situation comedies in which a woman either dominates or is at least coequal with the male lead character.[140] Not surprisingly, too, a number of studies also suggest that ethnic minority children prefer programs that feature performers from their own ethnic groups.[141]

One of the possibly surprising facts about children's television viewing is that they spend so much time viewing adult programs. In 1980, for example, the programs *Dallas, Love Boat, M*A*S*H, The Dukes of Hazzard,* and *Happy Days, Again* were among the most popular programs for every age group in the United States, including ages two to eleven.[142] Nielsen, presenting 1986–1987 data for children ages two to five and six to eleven, reports the following:

Children 2 to 5

22 percent of their total viewing occurs during prime time (8–11 P.M. Monday to Saturday, 7–11 P.M. Sundays).

16 percent occurs during the "early fringe" period (weekdays from 4:30 to 7:30 P.M.).

24 percent occurs weekdays from 10:00 A.M. to 4:30 P.M.

19 percent occurs Saturday 7:00 A.M. to 7:30 P.M. and Sunday 7:00 A.M. to prime time.

Children 6 to 11

28 percent of their viewing occurs during prime time.

17 percent occurs during the "early fringe" period

22 percent occurs Saturday and Sunday, daytime hours noted above.

5 percent occurs during the "late fringe" from 11:00 P.M. to 1:00 A.M.[143]

Unfortunately, we have no data on children's responses to adult television programs. We do, however, as we shall note later in this section, have some insightful speculations.

What do children see on television in children's programs? F. Earle Barcus, who analyzed fifty hours of such programming in Boston in 1981, speaks of the child's world on television as

predominantly populated by animated characters involved in comedy and adventure. . . . Prime concerns are with personal rivalries, crime, and domestic affairs; nature and animals, the entertainment world, and science and technology receive some attention. There is much less concern for religion, war, education, love and romance, and other aspects of public and private life.[144]

He found other interesting results. In studying male and female characters, he found, as have others, that males predominated and sex roles were traditional. Of 1,107 total characters identified by sex, 78 percent were male and, of the 244 animal characters, only 9 percent were female. Males were also better represented in important dramatic roles, making up 88 percent of the heroes. Females were less often shown as employed and, when they were, worked primarily as professional entertainers or clerical or household workers. In values, the female characters tended to uphold traditional ideals and more often sought altruistic goals such as respect for others and devotion to group, home, and family. Compared to men, they were unselfish, kinder, and warmer. The males were more active, independent, and violent and more apt to seek wealth, fame, and thrills, and to act out of hatred.[145]

The portrayal of minorities also shows a distorted picture of reality. Of the 1,145 characters, blacks represent 3.7 percent, Hispanics 3.1 percent, and Asians 0.8 percent. Of the major dramatic characters, blacks represent 2 percent and nonblack minorities 3.7 percent. Interestingly enough, when blacks are represented, their images are very favorable. They tend to be more serious, peaceful, and intelligent than nonethnics and have more altruistic goals than other ethnic groups. They represent 4.5 percent of the heroes but only 1.1 percent of the villains. In contrast, other ethnic characters represent 12.6 percent of the villains and only 2.7 percent of the heroes. On the whole, Barcus concludes, the programs originally produced for the Public Broadcasting Service provided more reasonable and balanced images of black and other ethnic groups than did those produced by commercial children's television.[146]

Some four out of ten program segments were relevant in some way to family or kinship relationships. Overall, the family was portrayed in a traditional and stereotyped manner. The father is rather stern and dominant and often engaged in work and adventure activities. The mother is portrayed as competent in her role, engages in household and daily living activities, and is more nurturing than the father. Single-parent families are considerably overrepresented, and many family problem areas such as financial difficulties, divorce, aging, and school troubles are not touched on.[147]

It is important to know the content of television programs; they present images of society and social relationships and models for children to follow. Yet knowing the content of TV in itself does not tell us how children are influenced. Children, as we shall note, are selective in their watching, and screen and interpret what they see. Children may well learn and be influenced by TV, but the effect is almost never direct.

Socializing Influences of Television

How might you study the influence of television on children? One neat way would be to find a community without television but into which it is to be introduced and study the children in the community before and after. Presumably—assuming there are no intruding influences—any changes would be the result of watching TV. A group of psychologists in British Columbia, Canada—Tannis MacBeth Williams and colleagues—were able to do just that.[148] They discovered a town that, in 1973, because of its geographical setting, was as yet without television reception but was about to receive it. They called the town *Notel*. Nearby they found two comparable communities; one received only one TV channel—they called it *Unitel*—and one received Canadian and U.S. networks—they called this town *Multitel*. These were to be "control" communities to allow the researchers to take intruding factors into consideration. Only if changes occurred in Notel and not in Unitel and Multitel could they then be said to be due to the effect of TV. They called their research a "natural experiment."

The researchers studied the three towns through observation and through giving various questionnaires and tests to children and adults before TV was introduced into Notel and again two years later. Their basic hypotheses were taken from the conclusions of the U.S. Surgeon General's Report of 1972 on the effects of television on children.[149] This report had been prepared at the request of a U.S. senator by a committee made up of a dozen academics and network research directors. With a budget of 1.5 million dollars, the committee hired a staff that commissioned twenty-three research projects (sixty research reports in all, since some projects produced more than one study) dealing with various facets of the basic question. But still the conclusions of the report were tentative and hedged, and the committee called for further research. Now, what did the British Columbia researchers find in their "natural experiment"?

On the use of television, their results are comparable to other studies. Children watch three to four hours a day. The authors note the difficulty, however, of getting meaningful precise data, especially for very young children. There is a great difference between "time in the room with the set on" and paying attention to a program. Neither reports by the children themselves nor ones by their parents are very reliable. Children may pop in and out of the TV room and while watching may also draw, play games, read comics, do homework, and converse with others.[150]

Williams and her colleagues asked first of all what activities in Notel were replaced when the children spent so many hours a week watching TV. The data here for children are limited but the authors do report that, following the introduction of television, children participated less in sports and community activities. In Notel, for children age twelve and under, the mean sports participation score (based on the number and frequency of participation in sports activities) before TV was introduced was 13.45; after TV was available, it was down to 9.62. For Multitel during the same period, the participation score actually increased from 5.10 to 7.57.[151] For total community activity, the participation score went down in Notel following the introduction of television from 64.03 to 41.38, over twice the drop in the same period for Multitel.[152]

Television, we have observed, has been criticized for its effect on a child's education. The British Columbia researchers asked: Does watching TV have a positive or negative effect on reading skills and creative thinking? In both cases, in this study, the results were against television. For reading, the authors explain the lower ability-to-read scores after the introduction of television by *displacement*. Learning to read, they say, requires practice, but once TV is available, the children spend so much of their time watching television programs that they practice reading less, and thus the reading ability scores go down.[153]

Likewise the creative thinking of the children fared worse after the introduction of television. Using a psychological test called the Alternate Uses Task in which children are asked to think of all the ways particular objects such as a knife, shoe, button, or key can be used, they found that Notel children before they had access to television scored higher than comparable Unitel and Multitel children but, two years later, when they all had television, their scores were essentially the same. The authors seek to explain:

These results may have occurred because watching television requires little or no mental elaboration . . . TV may encourage viewers to rely on ready-made ideas, that is, to be mentally passive. In addition, time spent with television may displace activities and experiences which otherwise would be helpful in problem-solving situations. These hypotheses gain some support from evidence that students who obtained higher creativity scores tended to read more books and participate in a greater variety of leisure activities than did students who obtained lower scores.[154]

We have noted that in the content of television shows, there are always more males than females and that most men and women depicted follow traditional sex roles. Other studies show that sex-role images enter into television preferences and responses. Boys prefer to watch programs with male actors and girls with female actors. Moreover the boys and girls pay more attention when the characters act in sex-role–typed ways.[155] But does the sex-biased content have any impact on the children's attitudes? The fact that one cannot disentangle the influence of television from other influences in the society makes this a very difficult question to study, but the British Columbia researchers did find clear results. Using a Sex Role Differentiation scale that asked in part how typical certain behaviors were of boys and girls their own age, the researchers found that before the Notel children had TV they expressed more egalitarian sex-role attitudes than the children in Unitel and Multitel but, two years later, after they had television, their perceptions of sex typing had increased and were little different from those of Unitel and Multitel children, which had not changed in the two-year period.[156]

The major emphasis of the 1972 Surgeon General's Report and, it seems, of most TV research on children was on the effect of aggression and violence in TV programs. This question, too, is enormously difficult to study because, as we shall note further below, aggression and violence are very difficult to define and, in one form or another, are so common in our society. In its review, the Surgeon General's Report states that the findings of various studies

converge in three respects: a preliminary and tentative indication of a causal relation between viewing violence on television and aggressive behavior; an indication that such relation operates only on some children (who are predisposed to be aggressive); and an indication that it operates only in some environmental contexts. Such tentative and limited conclusions are not very satisfying. They represent substantially more knowledge than we had two years ago, but they leave many questions unanswered.[157]

Williams and her colleagues sought to study this question of aggression by observing children's behavior during free play and by obtaining teacher and peer ratings of aggression for both Notel and the control communities before and after television was introduced into Notel. The authors acknowledge certain limitations in carrying out their research—especially the small number of children observed and the fact that the same children couldn't be studied directly two years later—but their results, they say, were clear and significant. The aggressive behavior of children in Notel increased significantly following the introduction of TV. The children produced many more physical acts of aggression and verbal aggressive remarks two years after getting TV than they had before, while for the control communities the changes in physical and verbal aggression were slight. The authors conclude:

> . . . there was a significant increase in the aggressive behavior of Notel children following the inception of television in the community. The increase occurred for both physical and verbal aggressive behavior; it occurred for both boys and girls; it occurred at more than one age level; it occurred for children who were initially low in aggressive behavior as well as those who were initially high in aggressive behavior; and it occurred for the same children studied longitudinally and same-aged children compared cross-sectionally.[158]

Thus, in general, the "natural experiment" of the British Columbia researchers finds that in various ways television does have a significant impact on children. Partly by the activities that are displaced while watching TV and partly by its content, television does affect the knowledge, behavior, and attitudes of children.

The researchers, like most researchers for the Surgeon General's Report, came to their conclusions through studying large groups of children and generalizing about their results. In some cases they observed children at play, in others they obtained teachers' and peer reports. But in most cases they used tests, scales, and other standardized devices, all tested for statistical significance. Assuming the tests and scales are appropriate and valid for the groups studied—and some academics would seriously question this—the studies point to general changes in the average behavior of the groups under study.

As valuable as these studies are, however, by their very nature they do not tell us much about the processes by which television content influences a child. They describe the children before and after they have access to TV, assuming the processes in between. Children, however, are not mesmerized by television; they are active and selective and interpret what they see. So complementing these more quantitative studies are those that deal in greater depth with the meaning and the interpretations children give to programs. Among the proponents of this type of study are Robert Hodge and David Tripp in Australia, who in their research ask how children interact with television content, how they interpret what they see, and how they incorporate the content into their lives.[159]

First, like others, they cite some of the cautions that complicate the problem of studying television's impact on children. One, which we noted before in our discussion of language, is that all communication involves a "modality"—the "how" and the context of a communication must be considered as well as its literal content. The problem is perhaps best seen in trying to define violence. Is the violence of the cartoon in which a cat is flattened by a steamroller (and returns to fight again) the same as the machine-gun shooting of a Rambo-type character? Is the violence of self-defense similar to the violence of the vicious criminal? Can gun-shooting in Westerns and detective stories be added to the newsclips of street riots, civil wars around the globe, and plane crashes, and further added to the goings-on in children's cartoons to produce a figure that can be called "the total amount of violence on television"? Obviously, even to the young child, these are not experienced and interpreted in the same way.

Hodge and Tripp cite examples from their interviews with children, this with a six-year-old:

INTERVIEWER: What about if somebody gets killed on television?
GEORGE: Um. . . . They're not really killed.
INTERVIEWER: They're not really killed on television?
GEORGE: They're just pretend bullets and they just pretend they're killed and they get all dead on purposely.

INTERVIEWER: I see . . . and what happens in life when somebody gets killed?
GEORGE: Um . . . they die.[160]

Hodge and Tripp write that the children recognized the processes of media production such as acting, pretending, or the use of tomato sauce. They write, too, of an interview in which nine-year-old girls speak of seeing a television program and then pulling the head off a doll and stabbing a Teddy bear. But this is all said with smiles and laughter, and the authors conclude, ". . . we need to take account of the modality of the action: stabbing, kissing or beheading Teddy or dolls, rather than people. These children are quite clear about the difference between cruelty to people, and cruelty to dolls. . . ." And also, they note, the difference between both of them and cartoons.[161]

Children assimilate what they see into their schema of reality. Hodge and Tripp give the example of an aboriginal black girl who was asked by an interviewer whether she liked "lot of fights and that sort of stuff on television?" The girl replied with a laugh: "Yeah, sometimes. If there's a black and a white I say 'come on Blackie.' "[162]

Another approach to the violence on television has been introduced by George Gerbner and Larry Gross of the Annenberg School of Communication at the University of Pennsylvania. They say that television programming, especially network drama, dramatizes and supports the conventional values, beliefs, and behavior of the society, and what is portrayed above all is *power*. Much of the action in network drama deals with "how to manage and maintain the social order." From this perspective, TV violence can be understood as "the key to the rule of power." It is the cheapest and quickest dramatic demonstration of who can and who cannot get away with what against whom. Violations and the enforcement of the rules of society, say Gerbner and Gross, are the major concern of about one-third of all male major characters (but very few women).

In studying the content of dramatic television, they find that

46 percent of all major characters commit violence and 55 percent suffer it. . . . Thus there are 12 victims for each 10 violents. The ratio for women is 13 victims, for non-white women 18 victims, and for old women 33 victims for every 10 violents. So, if and when involved, women, non-white women, and older women characters bear a

higher burden of relative risk and danger than do the majority types.[163]

Gerbner and Gross seek to ascertain the impact of this system of symbols by comparing heavy viewers of television with light viewers in the same demographic categories. When heavy viewers of television are compared with light viewers who in everyday life are exposed to similar risks, the authors find that heavy viewers have a stronger sense of danger and mistrust and a much greater sense of personal risk and suspicion. Gerbner and Gross conclude that the heavy viewers' "expressions of fear and interpersonal mistrust, assumptions about the chances of encountering violence, and images of police activities can be traced in part to television portrayals."

The basic conclusion of these authors is that television does indeed have a socializing impact, but its basic impact is not in stimulating violence. Rather, television programming cultivates a pervasive fear of violence. It is this fear that maintains power and compels acquiescence to power. However, not all violent incidents in TV programs are equivalent. One must always pay attention to the social content because "it is important who scares whom and who is 'trained' to be the victim."[164]

These further approaches offer more complex and sophisticated analyses of the influence of television violence on both children and adults. It is not enough to know that TV violence has an impact, we must also consider the context, meanings, and interpretations viewers give to the violence.

We have noted that in children's programming, male characters are more predominant than females (roughly by a ratio of four to one) and that sex roles tend to be traditional. These television images also, if the British Columbia research can be believed, do directly influence the attitudes of children. Hodge and Tripp, following their argument that television is refracted in a child's mind, seek to analyze this impact further and ask how boys and girls respond to such sex-role differences. And they find, as we would expect, that any influence is not direct. In one research, they asked children age eight to twelve to write on the question: "If I could be on television, I would be . . ." Of the boys, 87 percent chose a male figure and of the girls, 75 percent chose a female. When a group of children—this time age six to twelve—

were asked to name five TV characters who were important to them, boys chose 63 percent male figures and girls 64 percent female figures. Thus, the boys reflect the sex bias of the characters and the girls resist it. The authors conclude:

> . . . it would seem that the gender bias of television does not drastically diminish the significance of being female, for girls; rather, it enhances the importance of being male, for boys. In one sense it is the boys who are deprived: deprived of females among their significant others. . . . How can they understand females, if only 20 per cent of their constructs are deployed on women? In this analysis, television contributes more to girls' understanding of males than it does to boys' of females.[165]

Hodge and Tripp also find that the reaction of children to television cannot be separated from their social relationships. Following a group interview and analysis, they speak of the reaction of a relatively socially isolated girl (named Catherine) to Miss Piggy, a character on the program *The Muppets*:

> There is total opposition between her fantasy figure, Miss Piggy, boisterous and outgoing, and her social self, which is painfully shy and withdrawn. Miss Piggy seems to be a compensation representing what she is not, rather than a likely influence on her behaviour. We see two aspects of her self which are not integrated, and this lack of integration is related to her uneasy position in the group. . . .[166]

In contrast they cite the reaction of a much more self-assured girl, Emma:

> Emma is as self-confidently part of the group as Catherine is isolated. . . . Along with her social integration goes a greater integration of the fantasy figure and her social self. As well as her definite tone of voice, she uses gestural language, mimicking Miss Piggy, which is high-modality communication. However, she laughs as she does so. . . . There is less distance between Miss Piggy and Emma, but her laughter signals her awareness of such distance as there is.[167]

The authors conclude that in seeking to understand the meaning of television for children, one should give prime weight to their social relationships rather than the other way around. "It seems likely that the ideological meanings inscribed in general social relationships will have a powerful effect on the total meanings of the television experience. That is because the television content itself is but one integral part of the whole television experience. . . ."[168]

One other area in which TV influence has become a concern is that of advertising. Children who watch three to four hours of television per day are exposed to about 20,000 commercial messages per year,[169] and some students of TV audiences have noted that children's "involvement with commercials is as deep and intense as it is with programs."[170] Citizen groups have become concerned that children are vulnerable to manipulation because of their inability to understand and evaluate advertising. In one province of Canada (Quebec), the government went so far as to ban advertising directed at children under thirteen.

That children can be influenced by commercials is evidenced in their requests to parents to buy products advertised. One researcher reports a study that found that parents yielded to 87 percent of their children's requests for cereals, 42 percent for candy, and 16 percent for shampoo.[171]

However, here, too, despite evidence of the impact of commercials, it is clear that the television content is but part of a larger picture. Sometimes, in the examples noted above, the children's requests to their parents are turned into occasions for parental teaching about consumption and socialization for the role of consumer as noted in Chapter 3. More important, we have evidence that children, as they become older, become more sophisticated about such advertising. They are less likely to believe the commercials or accept the advertising claims. George A. Comstock, a senior research coordinator on the Surgeon General's Advisory Committee, wrote: "By the second grade, children begin to express distrust of commercials, and by the sixth grade 'global' distrust is said to exist."[172] Another group of reviewers put it more strongly: ". . . by age 11 children have become cynical about the purpose and credibility of commercials, feeling that they have been lied to in an attempt to get them to buy products which are not as desirable as the adman's copy would have it."[173]

Most of the research on children and television has dealt with programs produced for children. We have noted, however, that children often watch programs directed at adults. What influence might these programs have? Of especial importance here are the ideas of Joshua Meyrowitz, who, in a wide-ranging and insightful treatise, argues that the new electronic media, especially television, have led to a merging and overlapping of social spheres.[174] The distinctions between the public and the private, the masculine and the feminine, and especially childhood and adulthood have become blurred.

To a great degree in recent generations, children lived in a world apart from adults. But now, with relatively free access to TV programs, this is much less true. There are no prerequisites for watching television and age is no barrier. Children of all ages and adults watch the same programs, and it is more difficult to distinguish stages in development. Parents are no longer "gatekeepers" determining what their children will or will not experience, and children are thrust into an adult world. So children now see adults on television programs with all their problems, conflicts, and anxieties. Adults commit crimes and behave in ways considered deviant, they "deceive" and prepare "backstage" for the parts they play in public. Any mystification in changing from one role to another is gone. The mysteries and taboos of the past are mysteries and taboos no longer.

The "data" of Meyrowitz's theories are not the data of the laboratory or empirical researcher, and little is said about the processes by which children interpret or incorporate what they see into their thoughts or behavior. But the theories do have a basis in the fact that a new technology has changed the patterns of children's behavior. With such changes we may legitimately ask: "What are the broad and long-run implications for our ways of thought and our social relationships?"

In summary, it is apparent that the socializing influence of television is a very complex matter. Children's viewing habits, their developmental level, the interpretive framework they bring to viewing, the social relationships in which they participate and which influence their viewing framework—all of these mediate the broadcast program content for the child viewer. Television has power—power to attract a mass audience and to "deliver" that audience to advertisers. It has power to shape our understanding of events, to put before us portrayals of events and relationships that become our "knowledge" of them, however poorly that knowledge corresponds to reality. Yet the question may be asked—How far does it carry viewers into a world at odds with the society in which it operates? Are children encouraged to look for simple answers to complex problems? Are they discouraged from analyzing social relationships and social problems in depth? Are they sometimes encouraged to be passive when facing moral situations that call for active confrontation? Do they observe and respond to feelings and emotions that are beyond their comprehension? If television advertising stimulates children to be materialistic, as some allege, does it do more than reiterate a materialism that is built into the basic values of a consumption-oriented Western society? Or, on the other hand, does television offer children new experiences and new objects and models that they can meaningfully and insightfully incorporate into their developing selves? The answers to all such questions may be yes, depending upon the circumstances, but they are all easier to believe than to prove.

Other Agencies of Socialization *Church*

We have discussed the major agencies of socialization; others, too, may be of great significance, depending upon the child and the particular conditions of his or her life. The church, for example, although less important in modern America than in rural French Canada or early Puritan New England, may still be instrumental in teaching a child to distinguish the sacred from the profane and in instilling feelings of group solidarity. Community agencies, such as YMCAs and YWCAs, may have a marked influence, especially insofar as they help widen the outlook of ethnic and lower-class children. The summer camp, particularly for middle-class children who attend every year from age three to adolescence, may be important for relationships with both peers and authority figures. The carpool, a prominent feature of suburban life, also is a context in which socialization takes place.[175] We have already cited the rapidly increasing number of nursery schools and day-care centers and have indicated their importance.

Athletic teams, many formally organized by adults, are influential in the lives of many children, particularly boys. Gary Fine reports that in the Little League baseball program in 1983, there were 7,000 Little Leagues with over 48,000 teams for children and well over half a million Little Leaguers aged nine to twelve. The Little Leagues are formally organized, with rules set by the national organization. The children never negotiate. The adult coaches are responsible for the team and always represent it in disputes.[176]

The leagues have been established ostensibly for the benefit of the children, with the motto "Character, Courage, Loyalty." Quoting from the Official Rules:

> Little League Baseball is a program of service to youth. It is geared to provide an outlet of healthful activity and a training under good leadership in the atmosphere of wholesome community participation. The movement is dedicated to helping children become good and decent citizens. It strives to inspire them with a goal and to enrich their lives towards the day when they must take their places in the world. It establishes for them the rudiments of teamwork and fair play.[177]

However, says Gary Fine, the values that the adults are basically seeking to impart to the children become transformed into values more comprehensible and relevant to the lives the children are leading. So the coach may stress sportsmanship, but this becomes transformed by the preadolescents to controlling their aggression, fears, and tears. The coach talks of teamwork, but this to the children means "be loyal, don't break the bond of unity"; the coach says they have to hustle, but this becomes "publicly display a desire to win"; the coach talks of winning and losing, but this means "display the appropriate emotions, be tough or fearful when the situation calls for it." The children are being taught throughout to behave properly.[178] In teaching morals to young children, there is a certain amount of rhetoric and the result is always problematic.

Although specific effects of these other agencies of socialization remain somewhat elusive, they all function to weaken the child's ties with the family, give the child new statuses, teach different perspectives, and broaden his or her range of experience.

CHAPTER 6

Sex, Socialization, and Gender

The first statement anyone is likely to make about a healthy newborn baby is either "It's a boy" or "It's a girl." Newborns vary in several visible characteristics. Some are born with hair, some without. Some are very wrinkled, others less so. They vary in weight and in length. But among these differences, only the identification of the external genitalia, attesting to maleness or femaleness, results in the newborn being assigned to one of the most fundamental categories in society, the category of sex. This assignment sets in motion an ongoing series of beliefs, values, expectations, and conduct on the part of others with respect to the newborn, a series that will be highly consequential for the life that newborn baby will live in society. One of the great public issues of our time is whether the genital difference that separates newborns into males and females ought to be as widely significant in a person's life as it has been up to this point in human history.

The importance of external genitalia at birth lies in the fact that they signify biological differences that are not visible at birth. Male and female bodies will later differ considerably in appearance and functioning, and it is the social awareness of these later changes that gives importance to the initial visible differences.

Biologically, the infant genitalia forecast different roles in reproduction for males and females when the newborns reach sexual maturity. For women, the fact that they can bear and nurse children has, throughout history, been taken to be the most decisive fact about them. It has usually led to a belief and expectation, shared by men and women alike, that women *ought* to bear children. And since it was assumed that women *would* bear children, their social roles have, in one way or another, been shaped by their presumed and expected childbearing activities. The maintaining of a domestic household has most often been assigned to women because child care has been regarded as a "natural" sequel to childbearing, and homemaking a "natural" extension of the fact that women's childbearing and child caring restricted their freedom to move around. Their early socialization has, throughout history, generally been carried out with this later role in mind. In contrast, men have been freer to fight or to do work that takes them away from the household, at least since the time when they engaged in hunting and warfare and could use their greater speed and strength to advantage.

In important ways, then, women and men have always had different fates within any particular society (although there have also always been individual men and women whose lives were not typical for their own society). In our own time, however, being asked with new urgency are the questions: To what extent is the difference between male and female lives due to biological differences, to what extent due to society's *interpretations* of those differences? Is it inevitable that women be primarily responsible for child care and for maintaining a household? Why have military activities almost universally been organized and carried out by men? Is it because males are biologically more aggressive than females, or is it because adult men and women have socialized their young sons but not their young daughters to be prepared for military activity? In short, *How compelling is human biology for human social life?*

The question is more easily asked than answered. Only in the last few years has the question of sexual biology's relative importance for social organization received concentrated attention, and no conclusive answer is yet available. But the question itself has become enormously controversial under the impact of the women's movement. It has also become apparent that, under the conditions of a modern industrial society, the preferred social expectations for males and females are not comfortable for all persons of the sex to which they are presumed to apply, a fact that implies that sex-role expectations are not necessarily "natural," in the sense of being entirely based on biology. The fact that societies differ among themselves in what they expect from males and from females also suggests that human sexual biology cannot be absolutely decisive in determining the place that women and men have in society. But set over against these facts are others that point to certain general patterns that distinguish men from women and boys from girls. These different facts, if they are facts, have given rise to controversy, and we shall discuss these issues in this chapter.

The fundamental fact we are dealing with is that the person's sexual anatomy and prospective generative role in sexual reproduction form the basis for the much wider-in-scope social-role assignment. Babies with male sex organs at birth are foreseen as potential fathers; they are judged male, and they are socialized toward certain attitudes, self-concepts, and performances in behavior and conduct that are considered masculine—that is, appropriate for a male in his particular society. Babies with female organs at birth are foreseen as potential mothers; they are judged female, and they are socialized toward certain feminine attitudes, self-concepts, and performances that in noticeable ways are different from those toward which the male is socialized. We shall use the term *gender role* or *sex role* to refer to the attitudes, self-concepts, and conduct expected of a person of given sex in a particular society. The term "sex role" has long been in use for this purpose, but "gender role" is gaining wider acceptance as a way of emphasizing that roles assigned *because of* sex are *not determined by* a person's biological sex but rather by a society's *interpretations* of what is appropriate for each sex. The implication is that gender roles can be changed by changes in socialization. A fairly clear example of this is seen in the increased acceptance of athletic sports as appropriate for girls and women; tennis, golf, running, skiing, swimming, rowing, and other sports have gained wider acceptance as fitting activities for females, and the resulting increase in physical strength is increasingly recognized as compatible with femininity. To emphasize the possibility of such changes and to overcome the notion that roles are permanently fixed by biological constitution, some authors advocate that gender role replace sex role. As of now, both terms are still in use; they have the same meaning.

Gender-role socialization, like all socialization, involves many processes. Since these processes involve the impact of social organization upon babies and children defined by their biological sex, it will be helpful to discuss both biology and social organization to provide a background for discussing socialization to sex roles. We shall begin with biology.

SEX AND BIOLOGY

If any phenomenon in the human world can be considered an incontrovertible fact, it would be this: A human being can *either* beget a child *or* bear a child. No human being can do both. This difference in body functioning between males and females in reproduction is universal; it occurs in all human societies, and there is not a single known exception. Although there are cases of individual hermaphroditism—being born with genital organs that are not unambiguously male or female—there are no known cases in which that hermaphroditism enabled the person both to beget and to bear a child. In reproductive function, the two sexes are absolutely and unambiguously distinct. This much seems certain, and it has probably seemed certain to all of humanity since the beginning of human history. It may well be the basis for the elaboration in society of so many other expectations based on sex.

Not so long ago, to have called attention to sex differences in reproductive function would have been belaboring the obvious. This is no longer the case. Now it is necessary to gain increased precision and clarity concerning what is fixed and what is variable, because many of the characteristics of males and females that once seemed to be as thoroughly dichotomous and biological as their distinctive contributions to procreation are today less certainly so. The occurrence of cases of hermaphroditism has, in fact, prompted ever more careful study of just how a person's biological sex is formed. In a clinic of the Johns Hopkins Hospital that treats congenital abnormalities of the sex organs, John Money and Anke Ehrhardt, medical psychologists, have considered the implications of the 150 or so cases of diverse abnormalities that have been seen at the clinic over a period of many years. Their work has obliged them to think carefully about the stages by which sexual differentiation comes about. In order to understand various abnormalities, it is necessary to have a clear view of the normal process, and they have provided a useful summary. The discussion of biological development that follows is based largely on their account.[1]

A person's biological sex is established through a series of four main processes or stages, each of which contributes a component to biological sex. These four components are: (1) chro-

mosomal sex, (2) gonadal sex, (3) hormonal sex, and (4) morphologic sex.

Chromosomal Sex

Conception occurs when the father's sperm unites with the
mother's egg, or ovum. Each parent contributes twenty-
three chromosomes—strands of genes that control biological
development—to the fertilized egg, which is the first phase in the
development of a new individual. Twenty-two of the chromosomes determine the person's physical characteristics—eye
color, hair color, shape of head, height, and many others—except
sex. The twenty-third chromosome is known as the sex chromosome, and it occurs in two forms, known as X and Y. The
mother's egg always contains an X chromosome; the father's
sperm may contain either an X or a Y. When a sperm with an X
chromosome fertilizes the egg, a female child is conceived; its
chromosomal sex is XX. When a sperm with a Y chromosome
does so, a male child is conceived, and its chromosomal sex is XY.

Gonadal Sex

Chromosomal sex by itself does not result in a male or female
body. Rather, the chromosomes contain "coded information" or
"directions" for the next step in sexual development. For the first
six weeks after conception, the original fertilized egg, a single
cell, divides into an increasingly complex but still sexless embryo.
One embryonic organ is the gonad, a gland that will become
either an ovary or a testis. When the embryo is chromosomal XY,
the gonads begin to differentiate into a pair of testes, starting at
the sixth week after conception. When the embryo is chromosomal XX, the gonads begin to differentiate into a pair of ovaries,
starting at the twelfth week after conception. "The normal rule
in embryonic development is that the primordial gonad begins its
differentiation as a testis, if that is to be its fate, after the sixth
week of gestation, and about six weeks ahead of the timing of
ovarian differentiation."[2] Money and Ehrhardt do not comment
directly on whether the earlier development of the male gonads
has any significance. They do note that the way in which X and

Y chromosomes regulate gonadal differentiation is not yet understood.

Hormonal Sex

The testes or ovaries, once formed in the embryo or fetus, begin to produce chemical substances known as sex hormones. These hormones are important in three main ways. First, male sex hormones and female sex hormones are produced in both male and female gonads. Males produce far larger quantities of male hormones (androgens) than do females, and females produce far larger quantities of female sex hormones (estrogens) than do males. The quantitative differences are significant, but so also is the fact of overlap. Second, the fetal sex hormones control the development of the internal and external sexual anatomy. Evidence indicates that if no hormones were present in the fetus, it would develop as a female. Testicular hormones are necessary for the fetus to develop as a male. Third, the sex hormones apparently influence brain organization. Since male and female sex organs are different, the pattern of nerve endings is different, both in the sex organs and in the way these nerves are linked to the central nervous system.[3] There is also some evidence that hormones act directly on the brain during critical periods of fetal development. Another specialist states: "It would appear that following exposure of the brain during these periods to certain kinds of hormonal influences, a powerful imprinting process occurs on cells involved in complex regulatory circuits so that both behavior and endocrine functions may be profoundly modified in the adult animal. . . ."[4] This same author also cautions, however, "that information concerning the effects of hormones on the CNS [central nervous system] is limited, scattered, and for the greater part indirect."[5]

Sex hormones, biologists recognize, can have an influence on behavior. Among rhesus monkeys, for example, rough-and-tumble play and chasing and threatening behavior, although present in both sexes, are much more frequent in males than females. Likewise in human beings. Ehrhardt refers to one research in which boys and girls received abnormal doses of sex hormones during prenatal development. She writes:

Girls who were exposed to unusually high levels of androgen during their prenatal development were found to show high levels of physically energetic outdoor play and behavior and low levels of nurturant behavior in terms of parenting rehearsal. They were significantly different in these respects from matched normal controls and, in a separate study, from endocrinologically normal sisters. . . . In a number of separate studies, prenatal exposure to pharmacological doses of estrogen and progesterone [female sex hormones] was assessed, and it was found that those sex hormones were associated with the opposite effect, namely, relatively less physically energetic play behavior and an increase in more nurturant behavior as exhibited in doll play and infant care in girls and in less aggressive play behavior in boys.[6]

Ehrhardt goes on to say, however, that cultural influences are powerful and may outweigh biological dispositions.

Morphologic Sex

The sex of a newborn baby is identified not by its chromosomes or its hormones but by the form of its external genitalia; this is its morphologic sex, and this is the criterion that society uses in assigning sex roles. Some adult males are never able to produce sperm that can fertilize an egg. Despite this gonadal insufficiency, they are judged male because their morphological sex is male. Some women are unable to bear children. They are nonetheless judged female because their morphological sex is female.

The very existence of the Johns Hopkins clinic, among others, which treats cases of hermaphroditism, suggests that in modern society, at least, there is social pressure toward certainty of morphologic sex. There is no way of knowing, of course, how many parents who have hermaphroditic children do nothing to resolve the ambiguity. But neither is there any known sentiment specifically in favor of letting hermaphroditic children remain morphologically ambiguous throughout their lives. Sex roles change from period to period in our history; they vary from one society to another; and there are important changes both advocated and under way in our own society at the present time. Morphological sex appears to represent, however, an ultimate limit in the social acceptance of variation. Ambiguous sexual morphology is regarded in our society as something to be "corrected," brought into conformity (by surgery or hormone treatments) with one of the two acceptable morphologic sexes.[7]

SEX AND SOCIAL ORGANIZATION

A baby's morphological sex at birth affects the way that baby will be socialized in its society. Since societies differ in their norms, values, beliefs, and institutions, it would be reasonable to expect that socialization to sex roles would be as variable as these other aspects of society. Although sex-role socialization does indeed vary among societies, there also appear to be certain characteristic ways in which sex enters into social organization, and these characteristics constrain sex-role socialization within narrower limits than might otherwise be expected. We shall consider three such characteristics that seem to hold true of societies in general—authority, division of labor, and social status. These three aspects of social organization are spoken of by some authors as the *sex/gender system* and by others as *sex stratification*. [8]

Sex and Authority

Anthropologists do not agree on the interpretation to be given to the range of cultural patterns found in sex roles, power, and authority. *Power* is generally defined as the ability to influence others to obtain one's desired ends, and *authority* is defined as legitimate or legal power. One anthropologist, Michelle Z. Rosaldo, affirms that invariably men have both power and authority:

> My reading of the anthropological record leads me to conclude that human cultural and social forms have always been male dominated. By this, I mean not that men rule by right or even that men rule at all and certainly not that women everywhere are passive victims of a world that men define. Rather, I would point to a collection of related facts which seem to argue that in all known human groups—and no matter what prerogatives that women may in fact enjoy—the vast majority of opportunities for public influence and prestige, the ability to forge relationships, determine enmities, speak in public, use or forswear the use of force are all recognized as men's privilege and right . . . I know of no political system in which women individu-

ally or as a group . . . hold more offices or have more political clout than their male counterparts.[9]

Another pair of anthropologists, M. Kay Martin and Barbara Voorhies, speak of men as "almost always" having authority, but not necessarily power. "A survey of human societies," they say, "shows that positions of authority are almost always occupied by males. Technically speaking, there is no evidence for matriarchy, or rule by women . . . Amazonian or otherwise."[10] They go on to observe, however, that power is sometimes wielded by men, sometimes by women.

A third anthropologist, Peggy Reeves Sanday, does not deny that men have authority in most cultures, but argues that there are some societies in which women have equal authority with men, although in different spheres. Citing the Iroquois Confederacy, the League of Five Nations formed in the mid-fifteenth century by five Indian tribes in what is now upper New York state, she writes:

> In the symbolic, economic, and familial spheres the Iroquois were matriarchal, that is, female dominated. Iroquoian women headed the family longhouse, and much of the economic and ceremonial life centered on the agricultural activities of women. Men were responsible for hunting, war, and intertribal affairs. Although women appointed men to League positions and could veto their decisions, men dominated League deliberations. This tension between male and female spheres, in which females dominated village life and left intertribal life to men, suggests that the sexes were separate but equal, at least during the confederacy. Before the confederacy, when the individual nations stood alone and consisted of a set of loosely organized villages subsisting on the horticultural produce of women, females may have overshadowed the importance of males.[11]

Despite the divergence in the interpretation of cultural data, we recognize that authority is at least "almost always" in the hands of men and power is generally so. How is this to be explained? Can we give the origins of such a pattern? We find two common explanations. One, perhaps best expressed by sociologist Steven Goldberg, points to biological differences between men and women. Males produce more androgens, the male hormones, and therefore, he says, tend to be more aggressive; this aggressiveness lies at the foundation of their dominant position. "The male hormonal system gives men a head start (in terms of probabilities) that enables them to better deal with those elements of the societal environment for which aggression leads to success."[12] He does allow for the role of socialization. Societies, he continues, perceive that boys and girls show a different likelihood of asserting dominance and therefore, in their socialization, tend to build on and sometimes exaggerate the reality. The socialization process thus amplifies the initial biological tendencies and reinforces the biologically based differences.

Goldberg acknowledges that women may sometimes have power—in situations or activities in which men are not interested and therefore do not compete, when power is delegated to them, or through using "feminine ways" of "getting around" men—but such roads to power involve implicit, if not explicit, recognition that men have the final authority.

The other common explanation for the generally dominant position of males is more in line with the predilections of the women's movement and current intellectual ideologies; it points to historical, and especially economic, factors to explain male and female power positions. Sanday writes:

> Females *achieve* economic and political power or authority when environmental or historical circumstances grant them economic autonomy and make men dependent on female activities. Female economic and political power or authority is *ascribed* as a natural right due the female sex when a long-standing magico-religious association between maternity and fertility of the soil associates women with social continuity and the social good. The rights and duties attached to this emphasis give women formal power and control at the local level. Male power and authority, on the other hand, is part of the social and ritual equation of hunting, warfare, fertility, social continuity and the social good. The rights and duties associated with this emphasis give men formal power and control at the local and nonlocal levels. These rights and duties, however, do not necessarily exclude women from the realm of control.[13]

Martin and Voorhies, too, point to economic factors to explain the relationship that developed in the past between sex roles and power. They say that "power attaches itself to those who control the distribution of food or wealth, irrespective of sex,"[14] so that where women have such control, they may not have authority, but they do have power.

Accepting historical or economic explanations more readily

allows one to argue that the roles of men and women are not fixed; as societal conditions and ideologies change, so, too, may the adaptive roles of men and women. Martin and Voorhies thus continue:

> The major trend for men and women in the future, as we see it, is that gender roles will become increasingly unimportant. History teaches us that gender roles have been ubiquitous, occurring in every known society extant today, and in those of the reconstructed prehistoric past. But history does not teach us that these roles are fixed or inevitable. . . . Gender roles seem to be increasingly dysfunctional in complex societies. The division of persons into two groups is becoming increasingly opposed to the requirements of social segmentation required in industrialized urban environments. The plethora of different occupational specializations required in these societies are most efficiently met by training people for their occupational roles on the basis of talent and aptitude rather than on the anatomy of their reproductive systems. . . . Societies have perpetuated sex categories to facilitate socioeconomic interdependence and cooperation among group members. In industrial societies this interdependence is now insured by other, more complex and more appropriate forms of integration. Gender categories thus have much less adaptive significance in modern societies than in ancient ones.[15]

Although historical and economic explanations of power and authority differences between the sexes receive more attention today than do biological explanations, they fail to account for one significant fact. Whether one believes that males have dominant authority in *all* societies, as Rosaldo and Goldberg interpret the data, or whether one believes that men have authority in *almost all,* as Martin and Voorhies and Sanday interpret them, the historical and economic explanations fail to account for this great imbalance. The historical and economic explanations utilized by anthropologists and sociologists have been invaluable in showing that many sex-role differences believed to be biologically based are almost purely social constructions. They have also provided a solid basis in knowledge that has supported women in their efforts to gain a greater share in positions of authority. (There are more women mayors, judges, and legislators than formerly because it is more widely recognized that there are no biological grounds for excluding them from these offices.) Such explanations therefore open up the possibility that differences in authority and power may further diminish in the future. However, they fail to explain the enormous preponderance of authority attained by males throughout history.

In seeking to explain the origins of our sex-role patterns, it is impossible to be definitive. The biological and the environmental are inevitably intertwined in the development of any such societal forms, and any general interpretations involve considerable speculation. Perhaps, in its application to sex-role development in our own society, the judgment of John Money and Patricia Tucker is as good as any to be offered. They acknowledge the general hormonal differences between males and females—as borne out by psychological studies, males as a group are relatively more aggressive and females relatively more nurturant— yet they stress that the cultural influences (as we shall note in the pages to come) are powerful and may outweigh biological dispositions. Money and Tucker write:

> The prenatal sex hormone mix apparently does not create any new brain pathways or eliminate any that would otherwise be there. The wiring for all the affected behavior is present in both sexes. What your prenatal mix did was to lower the threshold so that it takes less of a push to switch you on to some behavior and to raise the threshold so that it takes more of a push to switch you on to other kinds. More androgen prenatally means that it takes *less* stimulus to evoke your response as far as strenuous physical activity or challenging your peers is concerned, and *more* stimulus to evoke your response to the helpless young, than would otherwise be the case. *How* you respond once you're over the threshold depends on many things— your age, health, strength, physical development, cultural heritage, gender schemas, environment, training, and experience—but not simply on your prenatal sex hormone exposure.
>
> Prenatally determined differences in sensitivity to stimuli help to explain why dominance behavior and activities involving a high expenditure of physical energy are more characteristic of boys' play than of girls', and why parental behavior is more characteristic of girls' play than of boys'. When nativists of the "anatomy is destiny" school and sex chauvinists cite this difference as evidence that men are predestined to be active and dominant, women to be passive and nurturant, however, they ignore the fact that all these behaviors are characteristic of both sexes, and they discount the heavy cultural reinforcement that maximizes the original slight difference in the thresholds.
>
> . . . The nativists and sex chauvinists are right to the extent that

if cultural influences were neutralized, one would still expect to find more men than women among those striving for dominance and those who prefer activities that demand a high expenditure of physical energy, and more women than men among those who prefer child care to other kinds of work. The prenatal sex hormone mix would still influence preferences. The point is that society need no longer insist that for a man to be a man he must be active and dominant, or for a woman to be a woman she must be passive and nurturant, no matter what capabilities and potential the interaction of nature and nurture may have given them.[16]

What remains an open question is how far cultural pressures will modify the patterns that have been built up over the centuries. The present period is perhaps the first in all human history in which an organized social movement has sought to change the direction of male and female power and authority sex roles. In recent years women, supported by government legislation and many educational, political, and professional groups, have taken an active hand to increase the numbers of women in positions of power and authority—in government agencies, political parties, business and professional organizations, and in such institutions as courts, schools, and churches. How far such a movement can go in the direction of equality in positions of power and authority is the difficult and unanswered question.

Sex and the Division of Labor

Most societies make some distinction between work that is appropriate for women and work that is appropriate for men. Anthropologist Roy D'Andrade, using data from 224 societies first compared by George Murdock, analyzes how these societies assign twenty-two subsistence activities and twenty manufacturing activities to the two sexes. For example, of 179 societies that hunt for their food, men always do the hunting in 166 societies and usually do it in the other 13. In contrast, of the 201 societies for which information is available on who does the cooking, it is always done by women in 158 societies, usually by women in 28, usually by men in 1, always by men in 5, and by either men or women in 9. The study reports that in 121 societies weapons are always made by men and never by women, and in no society studied is this type of work open equally to men and women. In contrast, in 29 societies, leather products are always made by men, while in another 32, they are always made by women. D'Andrade suggests that:

> One possible explanation for the sex differences found in the manufacture of objects is that the objects being made are intended for use in activities that are directly related to physical differences. Thus weapon making is anticipatory to activities that do involve physically strenuous and mobile behavior. . . . The thesis here . . . is that the division of labor by sex comes about as a result of generalization from activities directly related to physical sex differences to activities only indirectly related to these differences. . . .[17]

Clearly, this process of generalization proceeds differently from one society to another, since an occupation such as making leather products can be decisively assigned either to men or to women. Any link with biological sex in such an occupation seems tenuous indeed, but the connection is clearer in other occupations.

Although there are some difficult technical problems in studying the division of labor by sex in a large industrial society, certain general characteristics do emerge. Women still, although less so than in the past, tend to be concentrated in particular occupations. In the United States in 1979, women made up more than 90 percent of the labor force among registered nurses, typists, stitchers and sewers of garments, and cleaners and servants, and over 80 percent of librarians, elementary-school teachers, clerical workers, waiters and waitresses, nursing aides and orderlies, and hairdressers.[18] In Canada, where the patterns are somewhat similar to those in the United States, women in 1985 made up over 70 percent of the labor force in the fields of medicine and health, clerical work, and over 60 percent in teaching.[19]

The sex composition of an occupation can and does change, as has happened in several professions in the United States. Whereas 7 percent of physicians in 1970 were women, in 1980 the percentage was 13. Women were only 5 percent of lawyers and judges in 1970 but 14 percent in 1980; this will increase even more since in 1980 more than 33 percent of law students were women. In 1970 women made up 19 percent of college faculties, but this increased to 37 percent in 1980.[20] It may nonetheless take awhile before an occupation is regarded as equally appropriate for either sex. Occupations that are judged to be more appropriate for one sex may continue to be so regarded for a long time. Although few occupations in modern society are restricted 100 percent to males or females, the concentration of one sex in an occupation leads to its being widely regarded as "men's work" or "women's work." An occupation that has been regarded as more suitable for one sex can become redefined as more suitable for the other. When the label change is from "men's" to "women's," as in the case of bank tellers, the occupation may then be considered of less importance.[21]

These labels and associated beliefs, together with the social visibility of men and women in their jobs, affect children's perceptions and expectations. A journalist who writes about parent-child relations reports that, despite his and his wife's best efforts, their four-year-old daughter is

> already blanketed in stereotypes. She's had a woman pediatrician, but insists all doctors are men . . . her favorite activity is "dress-up"— second only to playing house—and practically the only garment she willingly wears is a dress. And lately, when furious, she has given up threatening personal retaliation. Instead she informs us that the boy up the street, a macho 4-year-old, a preschool protector and enforcer, will break our necks. All this would be even more disturbing, of course, if we felt alone in it. But we don't. Whenever we bring up the subject, someone else has a similar story.[22]

A study in the late 1970s presents the same general picture with some minor changes in the direction of greater equality. Kindergarten schoolboys most often would like to be policemen or firemen, but in later elementary grades they cite as exemplars (people they'd like to be like) famous athletes and political figures, followed by movie or TV stars. Kindergarten girls most often choose nursing as their occupational choice, to which they later add teachers and after that doctors, dentists, or veterinarians. As exemplars, as they move up to grade four, they most often cite movie or TV stars, followed far behind by famous athletes.[23]

Other studies also report that children strongly stereotype many jobs, but there are variations. One study found that grade six pupils listed a greater number of careers available to both sexes than did children in lower grades.[24] Another reported that girls in grade six believe men and women can perform in a variety of careers but chose the traditional female occupations for themselves.[25] A recent national survey in Canada of children age six to fourteen comes to a roughly similar conclusion. High proportions (at least two-thirds) of girls expect women to take on jobs traditionally male (doctors, store owners, bank managers, school principals, dentists, and police officers), but they don't aspire to these jobs themselves:

> It was as though girls did not apply to themselves their general belief in the equality of the sexes. Many of them seemed to be saying, "Yes, women can become doctors, but I expect to be a nurse", "Bank managers can be women as well as men, but I am going to be a teller", "Dental assistant is my career goal, although I know that women can be dentists".[26]

The authors also note, on the basis of their small-group discussions, that the girls almost without exception expected to marry and have children. The girls seemed to assume without question that a husband and father would provide for the family:

> Even grade eight girls of 14 years of age did not consider the possibility of their having to be in remunerative employment to support themselves or their children. There do not seem to be any unmarried mothers, deserted wives, widows, or divorcees among the imaginary women Canadian schoolgirls expect to become.[27]

Thus, with some minor variations, socialization in childhood tends to conform to the existing distribution of occupations by sex. Later in this chapter we shall describe how boys and girls tend to be socialized in different occupational directions. At this point, it is relevant to note that widespread beliefs about the particular aptitudes of men and women affect the assignment of occupations to one or the other sex. Women are believed to be more nurturing than men; the occupations that require nurturing, such as nursing, nursery school teaching, and social work, are held out to girls as the types of occupations they should seek to enter. Men are believed to be more direct and aggressive, and in line with this belief, occupations such as the military, firefighter, and corporation executive, among others, are held up as more suitable for boys to look ahead to. Socialization practices usually encourage movement toward occupations that are considered congruent with what are believed to be sex-linked temperamental characteristics and sex-linked abilities.

Sex and Social Status

In modern discussions of sex roles and socialization, few topics have received as much attention as the status of women. The implications of much of this discussion are pointed up in the very title of an article published in 1951 that gave the topic new prominence—"Women as a Minority Group." In this article sociologist Helen Mayer Hacker pointed out that women are discriminated against on the basis of physical and cultural characteristics, just as are members of ethnic minorities.[28] Discrimination has clearly played an important part in the differential status of men and women.

No one questions that males as a group have higher status than females as a group. Lipman-Blumen and Tickameyer state: "Perhaps one of the most theoretically interesting (and existentially frustrating) aspects of sex differentiation is its constancy and its invariant rank ordering: the male role is always more highly valued than the female role."[29] The discrepancy in value may be large or small and may take different forms. In rural Greece, "the word 'child' is synonymous with 'boy.' When asked how many children they have, parents answer 'I have two children and two girls,' meaning that they have two boys and two girls."[30] The negative attitude toward the female changes as soon as she becomes a mother: "From that moment she assumes a role that is idealized and considered 'holy'. Despised and suspected as a woman, she is revered, trusted, respected, and obeyed as a mother."[31] In Sweden, in contrast, the ideal of equality of treatment of boys and girls has been an explicit goal of the public schools since 1962; girls with interests in technology and science should be encouraged to develop them and "conventional attitudes toward these matters should be opposed."[32] As we shall note, however, the Swedish ideal has not yet completely come to pass.

Status differences between men and women do not remain fixed. As a rough generalization, it may be stated that as industrialization increasingly pervades society in all parts of the globe, societies will tend to abandon the type of pattern of which rural Greece is an example and will tend to move toward the pattern exemplified by the goal expressed in the Swedish school doctrine. Each country's circumstances are different, and there will therefore be national differences in the ways change takes place and in its speed.[33] At any given time, until status differences completely disappear, they will be visible in many ways. Authority and status tend to go together; as long as males have more authority, they will tend to have higher status. Currently women tend to be concentrated in lower-paid occupations and in lower-paid ranks of high-paid occupations. Regarding legal rights, since 1985 women in Canada are guaranteed equality in the Constitution. This step has yet to be taken in the United States.

The status differences between men and women are built into interpersonal behavior as well as into social institutions. Writing on the ways that nonverbal behaviors contribute to maintaining traditional sex roles, psychologists Irene Hanson Frieze and Sheila J. Ramsey cite research that shows that men do more touching than do women and that women are touched more by both sexes. In speaking of the uninvited touch, they conclude that "The higher status individual has the social right to breech the spatial boundaries of the lower ranked."[34] They add that:

> One of the major indicators of women's low status is their lack of territory. This symptom is itself a perpetuating factor since having space allows one privacy and the freedom to control what information about oneself will be made available to others as well as who or what will enter one's space. . . . From another point of view, nonverbal behaviors which communicate low status and submission are precisely those crucial to attributions of femininity. Traditional role behavior dictates that women take up the smallest amount of space, speak softly and politely, refrain from initiating prolonged eye contact, and present an affable exterior. A woman who rejects these low status behaviors is often accused of being too assertive or aggressive.[35]

SOCIALIZATION AGENTS AND PROCESSES

Boys and girls are born with different reproductive potential. The adults who receive them into society and who guide their participation in it, both initially and later, anticipate that boys and girls will come to have different patterns of participation when they are adults, patterns that are sex-appropriate and that are termed sex roles. The newborn baby does not, of course, have any awareness of himself or herself as a person of a particular sex. In the course of time he or she will develop such an awareness and a pervasive sense of self as a member of one sex or the other. This is the person's *sexual identity,* which may be defined as

> the image of self as a male or a female and convictions about what membership in that group implies. Sexual identity, the individual's basic, sex-typed self image, is built up gradually from early infancy. It is the result of learned conceptions about the self, as a male or as a female. It includes beliefs about how one *ought* to think, act, and feel by virtue of having been born male or female. It includes learned ideals of masculine and feminine behavior and the proper authority relationships between the sexes.[36]

A person's sexual identity is a part of his or her self-concept, which we discussed in Chapter 3.

The persons who socialize children attempt to lead boys and girls to develop sex-appropriate identities, according to whatever standards of appropriateness are current in the society and in the groups to which they belong or refer. For their part, children make their own observations of the social life that takes place around them and contribute to their own sexual identity by fitting their own feelings and behavior to the varieties of male and female behavior that are part of their observed world and world of interaction. Gary Fine, speaking of nine- to twelve-year-old boys, writes: ". . . they select from among the repertoire of behaviors that they perceive men (particularly media men and other role models) display. They select those behaviors that are congruent with their own needs for independence and separation from the world of girls and younger children."[37] Similarly girls would select those behaviors that are congruent with the needs they feel. The development of sexual identity and the development of sex roles are parts of the same complex process. In this section we shall present some of the main aspects of this process as now understood, with particular attention to the United States and Canada.

Before turning to specific agencies and processes, it is well to note the fact that socialization to sex roles is not a simple cumulative process. The time dimension, which we discussed in Chapter 3, introduces an important complication: the socially desired outcomes of socialization are different at different ages. Thus, Joseph Pleck finds this generalization emerging from several studies: "boys' socialization emphasizes physical strength and skill and the avoidance of anything feminine, including girls, but . . . men are rewarded primarily for intellectual and social skills and are expected to be capable of intimate relationships with women."[38] Phyllis Katz, in a detailed review of female sex-role development, concludes that there are three distinct stages (each with stages of its own) and that there are some important discontinuities. For example, she contrasts the nursery-school period with the grade-school period:

> in nursery school . . . boys are expected to be more physical, aggressive, exploratory, and independent, whereas girls are expected to be more docile, sociable, and dependent. Such expectations are widely held by both nursery-school teachers and parents. . . .
>
> . . . Stated sex-role expectations for boys and girls in a school environment are remarkably similar. Both sexes are expected to sit quietly, to pay attention to the teacher, and to master the rudimentary mysteries of reading and mathematics. Generally speaking, grade-school classrooms are not as obviously sex-typed as most nursery-school classrooms in terms of materials and play areas. Thus, if sex role socialization were primarily transmitted by adults, we would expect to find fewer behavioral differences between grade-school boys and girls than at earlier levels of development. This is not the case. More sex-related differences in socialization have been found in grade school than in the preschool period. . . . Boys and girls exhibit differential ability in mastering the early school environment (boys seem to have more difficulty), differential interests and activities (both in and after school), and strong preferences for same-sex friends. During the period of middle childhood, this peer group takes on an increasingly prominent role in determining what constitute appropriate standards of behavior. . . .[39]

A further disjunction occurs between childhood and adolescence:

> Thus there is a greater disparity between childhood and adolescent sex roles for females than for males. This disjunction occurs not only in dating behavior but also with regard to female perceptions of life

goals. Marriage becomes a much more significant goal for girls during adolescence than occupational success. In contrast to the childhood message, what is now being transmitted (by parents, media, and peers) is that although academic excellence and thinking about careers are fine, marriage and maternity are paramount.[40]

Katz underestimates the continuities of socialization. Girls do not, after all, first learn of the social desirability of marriage during adolescence. Parents and others have usually introduced this goal fairly early in childhood. But Katz is right to call attention to the fact that there are discontinuities and contradictions in the socialization process. The adolescent girl and young woman, like her male counterpart, has to sort out the many incoming messages and experiences of socialization and assemble them into some coherent identity, as we discussed in Chapter 3. Let us now look more closely at those messages dealing with sex roles.

Family Interaction

We have discussed the discrepancies between men and women in authority, positions in the work world, and in social status, and two of the main theories proposed to account for them—one based on biological predisposition and one based on men's discrimination against women. These two theories can be regarded as opposed to each other, but they can also be regarded as complementary; that is, the theory of male hormonal advantage in expressing dominance can help to explain why males have succeeded in discriminating against females and why there are no societies in which women have gained the authority that would enable them to discriminate against men.

A third theory, based mainly on the work of psychologists, can also be introduced here. It may be regarded as an alternative to the two just cited, or equally well as a third component joining them to result in a more inclusive theory. This third theory (or component) seeks to explain why women fail to achieve to a degree that is in keeping with their intelligence. Lois W. Hoffman states: "The failure of women to fulfill their intellectual potential has been adequately documented. . . . the precursors of the underachieving woman can be seen in the female child." She presents her theory as follows:

> It is our theory that the female child is given inadequate parental encouragement in early independence strivings. Furthermore, the separation of the self from the mother is more delayed or incomplete for the girl because she is the same sex with the same sex role expectations, and because girls have fewer conflicts with their parents. As a result, she does not develop confidence in her ability to cope independently with the environment. She retains her infantile fears of abandonment; safety and effectiveness lie in her affective ties.[41]

Hoffman draws on Erik Erikson's theory of development that emphasizes the ages between one and four as critical for the development of independence and competence. "By critical, we mean a period when independence and competence are more efficiently learned than at other times. There is a rapid building up of notions about the self and about the world."[42] Hoffman summarizes and interprets the available research bearing on her theory, recognizing that it remains incomplete. We shall draw upon her review, supplementing it with the references to some additional studies.

Boys and girls seem to differ from birth, with boys being somewhat more active than girls and girls being more sensitive to touch and to pain. The sex differences in sensitivity to touch and to pain are found in infants less than four days old and still in the hospital nursery.[43]

It is not clear from the available research what generalizations, if any, can be made about the way parents in our society treat infant girls and boys. Hoffman cites one study showing that mothers handle and stimulate males more than females, and another study that suggests that such maternal attentiveness stimulates exploratory behavior. A more recent study points to reciprocal roles of the parents with sons and daughters. That is, fathers hold their daughters close more frequently than they do their sons. However, the fathers provide more visual and tactile stimulation for their sons. Mothers show the reverse pattern: They hold their sons more closely than their daughters but more often provide stimulation to their daughters.[44]

Other researchers report that mothers talk more to baby daughters than to baby sons[45] and that both parents interrupt daughters more than sons, ages two to five.[46] Fathers, according to a number of studies, tend in their play to be more active, physically stimulating, and rough-and-tumble, sometimes arousing discomfort and anxiety in the child.[47] Psychologist K. Alison Clarke-Stewart raises the question whether this more active style of play by males is biologically based, but also notes that it is supported in our society by cultural expectations for fathers, especially with sons. Citing a study by B. J. Fagot, she writes: "Parents of boys, even university-educated, more 'liberated' parents, believe that mothers' and fathers' roles are different—the mother's role is to be a caregiver and the father's role is to play—and play with sons, all parents agree, can and should be rougher and more physical than play with daughters."[48]

Detailed studies of parental interactions with infants and babies are still relatively few in number and based on limited samples in limited settings. The facts are not easy to establish and the topic requires much careful research.

Studies of the preschool years give some support to Hoffman's theory that parents encourage the independence strivings of boys more than they do of girls. According to one study, when mothers are asked at what age they would first allow their children to use sharp scissors without adult supervision and at what age they would allow their children to begin playing away from home for long periods without telling where they will be, mothers of boys give earlier ages than do mothers of girls.[49] Several other studies have indicated that dependency is discouraged in preschool boys but is more acceptable on the part of girls. Generally, mothers seem to consider girls more vulnerable and fragile than boys and thus in greater need of protection. A Canadian study reports that both French-Canadian and English-Canadian mothers and fathers, when hearing a child's demand for comfort for a minor injury, would more likely withhold such comfort from a boy than from a girl.[50] Boys also are more often punished by spanking, which prompts a kind of reactive independence, while girls are more often punished with threats of loss of love, which prompts continuing obedience and dependence upon the parent who uses this power.[51]

Complementing the encouragement given to boys toward

earlier independence is their greater tendency to come into conflict with parental authority. They are therefore disciplined more often, and these experiences facilitate separation of the self from the parent. Hoffman then suggests:

> One implication of this is that girls need a little maternal rejection if they are to become independently competent and self-confident. And indeed a generalization that occurs in most recent reviews is that high achieving females had hostile mothers while high achieving males had warm ones. . . . Our interpretation of these findings then is that many girls experience too much maternal rapport and protection during their early years. Because of this they find themselves as adults unwilling (or unable) to face stress and with inadequate motivation for autonomous achievement. . . . The theoretical view presented in this paper is speculative but it appears to be consistent with the data.[52]

In assessing the differences between girls and boys that appear to result from different patterns of family interaction, Hoffman notes that several studies show that girls tend to underestimate their ability and to avoid difficult tasks, whereas boys are more self-confident and challenged by difficult tasks. Boys, she suggests, may even be pushed prematurely into independence. Ruth Hartley, in support, points out that the socialization of boys is often harsh and demanding. Boys are told to be "manly" much earlier than girls are told to be "ladylike." But the greater difficulty for boys is the fact that they are subject to demands to be manly, not a sissy, not feminine, and yet they are under the supervision of women most of the time during their early years.[53]

Toys and the Media

Although the differences in parental handling of infant girls and boys are still to be adequately researched and described, it nonetheless seems clear that those differences begin fairly early. By the time children are two or three years old, parents are applying fairly distinct conceptions of femininity and masculinity. Girls are considered to be feminine when they show interest in pretty clothes, domestic activities, and babies, and when they display social awareness and behave coquettishly. Boys are considered masculine when they show interest in objects or ideas, not persons, and in getting things to work.[54] Parents express their ideas, in part, by the toys they give to children. These conceptions also tend to be supported in picture books for children and in TV programs.

In recent years some research attention has turned to children's toys. All children are given cuddly toys to start, but thereafter standard toys for the boy represent the world of work and adventure—guns, trucks, tools, and building supplies. The standard toys for the girl are those of the mother role—dolls, dishes, and household appliances.[55] That adult gender-role expectations begin early is suggested by an experimental study in which adults were left alone with a three-month-old infant, not their own, and observed through a one-way mirror. Those adults who were told that the infant was a boy handed "him" a small rubber football; when the infant was identified as a girl, the adults handed "her" a Raggedy Ann doll.[56]

As early as thirteen months, according to one research finding, children show different toy preferences by sex.[57] Another study of two-year-olds found that girls preferred to play with dolls and soft toys while boys preferred to play with blocks and to manipulate objects. Parents, by giving positive or negative sanctions, reinforced these preferences.[58] A study of four-year-old nursery-school children found that boys spent more time in that part of the playroom where blocks, wheel toys, and carpenter's tools were located, while girls spent more time in the area having the doll houses, cooking equipment, and dress-up clothes.[59] These preferences in nursery-school activity may well result from earlier experiences in the home.

Jacquelynn Eccles and Lois Hoffman cite research which suggests that more than sex roles are communicated to children by the sex typing of toys. Intellectual development is also shaped by toys. They summarize:

> Boys' toys, more than girls' toys, afford inventive possibilities, encourage manipulation, and provide more information about the physical world. Furthermore, research suggests that some of the "masculine" toys, particularly blocks and building materials, develop skills that enhance abilities in dealing with spatial relationships and mathematics. . . . [Other data,] on the other hand, suggest that the toys and play activities of girls may be particularly valuable for

verbal development. Since these very skills are often cited as sex differences in abilities throughout the life cycle, it is quite possible that children's play is part of the preparation for adult occupations.[60]

With considerable publicity given to the sex-typing of toys and with pressure from women's groups, the pictures on toy boxes and the presentation in toy catalogs are not as sex-typed as they used to be. The box of a doctor's kit, for example, may now picture a girl as well as a boy. This was not always so. Sociologist Janet Chafetz in 1974 reported a research study carried out by her students, of the Christmas toy catalogs of Sears, Roebuck and of Montgomery Ward, the two largest mail-order companies in the United States. The catalogs were each divided into a boys' section and a girls' section; the latter was full of dolls, household goods (dishes, appliances), and beauty aids; the former featured athletic items, technological toys such as tractors and building materials, toy soldiers, guns, cars, as well as some male dolls of football player Joe Namath, G.I. Joe, and an astronaut. One illustration showed boys being served tea by girls. The catalog illustrations showed a total of thirteen boys and one girl riding a toy; twenty-nine boys and no girls operating a model vehicle (train, car, tractor); and twenty-nine boys and two girls operating construction toys.[61] Presumably adults' toy purchases tended to follow these conceptions of sex-appropriateness.

In discussing the media of mass communication as agencies of socialization, we noted that research on both children's and adult television programs reported a predominance of males over females and the common portrayal of traditional sex roles. We also noted in the British Columbia study of Notel, a town in which TV was newly introduced, that the children were more likely to express sex-role stereotypes two years after they had access to television programs than before.

We find a similar sex-biased content—with perhaps the same impact—in the advertising for children who, we have observed, are exposed to some 20,000 commercials a year. Advertising to children, it is reported, is a half-billion-dollar-a-year business.[62] Research by Charles Winick and his associates, who examined 236 commercials representing 127 products (mostly food, beverages, and snacks) and using real-life, animated, or puppet children, found that about 58 percent of the commercials had boy characters while about 35 percent had girls.[63] Another study of over 400 commercials and public service announcements in children's programs on a Saturday morning reported that almost 63 percent of human and cartoon characters were male. Chafetz, who studied 100 TV commercials as well as toy catalogs, reports that 79 of 83 narrators were male; 17 females were shown engaged in domestic activities as compared to 5 males; 8 males but no females were shown doing something mechanical; 40 males and 4 females were shown as physically active; 22 males and 2 females were shown in provider roles; 16 females and no males were shown as economically dependent; 15 females and 3 males were shown as responding to social pressure.[64]

Presumably these commercials are effective. Following the presentation of commercials that portrayed toys appropriate to one or the other sex, one study found that both boys and girls, age four to six, tended to choose the toys that were presented as gender appropriate.[65] An advertising executive who provides tips on how to "communicate" with children is quoted as saying "Boys are concerned with power and strength. Girls are concerned with looks and cuteness."[66] In a general comment on toy commercials, Brian Sutton-Smith has suggested that they

> have a pervasive rather than a decisive effect. Which is to say, few particular commercials necessarily compel all children and all parents to respond with active purchasing, but in general these commercials establish in the minds of parents and children the "orthodoxy" of what play is all about. Parents and children will undoubtedly suit themselves, and argue between themselves as to what they want to buy. They will not be overdetermined by the particular commercial, but the range of what they will think about is increasingly influenced, even confined by what they see on television.[67]

Two studies of the prize-winning Caldecott Medal picture books for preschool children report results substantially similar to those of toy catalogs and TV commercials. The Caldecott Medal is awarded by the Children's Service Committee of the American Library Association for the most distinguished picture book of the year. The winning books are ordered by most children's librarians throughout the country; parents look on library shelves for the gold seal that designates the winner; and sales may reach as high as 60,000 copies.[68] One of the studies, by Alleen

Pace Nilsen, examined the winning and runner-up books for a twenty-year period from 1951 to 1970, eighty books in all. Among the findings are: (1) fourteen of the titles include a male's name, while four include a female's; (2) the illustrations depicted a total of 579 males and 368 females; (3) in one book entitled *A Tree Is Nice,* the illustrations show eleven boys and three girls in the branches of trees, with all the girls in the lowest branches; "The other girls are pictured in such poses as waving to a boy who is high in a tree, dragging a little boy through the leaves, helping another little boy into a tree, standing with a sprinkling can, and standing dejectedly alone while the boys climb a magnificent tree."[69] Nilsen finds, further, that the percentage of girls in the illustrations declined from 46 percent in the 1951–1955 period to 26 percent in the 1966–1970 period.[70]

Weitzman and co-authors focused on the Caldecott winners for the 1966–1970 period, and they report 261 pictures of males and 23 pictures of females, a ratio of 11 to 1 or about 9 percent females. The apparent discrepancy between 9 percent and 26 percent in the two studies of the same set of books is possibly due to the fact that Nilsen was counting only children while the Weitzman group was counting all "males and females," including adults. The Weitzman group also made a separate count of animals, which was even more heavily weighted in favor of males, while Nilsen includes animal characters in her overall count of males and females. In sum, both studies agree that women, girls, and females are pictured less often than men, boys, and males. We note, however, how different procedures for counting and reporting figures can affect the presentation of a problem. In this instance, the differences did not happen to affect the basic results.

Both studies essentially agree also on the way the books present males and females:

> In the world of picture books, boys are active and girls are passive. Not only are boys presented in more exciting and adventuresome roles, but they engage in more varied pursuits and demand more independence. The more riotous activity is reserved for the boys. . . . In contrast, most of the girls in the picture books are passive and immobile . . . the girls are more often found indoors. . . . Even the youngest girls in the stories play traditional feminine roles, directed toward pleasing and helping their brothers and fathers. . . . While girls serve, boys lead.[71]

No doubt, with the pressure to open opportunities for girls and the publicity given to such studies, the new books for children point to less stereotyped images. We shall look forward to research both to confirm this tendency and to analyze its impact.

The School

Schools contribute to the differential socialization of boys and girls. But in appraising the impact of schools, it is useful to keep in mind the comment of educational sociologist Sara Lawrence Lightfoot:

> Teachers are not totally responsible for the socialization that occurs in classrooms. Children also socialize teachers into certain behaviors. Much of the sex-role patterning of boys and girls has been deeply rooted by the time the children enter school at five years of age. Without making her first move, the teacher sees boys building boats in the block corner and girls playing house in the doll corner.[72]

Another elementary-school teacher speaks of machismo among boys as a compelling force. By grades one and two, she writes, they have absorbed the macho kid, and for a third-grade boy to be labeled a sissy is a "fate worse than death."[73]

Even in nursery school, boys and girls act differently in some respects and are responded to differently by teachers. One study, which focused on fifteen female teachers of pupils age three to five, with twelve to seventeen pupils per class, found that boys ignore teachers more often and are more often aggressive, while girls more often stay within arm's reach of the teacher. There were no differences between the sexes in crying or in asking for help. Boys received more loud reprimands for disruptive behavior than did girls, but the boys also received more praise when they did what they were supposed to do.[74] In recent years some nursery schools have sought to treat boys and girls alike and minimize any particular sex-role socialization.[75]

In reviewing the school's role in sex-role stereotyping of girls, educational psychologist Betty Levy confirms the general trends that have emerged thus far in our analysis. She finds the following:

1. Traditional sex roles are reinforced through the authority structure of the elementary school. Eighty-five percent of all elementary school teachers are women; 78 percent of all elementary school principals are men.[76]
2. Teachers often separate boys and girls for seating, lining up, hanging up coats, and other activities, thus calling attention to sex distinctions.[77]
3. "Elementary schools reinforce girls' training for obedience, social and emotional dependence, and docility. That girls on the whole like school better than boys and perform better in most respects may be due in part to the consistency of the sex role demands of home and school."[78]
4. "The schools' emphasis on neatness, order, punctuality, and performance of often meaningless and monotonous tasks is an important part of the 'domesticating' function of schools, particularly in the case of girls."[79]

The high ratio of males to females that we reported for preschool picture books has also been found in a study of 134 elementary school readers put out by fourteen publishing companies and used in three suburban New Jersey towns. The study further reports that in sixty-seven stories, "one sex demeaned the other, sixty-five of these were directed against girls, only two against boys."[80]

Boys have not always been so overemphasized. At least one historical study that focuses on changes over the years points to an increasing emphasis on girls. In a study of introductory reading textbooks in the United States from colonial days through 1966, educational researcher Sara Goodman Zimet found that "From a character count, it was noted that textbook authors began to increase the number of female characters in the stories as formal education was opened to girls (between 1776 and 1835). This trend continued so that by 1898 and up through 1966, girl characters actually outnumbered boy characters in the texts."[81] She also finds, in keeping with an earlier study, that first-grade readers avoid aggressive themes and that dependency "was particularly frequent in the books . . . from 1921 to 1966, and was rewarded overwhelmingly for both sexes and all age levels. . . . Interestingly enough, the dependency model for the male was even more striking in frequency than for the female."[82] Zimet's study is confined to primers, the books children are presented in their first school-organized formal reading instruction. Many other studies sample from a larger (or at least a more varied) range of elementary school reading materials.[83]

Although most kinds of elementary school reading materials beyond the primers may emphasize males, this does not seem to make boys better readers than girls. Various studies show that from the second grade through the sixth, girls are better readers than boys. Caution is required, however, in any effort to find universal generalizations. A cross-cultural study of four countries where English is spoken revealed that in the elementary grades girls are better readers than boys in the United States and in English-speaking sections of Canada, while boys are the better readers in England and Nigeria. The explanation given is that:

> Teachers in our culture expect girls to excel in reading as compared to boys, and they do. . . . Reading ability of boys is more highly valued in England and Nigeria than it is in North America. In Nigeria, in fact, schooling has a very low priority for girls and most of the teachers are men. Sex differences in favor of boys even increased from second to sixth grades in Nigeria and England.[84]

The fact that girls generally read better than boys in North American elementary schools is one of the facts that has been offered in support of the view that elementary schools, far from giving support to males and fostering masculine stereotypes, actually are environments that are more compatible with the temperament of girls and have a "feminizing effect" on boys. One group of educators states the matter this way:

> There is little doubt that the character of American education is feminine, either by design or as a comfortable acceptance unintentionally adopted by the teachers and administrators developing the structure of the program. Standards of conduct, restricted environments for learning, the majority members of the instructional staff, academic and social expectations, and the physical setting for the school are all substantially feminine, with little regard for the male culture presented within the societal structure outside of the schools.[85]

These authors then present two sets of adjectives, one set describing societal expectations for boys and one set for girls. Boys are expected to be "active, adventuresome, brave, curious, dirty, imaginative, robust, outspoken, disheveled, rough," while girls are expected to be "neat, quiet, mannerly, pretty, clean, artistic, studious, sensitive, obedient, gentle."[86] They believe that the second list of characteristics" more aptly describes the type of child readily accepted in the classroom" and that girls will indeed fit that list better than will boys. Schools do, however, in their view, press boys toward becoming more neat, quiet, mannerly, and so on, thus exerting a "feminizing" effect.

Peer Games

The extent to which children create variations in their relationships independent of the adult world is at this time still a very open question. A case in point is the relationship of children's games to the larger society. Two psychologists have reviewed four surveys of children's games conducted between 1896 and 1959. Children studied were mostly between nine and fifteen years old. The researchers conclude that:

> Perhaps the most important generalizations arising out of this study concern the changing relationships between boys and girls. . . . [T]he responses of girls have become increasingly like those of boys as the sixty years have passed. . . . [This] is not unexpected, in the light of the well-known changes in woman's role in American culture during this period.[87]

They suggest that it is more deviant today than sixty years ago for a boy to play such things as dolls, hopscotch, jumprope, and other specifically girls' games. Though the authors do not delineate the societal changes, it may be pointed out that coeducation has increased greatly during this period and, in general, there is freer mingling between boys and girls. But insofar as there has been "acculturation" in games, the change has been largely in one direction. The pattern seems to be continuing, with relatively more girls now taking part in such sports as track and field, hockey, and basketball.[88]

Nevertheless, the play of girls has not become identical to that of boys. Significant differences remain. Sociologist Janet Lever studied 181 fifth-grade children, age ten and eleven, mostly white and middle class, in three schools. She observed them in schoolyards during recess, in physical education periods, and after school; she also had them keep a diary of their after-school activities for one week. She discovered that boys' play is more complex than girls' play. Complexity is indicated by six features:

1. Size of the play group.
2. Role differentiation—for example whether players have the same role, as in playing checkers, or different roles, as in playing baseball.
3. Player interdependence—a tennis player's move affects the opponent's next move, but in a game of darts, each player's throws are not affected much by what the other player does.
4. Explicitness of goals—play is a cooperative interaction that has no stated goal, no end point, no winners; formal games are competitive interactions aimed at a specific goal (getting a touchdown or scoring a run) and have a stated end point (such as completion of nine innings) that is simultaneous with the declaration of a winner.
5. Number and specificity of rules—a game of tag has few, baseball many.
6. Team formation—play never has teams; many games require teams, though some do not.

Lever found that on all six of these dimensions, boys' activities were more complex than girls'. Boys were observed typically engaged in team sports, with ten to twenty-five players; girls were seldom observed in groups as large as ten, and on those occasions they were doing cooperative circle songs. More typically, the girls would play tag, hopscotch, or jumprope, with two to six participants. Role differentiation is minimal in girls' play; most commonly they engage in activities in which there is a single role and all do the same thing, such as skating or riding bikes. They play some turn-taking games in which there are two roles, such as jumprope with the roles of rope-turner and rope-jumper, or central-person games with one person as "it" and the others all in a secondary role. Boys' play was most often in team sports with multiple roles.

Girls' play tends to require less interdependence than does boys'. Single-role play requires co-action rather than interaction; turn-taking games have a routine and don't require much decision making. When girls' play is interdependent, it is usually cooperative interdependence within a single group, for example, putting on a play. Boys are more likely to engage in competitive team activity, which calls for interdependence not only among members of a team but also in taking account of the actions and strategies of opponents. Even one-on-one basketball is inter-dependent because each player must make decisions that take account of what the opponent is doing.

Boys' games were found more often to have an elaborate organization of rules. There are more ambiguous situations in their games that require elaboration of rules or that lead to dis-putes in which rules must be interpreted and applied. Girls play cooperatively more than competitively; consequently, they seem to be less rule-conscious than boys. Finally, since boys are more involved in team play, more of their activity is simultaneously cooperative and competitive; they cooperate with members of their own team while competing against another team. Girls, in turn-taking games, more often compete within a single group as independent players, each one against all the others.

Lever suggests that these differences have implications for adult life. Different skills are fostered in boys' and in girls' play activities. The skills boys are probably sharpening are: ability to deal with diversity, where each person is performing a special task; ability to coordinate actions and maintain group cohesive-ness; ability to cope with impersonal rules; ability to work for collective as well as personal goals; ability to engage in face-to-face competition while maintaining self-control and sportsman-ship; and ability to engage in strategic thinking. In addition, team sports provide experience with clear-cut leadership positions. Gary Fine also notes that in competitive team play there are always winners and losers and, as sometime losers, boys learn not to take defeat as a blow to self-esteem—a characteristic that may well serve later in a competitive corporate environment.[89]

Girls' play and games tend to be spontaneous, imaginative, and less structured by rules. Competition tends to be indirect rather than face to face, individual rather than team-based. Lead-ership roles do not emerge as often. Girls' play occurs in smaller groups, and they often engage in conversation rather than play-ing anything at all. The overall result, Lever suggests, is that boys develop a greater ability to take the role of the "generalized other" and to view themselves from the position of a wider soci-ety, while girls develop empathy skills to take the role of the "particular other."

At this time, one can only hypothesize, rather than demonstrate, a relationship between these sex differences in childhood play and adult behavior. Lever points to the similarity between boys' play patterns and adult male roles and suggests the possibility that the earlier experiences serve a socializing function for the later roles. Further, she cites a study of twenty-five female executives that indicates these women were tomboys. Also suggestive is the fact that women leaders in the United States tend to come disproportionately from elite schools and colleges that do emphasize team sports for women. This suggests that providing girls greater experience in competitive team sports in childhood—a tendency that is well under way in high school athletics, especially basketball[90]—could be one way to increase their later ability to compete effectively for more demanding, higher-level jobs in complex organizations.[91]

Some of Lever's research findings receive direct support from other studies. In one research on the play activities of a group of eight- to thirteen-year-old black, working-class children in Philadelphia, anthropologist Marjorie Goodwin reports on the differences in the use of directives, that is, speech acts that try to get another person to do something. She says, "both girls and boys in our society have access to the same general language system, but detailed study of the talk they produce shows systematic differences in how the sexes put that common system to work."[92] She watched boys making slingshots and girls making rings from bottle rims. Although slingshots could be made individually, Goodwin points out that

> the activity of making slings became organized into a competition between two separate teams with a hierarchical organization of participants on each team. . . . The slingshot fight itself was preceded by an extended period during which, not only were weapons and slings prepared, but the organization of the group was also negotiated. All the elements in this process, such as where the preparation would occur, who would provide materials, who had rights to materials, the allocation of necessary tools, the spatial organization of participants, when the activity was to move from stage to stage, and so on, became the focus for status negotiations between the participants.[93]

The leaders of the two teams would issue directives as explicit commands—"Gimme the pliers." "Get off my steps." When such directives were accepted, as they sometimes were, the leadership status of the person issuing the directive was confirmed.

In making rings, the girls faced similar decisions about where to get the materials, where to carry on the activity, who would do what, and so forth. They did not form a hierarchical organization, however; the author notes that such organizations are uncommon in girls' games. Thus, there were no leaders issuing orders. Rather, directives took the form of suggestions in which speaker as well as hearer were potential agents of the action to be performed—"Let's ask her 'Do you have any bottles.' " "Let's use these first and then come back and get the rest cuz it's too many of them." In addition to suggesting, rather than ordering, the girls tended to leave open the time at which an action was to be performed, while the boys wanted an action completed "right now." Girls do use direct commands in certain specific situations, for example acting as teacher or mother while playing school or house, telling younger siblings what to do, ridiculing ostracized girls, and in responding to earlier attacks of age-mates. But girls tend to express ambivalence about their use of direct commands. Goodwin says: "Giving direct commands is taken to be an action which displays offensive character for girls though it is such a commonplace verbal behavior among boys as to not even be considered remarkable."[94]

In another study, this time of nine- to eleven-year-olds in elementary schools, sociologists Barrie Thorne and Zella Luria focus on the taken-for-granted segregation of boys and girls in their everyday activities. They observed schoolchildren in California, Michigan, and Massachusetts as they came together in playgrounds, classrooms, hallways and lunchrooms. When choosing seats, selecting companions for study or play, or arranging themselves in line, the boys and girls kept to members of their own sex. Their free activities likewise followed different patterns with the boys being generally rougher and less conformist.[95] As we shall note in the next section, the different styles of play also help shape the meanings of sexuality that are beginning to emerge in this age group.

The boundary between boys and girls that is taken for granted in segregated activities is reaffirmed in many heterosexual activities. Sex-divided classroom competitions such as spelling bees and math contests, cross-sex-chasing games provoked by teasing or pokes, playground invasions in which boys disrupt the games of girls (or less often vice versa) are means of calling attention to and reaffirming the boundaries.[96]

Socialization to Sexuality

Sexuality is popularly thought of as genital activity, the use of the sexual organs for reproduction, to express love, to experience sensual pleasure, or some combination of these aims. Some students of sexuality point out that this definition is too limited because genital activity is not isolated from other aspects of life. For example, a child's attitude toward genital activity may partly depend upon whether its parents talk about the genitals or not and, if so, with what emotions, what vocabulary, and in what tone of voice. These, in turn, reflect the parents' values, beliefs, and life style. With such considerations in mind, one author has proposed that sexuality can be considered as consisting of six related aspects: (1) gender role; (2) affection and intimacy; (3) family life style; (4) body image; (5) erotic experiences; and (6) reproduction. All of these aspects are interrelated, and socialization to sexuality would encompass socialization to all aspects. This view has considerable merit, as does the author's further statement that "The single most important area of learning affecting our sexuality is the set of messages that we receive throughout our lives about 'appropriate' masculine and feminine roles."[97]

Nevertheless, there is value, in a brief volume such as this, in focusing some attention on sexuality in the more restricted sense of erotic experience and body image. One reason is that we do not yet have a great deal of information about how all six aspects of sexuality affect each other. Second, sexuality in the narrower sense has been a troublesome issue in Western societies. As anthropologist Ruth Benedict pointed out almost a half-century ago, "From a comparative point of view, our culture goes to great extremes in emphasizing contrasts between the child and the adult. The child is sexless, the adult estimates his virility by his sexual activities. . . ."[98] While values, norms, and attitudes toward sexuality have been changing, and these changes have had some impact on socialization, the extent of the impact is still unclear. We shall attempt to present the main points of what is now known about socialization to sexuality, recognizing that knowledge in this area is still sketchy.

The first point to be made is that societies differ in their basic stance toward sexuality in general and toward children's sexuality in particular. This fact is important because socialization practices and outcomes tend to follow from the society's basic value position. Anthropologist Richard Currier has looked at this question and has expanded upon Benedict's statement. He states that the world's cultures can be classified into four main types, as regards their approach to sexuality, each type having the following characteristic features.

Sexually repressive cultures
    Are disposed toward denial of sexuality
    Consider sex to be a dangerous area of behavior
    Tend to prohibit all forms of sexuality except what is necessary for procreation
    Impose sexual ignorance on the young
    Strictly prohibit sex play in childhood

Sexually restrictive cultures
    Limit sexuality
    May give sexual license to one sex while requiring the other to be premaritally chaste
    Segregate the sexes early in life
    Discourage sex play in childhood
    Are a minority among primitive societies but the dominant type among civilizations

Sexually permissive cultures
    Are disposed toward tolerance of sexuality
    Loosely enforce formal prohibitions
    Technically forbid sexual play in childhood, but, as long as it is kept out of adult sight, pretend they don't know what is going on
    Consider premarital sexual activity normal

Sexually supportive cultures
    Are disposed toward the cultivation of sexuality
    Consider sexuality indispensable to human happiness
    Consider early sexual experience a necessary part of social and biological maturation
    Provide both sexual information and sexual opportunity to young people of all ages, who are encouraged to develop their sexual skills

According to this analysis, Western culture made a transition from repressive to restrictive between 1900 and 1950 and is currently in transition from restrictive to permissive. Looking into the future, the author concludes:

> Americans born after the 1960s thus represent the first American generation for whom the psychological release from juvenile celibacy occurred at puberty, rather than several years later, and it seems almost certain that this generation's attitude toward sex will consequently be quite different from that of its parents and grandparents. There is a distinct possibility that this generation will raise its own offspring in an atmosphere of genuine sexual permission.[99]

In the remainder of this section, our attention will be focused on socialization to sexuality in Western societies.

Adult sexual expression involves a complex combination of knowledge, attitudes, emotions, and body sensations that have been acquired and developed piecemeal over an extended period of time. These diverse elements begin to be introduced at birth. The infant's relationship with its parents involves many body experiences—nursing at the breast, being held, cuddled, and hugged, being diapered and bathed, being rocked. These experiences introduce the child to the sensuous aspects of life in an interpersonal context.[100] Parents and other adults do not usually view these early experiences as in any way connected to sexuality, but students of the subject seem to be in general agreement that the quality of these early experiences has some part in shaping later sexuality. Sociologists John Gagnon and William Simon, however, are skeptical about the importance of this early experience for later sexuality; we shall explain their view in a moment.

Some time during the first two years of life or so, the child discovers its own genitals with its own hands. He or she discovers that this part of the body yields a sensation that is different from that experienced elsewhere. During ages three to six, many children at some time or another play games in which they explore each other's bodies. A study of sixty teachers of preschool children in Bergen, Norway, for example, found that all of them had observed children playing doctor/nurse/patient or family-role games involving body exploration, genital manipulation, and "coitus training." Much of the play occurred in secluded areas of the kindergarten, where children undressed and explored each other. The teacher left the children alone unless they were inserting fingers or objects into the anus or vagina or pressuring an unwilling child to join in.[101]

The child's touching of its own genitals and its exploration of other children's in play are widely perceived by parents, teachers, and child development experts alike as early expressions of sexual drives. Self-manipulation is perceived as "masturbation" and sex play in young children is, in this society, regarded as "precocious sexuality"; both are usually discouraged or sharply prohibited. In fact, 40 percent of the Norwegian teachers felt that they ought to react negatively to the sexual behavior of the children because they thought the parents expected them to, although 98 percent of the teachers said it was natural for the children to exhibit sexual behavior.

Sociologists John Gagnon and William Simon have emphasized the importance of adult labeling activities in defining what is sexual. They take issue with Freud's view that the human infant and child behave in ways that are intrinsically sexual and that are thus continuous with later sexuality. They argue to the contrary:

> For the infant touching his penis, the activity cannot be sexual in the same sense as adult masturbation but is merely a diffusely pleasurable activity, like many other activities. Only through maturing and learning these adult labels for his experience and activity can the child come to masturbate in the adult sense of that word. . . . The naive external observer of this behavior often imputes to the child the complex set of motivational states that are generally associated (often wrongly) with physically homologous adult activities. . . . In general, it is possible that much of the power of sexuality may be a function of the fact that it has been defined as powerful or dangerous. . . . Thus it does not necessarily follow that the untrained infant or child will respond as powerfully or as complexly to his own seemingly sexual behavior as an adult observer.[102]

Gagnon and Simon are correct in emphasizing the importance of the adult definition of the situation. The adult who comes upon a child touching its own or another's genitals may become upset and indeed give more importance to the activity than the child does, and the adult reaction may lead to bewilderment, fear, or guilt on the part of the child. An adult who says or does nothing in this situation, allowing it to proceed until the child terminates it, implicitly defines the situation as permissible, and the child's reaction is less likely to be as bewildered, fearful, or guilty.

However, Gagnon and Simon seem to exaggerate the importance of the adult definition of the situation. Few would claim that the infant's touching his penis is masturbation in the adult sense of the word. But it is not necessary to prove that infant/child sexual activity is *the same* as adult in order to indicate that there is a connection between earlier experience and later. Their argument suggests an "oversocialized view of man." Consider this analogy. A young child may be physically beaten or sexually assaulted and experience considerable pain without a cognitive grasp of what a beating or sexual attack is. Because the child cannot yet label such experiences and may not actually *know* until some years later that it was abused, it does not follow that the abuse has no continued and lasting impact. In the same way, the feelings that come with exploring and touching one's genitals need not be specifically labeled as such by concepts and a vocabulary in order to be distinctively experienced and incorporated into a continuing sexual development.

Despite their possibly exaggerated reliance on labeling as the major factor in creating sexuality—so that biological sex drive is considered not very significant—these authors provide some useful observations and analyses of the labeling process and how it functions in socialization to sexuality. An important point is that quite commonly, adults do discover children engaged in what the adults call sex play and they define the behavior not in sexual terms but in moral terms ("dirty," "bad," "good boys and girls don't"). These judgments contribute to the child's developing feelings about the activities he or she was engaged in. But the adults usually do not explain why they disapprove of what the children have been doing. The result is that the children have some experiences that have been judged as bad but for which they have not been provided a vocabulary or cognitive understanding.

During the same earlier years, children are learning some words that have a sexual meaning to adults but not yet clearly so to children, who may, however, learn that the words are not "nice." Thus, in the Norwegian study, all the teachers reported children using words pertaining to sex organs, sex acts, and elimination in three different ways: (1) to exchange information among themselves; (2) to provoke adults; (3) to insult another child. Only the first of these is part of socialization to sexuality in the precise sense, although the use of vulgar sexual terms to provoke or insult persists in adult life.

Thus, in early or middle childhood (ages three to nine),

> The child possesses two tapes (to use the computer metaphor), one containing experiences, judged in certain ways; the other, words without experiences. His dilemma is to sort and merge them, attaching the proper words to the proper acts. The possession of words, experiences, and judgments, all unassembled, leaves the young child without a vocabulary with which to describe his emerging physical or psychic experiences.[103]

In our discussion of the peer group, we referred to its importance in sex education; studies of later childhood masturbation offer a specific illustration. Such studies show that between 56 percent and 85 percent of prepubescent boys (up to age thirteen) have masturbated, but no more than about 30 percent of prepubescent girls have.[104] There appear to be fairly pronounced sex differences in the social organization of masturbation. Girls tend to masturbate alone; boys often gather in groups. Boys tease about it; girls take it more seriously. Girls may exchange information with individual friends based on reading about sex; boys exchange information in peer groups. The implication is that girls are more likely to read about sex, boys to talk about it. In these groups, older boys sometimes correct—or add to— misunderstanding about sexuality among the younger, and they may discuss masturbation techniques with them. Giving and receiving sexual information in the group seems to reduce guilt and anxiety among the group members who, by exhibiting and playing with their penises in the secret but group setting, are usually violating earlier norms of modesty and self-restraint.[105]

In addition to masturbatory experiences as a component of socialization, children's sex play includes both heterosexual and homosexual experiences. About 70 percent of boys and about 30 percent of girls have engaged in some heterosexual play by age thirteen. About 40 percent of boys and about 30 percent of girls have engaged in some homosexual play by age thirteen. There are no data on the frequency of such play; individual children vary greatly, and it appears that some probably did no more than mutually expose genitals on a single occasion.

In these experiences, children may be learning about sensations and about the outsides of bodies, but not much about sexuality as reproduction. As Gagnon and Simon state:

> There is nothing in this peer-peer learning process which suggests that the children have any integrated body of sexual knowledge. The young boy with experience in sex play may not associate his first-hand knowledge of the anatomical differences between boys and girls with the fact that babies grow inside of his mother, and the biological facts of fertilization may never dawn on him at all. . . . It would seem safe to speculate that, except for menstruation, females are unlikely to have learned the facts in any more logical or coherent order. In the case of females, it is clear that the mother may often play a more decisive role because it is more appropriate that she inform her daughter of the dangers of sexuality and the possibility of menstruation. This is certainly not always the case since a fair number of females report that they first learned of menstruation when it occurred for them the first time.[106]

The Thorne/Luria study mentioned above contributes additional information and understanding about the role of peer groups in socialization to sexuality. Boys and girls develop somewhat distinct styles of interaction and even gender-differentiated subcultures. Although girls as well as boys know dirty words, boys are more likely to flaunt them in public and risk punishment. Boys get visibly excited when they break rules together. As Thorne and Luria put it, "Sports, dirty words, and testing the limits are part of what boys teach boys how to do. The assumption seems to be: dirty words, sports interest and knowledge, and transgression of politeness are closely connected."[107] Exploration of sexuality takes one form in the sharing, by fifth- and sixth-grade boys, of soft-core pornographic magazines such as *Playboy* and *Penthouse.*

The team sports and other group game activities, the use of dirty words in open exchanges that bring disapproval from teachers, the various kinds of rule-breaking and testing the patience of adults, the sharing and discussing of magazines with explicit sexual focus, all help to create a specifically masculine world. This includes particular care in avoiding connotations of homosexuality. By the fourth grade boys have begun to use homophobic labels such as "fag" or "queer" as terms of insult. By this age, too, or a bit later, they have begun to avoid physical contacts that are directly expressive of tenderness. Whereas kindergarten and first-grade boys touch each other easily, put an arm around another boy's shoulder, hug each other and hold hands, by the fourth or fifth grades such gestures are largely unacceptable and are replaced by poking, shoving, and mock gestures of violence.

The girls' subculture, Thorne and Luria find, is quite different. Girls tend to associate in pairs (dyads) as best friends, sometimes in a threesome (triad), rather than in larger groups as boys do. They talk about each other in terms of who is "nice" and who is "mean." As Lever also found, their activity is more often in the form of turn-taking than group competition. Sometimes girls stroke or comb their friends' hair. Further,

> Best friends monitor one another's emotions. They share secrets and become mutually vulnerable through self-disclosure, with an implicit demand that the expression of one's inadequacy will induce the friend to disclose a related inadequacy. In contrast, disclosure of weakness among boys is far more likely to be exposed to others through joking or horsing around.[108]

By the fifth and sixth grades, boys and girls begin to engage in certain kinds of ritual contact across the boundaries that demarcate their separate worlds. Taking up a point made by Gagnon and Simon, Thorne and Luria point out that

> Girls emphasize and learn about the emotional and romantic before the explicitly sexual. The sequence for boys is the reverse; commitment to sexual acts precedes commitment to emotion-laden, intimate relationships and the rhetoric of romantic love. Dating and courtship, Gagnon and Simon suggest, are processes in which each sex teaches the other what each wants and expects. The exchange, as they point out, does not always go smoothly. . . .[109]

During the elementary-school years, well before any dating, children prepare for the more active heterosexual interest that is to emerge in adolescence. "Invasions" to disrupt the play of the other sex group is one ritual. Another is threats of kissing. Although boys make such threats, Thorne and Luria report that girls more often use them to tease boys and make them run away.

Another form of teasing is for one child to say of another that he or she is "goin' with" or "has a crush on" someone of the opposite sex. One other kind of ritual deals with pollution; children use the idea that a person or group has "germs" or "cooties." Boys seem to attribute such contamination to girls more often than girls attribute it to boys. Games are played in which a child may touch another and yell "You've got cooties."

The general significance of these rituals and games is summarized by Thorne and Luria in these words:

> Gender-marked rituals of teasing, chasing, and pollution heighten the boundaries between boys and girls. They also convey assumptions which get worked into later sexual scripts: (1) that girls and boys are members of distinctive, opposing, and sometimes antagonistic groups; (2) that cross-gender contact is potentially sexual and contaminating, fraught with both pleasure and danger; and (3) that girls are more sexually-defined (and polluting) than boys.[110]

Of course, the worlds of boys and girls are not completely separate. Barrie Thorne in another report observes that some situations allow for interaction between boys and girls without strain—for example, when they are involved in absorbing tasks such as creating a radio show; or when principles of grouping other than gender, such as reading ability, are explicitly invoked; or when they are in less public and crowded settings and do not run the risk of being teased. Cross-sex contact can most readily be legitimated when adults take the responsibility for organizing the mixed-sex encounters.[111] However, the more common segregated activities and the sexual meanings in the teasing and ritualized heterosexual play do tend to maintain gender divisions, one result being that nonsexualized friendships between girls and boys are not easily achieved or maintained during this period of life.

There has always been strong opposition to sex education in the schools in the United States. A long-time educator in the sex education field, Lester Kirkendall, has explained this opposition as due to three main factors: (1) A popular fear that unbridled hedonism would be encouraged; (2) a belief that the innocence of children is violated by discussions of sexuality; and (3) a belief that sex education should be given in the home, not in the school.[112] However, sex education in the home is not yet a taken-for-granted aspect of socialization. A study in 1978 found that 20 percent of mothers of seventh-grade girls had never told their daughters about menstruation; 50 percent had not discussed the male's role in intercourse and reproduction; and 68 percent had not talked about birth control. Another study done in the late 1970s, based on questioning of 1,400 parents of three- to eleven-year-old children, showed that they "were generally not talking very much at all about sex-related topics." The results of the study suggest that the notion of a "father-son talk about the facts of life" is largely a myth. Both boys and girls directed most of their questions to their mothers. And parents largely had the attitude that once a topic was discussed with a child, it never needed to be brought up again.[113]

Children's curiosity is not satisfied by such brief consideration of the subject. Elementary-school teacher Raphaela Best writes of a school she observed:

> So, while the adults hemmed and hawed, the children went about learning and experimenting on their own, careful to protect the frightened adult world from the facts of life. They indulged the adult world's need for ignorance, all the while garnering what they could from whatever source they could to expand on their personal observations. They found ways to circumvent adult scrutiny and allay suspicion. . . . Under a multitude of pretexts they felt and touched one another without arousing the suspicion of watchful adults.[114]

One very important reason why children in our society receive a low amount of sexual information from parents, teachers, and other official agents of socialization is probably that all three major religious traditions in Western society have either repressive or restrictive sexual values. Judaism confines erotic behavior to legalized marriage. Catholicism sees erotic feelings and activity as dangerous and sinful; the only legitimate sexual expression is that aimed at procreation. Protestantism shares with Catholicism a general fear of sexual experience, although some Protestant denominations have developed programs on sexuality for junior and senior high school students.[115]

Despite the continuing restrictiveness among some socialization agents, the developing permissiveness that Currier referred to can also be noted. This may be seen by comparing sexual messages in public environments in our society with those in

China, a still more restrictive society, as Florence Ladd has done. She states, "In comparison to the Chinese, people in the United States in the 1970s present a wide range of public behavior and signs that express an intention to communicate information about sexuality. The ideologies, styles, and conventions of the United States and the People's Republic of China are contrasting patterns."[116] She mentions such public "messages" found in the U.S. (but not in China) as adult entertainment places, which may communicate to children that "there is an illicit dimension of sexuality that lacks candor and clarity." In the sexually oriented magazines on newsstands, "the images are memorable and powerful." Sexual graffiti are widespread and communicate various levels of information, "some for the general reader with the skills and comprehension of a second-grader" and some "elaborated in complex, esoteric statements." Ladd also comments that the separation and identification of toilets by sex in public places must communicate something: "Children know that at home family members and guests . . . of both sexes use the same toilets. The discerning five- or six-year-old who begins to distinguish between public and private toilet conventions must conclude that there is an element of sexual mistrust between females and males who are strangers."[117] Overall, she concludes:

> The frequency of environmental messages pertaining to sexuality is determined by social conventions and political policies. The limited range of publicly explicit messages in the People's Republic of China, in the Islamic world, and in other societies leads to speculation about the behavioral and attitudinal consequences of growing up in a society where public statements about sexuality are infrequent and rarely explicit.[118]

To which it is necessary to add that we don't yet know much about the consequences of growing up in a society where public statements about sexuality are fairly explicit and fairly frequent, while private messages to children remain inexplicit and infrequent.

The newest and most striking development in recent years in sexuality has been the spread of AIDS, the acquired immune deficiency syndrome. This disease, unknown until about 1980, has spread rapidly throughout the world, primarily through sexual contact but also through the use of unclean needles and blood transfusions, with over 80,000 cases reported worldwide by the spring of 1988 and with World Health Organization estimates of 500,000 to 3 million by 1992. As yet there is no cure or vaccination against the disease, and government health authorities and educators have been desperately concerned with the need to pass on to schoolchildren and others information on how best to prevent spreading the disease. Their suggestions, if followed, could point to a somewhat less permissive society.

From the perspective of socialization, the concern about AIDS goes beyond strict matters of sexuality and physical health. Dr. Jonathan Mann, director of the World Health Organization's special program for AIDS, speaks of a "rising wave of stigmatization" against those who are thought to transmit the disease—in Asia, against Westerners; in Europe, against Africans; and elsewhere, against homosexuals, prostitutes, and even hemophiliacs and others who have been infected by blood transfusions.[119] Such fears, anxieties, and hostilities show more than ever that sexuality cannot be kept apart from social relationships, ideologies, and the socialization of children.

GENDER ROLES AND IDENTITIES

Boys and girls are born into a society that expects them to become different kinds of people and to occupy different statuses because they are either male or female. As Betty Yorburg states, "In all societies, even those in which sex-typing is not extreme, a person's basic status is that of male or female, and this basic status determines what other statuses the person can or cannot have."[120] In our society many social institutions have been organized on the assumption that girls would grow up to become mothers and homemakers and boys would grow up to become economic providers. Some women have always departed from this assumption and have joined the labor force, and increasing numbers are doing so, as we have pointed out in Chapter 5. To a great degree, the work aspirations of girls and boys have been directed toward different occupations, which differ not only in content but also in that men's have higher prestige.

The fact that boys and girls are prepared for distinctive statuses and social roles means that they also tend to develop distinctive masculine and feminine identities. While there are different analyses of how and why these identities differ, there is widespread agreement that the masculine identity in our society emphasizes an orientation toward achievement, restraint in emotional expression, and a great deal of self-reliance.[121] The female identity emphasizes being helpful and supportive of children, men, bosses—what sociologist Jessie Bernard has called "the all-pervading function—stroking."[122] It appears that some girls and women who develop an identity that emphasizes independence and achievement rather than that of pleasing and comforting others often fear that they have formed an inappropriate identity. According to some research, even talented girls and women develop a "wish to fail" or a "fear of success" as a way of preserving a more traditional feminine identity,[123] although other research points to similar levels of success-avoidance among boys and men.[124] One line of research that seems to give some support to "success-avoidance" as a motive is that girls lose their early superiority over boys in reading ability, so that by the sixth grade boys tend to be equal. Also, whereas there have been no differences between the sexes in mathematical performance during the elementary school years, boys tend to perform significantly better than girls in mathematics during the high school years.[125] A review of numerous studies of sex differences in mathematics also indicates that girls are less likely than boys to take advanced courses in math because they less often consider math as useful for their career interests and aspirations. Math is widely seen as a masculine domain. Such differences between boys and girls have been reported as early as the seventh grade. Even mathematically talented girls, in order to maintain popularity and avoid peer rejection for sex-role deviance,[126] sometimes do not pursue advanced courses. Socialization into a feminine identity thus becomes, for some girls, a basis for closing out later socialization opportunities, even though the result is that they do not develop a talent that is socially valued when found in males.

The differences in masculine and feminine identities are manifested not only with regard to the ways in which males and females participate in schools, occupations, and other organized institutional settings. They are also manifested in behaviors that are relatively independent of specific organizational settings. For example, anthropologist Ray L. Birdwhistell has found that in several societies, including American, there are distinctive masculine and feminine ways of moving. These differ somewhat from one society to another, but each society distinguishes masculine and feminine forms of body movement.[127]

Differences between the sexes in the use of language is a growing area of research investigation. Several studies show that women's speech is more "correct," "proper," and polite than men's speech. Women do not swear as much as men, are less likely to use slang, and are more likely to use correct pronunciation (for example saying *-ing* rather than *-in'* at the end of a word). These differences have been found consistently in many settings—among children in a New England village; among both blacks and whites in Detroit and in North Carolina; in Chicago and New York City; in Norwich, England; and in Norway. Women's use of the higher prestige forms of language has often been placed in the context of male dominance and explained as an expression of the greater care that subordinate persons must exercise; or as an effort to compensate for their subordination by using language to indicate higher status; or as due to women's need to use appearances as indicators of morality or prestige, since they lack(ed) occupational status. The Norwich study, carried out by sociolinguist Peter Trudgill, suggests that

> working-class, nonstandard speech has positive connotations for male speakers of all social classes. On the one hand, males expressed the greater value attached to more correct forms (e.g., making comments such as "I talk horrible"), but on the other hand, they indicated in various ways that they were favorably disposed to nonstandard speech, which has strong connotations of masculinity, and may signal male solidarity.[128]

The findings concerning body movement and language usage point to some interesting questions that lie beyond the issue of dominance and subordination. While the pervasiveness of male dominance has been amply documented, the growing tendency to interpret all aspects of male and female sex roles and masculine and feminine identities as nothing more than manifestations of discrimination or power relationships, or both, rests on an apparent assumption that there is nothing sexual in the relations between the sexes, or, alternatively, that sexuality is only another form of power.[129] These interpretations do not inquire into the nature of sexuality and how it might figure in sex differences. For example, the fact that there are characteristic masculine and feminine ways of moving in each society, but that these characteristic differences vary from one society to another, suggests the possibility that both men and women *want* to create distinctions of masculinity and femininity. If this is so, then it is by no means certain that such differences would disappear if women were to gain authority and power fully equal to that of men. Only by adopting "an oversocialized view" of human functioning is it possible to interpret masculinity and femininity as entirely imposed from without. Such a view fails to take account of the gratifications that come from differences and the sources of separateness and autonomy within each person—his or her experience of bodily sensations; and thoughts, fantasies, and speculations about oneself and the world outside oneself. Such subjective experiences may be shared and may become the basis of distinctive conceptions of masculinity and femininity and of male and female sex roles; and they may, of course, change in the course of history. At any given time more than one conception of masculinity and femininity is current and available in a diverse and heterogeneous society.[130] In sum, the analyses of sex roles and sex identities in terms of power make clear that these phenomena can be shaped by power, but they do not demonstrate that the social organization of the sexes can be reduced to nothing but a power relationship.

The Special Case of Mothering

The fact that women have primary responsibility for the care and nurturance of infants and children is widely regarded as "natural," something that is biologically determined and part of a sequence that follows upon childbearing and lactation. But while the anatomy and physiology of women unmistakably restrict childbearing and lactation to the female sex, no biological basis for mothering—the activities of caring, nurturing, primary socializing—can be demonstrated. Challenging the widely held belief that mothering is natural for women, Nancy Chodorow asks, "Why is the person who routinely does all those activities that go into parenting not a man?"[131] Mothering is not only a set of specific activities but also a diffuse, affective, interpersonal involvement in a relationship. How does it happen, she asks, that women are the ones who are universally and normally expected to undertake that relationship?

Because mothering is more than a specific set of activities, Chodorow argues that it cannot be explained entirely as due to the more obvious aspects of socialization. Role training (giving girls dolls to play with), identification (giving her the opportunity to imitate a mother), and male enforcement of mothering (for example, by mass media that portray women mostly as mothers, or by public policies that make it difficult for women to do anything but become mothers) may contribute to the result; but these alone cannot account for "the tenacity of self-definition, self-concept, and psychological need to maintain aspects of traditional roles which continue even in the face of ideological shifts, counterinstruction, and the lessening of masculine coercion which the women's movement has produced."

The answer lies, in her analysis, in those aspects of the early socialization process that tend to create different personalities in girls as distinguished from boys. Parenting requires certain capacities in relating to infants and young children, and those capacities are generally fostered in girls but not in boys. Early social relations in the family are different for boys and for girls in crucial ways and tend to lead to different ways of relating to people generally, as well as to infants specifically.

A mother tends to experience a sense of oneness with her infant. But because a mother is of the same sex as a daughter, that sense of oneness is likely to be stronger and last longer than would be the case with a son. A mother tends to experience a son as a male opposite, as differentiated from her. Because the mother tends to foster or push this differentiation, the male child tends to become a more clearly separate person at an earlier age than the female. The longer-continuing sense of oneness that girls experience contributes to a lifelong greater capacity for entering into diffuse relationships, that is, relationships that are not defined by specific role obligations but are relationships in which the person has a good level of empathy for what another person (infant, child, or adult) needs and can respond to those needs. As a result of this and other family processes,

> growing girls come to define and experience themselves as continuous with others; . . . boys come to define themselves as more separate and distinct. . . . The basic feminine sense of self is connected to the

world, the basic masculine sense of self is separate. . . . Masculine
personality, then, comes to be defined more in terms of denial of
relation and connection (and denial of femininity), whereas feminine
personality tends to include a fundamental definition of self in relationship. Thus, relational abilities and preoccupations have been
extended in women's development and curtailed in men's.[132]

Boys and girls alike receive their basic parenting from a
woman, the mother. This common experience provides both
sexes with a basis for being parental when they grow up. But they
do not grow up to become equally involved in parenting. In
addition to girls defining themselves in terms of relationships
much more than boys do, boys' efforts to develop their masculinity lead them to turn away from "womanish" ways:

> Masculinity becomes an issue in a way that femininity does not.
> . . . Masculinity becomes an issue as a direct result of a boy's experi-
> ence of himself in his family, as a result of his being parented by a
> woman. For children of both genders, mothers represent regression
> and lack of autonomy. A boy associates these issues with his gender
> identification as well. Dependence on his mother, attachment to her,
> and identification with her represent that which is not masculine; a
> boy must reject dependence and deny attachment and identification.
> Masculine gender role training becomes much more rigid than femi-
> nine. A boy represses those qualities he takes to be feminine inside
> himself, and rejects and devalues women and whatever he considers
> to be feminine in the social world.[133]

Chodorow has attempted to show how mothering reproduces
itself, that is, how basic primary-care parenting is transmitted
from woman to daughter, almost never from woman to son. In
fact, a recent study by LaRossa and LaRossa of families in which
men do engage in some primary-care parenting found that when
fathers do take over these activities they define what they are
doing as "helping their wives," not as "sharing the child-
care."[134] They do not consider that they have an equal responsibility (and they do not put an equal amount of time into it).
Chodorow believes that men could, despite the deep personality
level of sexual (or gender) identity, become equally responsible
and participant with women in primary parenting. She believes
that the socialization to mothering is the process which maintains
male dominance. The social organization of parenting produces

sexual inequality. Equal parenting would, she believes, be better for children and for adult men and women. She sees some possibility that such a change could occur. Further, she believes that only when men have equal responsibility with women for primary parental care of infants will it be possible to have general social equality between the sexes.

EGALITARIAN IDEOLOGIES AND THE FUTURE

The differential socialization of boys and girls reflects the fact that adults anticipate that the children of each sex will, when they reach adulthood, occupy statuses that are different. While some advanced thinkers, as long as 200 years ago, considered that these statuses were unequal as well as different, it is only in modern times that concerted efforts have been made consciously to achieve equality of status for the two sexes. In concluding this chapter, we shall turn attention briefly to some of these efforts.

As we indicated above, Sweden since 1962 has sought to offer girls and boys equal access to all educational opportunities. The school curriculum provides that students, during their eighth-grade year, will have a three-week period of practical occupational experience in settings of their own choice. A study in one middle-sized Swedish town during the 1965–1966 school year revealed that the most frequently chosen placements by the boys were with auto mechanics, electricians, bakers, laboratory assistants, photographers, IBM data machine operators, draftsmen, salesmen, and jobs with the railroad, air force, and with the local military regiment. The girls chose placements with primary school teachers, kindergarten teachers, child nurses, saleswomen, hairdressers, office girls, nursing assistants, store decorators, travel bureau assistants, and in animal care. In Sweden as a whole for 1965 and 1966, the most popular work areas selected by girls were in public health and nursing. Swedish sociologist Rita Liljestrom notes that:

> The social changes in the Scandinavian countries up to the present time have meant, in effect, that a legal and formal equality has not been met by a corresponding equalization of roles. In spite of the

fact that many *outward* obstacles have been removed, there remain obstacles that are partly of another type having to do with deeply-rooted ideas, role expectations, role ideals, values, and habits among, for example, employers, work supervisors, fellow workers, husbands, and, not least, among women themselves.[135]

It would appear from this evidence that the socialization Swedish boys and girls received before becoming eighth-graders influenced them to select typically sex-stereotyped vocational settings despite the opportunity to make nonstereotyped choices.

The Soviet Union has long encouraged women to participate in the economic activity of the country. As two specialists in Soviet studies report:

> There is little doubt, from a perusal of the Soviet sources, that the woman who deliberately chooses to become a housewife and mother and to restrict her activities to husband, children and hearth is not considered a "complete" Soviet woman because she is not participating fully in the building of the new society and because her position and "dependence" are too strongly reminiscent of the bourgeois housewife of a former stigmatized past. . . . The woman who chooses to participate and earn her independence on the basis of her occupational and other achievements is likely to be defined as exemplary, *provided* she does not totally neglect her other functions.[136]

But despite the fact that the Soviet Union lost great numbers of men during World War II, so that in 1959, fourteen years after the war ended, women constituted 55 percent of the population, women have not attained occupational equality with men. "While women are engaged in practically all types of work, they are underrepresented in the occupations that embody directive, managerial, decision-making and executive functions, and they tend to be overrepresented in the subordinate and junior positions and in the menial jobs."[137]

A third example is the Israeli kibbutz (plural: kibbutzim). These are settlements that were established, mostly between 1910 and the late 1940s, under the inspiration of socialist ideology, by Jews from eastern Europe and the Middle East who made a determined effort to establish a society of equals. All property was held in common (although today there is private ownership of small personal items). Emancipation of women was (and is) a prominent ideal. Collective rearing of children from birth, and other collective institutions, freed women from traditional household confinement, and they took their place as full-time workers. Efforts were made to abolish all sex distinctions in role and identity that were not directly related to reproduction. The educational system, for example, minimizes sex distinctions: "There is . . . little evidence of direct sex-role instruction in Kibbutz childhood . . . a deemphasis of any juxtaposition of masculinity and femininity are part of the education process in the Kibbutz."[138] But the effort to minimize sex-role differences has not worked out as anticipated. Men have ended up in most of the jobs in agriculture, management, and other income-producing activities, while women predominate in child care, nursing, clothes supply store work, and kitchen work. One author writes: "many women began to have second thoughts about their 'liberation' from the household, especially from the care of their children. The need to be more with their children has been asserting itself very strongly among the mothers who were themselves born outside the Kibbutz as well as among those *sabras* born and reared in the Kibbutzim."[139]

The reactions of the women themselves to this division of labor and strengthening of the kibbutz family are not consistent. A study of one kibbutz reports that young women are dissatisfied and unhappy about their life and welfare.[140] A detailed report of women in another kibbutz notes that the question of their status as women rarely bothers them and that on the whole they are satisfied and feel a strong sense of personal self-fulfillment.[141] But whatever the reactions of the women themselves, the original goal of a society without significant social distinctions by sex has not come to pass.[142]

In the United States today, and somewhat less prominently in other countries, a new effort is under way to change the prevailing conceptions of masculinity and femininity, as well as the prevailing distributions of men and women in various occupations and the disparity between men and women in authority and status. These new efforts are based on the view that equality between the sexes cannot be achieved so long as stereotypical conceptions of masculinity and femininity divide humankind into two kinds of beings based on their morphological sex. Perhaps the best-known modern statement of this view was made by sociologist Alice S. Rossi:

> we need to reassert the claim to sex equality and to search for the means by which it can be achieved. By sex equality I mean a socially androgynous conception of the roles of men and women, in which they are equal and similar in such spheres as intellectual, artistic, political and occupational interests and participation, complementary only in those spheres dictated by physiological differences between the sexes. This assumes the traditional conceptions of masculine and feminine are inappropriate to the kind of world we can live in in the second half of the twentieth century. An androgynous conception of sex role means that each sex will cultivate some of the characteristics usually associated with the other in traditional sex role definitions. This means that tenderness and expressiveness should be cultivated in boys and socially approved in men, so that a male of any age in our society would be psychologically and socially free to express these qualities in his social relationships. It means that achievement need, workmanship and constructive aggression should be cultivated in girls and approved in women so that a female of any age would be similarly free to express these qualities in her social relationships. This is one of the points of contrast with the feminist goal of an earlier day: rather than a one-sided plea for women to adapt a masculine stance in the world, this definition of sex equality stresses the enlargement of the common ground on which men and women base their lives together by changing the social definitions of approved characteristics and behavior for both sexes.[143]

In a more recent statement of her position, Rossi recognizes the influence of sex hormones and other biological factors, but affirms that, through compensatory learning, we can encourage more androgyny in children. She writes:

> . . . the socially desirable attributes of both sexes can be acquired by each sex only if we properly identify their sources in both biology and culture. Biological predispositions make certain things easier for one sex to learn than the other; knowing this in advance could permit a specification of how to provide compensatory training for each sex, in rearing children within families, in teaching children in schools, or in training adults on the job.[144]

The crucial question then becomes: Could such a program be successfully established? In Sweden, the Soviet Union, and the

Israeli kibbutz where ambitious programs have been set up to rectify inequality, the results, we have observed, are limited, and nowhere, for example, do we find child care defined as a major male occupation.

A truly androgynous concept of sex roles would contemplate all occupations equally open to and perhaps equally chosen by both sexes. Clearly this is hard to contemplate and harder to achieve. Sumner, in his classic *Folkways,* said, "The mores can make anything right." Sociologist Robert E. Park agreed but added, "But they have a harder time making some things right than others."[145] The evidence seems to indicate that even drastic changes in social organization and socialization cannot readily *reduce inequality* between the sexes let alone *attain equality.* Revolutionary societies that succeed in drastically altering many prerevolutionary institutions seem not to succeed in equally drastically altering sex roles. This failure cannot be clearly attributed to hormonal differences between the sexes; the available evidence cannot be stretched to justify this conclusion. It is possible to argue that the failure lies in the "incorrigible" beliefs developed in an earlier time and carried over into revolutionary societies. This argument is plausible enough as far as it goes, but it does not explain why beliefs about sex roles should be more resistant to change than beliefs about other social institutions. At the present time, there is no explanation that is adequately supported by convincing evidence.

The most conservative among sociologists and the most radical among them agree that men have been dominant in virtually all, if not all, societies. Feminists argue that the fact of male dominance is a long-enduring injustice, one that can and should be brought to an end. Others affirm that the fact itself requires explanation; it has been an enduring fact that cannot be wished away. Many would go on to add that the fact has been used to create injustices that cannot be defended. Socialization processes have certainly helped to strengthen—indeed help create—societal beliefs that males and females are different, and these processes continue to play a significant part in preparing males and females for different identities and different patterns of social participation. There is sharp disagreement, however, on the outer limits of possible change in sex-role socialization. Certainly, the total pattern of sex-differentiated behavior to be found in one particular society at one particular period cannot be taken as evidence of a biologically based "natural" difference between the sexes. There are too many variations among societies, and too many changes in the history of our own society, to justify such a view. Throughout all these changes and variations, however, persists the irreducible fact of absolute difference between the sexes in reproductive role. The difference can be magnified or minimized in a society, but it cannot be abolished. But the persistence of difference does not necessarily predict the persistence of inequality.

CHAPTER 7

Socialization in Later Life

Socialization continues throughout life. After childhood one continues to enter new groups, to attain new statuses, to learn new roles and thereby to elaborate one's ways of participating in society. A freshman is socialized into the patterns of a college, an immigrant into the life of a new country, a recruit into the army, a new resident into a suburb, a medical student into the profession of medicine, a new patient into a hospital ward, and a bride into a life of marriage.

In some respects later socialization is continuous with that of childhood, in other respects it is discontinuous.[1] Let us first note some continuous aspects. In the home, at school, with the peer group, and through the mass media children acquire their "native language." They learn to speak, to read, and to write. Having developed this foundation in early socialization, they later acquire the capacity to preach sermons or read novels or write love letters, shopping lists, legal briefs, newspaper articles, or sales reports. They thus learn to use their native language in new and specialized ways, consonant with the particular adult statuses they attain and the expectations of their adult roles. Further, the general symbolic capacities that children begin to develop in infancy as they begin to acquire their human nature eventuate in their being able also to use special nonverbal symbol systems. They can learn to read music or blueprints or computer printouts—or, for that matter, tea leaves, smoke signals, or Tarot cards.

Children's symbolic capacities are not merely cognitive in nature. These capacities combine with sentiments in particular ways so that children can come to cherish people with whom they have never actually interacted. Thus popes, presidents, prime ministers, and other leaders, in the sense that they represent causes and ideals to which someone is committed, also represent aspects of that person's self. They are symbols of oneself (or parts of oneself) that strengthen the attachment to nation, church, political party, or social movement. This ability to so utilize others as symbols does not arise for the first time in adulthood. It is essentially a development from and a refinement of a capacity that first showed itself when the child was attracted to role models outside the family. The child's imagining himself or herself as police officer, heroic rescuer, or star athlete are the precursors.

Other examples of continuity readily come to mind. In interacting with and learning to talk in a family, a child learns from babyhood to take turns. Such turn-taking in conversations and in numerous other relationships becomes a taken-for-granted characteristic of daily life. Also in the early games of childhood, children learn to pursue a goal within a framework of rules. Their later ability to play bridge, chess, or tennis, or even to behave as expected in a bureaucratized office, is built on earlier experiences with such games as Simon Says or hide-and-seek. The later rules are more elaborate, but the orientation to rules is a refinement of the childhood orientation.

Other basic elements of the adult socialization process are also similar to those in childhood. There are socializing agents who teach, serve as models, and invite participation. Through their ability to offer gratifications and deprivations they induce cooperation and learning, and they endeavor to prevent disruptive deviance. The persons being socialized, on their part, through observation, participation, and role-taking, learn and internalize new expectations and develop new self-conceptions.

The continuities in socialization from childhood to adulthood are significant because adulthood is rooted in childhood. But there is also reason to believe that childhood socialization sets limits to what may be accomplished through adult socialization, even though we are not yet able to define those limits with any precision.[2] The human organism has great plasticity, as we discussed in Chapter 2, but that plasticity is not infinite. For example, it would appear virtually impossible for a person brought up in a rural slum who never advanced past grade five to, at age twenty-five, prepare for and successfully follow a professional career, or for a Vietnamese refugee speaking little English to launch into a career of national politics. This degree of discontinuity between childhood and adult socialization seems insurmountable.

Although certain aspects and certain kinds of adult socialization presuppose continuity with childhood socialization, it is nevertheless equally true that adult socialization, even in the ordinary course of events, is often discontinuous from that of childhood. Before we turn to these aspects we must say something about the period between childhood and adulthood—adolescence.

SOCIALIZATION IN ADOLESCENCE

We cannot do full justice to the literature on adolescence in the brief space available. We shall therefore confine ourselves to a discussion framed generally by this book and this chapter, focusing on generations and the basic question of life cycle continuity. How does adolescence fit into the cycle?

We may begin by noting that the delineation of adolescence as a distinct period of life is not simply derived from observing the biological organism's maturation but is, like childhood, a social invention. Many societies do not identify a distinct period of life as adolescence, and even Western societies did not do so before industrialization. Frank Musgrove goes so far as to claim that:

> The adolescent was invented at the same time as the steam-engine. The principal architect of the latter was Watt in 1765, of the former Rousseau in 1762. Having invented the adolescent, society has been faced with two major problems: how and where to accommodate him in the social structure, and how to make his behaviour accord with the specifications.[3]

This author further argues that the creation of the concept of adolescence as a distinct period was accompanied by the development of a special psychology of adolescence that largely created its own subject matter. He is claiming that the phenomena associated with adolescence are, in effect, the result of a large self-fulfilling prophecy—that is, because people started believing that there was such a stage of life as adolescence, with distinctive characteristics and problems, and started treating adolescents with such expectations, they elicited the behavior they had come to expect. There seems little doubt that in a general sense Musgrove is substantially correct. If the people we now call teenagers were still allowed to marry, participate fully and actively in the labor force, and otherwise function as adults instead of being set off as a distinct age group and kept in school, socialization in adolescence would not loom as a topic of discussion. In the American colonies, until the Revolution, fourteen-year-old boys could serve as executors of wills; at sixteen they became men, paying taxes and serving in the militia. Marriages in the middle teens were common. The age at which a young person went to work depended upon the family's financial situation and the youth's own physical capacity.[4]

The exclusion of youth from adult employment statuses and roles in the United States was accomplished gradually over the period of about 150 years from the Revolution to the Great Depression, and it reflected various social and economic forces. During this period there was increasing recognition of youth as a special age group (whose upper age limit generally came to be legally defined as eighteen for some purposes, twenty-one for others), and there was a correspondingly increased awareness of "youth problems." This awareness accompanied the increasing tendency of adolescents to remain in school until graduating from high school, where they remain assembled in a distinctive institution rather than being dispersed in the labor force among people of diverse ages. As educational aspirations and expectations continue to increase, the period of adolescence tends to be prolonged, so that in the middle class, at least, adolescence is sometimes thought to last until graduation from college. The term "youth" is increasingly used to refer to the age period roughly spanning ages sixteen to twenty-four or so.[5]

Should adolescent socialization be regarded as fundamentally continuous or discontinuous with the preceding socialization of childhood and the succeeding socialization of adulthood? The argument has gone through several cycles of enunciation and refutation. The argument for discontinuity gained notable support from an influential paper by Talcott Parsons, first published in the early 1940s and widely disseminated during the 1950s as an interest in the sociology of adolescence spread.[6] In this essay Parsons introduced the term "youth culture," whose most notable characteristics he considered to be an emphasis on irresponsibility and pleasure seeking—exemplified by concern with "having a good time," heterosocial activities, and athletics—which he contrasted with the emphasis on responsibility in adulthood. Some evidence that this emphasis on discontinuity was exaggerated was presented by Frederick Elkin and William Westley.[7]

The argument in favor of discontinuity was reinvigorated during the 1960s with the publication of a study by James S. Coleman of ten widely varying high schools in Illinois.[8] Coleman starts with the assumption that adolescents constitute a small society of their own, one that "maintains only a few threads of connection with the outside adult society." By means of questionnaires administered to the several thousand boys and girls in these high schools, Coleman found that they placed much greater value on athletics and popularity than on academic performance and that intellectual values generally had little to do with popularity among peers (although there were variations among schools in the importance attributed to scholarship by the students). He found further evidence of the "irresponsibility" pattern noted by Parsons—for example, great interest in cars (and activities and paraphernalia related to cars). He found, in effect, that adolescents are socialized into a subculture, a special society of their own peers dominated by their own values. And since the schools are identified by Coleman as society's established agency for preparing adolescents to participate in the adult world, he argues that the activities and values of adolescents are discontinuous with, and in opposition to, the world of adults.

Although there is no doubt that adolescents are in the process of becoming more independent of their parents and, consequently, are more responsive to their peers than they were at younger ages, and although their interests and values may differ from those ostensibly emphasized by the high school, it does not follow that adolescent socialization is peer-dominated and little influenced by adult values and norms. In reviewing Coleman's study, Bennett Berger argues that most of the adolescent values and interests noted by Coleman are more accurately understood as derivative from adults. For example, high school athletics depend greatly upon support by parents and local booster organizations. Further, parents are concerned about popularity and prestige. Emphasizing the continuity of adolescent and adult values, Berger comments, "From Coleman's treatment of the *adolescent* 'subculture' one might think that cars and masculine prowess and feminine glamour and social activities and sex and dating and wearing the right clothes and being from the right family were concerns entirely alien to American adults."[9] He points out that athletics, extracurricular activities, and social affairs are sponsored by the schools and are considered to be training grounds for adult responsibilities. Berger thus argues that Coleman's data tend to support conclusions nearly opposite from those Coleman himself draws from them and that much of what takes place during adolescence may be regarded as a rehearsal for adulthood or *anticipatory socialization* rather than as evidence for a discontinuous interval.

In summary, as Marie Jahoda and Neil Warren have pointed out,[10] one can find evidence to "prove" the existence of a youth culture, if one wishes; or one can likewise find evidence to bear out the contention that the fundamental fact of adolescent socialization is its continuity with and preparation for adulthood. The argument depends upon the groups studied, the data selected, and the conceptual approach adopted. Whether a youth group is working or middle class or of a given national or ethnic group, or whether its primary activities are delinquent behavior, rock music, school achievement, or sports are all relevant in judging the functions it serves and the degree of continuity with adulthood.[11]

In recent years the emphasis among social researchers has largely been on a life-span or life-course perspective that lays more stress on the continuity of development. Adolescence, it is suggested, should not be viewed apart from a person's past and anticipated future. The perspective also stresses the complexity of development and the contribution of the various social science disciplines. Historically, for example, it is noted that adolescence always occurs in a particular social context, and whether or not it is experienced in a period of depression, wartime, or calm and prosperity makes a difference in the way the adolescent sees the world and relates to others.[12]

In line with this perspective, some observers in recent years have suggested that age distinctions are becoming more blurred and people of all ages are mingling more freely. Adolescence here, as we know it, is viewed more as a characteristic of a particular historical period that is drawing to a close. Historian John Gillis concludes his study of age relationships in England and

Germany from 1770 to the present with a chapter entitled "End of Adolescence: Youth in the 1950s and 1960s." He notes that parental control of middle-class adolescents has declined so that by the 1960s

> Freedoms previously associated with university-age youth were being rapidly appropriated by adolescents, who, having access to larger allowances and greater mobility made possible by the automobile, were gaining something of the autonomy they had lost a century or so before. . . . In effect, adolescence, while still recognized in medical texts and psychological guides, is losing its status as a separate stage of life among the very class with whom it has been previously associated.[13]

Appropriate to this analysis is the generally decreasing attention in the literature to "generation gaps." In the United States, an advisory panel to the president reviewed the history of age relationships and made numerous recommendations that, if implemented, would reduce both the sharp segregation of one age group from another (for example, junior high school students from high school students) and also segregation of youth from adults. The main thrust of the report is in the direction of more effective socialization for adult roles of responsibility, particularly adult work roles. The panel was chaired by James S. Coleman, and the report tends to emphasize the idea that there has been a discontinuity between adolescence and adulthood that should now be replaced by greater continuity. The report suggests that the time is ripe for a change in age relationships, and that adolescence is no longer particularly valuable as a distinctive period of life in a modern industrial society such as the United States.[14] Associated with this perspective in recent years—1985 was officially International Youth Year—is a movement focusing attention on the problems facing young people and initiatives to extend their political and economic rights.[15]

SOCIALIZATION IN ADULTHOOD

In writing on change versus continuity, Lonnie Sherrod and Orville Brim, Jr., state: "Research . . . shows that important growth changes can occur across the full life span. The consequences of early developmental experiences may be transformed again and again by later experiences, and the course of development may remain malleable into old age, even up to death."[16] There are several reasons why socialization does not terminate with childhood or even adolescence. One is that individuals enter into new statuses with new role expectations when they reach adulthood and they must learn how to function in them. Earlier socialization gives some preparation, but much of what one needs to know can only be learned when one is actually in the new situation. Thus, boys and girls receive considerable anticipatory socialization for marriage throughout their lives prior to marriage—by observing their own parents and other married couples, by talking about it with their peers, by vicariously experiencing various kinds of marriages portrayed in the mass media, and even by temporarily sharing living quarters. But it is only when they have made the commitment to marriage and are in the new socially recognized status that they adapt themselves to functioning completely as actual marriage partners.

A second reason is that many groups, statuses, and roles become known to us only after we have reached adulthood. This is particularly evident with regard to occupations. Only a relatively small number of occupations are known to children and young adolescents. As we noted earlier, the mass media portray a much smaller array of occupations than exists in the actual world, and this picture is only moderately amplified through the child's personal acquaintance and school learning. So, too, for parenthood. The anticipatory socialization of doll-playing, watching over younger siblings, or care of someone else's children can be only a partial training for the role of actual parenthood.

A third reason is that the person continues in adulthood to encounter people who become for him or her new significant others. Some of them may be one's own peers; others may be senior in age or social status or both; they may even be one's own children. Through encounters a woman or man may learn to value skiing, or drug taking, or working in community endeavors, or playing the stock market, or any of other innumerable ideas and activities.

Encounters with new significant others may occur in various ways. The mass media of communication provide one avenue. For example, during the 1930s and 1940s and even after—the era of "big stars"—film actresses became significant others to many moviegoers who copied their hairstyles and in other ways sought to model themselves after one or another "glamor girl." In the 1960s President John F. Kennedy in the United States and Prime Minister Pierre Trudeau in Canada, known through the media, especially television, were widely believed to have stimulated a heightened interest in politics. And in the early 1980s actress Jane Fonda, singer Olivia Newton-John, and others, through songs, films, radio, television, and books, helped influence innumerable women to take part in body building and physical fitness programs.

New significant others can be neighbors as well as distant figures. Moving into a new house results in new patterns of informal interaction, and new neighbors become important to each other as sources of mutual expectations.[17] The role of neighbor itself may have to be learned anew, especially for the person who previously lived in a big-city apartment and now becomes a homeowner. A norm of casual accessibility, rather than a norm of determined insularity, is likely to govern, and this may entail willingness to borrow and lend (lawn mowers and cups of sugar), as well as routine forms of cooperation, such as participating in a carpool or taking in the neighbors' mail when they are away on vacation.

One major consideration underlying all the reasons cited for the continuing importance of socialization in adult life is the fact that both maturation and previous socialization present new demands and new opportunities to the person. Generally speaking, childhood socialization endows the child with the capacities for participating in adult society in *some* ways. Adult socialization makes possible one's participation in *specific* ways, through participation in particular institutions of society. Following Erik Erikson, we may say that the period through adolescence ordinarily results in the establishment of the person's core identity. Although his or her identity will be further developed and modified (and, in certain extreme situations, such as battlefield fighting, imprisonment, religious conversion, or hospitalization for mental illness, drastically altered), the establishment of a core identity provides a kind of platform from which a person may *launch himself or herself* into further socialization. The importance of the establishment of a core identity is that it provides the person with the opportunities and the capacities for *choice,* and this is one of the fundamental distinctions between child and adult socialization (recognizing, of course, that external circumstances condition choice and that, at times, for example, during an economic depression, these circumstances can be quite limiting). When they reach biological sexual maturity, people may choose to lead celibate or active sexual lives. They may choose to marry or to remain single or to live in a commune; to become parents or not, to have few children or many. They may choose to pursue a college education or go to work as soon as they can find jobs. When they go to work, they may seek to work for a large bureaucratic enterprise or a smaller more personal organization; or they may remain relatively independent, as taxi drivers, traveling sales representatives, lawyers, or physicians. With all such choices, people are also choosing environments in which they will be further socialized, although they will have no more than a vague idea of what their later socialization experiences will be until they are actually enacting the choices they have made and interacting with others whose choices have brought them into mutual contact.

In a stable society or institution, fully socialized persons have both internalized the correct beliefs and display the appropriate behavior for their positions. But we know that socialization is not always fully successful. Irving Rosow, by distinguishing between beliefs and behavior and by asking whether an individual adopts both, neither, or just one of the two, classifies people into four types. The *socialized* person adopts both the values and the behavior of the positions into which he or she is being socialized, the *unsocialized* person adopts neither. In between are the *dilettante* who adopts the values and not the behavior and the *chameleon* who displays the expected behavior but does not subscribe to the values. The most suggestive distinction is between the socialized person and the chameleon since they are similar in behavior but different in their commitment to values. Rosow contends that the chameleon type of outcome to socialization, in which the person behaves contrary to what he really feels, is found in many different relationships:

> the stereotyped complaisance of many Negroes in traditional contacts with whites, in the orientation of prostitutes to clients, in the involuntary union member in a closed shop, in the married homo-

sexual, in the unskilled worker in the marginal labor market who has no occupational or organizational identity but fits tolerably into a diversity of work situations. It is also familiar in the typical adjustment of most draftees to military life, in the adaptation of lower ranks of large-scale organizations . . .[18]

Rosow then goes on to argue that "chameleon conformity may be the most common pattern in complex societies." In this view, full socialization is concentrated in a few areas of a person's life. Since people are not fully committed to the various positions they occupy and the groups to which they belong, their socialization types will differ with each of them, so that a person is "a chameleon in one, a dilettante in a second, and fully socialized in a third."

The Contexts of Adult Socialization

Important aspects of adult socialization take place in formally organized settings such as colleges and trade schools, work organizations, professional associations, and the military services. There are also special settings—such as reformatories and mental hospitals—for those whose earlier socialization comes to be adjudged so seriously faulty that their behavior is deemed to fall outside the range of socially accepted outcomes of socialization.

Stanton Wheeler has attempted to identify some of the main features of these adult socialization settings, features more or less common to all of them, regardless of type.[19] He also notes some important differences between "developmental" socialization organizations as a type (schools, colleges, work organizations) and "resocialization" organizations (prisons, mental hospitals) that seek to correct some deficiency in earlier socialization. The latter merit more extended treatment than can be given them here; we shall therefore consider only the developmental organizations, which ordinarily result in socially acceptable socialization outcomes.

The person who enters an organization may be designated a *recruit*. The organization has goals of its own that lead to its providing goals to the recruit. When these are specific goals, such as teaching typing or engineering, the organization is concerned with role socialization. When they are general, such as teaching liberal arts, the concern is with status socialization—preparing the recruit to occupy a generalized status in life and to enact an associated life style. Some organizations may be concerned with both types 6f goals.[20]

Recruits move through an organization in a sequence of steps. Organizations that have great control over entry procedures may be able to provide an adequate period of anticipatory socialization. Even so, recruits often experience "reality shock" upon entry—what they had anticipated was either misleading or seriously incomplete. The situation in which they find themselves is unexpected—as when first-year college students are jolted by the amount of work they are expected to do or graduates of secretarial school, expecting to be executive secretaries, are assigned routine filing.

Usually there are entry procedures of some kind, in which information is exchanged. The recruits receive "an orientation" and learn somewhat more definitely what is expected of them. The socializing agents, in turn, form initial impressions of the recruits and therefore anticipations of what may be expected from them in the way of performance. Of course, other information about the recruits may have been acquired earlier, information from application forms, tests, letters of recommendation, interviews, and transcripts of school grades.

Organizations generally have definite expectations concerning the length of time the recruit is expected to stay in the socialization program. After that time he or she goes through specified exit procedures: graduation from college, assignment to independent responsibilities in a work organization, qualifying examinations for such professions as law or medicine.

The socialization process in formal organizations is not governed entirely by the organization and its officially designated agents. Recruits respond to the situations presented to them and often develop their own norms. An illustration of this is provided in a study of medical students by Howard S. Becker and his associates.[21] Beginning medical students, they found, enter with the expectation of learning everything that is taught them. In the course of the first few weeks they begin to feel overloaded and realize they have set themselves an almost impossible task, so they shift their perspective to trying to learn "only the things that are important." Before the first year is over, the emphasis has shifted to learning what the students think the faculty wants them to know and will ask about on examinations. Student and faculty perspectives differ as to what students should learn and how to judge how much they have learned.

Wilbert Moore has noted that punishment—in the form of heavy workload, great isolation, or required performance of unpleasant tasks and duties—is a component in all socialization to occupations that have high standards of competence and performance and that exhibit high identification of members with the collectivity of fellow practitioners.[22]

All adult socialization leads to some changes in self-image. The formation of a specific occupational identity results, Moore suggests, from these main factors:

1. Learning the language and skills of an occupation
2. Surviving the ordeals that have punished the recruits and their colleagues
3. Accepting fellow recruits and adult role models as significant others for oneself
4. Internalizing the occupational norms, so that self-respect becomes a powerful constraint on poor performance or violation of standards
5. Continuing to be aware of peers as purveyors of potential sanctions
6. Being aware of formal reinforcements, the most important of which is the lack of a market for the services of poor performers

This is, of course, again in Rosow's terms, a model of full socialization; it does not throw much light on how dilettantes and chameleons are produced or on the fact that some of them even do quite well in the market. Questions raised by such observations, however, have not yet been studied carefully.

The above discussion has focused on the more or less formal organizational context of socialization into occupations. This, of course, is only one context of adult socialization. Other contexts in which the socialization is less formal might be the neighborhood into which one moves; the voluntary organization, church, or recreational club of which one becomes a member; or the spouse's extended family into which one is introduced. All of these are contexts in which one begins as a recruit or new member and into which one becomes socialized.

Socialization for Growing Old and Dying

In recent years a new discipline has developed—gerontology— concerned with the basic question: What is aging? The long- accepted answer had been that it was basically a biological process with some secondary psychological aspects ("You're as young as you feel"). Increasingly, however, investigators are ask- ing whether there may not be self-fulfilling prophecies built into the process, that is, the elderly were acting as they thought others expected them to act.

According to one early theory, aging individuals are moti- vated naturally to disengage from and relinquish the active roles for which they have been socialized in earlier life;[23] but numerous authors have questioned this view. Some suggest that aging in- dividuals do not seek disengagement from social participation; rather, society operates in many ways to withdraw roles from aging individuals, roles that they might well wish to continue. They are socialized to accept the withdrawal of roles. This is most easily shown with regard to work roles. Retirement is formally defined in many organizations as occurring at a certain age. In- dividuals are expected to retire at that age and are socialized to define their leaving work as retirement (though other norms might define it as discriminatory exclusion from the labor mar- ket). There is anticipatory socialization for retirement: The per- son's "work role deteriorates around him." He or she may be bypassed for promotion or barred from retraining programs available to younger workers. Performance expectations may rise to levels unattainable by the older worker, resulting in subtle depreciation of his or her performance.

Currently, the most common view among gerontologists is that many patterns of retirement are possible. Vern L. Bengtson, reviewing one major comparative research, concludes: "Far from there being universal patterns of disengagement and decline of nonfamily roles in retirement, there appear to be several patterns of retirement. These patterns vary not only between occupations but also between apparently similar urban contexts of Western industrialized societies."[24] Older people, if healthy and provided with useful social roles, if they wish need not "disengage." There is no single pattern of aging and no single life style the elderly need follow; they may actively participate in family life, voluntary organizations, various leisure activities, and even productive labor. In the late 1980s the entire concept of mandatory withdrawal from work and other activities is less accepted and, concomitantly, we have witnessed a growing interest in socialization for growing old.

The final and inevitable step for the elderly, as well as for younger people with terminal illnesses, is death. Until recently in our North American society, death was surrounded by numerous taboos and was a topic to be avoided in conversation, if not in thought. Those who were dying were encouraged to think they would recover, and when they died, others spoke of their "passing away" and "breathing their last." Children were "protected" by excluding them from attendance at funerals and the emotional experiences of surrounding adults. In recent years, however, for social scientists and many in the public at large, the taboos have been lifted. Researchers and popular writers now openly discuss the fear of death; the grief of the dying and those who feel close to them; and the relationships among the dying, their families, and the attending medical personnel. Socialization for death and dying has been given a legitimacy unknown a generation ago.[25]

As society changes, more and more life situations formerly left to chance and to individual adjustment are coming to be defined as situations for which the person should be formally socialized. The replacement of apprenticeship by more formalized training programs for work has long been accepted. Increasingly, marriage and parenthood themselves are thought to require formal socialization. And more recently, with more and more people living to advanced age, the need for education for retirement from mature social roles has become a common cry. And still more recently, programs have been introduced to prepare people both to die and to accept the death of others. In modern industrial societies the concern with the outcomes of socialization does not abate.

More than ever before among social scientists, socialization is recognized as a lifelong activity. Few would argue, as did Freud, that the self is established in early life and that little basic change occurs thereafter. As we go through life, depending upon our individual characteristics and experiences and the period in which we live, we change. These changes, as we move through different positions, may be relatively smooth or abrupt. They may involve continual movement in particular directions and back and forth movements in others. We are constantly being socialized, socializing others, and participating in our own socialization. Thus, socialization in childhood, our focus in this volume, is far from a determining process; yet it is always the foundation on which subsequent development and growth are based.

NOTES AND REFERENCES

Chapter 1: Socialization Defined

1. Aage B. Sorensen, Franz E. Weinert, and Lonnie R. Sherrod (eds.), *Human Development and the Life Course: Multidisciplinary Perspectives* (Hillsdale, N.J.: Lawrence Erlbaum Associates, 1986).

Chapter 2: Preconditions for Socialization

1. For an insightful discussion of problems in socializing the blind, see Robert A. Scott, "The Socialization of Blind Children," in David A. Goslin (ed.), *Handbook of Socialization Theory and Research* (Chicago: Rand McNally, 1969), pp. 1025–1046.
2. Robert L. Fantz, "Visual Perception and Experience in Early Infancy: A Look at the Hidden Side of Behavior Development," in Harold W. Stevenson, Eckhard H. Hess, and Harriet L. Rheingold (eds.), *Early Behavior: Comparative and Developmental Approaches* (New York: Wiley, 1967), p. 190.
3. Helen McK. Doan, "Early Stimulation: A Rationale," *Canada's Mental Health,* 24 (June 1976), 10.
4. Fantz, op. cit., p. 218. Italics in original.
5. W. H. Thorpe, *Animal Nature and Human Nature* (Garden City, N.Y.: Anchor Books, 1974), p. 223.
6. Doan, op. cit., p. 9.
7. Kenneth Kaye, *The Mental and Social Life of Babies* (Chicago: University of Chicago Press, 1982), p. 219.
8. Anneliese F. Korner, "Individual Differences at Birth: Implications for Early Experience and Later Development," *American Journal of Orthopsychiatry,* 41 (1971), 608–619; Susan Goldberg, "Social Competence in Infancy," *Merrill-Palmer Quarterly,* 23 (1977), 163–177.
9. Lois Barclay Murphy and Alice E. Moriarty, *Vulnerability, Coping, and Growth: From Infancy to Adolescence* (New Haven, Conn.: Yale University Press, 1976), p. 49.
10. M. P. M. Richards, discussion comment in H. R. Schaffer (ed.), *The Origins of Human Social Relations* (New York: Academic Press, 1971), pp. 210–211.
11. The difficulty of distinguishing the hereditary from the environmental is especially evident in analyzing identical twins reared apart. See

283

Susan L. Farber, *Identical Twins Reared Apart: A Reanalysis* (New York: Basic Books, 1981).

12. A listing of fifty-three recorded cases beginning with the "Hesse wolfchild," discovered in 1344, down to the "Teheran ape-child," discovered in 1961, is given in Lucien Malson, *Wolf Children and the Problem of Human Nature* (New York: Monthly Review Press, 1972), pp. 80–82.

13. Harlan Lane, *The Wild Boy of Aveyron* (Cambridge, Mass.: Harvard University Press, 1976). This book is our major source for the material that follows.

14. Ibid., p. 37. This quotation is from one of several reports on the boy, written by different specialists of the time.

15. Ibid., p. 56.

16. Ibid., p. 99.

17. Ibid., p. 101.

18. Ibid., p. 102.

19. Ibid., pp. 155 ff.

20. Ibid., pp. 179–180.

21. Ibid., p. 182.

22. Ibid., p. 153, p. 167. Itard wrote two reports to the Ministry of the Interior on his work with Victor. These are reprinted, in English translation, in Malson, op. cit. The French film director François Truffaut in 1970 made a film, *The Wild Child*, based on Victor's capture and life with Itard.

23. E. H. Lenneberg, *Biological Foundations of Language* (New York: Wiley, 1967), cited in Dan I. Slobin, *Psycholinguistics* (Glenview, Ill.: Scott, Foresman, 1971), p. 56.

24. Roger Shattuck, *The Forbidden Experiment: The Story of the Wild Boy of Aveyron* (New York: Farrar Straus Giroux, 1980), pp. 165–170.

25. Kingsley Davis, "Final Note on a Case of Extreme Isolation," *American Journal of Sociology*, 52 (1947), 432–437.

26. Susan Curtiss, *Genie: A Psycholinguistic Study of a Modern-Day "Wild Child"* (New York: Academic Press, 1977); Maya Pines, "Civilizing of Genie," *Psychology Today*, 51 (September 1981), 28–34.

27. J. H. Plumb, "The Great Change in Children," in Arlene Skolnick (ed.), *Rethinking Childhood* (Boston: Little, Brown, 1976).

28. Anthony Synnott, "Little Angels, Little Devils: A Sociology of Children," *Canadian Review of Sociology and Anthropology*, 20 (1983), 79–95.

29. Derek Fraser, *The Evolution of the British Welfare State* (New York: Barnes and Noble, 1973), Chap. 1.

30. Viviana Zelizer, *Pricing the Priceless Child* (New York: Basic Books, 1985), p. 11.

31. Ibid., p. 227.

32. Robert S. Weiss, *Going It Alone: Family Life and Social Situation of the Single Parent* (New York: Basic Books, 1979), Chap. 4.

33. Joshua Meyrowitz, *No Sense of Place: The Impact of Electronic Media on Social Behavior* (New York: Oxford University Press, 1985), p. 256.

34. Ibid., pp. vii–viii.

Chapter 3: The Processes and Outcomes of Socialization

1. Alex Inkeles, "Society, Social Structure and Child Socialization," in John A. Clausen (ed.), *Socialization and Society* (Boston: Little, Brown, 1968).

2. M. Brewster Smith, "Competence and Socialization," ibid.

3. Inkeles, op. cit., pp. 87–88.

4. The evidence on nutrition and learning is evaluated in Herbert G. Birch, M.D., and Joan Dye Gussow, *Disadvantaged Children: Health, Nutrition and School Failure* (New York: Harcourt, Brace/Grune & Stratton, 1970). See also: Nevin S. Scrimshaw and J. E. Gordon (eds.), *Malnutrition, Learning and Behavior* (Cambridge, Mass.: M.I.T. Press, 1968); Ruth L. Pike and Myrtle L. Brown, *Nutrition: An Integrated Approach*, 2nd ed. (New York: Wiley, 1975), p. 756; Ernesto Pollitt, *Poverty and Malnutrition in Latin America: Early Childhood Intervention Programs* (New York: Praeger Publishers, 1979); and Judith B. Balderston et al., *Malnourished Children of the Rural Poor* (Boston: Auburn House, 1981).

5. W. Lloyd Warner, Robert J. Havighurst, Martin B. Loeb, *Who Shall Be Educated?* (New York: Harper and Brothers, 1944).

6. The concept of the infant as evocative is discussed in Gerald Handel, "Analysis of Correlative Meaning: The TAT in the Study of Whole Families," in Gerald Handel (ed.), *The Psychosocial Interior of the Family* (Chicago: Aldine, 1967), pp. 104–106.

7. Bettye M. Caldwell, "The Effects of Infant Care," in Martin L. Hoffman and Lois Wladis Hoffman (eds.), *Review of Child Development Research*, Vol. 1 (New York: Russell Sage Foundation, 1964).

8. Leon J. Yarrow, "Separation from Parents During Early Childhood," in Hoffman and Hoffman, op. cit., p. 98.

9. Dale C. Farran and Craig T. Ramey, "Infant Day Care and Attachment Behavior toward Mothers and Teachers," *Child Development*, 48 (1977), 1112–1116.

10. Jerome Kagan, *The Growth of the Child* (New York: Norton, 1978), p. 215.

11. M. Kotelchuk, "The Nature of the Child's Tie to the Father" (unpublished Ph.D. dissertation, Harvard University, 1971), cited in Helen Wortis and Clara Rabinowitz (eds.), *The Women's Movement: Social and Psychological Perspectives* (New York: AMS Press, 1972), p. 34.

12. M. Ainsworth, "The Development of Infant-Mother Interaction Among the Ganda," in B. M. Foss (ed.), *Determinants of Infant Behavior,* Vol. 2 (New York: Wiley, 1963), cited in Yarrow, op. cit.

13. The impact of newborn infants on adults is beginning to be studied by psychologists. See Michael Lewis and Leonard A. Rosenblum (eds.), *The Effect of the Infant on Its Caregiver* (New York: Wiley, 1974). All of the contributions to that volume deal with mother-infant interaction. Studies of the effects of newborn infants on the whole family have not, so far as we know, been carried out. This is a topic that is ripe for development.

14. William Caudill, "Tiny Dramas: Vocal Communication between Mother and Infant in Japanese and American Families," Chap. 3 in William P. Lebra (ed.), *Transcultural Research in Mental Health* (Honolulu: University Press of Hawaii, 1972), p. 43. Caudill believes (p. 47, fn. 15) that although his particular study dealt only with firstborn infants in middle-class families, his findings apply to the two societies more broadly.

15. Joy Hendry, *Becoming Japanese: the World of the Pre-School Child* (Honolulu: University of Hawaii Press, 1986), pp. 19, 98, 154.

16. Some examples of the different ways in which the infant's cry is symbolically interpreted by mothers are reported in the section "Leaving the Baby to Cry" in John and Elizabeth Newson, *Infant Care in an Urban Community* (New York: International Universities Press, 1963), Chap. 6, "The Roots of Socialization," pp. 87–99.

17. T. G. R. Bower, *A Primer of Infant Development* (San Francisco: W. H. Freeman, 1977).

18. This account of the work of these linguistic scholars is adapted from James J. Jenkins, "The Acquisition of Language," in David A. Goslin (ed.), *Handbook of Socialization Theory and Research* (Chicago: Rand McNally, 1969), Chap. 13.

19. Ibid., p. 675.

20. Ibid., p. 679.

21. Sigmund Freud, "Three Contributions to the Theory of Sex," in A. A. Brill (ed.), *The Basic Writings of Sigmund Freud,* Book III (New York: Modern Library, 1938), p. 581.

22. Ernest G. Schachtel, *Metamorphosis* (New York: Basic Books, 1959), Chap. 12, "On Memory and Childhood Amnesia," pp. 287–289.

23. Harold Garfinkel, "Studies of the Routine Grounds of Everyday Activities," *Social Problems,* 11 (Winter 1964) pp. 227–228.

24. Susan Ervin-Tripp, "Wait for Me, Roller Skate!" in Susan Ervin-Tripp and Claudia Mitchell-Kernan (eds.), *Child Discourse* (New York: Academic Press, 1977).

25. A convenient introduction to the concept of communication modalities is given in an article by one of Bateson's co-workers, Jay Haley, "The Family of the Schizophrenic: A Model System," *Journal of Nervous and Mental Disease*, 129 (1959), 357–374. Reprinted in Gerald Handel (ed.), *The Psychosocial Interior of the Family*, 2nd ed. (Chicago: Aldine, 1972), pp. 251–275.
26. Mead does not himself use these examples. His most influential work is presented in George H. Mead, *Mind, Self and Society* (Chicago: University of Chicago Press, 1934). Interpretation and elaboration of his work are found in Herbert Blumer, *Symbolic Interactionism* (Englewood Cliffs, N.J.: Prentice-Hall, 1969); Jerome Manis and Bernard Meltzer (eds.), *Symbolic Interaction* (Boston: Allyn and Bacon, 1967); and Arnold M. Rose (ed.), *Human Behavior and Social Processes, An Interactionist Approach* (Boston: Houghton Mifflin, 1962).
27. Mead, op. cit., p. 151.
28. Mead, op. cit., p. 155.
29. Ralph H. Turner, "Role-Taking: Process Versus Conformity," in Arnold M. Rose (ed.), *Human Behavior and Social Processes* (Boston: Houghton Mifflin, 1962), pp. 22–23.
30. Mead, op. cit., pp. 176–178.
31. Donald W. Ball, "Toward a Sociology of Toys," *Sociological Quarterly*, 8 (Autumn 1967), 447–458.
32. Sherry Turkle, *The Second Self: Computers and the Human Spirit* (New York: Simon and Schuster, 1984).
33. Sheldon Stryker, *Symbolic Interactionism* (Menlo Park, Calif.: Benjamin/Cummings Publishing Co., 1980), pp. 62–63.
34. Jean Piaget and Barbel Inhelder, *The Psychology of the Child* (New York: Basic Books, 1969).
35. Philippe Ariès, *Centuries of Childhood* (New York: Knopf, 1962), pp. 128 and 411. Ariès's thesis has been subjected to intense examination by other scholars. They generally support his basic analysis, although with various qualifications and modifications. See David Hunt, *Parents and Children in History: Psychology of Family Life in Early Modern France* (New York: Basic Books, 1970); John R. Gillis, *Youth and History* (New York: Academic Press, 1974); and Lloyd deMause (ed.), *The History of Childhood* (New York: The Psychohistory Press, 1974), particularly Chap. 3, Mary Martin McLaughlin, "Survivors and Surrogates: Children and Parents from the Ninth to the Thirteenth Centuries," and Chap. 5, M. J. Tucker, "The Child as Beginning and End: Fifteenth and Sixteenth Century English Childhood," and works cited therein.

36. Ariès, op. cit., pp. 176–177.

37. Robert K. Merton, *Social Theory and Social Structure* (New York: Free Press, 1968).

38. The following summary of Erikson's approach is adapted from two of his works, *Childhood and Society* (New York: Norton, 1950) and *Identity: Youth and Crisis* (New York: Norton, 1968).

39. Erikson, *Identity: Youth and Crisis*, p. 124.

40. Ibid., p. 132.

41. Erikson, *Childhood and Society*, p. 231.

42. Alice S. Rossi, "Transition to Parenthood," *Journal of Marriage and Family*, 30 (February 1968), 26–39.

43. Erikson, *Identity: Youth and Crisis*, p. 139.

44. Erikson, *Childhood and Society*, Chap. 3, "Hunters Across the Prairie." For a different interpretation of identity problems of Indians—though not of the Sioux specifically—see Ann Beuf, *Red Children in White America* (Philadelphia: University of Pennsylvania Press, 1977).

45. Albert J. Reiss, "Social Organization and Socialization: Variations on a Theme about Generations" (unpublished paper, 1965), cited in Eleanor E. Maccoby, "The Development of Moral Values and Behavior in Childhood," in Clausen (ed.), op. cit.

46. For one such analysis, see Glen H. Elder, Jr., *Children of the Great Depression* (Chicago: University of Chicago Press, 1974).

47. Lillian Troll and Vern L. Bengtson, with the assistance of Dianne McFarland, "Generations in the Family," in Wesley Burr et al. (eds.), *Contemporary Theories about the Family*, Vol. 1 (New York: Free Press, 1979). See also Vern L. Bengtson and Lillian Troll, "Youth and Their Parents: Feedback and Intergenerational Influence in Socialization," in Richard M. Lerner and Graham B. Spanier (eds.), *Child Influences on Marital and Family Interaction* (New York: Academic Press, 1978).

48. Glen H. Elder, Jr., Avshalom Caspi, and Geraldine Downey, "Problem Behavior and Family Relationships: Life Course and Intergenerational Themes," in Aage B. Sorensen, Franz E. Weinert, and Lonnie R. Sherrod, *Human Development and the Life Course* (Hillsdale, N.J.: Lawrence Erlbaum Associates, 1986), p. 334.

49. Erikson, *Identity: Youth and Crisis*, pp. 257–258.

50. Erving Goffman, "On Face-Work," in Erving Goffman, *Interaction Ritual* (Garden City, N.Y.: Doubleday Anchor, 1967).

51. Norman Denzin, *Childhood Socialization* (San Francisco: Jossey-Bass, 1977), p. 72.

52. Gary Alan Fine, "Friends, Impression Management, and Preadolescent Behavior," in Steven R. Asher and John M. Gottman (eds.), *The*

Development of Children's Friendships (Cambridge: Cambridge University Press, 1981), p. 35.

53. Erving Goffman, "The Nature of Deference and Demeanor," in Goffman, *Interaction Ritual*, p. 47.

54. William A. Corsaro, "We're friends, right? Children's Use of Access Rituals in a Nursery School," *Language in Society,* 8 (1979), 315–336.

55. Viktor Gecas, "The Self-Concept," *Annual Review of Sociology,* Vol. 8 (Palo Alto, Calif.: Annual Reviews, 1982), pp. 1–33.

56. Morris Rosenberg, *Conceiving the Self* (New York: Basic Books, 1979), p. 7.

57. Betty Yorburg, *Sexual Identity* (New York: Wiley, 1974), pp. 1, 4.

58. Rosenberg, op. cit., pp. 9–17.

59. Erik H. Erikson, *Identity and the Life Cycle* (New York: Norton, 1980), p. 122.

60. Gregory Stone, "Appearance and the Self," in Arnold Rose (ed.), *Human Behavior and Social Processes* (Boston: Houghton Mifflin, 1962), p. 93.

61. Lee Rainwater, *Behind Ghetto Walls* (Chicago: Aldine, 1970), p. 375.

62. Sheldon Stryker, op. cit., pp. 60–61.

63. Charles Horton Cooley, *Social Organization* (New York: Scribner, 1909), p. 27.

64. Ibid., p. 30.

65. Thomas J. Scheff, "Toward Integration in the Social Psychology of Emotions," *Annual Review of Sociology,* Vol. 9 (Palo Alto, Calif.: Annual Reviews, 1983), pp. 333–354.

66. Scheff, "Toward Integration"; Steven L. Gordon, "The Sociology of Sentiments and Emotion," in Morris Rosenberg and Ralph H. Turner (eds.), *Social Psychology* (New York: Basic Books, 1981), pp. 562–592.

67. Carol Zander Malatesta and Jeanette M. Haviland, "Signals, Symbols, and Socialization: The Modification of Emotional Expression in Human Development," in Michael Lewis and Carolyn Saarni (eds.), *The Socialization of Emotions* (New York: Plenum Press, 1985), pp. 89–116.

68. Ibid., pp. 103–113.

69. Ibid. See also Leila Beckwith, "Parent-Infant Interaction and Infants' Social-Emotional Development," in Allen W. Gottfried and Catherine Caldwell Brown (eds.), *Play Interactions* (Lexington, Mass.: Lexington Books, 1986), pp. 279–292.

70. Arlie Russell Hochschild, "Emotion Work, Feeling Rules, and Social Structure," *American Journal of Sociology,* 85:3 (1979), 551–575.

71. Gordon, "Sociology of Sentiment," p. 566.

72. Sandra Kenyon Schwartz, "Preschoolers and Politics," in David C. Schwartz and Sandra Kenyon Schwartz (eds.), *New Directions in Political Socialization* (New York: Free Press, 1975).

73. Stanley W. Moore, James Lare, and Kenneth A. Wagner, *The Child's Political World* (New York: Praeger, 1985), p. 44.

74. Fred I. Greenstein, *Children and Politics,* rev. ed. (New Haven: Yale University Press, 1969), p. 45.

75. Moore, Lare, and Wagner, op. cit., pp. 72–73.

76. Eugene Green, "The Political Socialization of Black Inner-City Children," in Anthony M. Orum (ed.), *The Seeds of Politics* (Englewood Cliffs, N.J.: Prentice-Hall, 1972), p. 183.

77. Dean Jaros, Herbert Hirsch, and Frederic J. Fleron, Jr., "The Malevolent Leader: Political Socialization in an American Sub-Culture," in Orum, op. cit., p. 209.

78. Bernard Goldstein and Jack Oldham, *Children and Work: A Study of Socialization* (New Brunswick, N.J.: Transaction, 1979), p. 172.

79. Scott Ward, Daniel B. Wackman, and Ellen Wartella, *How Children Learn to Buy* (Beverly Hills, Calif.: Sage, 1977), p. 18.

Chapter 4: Socialization and Subcultural Patterns

1. The idea of different cultures is most strongly embodied in Oscar Lewis's notion of a "culture of poverty." This and related ideas are discussed and challenged in a carefully reasoned work by Charles A. Valentine, *Culture and Poverty: Critique and Counter-Proposals* (Chicago: University of Chicago Press, 1968).

2. Ibid., p. 106.

3. Anne Moody, *Coming of Age in Mississippi, An Autobiography* (New York: Delta, 1970), p. 23.

4. See, for example, Arthur J. Vidich and Joseph Bensman, *Small Town in Mass Society* (Princeton, N.J.: Princeton University Press, enlarged edition, 1969).

5. William Graham Sumner, *Folkways* (Boston: Ginn, 1906), p. 13.

6. Tamotsu Shibutani and Kian M. Kwan, *Ethnic Stratification* (New York: Macmillan, 1965), p. 109.

7. Writings that exemplify this belief include Nelson N. Foote and Leonard S. Cottrell, Jr., *Identity and Interpersonal Competence* (Chicago: University of Chicago Press, 1955); Ronald Lippitt, "Improving the Socialization Process," in John A. Clausen (ed.), *Socialization and Society* (Boston: Little, Brown, 1968); and Eugene A. Weinstein, "The Development of Interpersonal Competence," in David A. Goslin (ed.), *Handbook of Socialization Theory and Research* (Chicago: Rand McNally, 1969).

8. Richard P. Coleman and Lee Rainwater, *Social Standing in America* (New York: Basic Books, 1978), p. 22.

9. Bernd Baldus and Verna Tribe, "The Development of Perceptions and Evaluations of Social Inequality Among Public School Children," *Canadian Review of Sociology and Anthropology,* 15 (February 1978), 50–60.

10. Hyman Rodman, "The Lower-Class Value Stretch," *Social Forces,* 42 (December 1963), 205.

11. Bernard Farber, *Family: Organization and Interaction* (San Francisco: Chandler, 1964), pp. 368–374.

12. John R. Seeley, R. A. Sim, and E. W. Looseley, *Crestwood Heights: A Study of the Culture of Suburban Life* (New York: Basic Books, 1956; paperback edition, New York: Wiley, 1963), p. 470.

13. Ibid., p. 306.

14. John N. Edwards, "Organizational and Leadership Status," *Sociological Inquiry,* 39 (1969), 49–56.

15. Elliott A. Medrich, Judith Roizen, Victor Rubin, and Stuart Buckley, *The Serious Business of Growing Up: A Study of Children's Lives Outside School* (Berkeley, Calif.: University of California Press, 1982), pp. 191–193.

16. Lydia O'Donnell and Ann Stueve, "Mothers as Social Agents: Structuring the Community Activities of School Aged Children," in Helena Z. Lopata and Joseph H. Pleck (eds.), *Research in the Interweave of Social Roles: Families and Jobs,* Vol. 3 (Greenwich, Conn.: JAI Press, 1983), pp. 113–129.

17. Ibid., pp. 116, 120.

18. Melvin J. Kohn, "The Effects of Social Class on Parental Values and Practices," in David Reiss and Howard A. Hoffman (eds.), *The American Family* (New York: Plenum Press, 1979), pp. 45–68; Melvin J. Kohn, "Social Class and Parent-Child Relationships: An Interpretation," *American Journal of Sociology,* 68 (January 1963), 471–480. Kohn, more than anyone else, has made the case linking occupations, values, and socialization processes, and many of our ideas are derived from his work. For a detailed review and evaluation of studies discussing the relationship between social class and child-rearing practices, see Viktor Gecas, "The Influence of Social Class on Socialization," in Wesley R. Burr et al., *Contemporary Theories About the Family,* Vol. 1 (New York: Free Press, 1979), pp. 365–403.

19. Rosanna Hertz, *More Equal Than Others: Women and Men in Dual-Career Marriages* (Berkeley: University of California Press, 1986), p. 61.

20. Lynda Lytle Holmstrom, *The Two-Career Family* (Cambridge, Mass.: Schenkman, 1973), p. 17.

21. Lillian B. Rubin, *Worlds of Pain* (New York: Basic Books, 1976), pp. 85–86.

22. Ibid., p. 128.

23. Wallace E. Lambert, Josiane F. Hamers, and Nancy Frasure-Smith,

Child-Rearing Values: A Cross-National Study (New York: Praeger, 1979), p. 349.

24. Allen D. Grimshaw, "Talk and Social Control," in Morris Rosenberg and Ralph H. Turner (eds.), *Social Psychology: Sociological Perspectives* (New York: Basic Books, 1981), p. 230.

25. Basil Bernstein, "Social Class and Linguistic Development: A Theory of Social Learning," in A. H. Halsey, Jean Floud, and C. Arnold Anderson (eds.), *Education, Economy and Society* (New York: Free Press, 1961), pp. 288–314. For a more recent review and critique, see Jerome Karabel and A. H. Halsey (eds.), *Power and Ideology in Education* (New York: Oxford University Press, 1977), especially pp. 62–71.

26. Robert D. Hess, Virginia Shipman, and David Jackson, "Early Experience and the Socialization of Cognitive Modes in Children," *Child Development,* 36 (December 1965), 869–886.

27. Louis Schneider and Sverre Lysgaard, "The Deferred Gratification Pattern: A Preliminary Study," *American Sociological Review,* 18 (April 1953), 142–149.

28. Allison Davis, "Socialization and Adolescent Personality," *Adolescence, Forty-Third Yearbook,* Part I (Chicago: National Society for the Study of Education, 1944), Chap. 11.

29. Duane F. Alwin, "Trends in Parental Socialization Values: Detroit, 1959–1983," *American Journal of Sociology,* 90 (1984), 359–382.

30. Duane F. Alwin, "From Obedience to Autonomy: Changes in Traits Desired in Children, 1924–78," *Public Opinion Quarterly,* in press.

31. Duane F. Alwin, "Historical Changes in Parental Orientations in Children," in Patricia A. Adler and Peter Adler (eds.), *Sociological Studies of Child Development,* Vol. 3 (Greenwich, Conn.: JAI Press), forthcoming.

32. Albert K. Cohen and Harold M. Hodges, Jr., "Characteristics of the Lower-Blue-Collar Class," *Social Problems,* 10 (Spring 1963), 303–334. Our account of lower-class subculture draws mainly on this article, unless otherwise indicated.

33. Ibid., p. 322.

34. Eleanor Pavenstedt, "A Comparison of the Child-Rearing Environment of Upper Lower and Very Lower Class Families," *American Journal of Orthopsychiatry,* 35 (January 1965), 89–98. The quotation is taken from the summary given in Bernard Goldstein, *Low Income Youth in Urban Areas: A Critical Review of the Literature* (New York: Holt, Rinehart and Winston, 1967), p. 11. See also Joseph T. Howell, *Hard Living on Clay Street: Portraits of Blue Collar Families* (Garden City, N.Y.: Anchor Books, 1973).

35. Rodman, op. cit., p. 309.

36. Luther P. Jackson, "Telling It Like It Is!" (Washington, D.C.: Health and Welfare Council of the Capital Area, 1966), quoted in Elizabeth Herzog, *About the Poor: Some Facts and Some Fictions* (Washington, D.C.: U.S. Department of Health, Education and Welfare, 1968), Chap. 1, "Problem Populations: 'They' and 'We.'"

37. Valerie Suransky, *The Erosion of Childhood* (Chicago: University of Chicago Press, 1982), p. 138.

38. Ibid., pp. 66, 82–85.

39. Ibid., pp. 75, 86.

40. Ibid., pp. 152–153. Also see Sally Lubeck, *Sandbox Society: Early Education in Black and White America: A Comparative Ethnography* (Philadelphia: Palmer Press, 1985).

41. The account that follows is adapted from Harry M. Caudill, *Night Comes to the Cumberlands: A Biography of a Depressed Area* (Boston: Little, Brown, 1962).

42. Ibid., p. 51.

43. Ibid., p. 146.

44. Ibid., pp. 337–338.

45. Richard A. Ball, "A Poverty Case: The Analgesic Subculture of the Southern Appalachians," *American Sociological Review,* 33 (December 1968), 885–895.

46. Jack E. Weller, *Yesterday's People: Life in Contemporary Appalachia* (Lexington: University of Kentucky Press, 1965), pp. 47–48.

47. Harry M. Caudill, *The Watches of the Night* (Boston: Little, Brown, 1976). For a fascinating report of how one hopeful Appalachian community was destroyed when a poorly constructed dam burst and flooded the area, see Kai T. Erikson, *Everything in Its Path: Destruction of Community in the Buffalo Creek Flood* (New York: Simon and Schuster, 1976).

48. Rex A. Lucas, *Minetown, Milltown, Railtown* (Toronto: University of Toronto Press, 1971).

49. Frank H. Epp, "Mennonites," *The Canadian Encyclopedia* (Edmonton: Hurtig, 1985), pp. 1117–1118.

50. John F. Peters, "Socialization Among the Old Order Mennonites," Paper presented at the XI World Congress of Sociology, New Delhi, India, August 1986; John F. Peters, "Old Order Mennonite Ethnic Maintenance," Paper presented at meetings of the Canadian Learned Society, Winnipeg, June 1986.

51. Peters, "Socialization Among the Old Order Mennonites," p. 12.

52. Ibid., p. 11.

53. For an excellent book of readings covering most facets of commune life, see Rosabeth Moss Kanter (ed.), *Communes: Creating and Managing the Collective Life* (New York: Harper & Row, 1973).

54. Benjamin D. Zablocki and Rosabeth M. Kanter, "The Differentiation of Life-Styles," in Alex Inkeles et al. (eds.), *Annual Review of Sociology*, Vol. 2 (Palo Alto, Calif.: Annual Reviews), pp. 262–298.

55. See A. I. Rabin and Benjamin Beit-Hallahmi, *Twenty Years Later: Kibbutz Children Grown Up* (New York: Springer Publishing Company, 1982); Suzanne Keller, "The Family in the Kibbutz: What Lessons for Us?" in Michal Palgi, Joseph R. Blasi, Menachem Rosner, and Marilyn Safir (eds.), *Sexual Equality: The Israeli Kibbutz Tests the Theories*, Vol. 6 (Norwood, Pa.: Norwood Editions, 1983), pp. 227–251; Yonina Talmon, *Family and Community in the Kibbutz* (Cambridge, Mass.: Harvard University Press, 1972); Bruno Bettelheim, *Children of the Dream* (New York: Macmillan, 1969).

56. Bennett M. Berger, *The Survival of a Counterculture* (Berkeley: University of California Press, 1981).

57. Ibid., p. 60.

58. Bennett M. Berger et al., "Child-Rearing Practices of the Communal Family," Progress Report to the National Institute of Mental Health, 1971. Cited in Kanter, op. cit.

59. Berger, *The Survival of a Counterculture*, pp. 60–63.

60. Berger et al., "Child-Rearing Practices of the Communal Family," op. cit., p. 358.

61. Berger, *The Survival of a Counterculture*, pp. 84–85.

62. Ibid., p. 73.

63. Sonya Rudikoff, "O Pioneers! Reflections on the Whole Earth People," *Commentary*, 54 (July 1972), 62–74.

64. One recent report comparing children up to the age of six of "nonconventional" families—of which communes are one type—with "conventional" families finds no significant differences in tests of intellectual functioning, health, or socioemotional adjustment. Thomas S. Weisner, "Implementing New Relationship Styles in American Families," in Willard W. Hartup and Zick Rubin (eds.), *Relationships and Development* (Hillsdale, N.J.: Lawrence Erlbaum Associates, 1986), pp. 185–206.

65. For a discussion of the difficulties with the concept of race and its abandonment by many scientists as no longer useful, see J. Z. Young, *An Introduction to the Study of Man* (Oxford: Oxford University Press, 1971), Chap. 41.

66. The suggestion has been made that *generation* is a less useful concept than *cohort*, which is defined as "the aggregate of individuals (within some population definition) who experienced the same event within the same time interval." See Norman B. Ryder, "The Cohort as a Concept in the Study of Social Change," *American Sociological Review*, 30 (December 1965) 843–861. The implication of this approach in the present context would be that children of immigrants ("second

generation") in, say, 1880 had different socialization experiences from children of immigrants in 1985. Although this is undoubtedly true, it does not mean that the fact of being second generation may not have common features regardless of the time at which it occurs.

67. Suzanne Ziegler, "Ethnic Diversity and Children," in William Michelson et al., *The Child in the City: Changes and Challenges* (Toronto: University of Toronto Press, 1977), p. 375.

68. Frances E. Aboud, "Ethnic Self-Identity," in R. C. Gardner and E. Kalin (eds.), *A Canadian Social Psychology of Ethnic Relations* (Toronto: Methuen, 1981), p. 43.

69. Judith D. R. Porter, *Black Child, White Child* (Cambridge, Mass.: Harvard University Press, 1971), p. 86.

70. Aboud, op. cit., p. 52.

71. Gordon Allport, *Becoming* (New Haven, Conn.: Yale University Press, 1955), pp. 36–56.

72. Frederick Elkin, "Family, Socialization and Ethnic Identity," in K. Ishwaran (ed.), *The Canadian Family* (Toronto: Gage Publishing, 1983), pp. 145–158.

73. Jeffrey G. Reitz, "Language and Ethnic Community Survival," *Canadian Review of Sociology and Anthropology*, Supplementary Issue (1974), 118.

74. C. Antoniou, *Greek Family Life* (Toronto: Ontario Ministry of Culture and Recreation: Multicultural Development Branch, 1974), p. 1.

75. Evelyn Kallen, *Spanning the Generations: A Study in Jewish Identity* (Toronto: Longman Canada, 1977), p. 66.

76. Ernesto Galarza, *Barrio Boy* (Notre Dame, Ind.: University of Notre Dame Press, 1971), pp. 211–212.

77. Kurt Lewin, *Resolving Social Conflicts* (New York: Harper & Row, 1948).

78. Robert K. Merton, *Social Theory and Social Structure* (New York: Free Press, 1968), pp. 281 ff. In the sociological literature, the term "reference group" sometimes has other meanings. See Tamotsu Shibutani, "Reference Groups as Perspectives," *American Journal of Sociology*, 60 (May 1955), 562–569.

79. Morris Rosenberg, "Summary," in Margaret B. Spencer, Geraldine K. Brookins, and Walter R. Allen, *Beginnings: the Social and Affective Development of Black Children* (Hillsdale, N.J.: Lawrence Erlbaum Associates, 1985), pp. 155–171.

80. Lee Rainwater, *Behind Ghetto Walls: Black Families in a Federal Slum* (Chicago: Aldine, 1970), pp. 385–386. See also p. 75.

81. Shibutani and Kwan, op. cit., p. 357.

82. Reported in Beatrice Griffith, *American Me* (Boston: Houghton Mifflin, 1948), p. 151.

83. Selma Berrol, "Ethnicity and American Children," in Joseph M.

Hawes and N. Ray Hiner, *American Childhood* (Westport, Conn: Greenwood Press. 1985), p. 363.

84. Grace Anderson and David Higgs, *A Future to Inherit: The Portuguese Communities of Canada* (Toronto: McClelland and Stewart, 1976), p. 133.

85. Hylan Lewis, Foreword to Elliot Liebow, *Tally's Corner: A Study of Negro Streetcorner Men* (Boston: Little, Brown, 1967), p. vii.

86. Walt Wolfram, *Sociolinguistic Aspects of Assimilation: Puerto Rican English in New York City* (Arlington, Va.: Center for Applied Linguistics, 1974), p. 31.

87. Richard Gambino, "La famiglia: Four generations of Italian-Americans," in Joseph Ryan (ed.), *White Ethnics: Their Life in Working Class America* (Englewood Cliffs, N.J.: Prentice-Hall, 1973), p. 45.

88. Berrol, op. cit., pp. 352–356.

89. Shih-Shan Henry Tsai, *The Chinese Experience in America* (Bloomington: Indiana University Press, 1986), pp. 161–165.

90. Stephen T. Boggs with the assistance of Karen Watson-Gegeo and George McNillen, *Speaking, Relating, and Learning. A Study of Hawaiian Children at Home and at School* (Norwood, N.J.: Ablex, 1985).

91. Ibid., p. 69.

92. Ibid., p. 120.

93. Bernard C. Rosen, "Race, Ethnicity and the Achievement Syndrome," *American Sociological Review,* 24 (1959), 47–60.

94. Richard D. Alba, *Italian Americans: Into the Twilight of Ethnicity* (Englewood Cliffs, N.J.: Prentice-Hall, 1985), p. 141.

95. W. Lloyd Warner, *American Life: Dream and Reality* (Chicago: University of Chicago Press, 1953), p. 171.

96. Nathan Glazer and Daniel P. Moynihan, *Beyond the Melting Pot: The Negroes, Puerto Ricans, Jews, Italians, and Irish of New York City* (Cambridge, Mass.: M.I.T. Press, 1963), p. 310.

97. Nathan Glazer and Daniel P. Moynihan (eds.), *Ethnicity: Theory and Experience* (Cambridge, Mass.: Harvard University Press, 1975), pp. 1–26.

98. Jean Burnet, "Ethnicity: Canadian Experience and Policy," *Sociological Focus,* 9 (1976), 199.

99. Richard D. Alba, op. cit., pp. 153–154.

100. Bernard Farber and Leonard Gordon, "Accounting for Jewish Intermarriage: An Assessment of National and Community Studies," *Contemporary Jewry,* 6 (1982), 47–75; Darrell Montero, "The Japanese Americans: Changing Patterns of Assimilation over Three Generations," *American Sociological Review,* 46 (1981), 829–839; Eric Woodrum, "An Assessment of Japanese American Assimilation, Pluralism, and Subordination," *American Journal of Sociology,* 87 (1981), 157–169.

101. Herbert Gans, "Symbolic Ethnicity: The Future of Ethnic Groups and Cultures in America," in H. J. Gans, N. Glazer, J. R. Gusfield, and C. Jencks (eds.), *On the Making of Americans: Essays in Honor of David Riesman* (Philadelphia: University of Pennsylvania Press, 1979), pp. 193–220.

102. Richard D. Alba, op. cit., p. 173.

Chapter 5: Agencies of Socialization

1. See David Riesman, with Reuel Denny and Nathan Glazer, *The Lonely Crowd: A Study of the Changing American Character* (New Haven, Conn.: Yale University Press, 1950).

2. Robert K. Merton, *Social Theory and Social Structure* (New York: Free Press, 1968), enlarged ed., chap. entitled "Manifest and Latent Functions."

3. Allen Kassof, *The Soviet Youth Program: Regimentation and Rebellion* (Cambridge, Mass.: Harvard University Press, 1965), pp. 170, 173.

4. Dennis Wrong, "The Oversocialized Conception of Man in Modern Sociology," *American Sociological Review,* 26 (April 1961), 183–193. An enlarged version of this article is printed in *Psychoanalysis and the Psychoanalytic Review,* 49 (Summer 1962), where it is accompanied by a rebuttal from Talcott Parsons entitled "Individual Autonomy and Social Pressure: An Answer to Dennis H. Wrong," pp. 70–79.

5. Jean Evans, *Three Men* (New York: Knopf, 1950), p. 11.

6. Elaboration of the family's mediating role is presented in Gerald Handel (ed.), *The Psychosocial Interior of the Family,* 2nd ed. (Chicago: Aldine, 1972), Part III, "The Family as Mediator of the Culture."

7. David A. Schulz, *Coming Up Black: Patterns of Ghetto Socialization* (Englewood Cliffs, N.J.: Prentice-Hall, 1969).

8. This analysis is developed by Lee Rainwater, "Crucible of Identity: "The Negro Lower-Class Family," *Daedalus, Journal of the American Academy of Arts and Sciences,* 95 (1966), 172–216.

9. Handel, op. cit.; Robert D. Hess and Gerald Handel, *Family Worlds* (Chicago: University of Chicago Press, 1959).

10. Talcott Parsons and Robert F. Bales, *Family, Socialization and Interaction Process* (Glencoe, Ill.: Free Press, 1955), Chap. 2, "Family Structure and the Socialization of the Child."

11. Lillian Troll and Vern Bengtson, with the assistance of Dianne McFarland, "Generations in the Family," in Wesley Burr et al. (eds.), *Contemporary Theories About the Family,* Vol. 1 (New York: Free Press, 1979), p. 130.

12. Herbert J. Gans, *The Urban Villagers: Group and Class in the Life of Italian-Americans,* updated and expanded edition (New York: Free Press, 1982).

13. Jack E. Weller, *Yesterday's People: Life in Contemporary Appalachia* (Lexington: University of Kentucky Press, 1965).

14. Gans, op. cit., pp. 54, 59–60.

15. Rhona Rapoport, Robert H. Rapoport, Z. Strelitz, and S. Kew, *Fathers, Mothers, and Society* (New York: Basic Books, 1977).

16. Ezra F. Vogel and Norman W. Bell, "The Emotionally Disturbed Child as the Family Scapegoat," in N. W. Bell and E. F. Vogel (eds.), *A Modern Introduction to the Family* (Glencoe, Ill.: Free Press, 1960), pp. 412–427.

17. Michael E. Lamb (ed.), *The Role of the Father in Child Development*, 2nd ed. (New York: Wiley, 1981).

18. Ross D. Parke, "Fathers: An Intrafamilial Perspective," in Michael W. Yogman and T. Berry Brazelton, *In Support of Families* (Cambridge, Mass.: Harvard University Press, 1986), pp. 59–68.

19. Bryan E. Robinson and Robert L. Barret, *The Developing Father. Emerging Roles in Contemporary Society* (New York: Guilford Press, 1986), p. 41.

20. Ross D. Parke, *Fathers* (Cambridge, Mass.: Harvard University Press, 1981), p. 27; Diane Ehrensaft, "Dual Parenting and the Duel of Intimacy," in G. Handel (ed.), *The Psychosocial Interior of the Family*, 3rd ed. (New York: Aldine, 1985), pp. 323–337.

21. Robinson and Barret, *Developing Father*, p. 87.

22. Debra G. Klinman and Rhiana Kohl, *Fatherhood U.S.A. The First National Guide to Programs, Services, and Resources for and about Fathers* (New York: Garland Publishing, 1984).

23. Lamb, op. cit.; Michael W. Yogman, "Development of the Father-Infant Relationship," in Hiram E. Fitzgerald, Barry M. Lest, and Michael W. Yogman (eds.), *Theory and Research in Behavioral Pediatrics*, Vol. 1 (New York: Plenum Press, 1982).

24. Jay D. Schvaneveldt and Marilyn Ihinger, "Sibling Relationships in the Family," in Burr, op. cit., pp. 453–468. See also Gerald Handel, "Beyond Sibling Rivalry: An Empirically Grounded Theory of Sibling Relationships," in Patricia A. Adler and Peter Adler (eds.), *Sociological Studies of Child Development*, Vol. 1 (Greenwich, Conn.: JAI Press, 1986), pp. 105–122.

25. James H. S. Bossard and Eleanor Stoker Boll, *The Sociology of Child Development*, 4th ed. (New York: Harper & Row, 1966), pp. 39–40.

26. Orville G. Brim, Jr., "Family Structure and Sex Role Learning by Children: A Further Analysis of Helen Koch's Data," *Sociometry*, 21 (1958), 1–15.

27. Cited in Robert W. Emery, E. Mavis Hetherington, and Lisabeth F. DiLalla, "Divorce, Children and Social Policy," in Harold W. Stevenson and Alberta E. Siegel (eds.), *Child Development Research and*

Social Policy (Chicago: University of Chicago Press, 1984), pp. 189–190.

28. Arthur J. Norton and Paul C. Glick, "One Parent Families: A Social and Economic Profile," *Family Relations,* 35 (1986), 16.

29. Emily B. Visher and John S. Visher, *Stepfamilies* (New York: Brunner/Mazel, 1979), p. 4.

30. Norton and Glick, op. cit., p. 16.

31. Judith S. Wallerstein and Joan B. Kelly, *Surviving the Breakup* (New York: Basic Books, 1980), pp. 34, 111–112.

32. Judith S. Wallerstein and Joan B. Kelly, "The Effects of Parental Divorce: Experiences of the Child in Later Latency," *American Journal of Orthopsychiatry,* 46 (April 1976), reprinted in Arlen Skolnick and Jerome H. Skolnick, *Family in Transition,* 3rd ed. (Boston: Little, Brown, 1980), p. 446.

33. Ibid., p. 306.

34. Kathleen A. Camara, "Family Adaptation to Divorce," in Michael W. Yogman and T. Berry Brazelton (eds.), *In Support of Families* (Cambridge, Mass.: Harvard University Press, 1986), p. 188.

35. Ibid., pp. 186–192.

36. Lucile Duberman, *The Reconstituted Family: A Study of Remarried Couples and Their Children* (Chicago: Nelson-Hall, 1975), pp. 109–110; Visher and Visher, op. cit., p. 154.

37. Gerald Handel, "Views of a Changing Interior," in G. Handel (ed.), *The Psychosocial Interior of the Family,* 2nd ed. (Chicago: Aldine, 1972), p. vii.

38. Wallerstein and Kelly, *Surviving the Breakup,* pp. 293–295.

39. Cited in Gwen G. Morgan, "Supplemental Care for Young Children," in Yogman and Brazelton, op. cit., p. 156.

40. Virginia Sapiro, *Women in American Society* (Palo Alto, Calif.: Mayfield, 1986), p. 31.

41. *Women in the Labour Force,* 1986–1987 ed. (Ottawa: Labour Canada, 1987), p. 20.

42. Lois W. Hoffman, "Effects on Child," in Lois Wladis Hoffman and F. Ivan Nye, with others, *Working Mothers: An Evaluative Review of the Consequences for Wife, Mother and Child* (San Francisco: Jossey-Bass, 1974), p. 147.

43. E. M. Rallings and F. Ivan Nye, "Wife-Mother Employment, Family, and Society," in Burr, op. cit., pp. 203–226.

44. Cited in Robert A. Lewis, "Men's Changing Roles in Marriage and the Family," in Robert A. Lewis and Marvin B. Sussman (eds.), *Men's Changing Roles in the Family* (New York: Haworth Press, 1986), p. 6.

45. Cited in Joseph Pleck, Michael E. Lamb, and James A. Levine, "Epi-

log: Facilitating Future Change in Men's Family Roles," in Robert A. Lewis and Marvin B. Sussman, op. cit., p. 11.

46. Theodore Caplow et al., *Middletown Families: Fifty Years of Change and Continuity* (Minneapolis: University of Minnesota Press, 1982), p. 369.

47. Bonnie E. Carlson, "The Father's Contribution to Child Care: Effects on Children's Perceptions of Parental Roles," *American Journal of Orthopsychiatry,* 54 (1984), 123–136.

48. Bonnie Carlson, "Preschoolers' Sex-Role Identity, Father-Role Perceptions, and Paternal Family Participation," *Journal of Family Issues,* 2 (June 1981), 238–255.

49. Richard A. Winnett and Michael S. Neale, "Flexible Work Schedules and Family Time Allocations: Assessment of a System Change on Individual Behavior Using Self-Report Logs," *Journal of Applied Behavior Analysis,* 14 (1981), 39–46; Richard A. Winnett, Michael S. Neale, and Kenneth R. Williams, "The Effects of Flexible Work Schedules on Urban Families with Young Children: Quasi-Experimental Ecological Studies," *American Journal of Community Psychology,* 10 (1982), 49–64.

50. S. Kamerman, *Infant Care Usage in the United States,* Report presented to National Academy of Sciences Ad Hoc Committee on Policy Issues in Child Care for Infants and Toddlers, Washington, D.C., 1986. Cited in Jay Belsky, "Infant Day Care: A Cause for Concern?" *Zero to Three,* Vol. 7 (September 1986), p. 1; Royal Bank of Canada, *Reporter* (Toronto), Spring 1986, p. 15.

51. Jerome Kagan, *The Growth of the Child* (New York: Norton, 1978), p. 262.

52. Jay Belsky and L. D. Steinberg, "The Effects of Day Care: A Critical Review," *Child Development,* 49 (1978), 929–949.

53. Belsky, op. cit, pp. 1–7; Deborah Phillips, Kathleen McCartney, Sandra Scarr, and Carolee Howes, "Selective Review of Infant Day Care Research: A Cause for Concern," *Zero to Three* (February 1987), pp. 18–21.

54. Sandra L. Hofferth and Kristin A. Moore, "Women's Employment and Marriage," in Ralph E. Smith (ed.), *The Subtle Revolution: Women at Work* (Washington, D.C.: The Urban Institute, 1979), p. 148.

55. Martha Power, "The Ritualization of Emotional Conduct in Early Childhood," in Norman Denzin (ed.), *Studies in Symbolic Interaction,* Vol. 6 (Greenwich, Conn.: JAI Press, 1985), p. 226.

56. Ibid., p. 220.

57. Rosanna Hertz, *More Equal Than Others: Women and Men in Dual-Career Marriages* (Berkeley: University of California Press, 1986), p. xiv.

58. Fran Pepitone-Rockwell (ed.), *Dual-Career Couples* (Beverly Hills, Calif.: Sage, 1980); Joan Aldous (ed.), *Two Paychecks: Life in Dual-*

Earner Families (Beverly Hills, Calif.: Sage, 1982); Lucia A. Gilbert, *Men in Dual-Career Families: Current Realities and Future Prospects* (Hillsdale, N.J.: Lawrence Erlbaum Associates, 1985).

59. Philo C. Wasburn, "The Public School as an Agent of Political Socialization," *Quarterly Journal of Ideology,* 10:2 (1986), 24.
60. Ibid.
61. Ibid., p. 25.
62. Ibid.
63. Ibid., p. 26.
64. Ibid., pp. 26, 32.
65. Edmund J. King, *Education and Social Change* (Oxford: Pergamon Press, 1966), p. 3.
66. David A. Goslin, *The School in Contemporary Society* (Glenview, Ill.: Scott, Foresman, 1965), p. 84.
67. Albert J. Reiss, Jr., Introduction to A. J. Reiss, Jr. (ed.), *Schools in a Changing Society* (New York: Free Press, 1965), p. 2.
68. Patricia Cayo Sexton, *Education and Income* (New York: Viking, 1961), reports on one major North American city.
69. S. John Eggleston, *The Social Context of the School* (London: Routledge and Kegan Paul, 1967), p. 26. The quotation describes a study carried out and reported by J. W. B. Douglas, *The Home and the School* (London: MacGibbon and Kee, 1964).
70. Ray C. Rist, *The Urban School: A Factory for Failure* (Cambridge, Mass.: M.I.T. Press, 1973), pp. 241–242. Italics in original.
71. Sarane Spence Boocock, *Sociology of Education: An Introduction,* 2nd ed. (Boston: Houghton Mifflin, 1980).
72. Christopher J. Hurn, *The Limits and Possibilities of Schooling: An Introduction to the Sociology of Education* (Boston: Allyn & Bacon, 1985), p. 150. Also see Helen Gouldner, *Teacher's Pets, Troublemakers, and Nobodies: Black Children in Elementary School* (Westport, Conn.: Greenwood, 1978).
73. Basil Bernstein, "Social Class and Linguistic Development: A Theory of Social Learning," in A. H. Halsey, Jean Floud, and C. Arnold Anderson (eds.), *Education, Economy and Society* (New York: Free Press, 1961). A follow-up of Bernstein's work will be found in three volumes: Bernstein (ed.), *Class, Codes and Control* (London: Routledge and Kegan Paul, 1971, 1973, 1975).
74. Robert D. Hess and Virginia C. Shipman, "Maternal Influences upon Early Learning: The Cognitive Environments of Urban Pre-School Children," in R. D. Hess and R. M. Bear (eds.), *Early Education: Current Theory, Research, and Action* (Chicago: Aldine, 1968), p. 103.
75. James Coleman et al., *Equality of Educational Opportunity* (Washing-

ton, D.C.: U.S. Government Printing Office, 1966); Christopher Jencks et al., *Inequality* (New York: Basic Books, 1972).

76. For a review of these studies, see Maurice R. Berube, *Education and Poverty: Effective Schooling in the United States and Cuba* (Westport, Conn.: Greenwood Press, 1984). Also see Michael Rutter et al., *Fifteen Thousand Hours* (Cambridge, Mass.: Harvard University Press, 1979); and Sara Lawrence Lightfoot, *Worlds Apart: Relationships between Families and Schools* (New York: Basic Books, 1978), pp. 171–175.

77. James Coleman, *High School Achievement: Public, Catholic and Other Private Schools Compared* (New York: Basic Books, 1982). A prepublication version of the book, entitled *Public and Private Schools*, was discussed by several critics in *Harvard Educational Review*, 51:4 (November 1981), 481–545.

78. See Berube, op. cit.

79. A. H. Halsey, A. F. Heath, and J. M. Ridge, *Origins and Destinations: Family, Class and Education in Modern Britain* (New York: Oxford University Press, 1980), p. 188.

80. David L. Featherman and Robert M. Hauser, *Opportunity and Change* (New York: Academic Press, 1978), p. 92.

81. Philip W. Jackson, *Life in Classrooms* (New York: Holt, Rinehart and Winston, 1968), p. 5.

82. Ibid., p. 18.

83. R. Timothy Sieber, "Socialization Implications of School Discipline, or How First-Graders Are Taught to 'Listen,' " in R. Timothy Sieber and Andrew J. Gordon, eds., *Children and Their Organizations: Investigations in American Culture* (Boston: G. K. Hall, 1981), pp. 18–43.

84. Gouldner, op. cit., p. 58.

85. Jackson, *Life in Classrooms*, p. 20.

86. Rist, op. cit., pp. 85–86.

87. Nancy L. Karweit, "Time in School," in Alan C. Kerckhoff and Ronald G. Corwin, eds., *Research in Sociology of Education and Socialization*, Vol. 2 (Greenwich, Conn.: JAI Press, 1981), pp. 77–110; Sarane Spence Boocock, "The Social Organization of the Classroom," in Ralph H. Turner, James Coleman, and Renee C. Fox (eds.), *Annual Review of Sociology*, Vol. 4 (Palo Alto, Calif.: Annual Reviews, 1978), pp. 1–28.

88. Talcott Parsons, "The School Class as a Social System: Some of Its Functions in American Society," *Harvard Educational Review*, 29 (1959), 297–318, reprinted in Talcott Parsons, *Social Structure and Personality* (New York: Free Press, 1964).

89. Merton, op. cit.

90. Robert Rosenthal and Lenore Jacobson, *Pygmalion in the Classroom: Teacher Expectation and Pupils' Intellectual Development* (New York: Holt,

Rinehart and Winston, 1968), p. vii. This book also includes a summary of other pertinent research on self-fulfilling prophecies.

91. Ibid., p. 70.
92. H. M. Cooper, "Pygmalion Grows Up: A Model for Teacher Expectation Communication and Performance Influence," *Review of Educational Research*, 49 (1979), 389–410; R. Rosenthal and D. B. Rubin, "Interpersonal Expectancy Effects: The First 34 Studies," *The Behavioral and Brain Sciences*, 1 (1978), 377–386.
93. Eleanor Burke Leacock, *Teaching and Learning in City Schools: A Comparative Study* (New York: Basic Books, 1969).
94. Ibid., p. 205.
95. John U. Ogbu, *The Next Generation: An Ethnography of Education in an Urban Neighborhood* (New York: Academic Press, 1974), p. 97. In original, the emphasis was in boldface.
96. Ibid., p. 98.
97. Ibid., p. 2.
98. Ibid., p. 13.
99. Ibid., p. 143.
100. Ibid., p. 258.
101. John U. Ogbu, "A Cultural Ecology of Competence among Inner-City Blacks," in Margaret B. Spencer, Geraldine K. Brookins, and Walter R. Allen, *Beginnings: The Social and Affective Development of Black Children* (Hillsdale, N.J.: Lawrence Erlbaum Associates, 1985), p. 57.
102. Iona and Peter Opie, *Children's Games in Street and Playground* (Oxford: Oxford University Press, 1969), p. 17.
103. Ibid., p. 18.
104. Mary and Herbert Knapp, *One Potato, Two Potato* (New York: Norton, 1976), p. 29.
105. Philippe Ariès, "Games, Fashions and Society," in Ariès et al., *The World of Children* (London: Paul Hamlyn, 1966), pp. 101–111.
106. Opie and Opie, op. cit., p. 10.
107. Iona and Peter Opie, *The Lore and Language of Schoolchildren* (Oxford: Oxford University Press, 1959).
108. Knapp and Knapp, *One Potato, Two Potato*, p. 12.
109. Sue Parrott, "Games Children Play: Ethnography of Second-Grade Recess," in James P. Spradley and David W. McCurdy (eds.), *The Cultural Experience* (Chicago: Science Research Associates, 1972), pp. 207–219.
110. Gary A. Fine, *With the Boys: Little League Baseball and Preadolescent Culture* (Chicago: University of Chicago Press, 1987), Chap. 7.
111. Harry Webb, "Professionalization of Attitudes toward Play among Adolescents," in Gerald S. Kenyon (ed.), *Aspects of Contemporary Sport Sociology* (Chicago: The Athletic Institute, 1969), p. 164.

112. Ibid., p. 178.

113. Janet Lever, "Soccer as a Brazilian Way of Life," in Gregory P. Stone (ed.), *Games, Sport and Power* (New Brunswick, N.J.: Transaction Books, 1972), p. 148.

114. Janet Lever, *Soccer Madness* (Chicago: University of Chicago Press, 1984), pp. 130–135.

115. Ariès, op. cit., p. 107.

116. Willard W. Hartup, "Peer Relations and the Growth of Social Competence," in Martha W. Kent and Jon E. Rolf (eds.), *Primary Prevention of Psychopathology*, Vol. 3, *Social Competence in Children* (Hanover, N.H.: University Press of New England, 1979), pp. 150–170.

117. Edward Devereux, "Backyard versus Little League Baseball: The Impoverishment of Children's Games," in Daniel M. Landers (ed.), *Social Problems in Athletics* (Urbana: University of Illinois Press, 1976), pp. 48–49.

118. James Youniss, *Parents and Peers in Social Development* (Chicago: University of Chicago Press, 1980).

119. William A. Corsaro, *Friendship and Peer Culture in the Early Years* (Norwood, N.J.: Ablex, 1985), p. 269.

120. Merton, op. cit., p. 302.

121. Harry Stack Sullivan, *The Interpersonal Theory of Psychiatry* (New York: Norton, 1953), p. 245.

122. Michael P. Farrell, "Friendship between Men," in Lewis and Sussman, op. cit., pp. 169–174.

123. Hartup, op. cit., p. 156.

124. Ibid., p. 157. See also Carlfred B. Broderick, "Social Heterosexual Development Among Urban Negroes and Whites," *Journal of Marriage and Family*, 27 (May 1965), 200–203; Carlfred B. Broderick, "Sexual Behavior among Preadolescents," *Journal of Social Issues*, 22 (April 1966), 6–21; and Boone E. Hammond and Joyce A. Ladner, "Socialization into Sexual Behavior in a Negro Slum Ghetto," in Carlfred B. Broderick and Jessie Bernard (eds.), *The Individual, Sex and Society* (Baltimore: The Johns Hopkins Press, 1969).

125. Opie and Opie, *Lore and Language*, p. 97.

126. Mary Ellen Goodman, *Culture of Childhood* (New York: Teachers College Press, 1970), pp. 138–139.

127. Brian Sutton-Smith, "Towards an Anthropology of Play," in Phillips Stevens, Jr. (ed.), *Studies in the Anthropology of Play: Papers in Memory of B. Allan Tindall* (West Point, N.Y.: Leisure Press, 1977), pp. 222–232. Also see Helen B. Schwartzman, *Transformations: The Anthropology of Children's Play* (New York: Plenum Press, 1978).

128. Among the general works dealing with mass communications are Charles R. Wright, *Mass Communication: A Sociological Perspective*, 2nd ed. (New York: Random House, 1975); and Lewis Anthony Dexter

and David Manning White (eds.), *People, Society and Mass Communications* (New York: Free Press, 1964). See also F. Gerald Kline and Phillip J. Tichenor (eds.), *Current Perspectives in Mass Communication* (Beverly Hills, Calif.: Sage Publications, 1972), Vol. 1, Sage Annual Reviews of Communication Research.

129. Donald Horton and R. Richard Wohl, "Mass Communication and Para-Social Interaction," *Psychiatry*, 19 (August 1956), 215.

130. Melvin L. DeFleur and Lois B. DeFleur, "The Relative Contribution of Television as a Learning Source for Children's Occupational Knowledge," *American Sociological Review*, 32 (October 1967), 777–789. See also a study by Melvin L. DeFleur, "Occupational Roles as Portrayed on Television," *Public Opinion Quarterly*, 28 (Spring 1964), 57–74, which shows that the occupational roles portrayed on television are disproportionately higher status compared to the distribution of occupations in the actual work world. Television thus does not present children with a realistic array of occupational models.

131. John R. Rossiter, "Source Effects and Self-Concept Appeals in Children's Television Advertising," in Richard P. Adler et al., *The Effects of Television Advertising on Children* (Lexington, Mass.: Lexington Books, 1980), p. 67.

132. Anthony Comstock, *Traps for the Young* (Cambridge, Mass.: Belknap Press of Harvard University Press, 1967 reissue, p. 13; original publication: New York: Funk & Wagnalls, 1883).

133. Fredric Wertham, *Seduction of the Innocent* (New York: Rinehart, 1953.)

134. Neil Postman, *Amusing Ourselves to Death: Public Discourse in the Age of Show Business* (New York: Viking Books, 1985); Marie Winn, *The Plug-In Drug,* rev. ed. (New York: Penguin Books, 1985.)

135. Tipper Gore, *Raising PG Kids in an X-Rated Society* (Nashville, Tenn.: Abingdon Press, 1987).

136. *Television Audience 1987* (New York: Nielsen Television Index, 1987).

137. Jack Lyle and Heidi R. Hoffman, "Children's Use of Television and Other Media," in Eli A. Rubenstein, George A. Comstock, and John P. Murray (eds.), *Television and Social Behavior, Reports and Papers* (Washington, D.C.: U.S. Government Printing Office, 1972), pp. 192–193, 137–138.

138. Bradley S. Greenberg and Brenda Dervin, with the assistance of Joseph R. Dominick and John Bowes, *Use of the Mass Media by the Urban Poor. Findings of Three Research Projects, with an Annotated Bibliography* (New York: Praeger, 1970), p. 70.

139. Lyle and Hoffman, "Children's Use," Table 13, p. 147; and Lyle and Hoffman, "Pre-School Age Children," Table 5, p. 262.

140. Lyle and Hoffman, "Children's Use," pp. 148–149.
141. George Comstock and Robin E. Cobbey, "Television and the Children of Ethnic Minorities: Perspectives from Research," in Gordon L. Berry and Claudia Mitchell-Kernan (eds.), *Television and the Socialization of the Minority Child* (New York: Academic Press, 1982), pp. 245–259.
142. A. C. Nielsen, *Nielsen Report on Television* (Northbrook, Ill.: A. C. Nielsen Co., 1981), pp. 14–15. Cited in Meyrowitz, *No Sense of Place*, p. 150.
143. *Television Audience,* 1987, op. cit.
144. F. Earle Barcus, *Images of Life on Children's Television: Sex Roles, Minorities, and Families* (New York: Praeger, 1983), p. 16.
145. Ibid., Part II, pp. 19–65.
146. Ibid., Part III, pp. 69–115.
147. Ibid., Part IV, pp. 119–155.
148. Tannis MacBeth Williams (ed.), *The Impact of Television: A Natural Experiment in Three Communities* (Orlando, Fla.: Academic Press, 1986).
149. *Television and Growing Up: The Impact of Televised Violence,* Report to the Surgeon General, United States Public Health Service, from the Surgeon General's Scientific Advisory Committee on Television and Social Behavior (Washington, D.C.: U.S. Government Printing Office, 1972). For an update on the technical research, which gives a much lesser role to violence and aggression, see David Pearl, Lorraine Bouthilet, and Joyce Lazar (eds.), *Television and Behavior: Ten Years of Scientific Progress and Implications for the Eighties,* Vols. 1 and 2 (Rockville, Md.: National Institute of Mental Health, 1982).
150. T. M. Williams and Michael C. Boyes, "Television-Viewing Patterns and Use of Other Media," in Williams (ed.), op. cit., Chap. 5.
151. T. M. Williams and A. Gordon Handford, "Television and Other Leisure Activities," in Williams (ed.), op. cit., Chap. 4, Table A.48, p. 193.
152. Ibid., Table 4.A3, p. 190.
153. Raymond S. Corteen and T. M. Williams "Television and Reading Skills," in Williams (ed.), op. cit., Chap. 2.
154. T. M. Williams, "Summary, Conclusions, and Implications," in Williams (ed.), op. cit., pp. 397–398. Also see Chap. 3 by Linda Faye Harrison and T. M. Williams.
155. Joyce N. Sprafkin and Robert M. Liebert, "Sex Typing and Children's Television," in Gaye Tuchman et al. (eds.), *Hearth and Home:*

Images of Women in Mass Media: (New York: Oxford University Press, 1978), pp. 228–239.

156. Meredith M. Kimball, "Television and Sex-Role Attitudes," in Williams (ed.), op. cit., Chap. 6.

157. *Television and Growing Up: The Impact of Televised Violence,* op. cit., p. 186. Also in summary chapter, pp. 18–19.

158. Lesley A. Joy, Meredith M. Kimball, and Merle L. Zabrack, "Television and Children's Aggressive Behavior," in Williams (ed.), op. cit. p. 334. Also see Chap. 7.

159. Robert Hodge and David Tripp, *Children and Television* (Cambridge: Polity Press, 1986).

160. Ibid., p. 112.

161. Ibid., p. 115.

162. Ibid., p. 140.

163. George Gerbner and Larry Gross, "The Violent Face of Television and Its Lessons," in Edward L. Palmer and Aimee Dorr (eds.), *Children and the Faces of Television* (New York: Academic Press, 1980); pp. 152–153.

164. Ibid., p. 160.

165. Hodge and Tripp, op. cit., pp. 94–95. Also see pp. 85–95.

166. Ibid., pp. 155–156.

167. Ibid., p. 156.

168. Ibid., p. 158.

169. Adler and Faber, op. cit., p. 17.

170. Ira O. Glick and Sidney J. Levy, *Living with Television* (Chicago: Aldine, 1962), p. 206.

171. Laurene Krasny Meringoff, "The Effects of Children's Television Food Advertising," and Thomas S. Robertson, "Television Advertising and Parent-Child Relations," in Adler, op. cit.

172. George A. Comstock, "The Effects of Television on Children and Adolescents: The Evidence So Far," *Journal of Communication,* 25 (Autumn 1975), 27.

173. Robert M. Liebert, John M. Neale, and Emily S. Davidson, *The Early Window: Effects of Television on Children and Youth* (New York: Pergamon, 1973), p. 157.

174. Joshua Meyrowitz, *No Sense of Place: The Impact of Electronic Media on Social Behavior* (New York: Oxford University Press, 1985).

175. Patricia A. Adler and Peter Adler, "The Carpool: A Socializing Adjunct to the Educational Experience," *Sociology of Education* 57 (October 1984), 200–210.

176. Fine, op. cit., pp. 5, 20–21.

177. Ibid., p. 61.

178. Ibid., p. 79.

Chapter 6: Sex, Socialization, and Gender

1. John Money and Anke A. Ehrhardt, *Man & Woman, Boy & Girl* (Baltimore, Md.: The Johns Hopkins University Press, 1972). Another useful summary, placing sexual reproduction in the framework of evolutionary biology, is that of anthropologists M. Kay Martin and Barbara Voorhies, *Female of the Species* (New York: Columbia University Press, 1975), Chap. 2.

2. Ibid., p. 7.

3. Money and Ehrhardt write, "Normal differentiation of genital morphology entails a dimorphic sex difference in the arrangement of the peripheral nerves of sex which, in turn, entails some degree of dimorphism in the representation of the periphery at the centrum of the central nervous system, that is to say, in the structures and pathways of the brain." Ibid., p. 8. See also Money and Ehrhardt, op. cit., p. 49.

4. Joan Vernikos-Danellis, "Effects of Hormones on the Central Nervous System," in Seymour Levine (ed.), *Hormones and Behavior* (New York: Academic Press, 1972), pp. 12–13.

5. Ibid., p. 50. A more skeptical view is taken by neuroanatomist Ruth H. Bleier, "Brain, Body, and Behavior," in Joan I. Roberts (ed.), *Beyond Intellectual Sexism. A New Woman, A New Reality* (New York: David McKay, 1976).

6. Anke A. Ehrhardt, "The Psychobiology of Gender," in Alice S. Rossi (ed.), *Gender and the Life Course* (New York: Aldine, 1985), p. 91.

7. Psychologist David Tresemer has noted that not all societies are as insistent upon two morphological sexes. David Tresemer, "Assumptions Made About Gender Roles," in Marcia Millman and Rosabeth Moss Kanter (eds.), *Another Voice: Feminist Perspectives on Social Life and Social Science* (Garden City, N.Y.: Anchor Books, 1975), pp. 314–315. But see also Martin and Voorhies, op. cit., pp. 88–89.

8. Jean Stockard and Miriam M. Johnson, *Sex Roles: Sex Inequality and Sex Role Development* (Englewood Cliffs, N.J.: Prentice-Hall, 1980), p. 4.

9. Michelle Z. Rosaldo, "The Use and Abuse of Anthropology: Reflections on Feminism and Cross-Cultural Understanding," *Signs: Journal of Women in Culture and Society,* 5 (Spring 1980), 394–395.

10. Martin and Voorhies, op. cit., p. 10.

11. Peggy Reeves Sanday, *Female Power and Male Dominance* (Cambridge: Cambridge University Press, 1981), p. 28. See also Judith K. Brown, "Iroquois Women: An Ethnohistoric Note," in Rayna R. Reiter (ed.), *Toward an Anthropology of Women* (New York: Monthly Review Press, 1975).

12. Steven Goldberg, *The Inevitability of Patriarchy* (New York: William Morrow, paperback edition, 1974), p. 98.

13. Sanday, op. cit., p. 114.

14. Martin and Voorhies, op. cit., pp. 10–11.

15. Ibid., pp. 406–408.

16. John Money and Patricia Tucker, *Sexual Signatures: On Being a Man or a Woman* (Boston: Little, Brown, 1975), Chap. 3, "Sex Hormones on the Brain," pp. 78–80.

17. Roy G. D'Andrade, "Sex Differences and Cultural Institutions," in Eleanor E. Maccoby (ed.), *The Development of Sex Differences* (Stanford, Calif.: Stanford University Press, 1966), pp. 177–178.

18. U.S. Department of Labor, 1980. Cited in Jacquelynn S. Eccles and Lois W. Hoffman, "Sex Roles, Socialization, and Occupational Behavior," in Harold W. Stevenson and Alberta E. Siegel, (eds.) *Child Development Research and Social Policy* (Chicago: University of Chicago Press, 1984), pp. 372–373.

19. Women's Bureau, *Women in the Labour Force,* 1986–1987 edition (Ottawa: Labour Canada, 1987), p. 17.

20. Natalie J. Sokoloff, "The Increase of Black and White Women in the Professions: A Contradictory Process," in Christine Bose and Glenna Spitze (eds.), *Ingredients for Women's Employment Policy* (Albany: State University of New York Press, 1987), Table 3.1, p. 57.

21. Jane E. Prather, "When the Girls Move In: A Sociological Analysis of the Feminization of the Bank Teller's Job," *Journal of Marriage and the Family,* 33 (November 1971), 777–782.

22. Richard Flaste, "The Frustrating Battle Against Sex Stereotyping," *The New York Times,* November 12, 1976, p. B5.

23. Stanley W. Moore, James Lare, and Kenneth A. Wagner, *The Child's Political World* (New York: Praeger, 1985), pp. 213–217.

24. C. Bacon and R. M. Lerner, "Effects of Maternal Employment Status on the Development of Vocational Role Perception in Females," *Journal of Genetic Psychology,* 126 (1975), 187–193.

25. C. H. Gregg and K. Dobson, "Occupational and Sex-role Stereotyping and Occupational Interests in Children," *Elementary School Guidance and Counseling, 1980,* 15 (1980), 66–75.

26. Women's Bureau, *When I Grow Up: Career Expectations and Aspirations of Canadian Schoolchildren* (Ottawa: Labour Canada, 1986), p. 55.

27. Ibid., p. 56.

28. Helen Mayer Hacker, "Women as a Minority Group," *Social Forces,* 30 (October 1951), 60–69. This paper has been reprinted in many anthologies. The notion that women are discriminated against in ways paralleling discrimination against blacks was set forth a few years earlier by the noted Swedish social scientist Gunnar Myrdal in "A Parallel to the Negro Problem," in his monumental study, *An American Dilemma: The Negro Problem and Modern Democracy* (New York: Harper & Brothers, 1944), Appendix 5.

29. Jean Lipman-Blumen and Ann Tickameyer, "Sex Roles in Transi-

tion: A Ten-Year Perspective," in *Annual Review of Sociology,* Vol. 1 (Palo Alto, Calif.: Annual Reviews, 1975), pp. 313–314. This article presents the most comprehensive summary known to us of the literature on sex roles. Also valuable in the present context is the briefer summary by Arlie Hochschild, "A Review of Sex Role Research," *American Journal of Sociology,* 78 (January 1973), 1011–1029.

30. C. D. Spinellis, Vasso Vassiliou, and George Vassiliou, "Milieu Development and Male-Female Roles in Contemporary Greece," in Georgene H. Seward and Robert C. Williamson, *Sex Roles in Changing Society* (New York: Random House, 1970), p. 313.

31. Ibid.

32. Rita Liljestrom, "The Swedish Model," in Seward and Williamson, op. cit., pp. 205–206.

33. The literature on the history of sex-role and sex-status changes in the United States is large. One valuable discussion is Peter Gabriel Filene, *Him/Her/Self: Sex Roles in Modern America* (New York: Harcourt, Brace, Jovanovich, 1974).

34. Irene Hanson Frieze and Sheila J. Ramsey, "Nonverbal Maintenance of Traditional Sex Roles," *Journal of Social Issues,* 32 (Summer 1976), 136.

35. Ibid., p. 139. For a classic discussion of how such restrictions were experienced by a talented and creative woman, see Virginia Woolf, *A Room of One's Own* (New York: Harcourt, Brace, 1929).

36. Betty Yorburg, *Sexual Identity: Sex Roles and Social Change* (New York: Wiley, 1974), p. 1.

37. Fine, *With the Boys,* p. 185.

38. Joseph H. Pleck, *The Myth of Masculinity* (Cambridge, Mass.: M.I.T. Press, 1981), p. 143.

39. Phyllis A. Katz, "The Development of Female Identity," in Claire E. Kopp (ed.), *Becoming Female* (New York: Plenum Press, 1979), pp. 14–16.

40. Ibid., p. 19.

41. Lois W. Hoffman, "Early Childhood Experiences and Women's Achievement Motives," in Martha T. Mednick, Sandra Schwartz Tangri, and Lois Wladis Hoffman (eds.), *Women and Achievement: Social and Motivational Analysis* (Washington, D.C.: Hemisphere Publishing, 1975), pp. 129, 136. Hoffman's contention gains some cross-cultural support from an earlier study of eighty-two societies that found that 85 percent of them socialized boys to self-reliance to a greater extent than girls. Also, 85 percent of them socialized only boys to be achievers, and only 15 percent showed no significant differences in the treatment of girls and boys in this regard. See Herbert A. Barry, Margaret K. Bacon, and Irvin L. Child, "A Cross-Cultural Survey of Some Sex Differences in Socialization," *Journal of*

Abnormal and Social Psychology, 55 (1957), 327–332, findings summarized in Martin and Voorhies, op. cit., pp. 68, 76.

42. Ibid., p. 136.
43. K. Alison Clarke-Stewart, "The Father's Contribution to Children's Cognitive and Social Development in Early Childhood," in Frank A. Pedersen (ed.), *The Father-Infant Relationship* (New York: Praeger, 1980), pp. 111–146.
44. Ross D. Parke and Douglas B. Sawin, "The Family in Early Infancy: Social Interactional and Attitudinal Analyses," in Pedersen (ed.), op. cit., pp. 44–70.
45. Clarke-Stewart, op. cit., p. 141; H. L. Frisch, "Sex Stereotypes in Adult-Infant Play," *Child Development,* 48 (1977), 1671–1675.
46. E. B. Greif, "Sex Differences in Parent-Child Conversations," *Women's Studies International Quarterly,* 3 (1980), 253–258.
47. Clarke-Stewart, op. cit., p. 139.
48. Ibid., p. 140.
49. Hoffman, op. cit., p. 139.
50. W. E. Lambert, A. Yackley, and R. N. Hein, "Child Training Values of English Canadian and French Canadian Parents," *Canadian Journal of Behavioral Science,* 3 (1971), 217–236.
51. Hoffman, op. cit., pp. 140–141; Weitzman, op. cit., pp. 116, 118.
52. Hoffman, op. cit., pp. 143–144. For a slightly different emphasis, see the interpretation in Aletha Huston Stein and Margaret M. Bailey, "The Socialization of Achievement Orientation in Females," *Psychological Bulletin,* 80:5 (1973), 345–366 and 358 ff.
53. Ruth E. Hartley, "Sex Role Pressures and the Socialization of the Male Child," reprinted from *Psychological Reports* (1959), in Judith Stacey, Susan Bereaud, and Joan Daniels (eds.), *And Jill Came Tumbling After: Sexism in American Education* (New York: Dell, 1974).
54. Evelyn Goodenough Pitcher, "Male and Female," in Stacey et al., op. cit., p. 81.
55. Mary Ann Kacerguis and Gerald R. Adams, "Implications of Sex Typed Child Rearing Practices, Toys, and Mass Media Materials in Restricting Occupational Choices of Women," *Family Coordinator,* 28 (1979), 368–375.
56. Carol A. Seavy, Phyllis A. Katz, and Sue R. Zalk, "Baby X: The Effect of Gender Labels on Adult Responses to Infants," *Sex Roles,* 1 (1975), 103–109.
57. Eleanor Emmons Maccoby and Carol Nagy Jacklin, *The Psychology of Sex Differences* (Stanford, Calif.: Stanford University Press, 1974), p. 278.
58. Beverly I. Fagot, "The Socialization of Sex Differences in Early Childhood," unpublished paper, 1978, cited in Jean Stockard and

Miriam M. Johnson, *Sex Roles* (Englewood Cliffs, N.J.: Prentice-Hall, 1980), p. 184.

59. Ibid., p. 279.
60. Jacquelynne S. Eccles and Lois W. Hoffman, "Sex Roles, Socialization, and Occupational Behavior," in Harold W. Stevenson and Alberta E. Siegel (eds.), *Child Development Research and Social Policy*, Vol. 1 (Chicago: University of Chicago Press, 1984), p. 388.
61. Janet Saltzman Chafetz, *Masculine/Feminine or Human? An Overview of the Sociology of Sex Roles* (Itasca, Ill.: F. E. Peacock Publishers, 1974), p. 81.
62. John Ferri, " 'Born to shop' electronic age kids are spending billions on themselves," *Sunday Star* (Toronto), September 6, 1987, p. 1.
63. Charles Winick, Lorne G. Williamson, Stuart F. Chuzmir, and Mariann Pezzella Winick, *Children's Television Commercials: A Content Analysis* (New York: Praeger, 1973), p. 27.
64. Chafetz, op. cit., p. 82.
65. Nancy J. Cobb, Judith Stevens-Long, and Steven Goldstein, "The Influence of Televised Models on Toy Preferences in Children," *Sex Roles*, 8 (1982), 1075–1080.
66. Ferri, op. cit., p. A14.
67. Brian Sutton-Smith, *Toys as Culture* (New York: Gardner Press, 1986), p. 190.
68. Information from Alleen Pace Nilsen, "Women in Children's Literature," *College English* (May 1971), in Diane Gersoni-Stavn, *Sexism and Youth* (New York: R.R. Bowker, 1974) and from Lenore J. Weitzman, Deborah Eiffler, Elizabeth Hokada, and Catherine Ross, "Sex-Role Socialization in Picture Books for Pre-School Children," *American Journal of Sociology*, 77:6 (May 1972).
69. Nilsen in Gersoni-Stavn, op. cit., p. 168.
70. Ibid., p. 169.
71. Weitzman et al., op. cit., pp. 179–180. This study also included other works in addition to Caldecott winners and runners-up; the other works were substantially similar in their portrayals of sex roles.
72. Sara Lawrence Lightfoot, "Sociology of Women: Perspectives on Women," in Millman and Kanter, op. cit., p. 136.
73. Raphaela Best, *We've All Got Scars: What Boys and Girls Learn in Elementary School* (Bloomington: Indiana University Press, 1983), p. 22.
74. L. A. Serbin, K. D. O'Leary, R. N. Kent, and I. J. Tonick, "A Comparison of Teacher Response to the Pre-Academic and Problem Behavior of Boys and Girls," *Child Development*, 44 (1973), 796–804, summarized in Eleanor Emmons Maccoby and Carol Nagy Jacklin, *The Psychology of Sex Differences* (Stanford, Calif.: Stanford University Press, 1974), p. 579. For a study of a nursery school that seeks to

minimize sex-role socialization, see Carole Joffe, "Sex Role Socialization and the Nursery School: As the Twig Is Bent," *Journal of
Marriage and the Family,* 33 (August 1971), 467–475.

75. See Joffe, op. cit.
76. Betty Levy, "The School's Role in the Sex-Role Stereotyping of
Girls: A Feminist Review of the Literature," in Gersoni-Stavn, op.
cit., p. 58.
77. Ibid., pp. 59–60.
78. Ibid., p. 53.
79. Ibid., p. 54.
80. Women on Words and Images, "Look Jane Look. See Sex Stereotypes," in Stacey, Bereaud, and Daniels, op. cit., p. 169. This is an
excerpt from a report entitled "Dick and Jane as Victims: Sex Stereotyping in Children's Readers." Somewhat different excerpts from it
are reprinted in Gersoni-Stavn, op. cit.
81. Sara Goodman Zimet, "Males and Females in American Primers
from Colonial Days to the Present," in Sara Goodman Zimet (ed.),
*What Children Read in School: Critical Analysis of Primary Reading Text-
books* (New York: Grune & Stratton, 1972), p. 83.
82. Ibid., pp. 83 and 121. See also the discussion in Clarice Stasz Stoll,
Female & Male: Socialization, Social Roles, and Social Structure (Dubuque,
Iowa: William C. Brown, 1974), pp. 102–104. As Stoll notes, different studies have used different categories for assessing how the two
sexes are presented in textbooks.
83. For feminist evaluations of diverse categories of children's literature, see Gersoni-Stavn, op. cit., "Books: Propaganda and the Sins
of Omission," Part 3.
84. Eleanor J. Gibson and Harry Levin, *The Psychology of Reading* (Cambridge, Mass.: M.I.T. Press, 1975), p. 270.
85. David E. Austin, Velma B. Clark, and Gladys W. Fitchett, *Reading
Rights for Boys: Sex Role in Language Experience* (New York: Appleton-
Century-Crofts, 1971), p. 1.
86. Ibid., p. 2.
87. B. Sutton-Smith and B. G. Rosenberg, "Sixty Years of Historical
Change in the Game Preferences of American Children," in R. E.
Herron and Brian Sutton-Smith (eds.), *Child's Play* (New York:
Wiley, 1971), p. 48.
88. A similar conclusion is reached by Charles Winick, *The New People:
Desexualization in American Life* (New York: Pegasus, 1968), pp. 217 ff.
89. Fine, op. cit., p. 263.
90. Eccles and Hoffman, op. cit., p. 403.
91. Janet Lever, "Sex Differences in the Complexity of Children's Play,"
American Sociological Review, 43 (August 1978), 471–482.

92. Marjorie Harness Goodwin, "Directive-Response Speech Sequences in Girls' and Boys' Task Activities," in Sally McConnell-Ginet, Ruth Borker, and Nelly Furman (eds.), *Women and Language in Literature and Society* (New York: Praeger, 1980), p. 157.
93. Ibid., p. 158.
94. Ibid., p. 170.
95. Barrie Thorne and Zella Luria, "Sexuality and Gender in Children's Daily Worlds," *Social Problems,* 33 (1986), 176–190.
96. Barrie Thorne, "Girls and Boys Together . . . But Mostly Apart: Gender Arrangements in Elementary Schools," in Willard W. Hartup and Zick Rubin (eds.), *Relationships and Development* (Hillsdale, N.J.: Lawrence Erlbaum Associates, 1986), pp. 171–180.
97. Elizabeth J. Roberts, "Dimensions of Sexual Learning in Childhood," in Elizabeth J. Roberts (ed.), *Childhood Sexual Learning* (Cambridge, Mass.: Ballinger, 1980), p. 6.
98. Ruth Benedict, "Continuities and Discontinuities in Cultural Conditioning," in Clyde Kluckhohn and Henry A. Murray (eds.), *Personality in Nature, Society, and Culture* (New York: Knopf, 1948), p. 415.
99. Richard L. Currier, "Juvenile Sexuality in Global Perspective," in Larry L. Constantine and Floyd M. Martinson (eds.), *Children and Sex: New Findings, New Perspectives* (Boston: Little, Brown, 1981).
100. Roberts, op. cit.; Eileen Higham, "Sexuality in the Infant and Neonate: Birth to Two Years," in Benjamin B. Wolman and John Money (eds.), *Handbook of Human Sexuality* (Englewood Cliffs, N.J.: Prentice-Hall, 1980), Chap. 2.
101. Bjorn Helge Gundersen, Per Steinar Melas, and Jens E. Sklar, "Sexual Behavior of Preschool Children: Teachers' Observations," in Constantine and Martinson, op. cit., Chap. 5.
102. John H. Gagnon and William Simon, *Sexual Conduct: The Social Sources of Human Sexuality* (Chicago: Aldine, 1973), pp. 14–16.
103. Ibid., p. 39.
104. Carlfred B. Broderick, "Sexual Behavior Among Preadolescents," Chap. 2, p. 25; and James Elias and Paul Gebhard, "Sexuality and Sexual Learning in Childhood," Chap. 3, p. 40; both in Anne McCreary Juhasz (ed.), *Sexual Development and Behavior* (Homewood, Ill.: Dorsey Press, 1973).
105. Thore Langfeldt, "Childhood Masturbation: Individual and Social Organization," in Constantine and Martinson, op. cit., Chap. 6.
106. Gagnon and Simon, op. cit., p. 40.
107. Thorne and Luria, "Sexuality and Gender in Children's Daily Worlds," p. 181.
108. Ibid., p. 183.
109. Ibid., p. 184.

110. Ibid., pp. 187–188.

111. Thorne, "Girls and Boys Together . . ."

112. Lester A. Kirkendall, "Sex Education in the United States: A Historical Perspective," in Lorna Brown (ed.), *Sex Education in the Eighties* (New York: Plenum Press, 1981).

113. Gary F. Kelly, "Parents as Sex Educators," in Brown, op. cit.

114. Raphaela Best, op. cit., p. 109.

115. Sheila Collins, "Religion and the Sexual Learning of Children," in Roberts, op. cit., Chap. 8.

116. Florence C. Ladd, "Human Sexuality: Messages in Public Environments," in Roberts, op. cit., Chap. 9, p. 245.

117. Ibid., p. 254.

118. Ibid., pp. 256–257.

119. Cited in "AIDS and Sex," *Maclean's,* August 31, 1987, p. 31.

120. Yorburg, op. cit., p. 153.

121. This summary draws on Joseph H. Pleck, "The Male Sex Role: Definitions, Problems, and Sources of Change," *Journal of Social Issues,* 32:3 (1976), 155–164; Deborah S. David and Robert Brannon (eds.), *The Forty-Nine Percent Majority: The Male Sex Role* (Reading, Mass.: Addison-Wesley, 1976); Ruth E. Hartley, "American Core Culture: Changes and Continuities," in Seward and Williamson, op. cit.; and Yorburg, op. cit., Chap. 5.

122. Jessie Bernard, *Women and the Public Interest: An Essay on Policy and Protest* (Chicago: Aldine-Atherton, 1971), Chap. 5.

123. Some of the recent literature on this subject is reviewed by Maccoby and Jacklin, op. cit., pp. 140–141.

124. David Tresemer, *Fear of Success* (New York: Plenum Press, 1977), cited in Stockard and Johnson, op. cit., p. 165.

125. Eleanor E. Maccoby, "Sex Differences in Intellectual Functioning," in Eleanor E. Maccoby (ed.), *The Development of Sex Differences* (Stanford, Calif.: Stanford University Press, 1966); Alice S. Rossi, "Women in Science: Why So Few?" *Science,* May 28, 1965, pp. 1196–1202, reprinted in Constantina Safillos-Rothschild (ed.), *Toward a Sociology of Women* (Lexington, Mass.: Xerox Publishing, 1972), pp. 149 ff.

126. Lynn Fox, Dianne Tobin, and Linda Brody, "Sex Role Socialization and Achievement in Mathematics," in Michelle Andrisin Wittig and Anne C. Petersen (eds.), *Sex-Related Differences in Cognitive Functioning* (New York: Academic Press, 1979), Chap. 12.

127. Ray L. Birdwhistell, *Kinesics and Context: Essays on Body Motion Communication* (Philadelphia: University of Pennsylvania Press, 1970), Chap. 6, "Masculinity and Femininity as Display."

128. The information on language differences in this paragraph is taken

from Barrie Thorne and Nancy Henley, "Difference and Dominance: An Overview of Language, Gender, and Society," in Barrie Thorne and Nancy Henley (eds.), *Language and Sex: Difference and Dominance* (Rowley, Mass.: Newbury House Publishers, 1975). The quotation is from p. 18.

129. For discussions of various interpretations of relations between the sexes as power relationships, see Lipman-Blumen and Tickameyer, op. cit., pp. 313–321; Hochschild, op. cit.; and Hans Peter Dreitzel (ed.), *Family, Marriage and the Struggle of the Sexes. Recent Sociology No. 4* (New York: Macmillan, 1972).

130. Filene, op. cit.; David and Brannon, op. cit.; Yorburg, op. cit.

131. Nancy Chodorow, *The Reproduction of Mothering* (Berkeley: University of California Press, 1978), p. 11.

132. Ibid., p. 169.

133. Ibid., p. 181.

134. Ralph LaRossa and Maureen Mulligan LaRossa, *Transition to Parenthood: How Infants Change Families* (Beverly Hills, Calif.: Sage, 1981), p. 57.

135. Liljestrom, op. cit., pp. 205 ff.

136. Mark G. Field and Karen I. Flynn, "Worker, Mother, Housewife: Soviet Woman Today," in Seward and Williamson, op. cit., pp. 270–271.

137. Ibid., p. 262.

138. Albert I. Rabin, "The Sexes: Ideology and Reality in the Israeli Kibbutz," in Seward and Williamson, op. cit., Chap. 13. See also Melford Spiro, *Children of the Kibbutz,* 2nd ed. (Cambridge, Mass.: Harvard University Press, 1975), pp. 236–248.

139. Rabin, op. cit., p. 305. See also Martha Mednick, "Social Change and Sex-Role Inertia: The Case of the Kibbutz," in Michal Palgi, Joseph R. Blasi, Menachem Rosner, and Marilyn Safir (eds.), *Sexual Equality: The Israeli Kibbutz Tests the Theories,* Vol. 6 (Norwood, Pa.: Norwood Editions, 1983), pp. 69–90.

140. Amia Lieblich, *Kibbutz Makom* (New York: Pantheon Books, 1981).

141. Aviva Zamir, *Mothers and Daughters: Interviews with Kibbutz Women,* Vol. 12 (Norwood, Pa.: Norwood Editions, 1986).

142. Some researchers argue that the Israeli kibbutz, because of its social structure and unique history, does not serve as a good test case for purposes of comparative research. See Joseph R. Blasi, "Epilogue," in Palgi, Blasi, Rosner, and Safir, op. cit., pp. 305–315.

143. Alice S. Rossi, "Equality Between the Sexes: An Immodest Proposal," *Daedalus,* 93 (Spring 1964), 608. Rossi later published an important modification of her views. Alice S. Rossi, "A Biosocial Perspective on Parenting," *Daedalus,* 106 (Spring 1977), 1–31.

144. Alice S. Rossi, "Gender and Parenthood," in Alice S. Rossi (ed.), *Gender and the Life Course* (New York: Aldine, 1985), pp. 185–186.

145. Robert Redfield, "The Universally Human and the Culturally Variable," in Margaret Park Redfield (ed.), *Human Nature and the Study of Society: The Papers of Robert Redfield,* Vol. 1 (Chicago: University of Chicago Press, 1962), pp. 451–452.

Chapter 7: Socialization in Later Life

1. The dual character of socialization throughout the life cycle was first enunciated in what became a classic paper by anthropologist Ruth Benedict, "Continuities and Discontinuities in Cultural Conditioning," *Psychiatry,* 1 (1938), 161–167.

2. George Bernard Shaw's play *Pygmalion,* in which a professor of linguistics teaches a Cockney flower girl to become a "lady," dramatizes an effort to explore the limits of adult socialization. Since the girl had not merely to learn new things for which her previous experience had not prepared her but also to forget some things she had learned thoroughly, the play is, strictly speaking, about *resocialization,* the term commonly used to describe socialization that requires the abandonment of previous socialization.

3. Frank Musgrove, *Youth and Social Order* (Bloomington: Indiana University Press, 1964), p. 33.

4. Beatrice Vulcan, "American Social Policy Toward Youth and Youth Employment," in Melvin Herman, Stanley Sadofsky, and Bernard Rosenberg (eds.), *Work, Youth and Unemployment* (New York: Crowell, 1968), p. 8.

5. This trend is discussed by Kenneth Keniston, "Youth: A New Stage of Life," *American Scholar,* 39 (Autumn 1970), 631–654.

6. Talcott Parsons, "Age and Sex in the Social Structure of the United States," *American Sociological Review,* 7 (1942), 604–616, reprinted in Talcott Parsons, *Essays in Sociological Theory,* 2nd ed. (New York: Free Press, 1954).

7. Frederick Elkin and William A. Westley, "The Myth of Adolescent Culture," *American Sociological Review,* 20 (1955), 680–684; and William A. Westley and Frederick Elkin, "The Protective Environment and Adolescent Socialization," *Social Forces,* 35 (1957), 243–249. Parsons himself tempered his views in a later report. See Talcott Parsons, "Youth in the Context of American Society," *Daedalus,* 41 (1962), 97–123.

8. James S. Coleman, *The Adolescent Society: The Social Life of the Teenager and Its Impact on Education* (New York: Free Press, 1961).

9. Bennett M. Berger, "Adolescence and Beyond," *Social Problems,* 10 (1963), 394–408.

10. Marie Jahoda and Neil Warren, "The Myths of Youth," *Sociology of Education,* 38 (Winter 1965), 147.

11. See Michael Brake, *Comparative Youth Culture* (London: Routledge and Kegan Paul, 1985).

12. Diane M. Bush and Roberta G. Simmons, "Socialization Processes over the Life Course," in Morris Rosenberg and Ralph H. Turner (eds.), *Social Psychology: Sociological Perspectives* (New York: Basic Books, 1981), pp. 133–164.

13. John Gillis, *Youth and History: Tradition and Change in European Age Relations, 1770–Present* (New York: Academic Press, 1974), pp. 187, 191.

14. James S. Coleman and others, *Youth: Transition to Adulthood* (Chicago: University of Chicago Press, 1974). The volume is a Report of the Panel on Youth of the President's Science Advisory Committee.

15. Bob Franklin (ed.), *The Rights of Children* (Oxford: Basil Blackwell, 1986).

16. Lonnie R. Sherrod and Orville G. Brim, Jr., "Epilogue: Retrospective and Prospective Views of Life-Course Research on Human Development," in Aage B. Sorensen, Franz E. Weinert, and Lonnie R. Sherrod (eds.), *Human Development and the Life Course* (Hillsdale, N.J.: Lawrence Erlbaum Associates, 1986), p. 560.

17. Herbert Gans's Study, *The Levittowners: Ways of Life and Politics in a New Suburban Community* (New York: Vintage Books, 1969), is written as a community study, but many of his observations bear directly on adult socialization.

18. Irving Rosow, "Forms and Functions of Adult Socialization," *Social Forces,* 44 (September 1965), p. 43.

19. Stanton Wheeler, "The Structure of Formally Organized Socialization Settings," in Orville G. Brim, Jr., and Stanton Wheeler, *Socialization After Childhood: Two Essays* (New York: Wiley, 1966).

20. Charles E. Bidwell, unpublished paper cited by Wheeler, op. cit., p. 70.

21. Howard S. Becker, Blanche Geer, Everett C. Hughes, and Anselm L. Strauss, *Boys in White: Student Culture in Medical School* (Chicago: University of Chicago Press, 1961). See also Fred Davis, "Professional Socialization as Subjective Experience," in Howard S. Becker et al. (eds.), *Institutions and the Person* (Chicago: Aldine, 1968).

22. Wilbert E. Moore, "Occupational Socialization," in David A. Goslin (ed.), *Handbook of Socialization Theory and Research* (Chicago: Rand McNally, 1969), Chap. 21. See also Dan C. Lortie, "Shared Ordeal and Induction to Work," in Becker et al., *Institutions and the Person.*

23. Elaine Cumming and William E. Henry, *Growing Old: The Process of Disengagement* (New York: Basic Books, 1961).

24. Vern L. Bengtson, "Comparative Perspectives on the Microsociology of Aging: Methodological Problems and Theoretical Issues," in Victor W. Marshall (ed.), *Later Life: The Social Psychology of Aging* (Beverly Hills, Calif.: Sage Publications, 1986), pp. 312–313.
25. See Kathy Charmaz, *The Social Reality of Death in Contemporary America* (Reading, Mass.: Addison-Wesley, 1980).

SELECTED READINGS

Adler, Patricia A., and Peter Adler (eds.). *Sociological Studies of Child Development,* Vol. 1. Greenwich, Conn.: JAI Press, 1986.
> This is the first volume of a new Research Annual series. Its appearance signals a revival of interest among sociologists in studying socialization and a broad range of topics pertaining to social processes and social relationships in childhood.

Ariès, Philippe. *Centuries of Childhood.* New York: Random House, 1962.
> The author combines the skills of history, sociology, and art criticism to trace the emergence of the concept of childhood as a distinctive period of the life cycle.

Berger, Bennett M. *The Survival of a Counterculture.* Berkeley: University of California Press, 1981.
> An analysis of the ideology and everyday life of the members of rural communes, including their efforts at new approaches to socialization.

Bronfenbrenner, Urie. *Two Worlds of Childhood: U.S. and U.S.S.R.* New York: Russell Sage Foundation, 1970.
> Bronfenbrenner compares socialization in the societies of the world's two superpowers. He feels strongly that peer groups and television have undue influence on socialization of American children.

Clark, Reginald M. *Family Life and School Achievement. Why Poor Black Children Succeed or Fail.* Chicago: University of Chicago Press, 1983.
> This intensive study of ten families, comparing low achievers and high achievers from single-parent and two-parent families, concludes that family structure is less important than the socialization processes in the family. Parents who are able to provide "school survival skills" provide socialization that is advantageous for the child's school success.

Clausen, John A. (ed.). *Socialization and Society.* Boston: Little, Brown, 1968.
> Eight encyclopedic chapters examine the concept of socialization as used in several disciplines, cross-culturally, and at various phases in the life cycle.

Corsaro, William A. *Friendship and Peer Culture in the Early Years.* Norwood, N.J.: Ablex, 1985.
> Using videotaped peer interaction episodes, Corsaro studied three- and four-year-old children in a nursery school. He seeks to understand the meanings children themselves give to their peer-group play.

Erikson, Erik H. *Childhood and Society.* New York: Norton, 1950.
> Erikson employs a modified psychoanalytic approach in discussing stages of development and in analyzing the relationship between childhood training and cultural characteristics. These ideas are further developed in the same author's *Identity: Youth and Crisis,* Norton, 1968, and his *Identity and the Life Cycle,* Norton, 1980.

Ervin-Tripp, Susan, and Claudia Mitchell-Kernan (eds.). *Child Discourse.* New York: Academic Press, 1977.
> How do children use language? This is the central question in this collection of papers by linguists, anthropologists, and psychologists on the speech and communication of children.

Fine, Gary Alan. *With the Boys: Little League Baseball and Preadolescent Culture.* Chicago: University of Chicago Press, 1987.
> In this study of boys who participate in Little League baseball, Fine considers both the socialization that derives from an adult-directed sports activity and the subculture of preadolescent boys.

Goffman, Erving. *Asylums: Essays on the Social Situation of Mental Patients and Other Inmates.* New York: Doubleday Anchor, 1961.
> In this classic study, Goffman analyzes the efforts of total institutions, especially the mental asylum, to resocialize their inmates.

Goldstein, Bernard, and Jack Oldham. *Children and Work: A Study of Socialization.* New Brunswick, N.J.: Transaction Books, 1979.
> The authors studied elementary school children in order to learn about their work experiences and their attitudes toward work and occupations.

Goslin, David A. *Handbook of Socialization Theory and Research.* Chicago: Rand McNally, 1969.
> This reference work has useful chapters on many aspects of socialization.

Greven, Philip J., Jr. *Child-Rearing Concepts, 1628–1861: Historical Sources.* Itasca, Ill.: F. E. Peacock Publishers, 1973.

This collection of essays and sermons by early American Christian writers documents their emphasis on controlling and suppressing the child's will. The last essay in the collection signals the beginning of a change in 1861.

Hartup, Willard W., and Zick Rubin (eds). *Relationships and Development,* Hillsdale, N.J.: Lawrence Erlbaum Associates, 1986.
This volume, with papers from a conference in June 1982, focuses on the links between children's relationships with other people and their social and emotional development. Contributors include representatives from developmental psychology, clinical psychology, sociology, and anthropology.

Hawes, Joseph M., and N. Ray Hiner (eds.). *American Childhood: A Research Guide and Historical Handbook.* Westport, Conn: Greenwood Press, 1985.
Edited by two historians, this encyclopedic volume reviews childhood in the United States from the seventeenth century to the early 1980s. Included are chapters on children's literature, native Indians, the child reform movement, and postwar baby boom.

Hess, Robert D., and Gerald Handel. *Family Worlds: A Psychosocial Approach to Family Life.* Chicago: University of Chicago Press, 1959.
Five midwestern families of different social class levels are analyzed, using data obtained from the children and parents of each family, to show how the family group functions as a socializing agency.

Hiner, N. Ray, and Joseph M. Hawes (eds.). *Growing Up in America: Children in Historical Perspective.* Urbana: University of Illinois Press, 1985.
This anthology begins with a chapter on colonial New England, includes discussions on infant abandonment, the juvenile court movement, the play of slave children and childhood in an urban black ghetto, and concludes with a discussion of the government's *Infant Care* bulletin and Spock's *Baby and Child Care.*

Hobbs, Nicholas. *The Futures of Children.* San Francisco: Jossey-Bass, 1975.
Hobbs examines the practices of classifying and labeling exceptional children, and he discusses the social consequences of such labeling.

Hunt, David. *Parents and Children in History: The Psychology of Family Life in Early Modern France.* New York: Basic Books, 1970.

This critical review of Philippe Ariès's work challenges it in some respects and supports it in others.

Journal of Family Issues, Vol. 4, June 1983.
This issue is devoted to television and the family. The articles, which are largely theoretical, stress that television viewing often occurs in a family context and that, especially for children, the impact of television is mediated by family relationships and family interaction.

Kagan, Jerome. *The Nature of the Child.* New York: Basic Books, 1984.
Kagan, a professor of developmental psychology, presents his considered judgments on themes of development, including inherent and environmental forces, continuity and discontinuity, and the necessity of a subjective frame of reference.

Kieffer, Christie W. *Changing Cultures, Changing Lives.* San Francisco: Jossey-Bass, 1974.
Kieffer traces the impact of historical changes on values and personality development of three generations of Japanese-Americans in San Francisco.

Lamb, Michael E. (ed.). *The Father's Role: Applied Perspectives.* New York: Wiley, 1986.
The papers in this book are directed to social service providers and "provide comprehensive and practically oriented summaries of the literature on fatherhood." The authors are all scholars with clinical orientations or experience.

McTear, Michael. *Children's Conversations.* Oxford: Basil Blackwell, 1985.
Research into the language of children has become a major area of study in linguistics and child development. In this book McTear focuses on "discourse analysis" and the development of conversational abilities in young children.

Marsella, Anthony J., George DeVos, and Francis L. K. Hsu (eds.). *Culture and Self. Asian and Western Perspectives.* New York: Tavistock Publications, 1985.
An informative set of essays exploring the Western views of self and four Asian perspectives: Japanese, Hindu, Confucian, and contemporary Chinese.

Meyrowitz, Joshua. *No Sense of Place: The Impact of Electronic Media on Social Behavior.* New York: Oxford University Press, 1985.
The author argues that the widespread use of television and other electronic media is largely responsible for many social

changes of recent years. The media have reorganized the settings in which people interact, and many in our society today have "no sense of place."

Middleton, John (ed.). *From Child to Adult: Studies in the Anthropology of Education.* Garden City, N.Y.: The Natural History Press, 1970.
This collection of studies by anthropologists discusses the educational systems in small-scale societies around the world.

Parr, Joy (ed.). *Childhood and Family in Canadian History.* Toronto: McClelland and Stewart, 1982.
This is a collection of essays, primarily by historians, describing various facets of childhood life in Canada from the seventeenth century onward.

Parsons, Talcott. *Social Structure and Personality.* New York: Free Press, 1964.
These essays by a leading American sociologist examine various aspects of the social structure as they shape socialization.

Piaget, Jean. *The Language and Thought of the Child.* Rev. ed. London: Routledge and Kegan Paul, 1932.
This is one of the earliest and most significant books by this major figure in the study of child development.

Riesman, David, in collaboration with Reuel Denney and Nathan Glazer. *The Lonely Crowd: A Study of the Changing American Character.* New Haven, Conn.: Yale University Press, 1950.
This imaginative study became an almost instant classic; it presents a detailed picture of how social change affects socialization agencies and processes.

Rist, Ray C. *The Invisible Children: School Integration in American Society.* Cambridge, Mass.: Harvard University Press, 1978.
This is a case study of a white upper-middle-class elementary school in Portland, Oregon, into which were voluntarily transferred a number of black children. They became, says Rist, essentially invisible as a distinctive cultural group.

Schulz, David A. *Coming Up Black: Patterns of Ghetto Socialization.* Englewood Cliffs, N.J.: Prentice-Hall, 1969.
This intensive study of ten families living in a problem-ridden public-housing project points up some of the special problems besetting black children from low-income families in the course of their socialization.

Schwartzman, Helen B. *Transformations: The Anthropology of Children's Play.* New York: Plenum Press, 1979.

This volume presents a survey of anthropological research on children's play and an analysis in terms of theories of culture.

Sieber, Timothy, and Andrew J. Gordon (eds.). *Children and Their Organizations: Investigations in American Culture.* Boston: G. K. Hall & Co., 1981.
This collection of readings, mostly by anthropologists, reports on socialization in a variety of settings including a girls' summer camp, a first-grade class, a drug-abuse program, and an army basic-combat-training unit.

Spencer, Margaret B., Geraldine K. Brookins, and Walter R. Allen, eds. *Beginnings: the Social and Affective Development of Black Children.* Hillsdale, N.J.: Lawrence Erlbaum Associates, 1985.
In this fine collection of reports, both theoretical and empirical, the authors examine black children from the perspective of the black cultural environment with its own historical experiences and current circumstances. Euro-American attitudes and models, the authors suggest, give a false picture.

Stockard, Jean, and Miriam M. Johnson. *Sex Roles: Sex Inequality and Sex Role Development.* Englewood Cliffs, N.J.: Prentice-Hall, 1980.
This volume presents a systematic overview of facts and theories of sex-role development. Sociological, biological, and psychological aspects are discussed.

Strauss, Anselm (ed.). Rev. ed. *George Herbert Mead on Social Psychology.* Chicago: University of Chicago Press, 1964.
This volume consists of selections from the writings of Mead, noted as the originator of the symbolic interactionist view of self and society.

Suransky, Valerie P. *The Erosion of Childhood.* Chicago: University of Chicago Press, 1982.
Suransky reviews the central orientations of five very different day-care centers and argues that our behavioral orientation and postindustrial technology are eroding the very essence of a natural childhood.

Sutton-Smith, Brian. *Toys as Culture.* New York: Gardner Press, 1986.
Toys, according to Sutton-Smith, are intimately related to many larger cultural patterns in the family, technology, education, and marketplace. They are a "small peep hole" through which we may analyze a culture.

Trudgill, Peter. *Sociolinguistics: An Introduction.* Harmondsworth: Penguin, 1974.

Sociolinguistics is a growing field with great import for socialization. This book is a general introduction.

Wallerstein, Judith S., and Joan B. Kelly. *Surviving the Breakup.* New York: Basic Books, 1980.

The authors studied 60 families with 131 children from the time of marital separation through a five-year follow-up.

Whiting, Beatrice B. (ed.). *Six Cultures: Studies of Child Rearing.* New York: Wiley, 1963.

Six teams of anthropologists and associates, each working separately but following the same basic outline, consider the relationships between child training practices and personality differences in communities in Kenya, India, Okinawa, the Philippines, Mexico, and New England.

Name Index

327

Subject Index

ABOUT THE AUTHORS

Frederick Elkin is professor emeritus of sociology at York University, Toronto. Formerly he taught at the University of Montreal, McGill University, and the University of Missouri. He is a member of the Professional Advisory Committee of Dellcrest Children's Centre, Toronto, a former Molson Fellow of the Vanier Institute of the Family, Ottawa, and an ex-president of the Canadian Sociology and Anthropology Association.

In addition to having made numerous contributions to journal literature and to edited works, Professor Elkin is the author of *Family in Canada* (1964) and *Rebels and Colleagues: Advertising and Social Change in French Canada* (1973), and co-editor of *Volunteers, Voluntary Associations, and Development* (1981).

Gerald Handel is professor of sociology at the City College and the Graduate Center of the City University of New York. He has taught in the Committee on Human Development at the University of Chicago and in the summer session at Harvard University. He was associate editor of the *Journal of Marriage and Family* from 1969 to 1975.

Professor Handel is the author of *Social Welfare in Western Society* (1982) and co-author of *Family Worlds* (1959) and *Working-man's Wife* (1959). He edited *The Psychosocial Interior of the Family* (1967; 3rd ed., 1985). His study entitled "A Children's New York: Boys at Play in Yorkville" appears as a chapter in *The Apple Sliced: Sociological Studies of New York City* (1983), which he co-edited.